ENGLISH LYRIC POETRY

English Lyric Poetry is the most comprehensive reassessment of lyric poetry of the early seventeenth century to appear in recent years. The study is directed at both beginning and more advanced students of literature and responds to specialized scholarly inquiries pursued of late in relation to specific poets. Jonathan F.S. Post seeks to assimilate many of the post-New Critical theoretical concerns with readings of the major and minor, male and female, authors of the period.

Donne, Jonson, the Spenserians, Herbert, Vaughan, Milton, Marvell, as well as Cavalier and women poets, all receive sustained, fresh, detailed analysis. In widening the scope of critical commentary, this lively and engaging literary history avoids the limitations of much recent criticism as it explores the imaginative life of the lyric in the early seventeenth century.

Jonathan F.S. Post is Professor of English at the University of California at Los Angeles, USA.

ENGLISH LYRIC POETRY

The early seventeenth century

Jonathan F.S. Post

London and New York

First published 1999
by Routledge
11 New Fetter Lane, London EC4P 4EE

Simultaneously published in the USA and Canada
by Routledge
29 West 35th Street, New York, NY 10001

First published in paperback 2002

Routledge is an imprint of the Taylor & Francis Group

Typeset in Goudy by Routledge
Printed and bound in Great Britain by Biddles Ltd,
Guildford and King's Lynn

British Library Cataloguing in Publication Data
A catalogue record for this book is available from the British Library

Library of Congress Cataloguing in Publication Data
Post, Jonathan, F. S., 1947–
English lyric poetry : the early seventeenth century / Jonathan F. S. Post
p. cm.
Includes bibliographical references and index.
1. English poetry–Early modern, 1500–1700–History and criticism.
2. England–Intellectual life–17th century. I. Title.
PR541.P67 1999 98–48933
821'.040904–dc21 CIP

ISBN 0–415–02949–X (hbk)
ISBN 0–415–20858–0 (pbk)

U.T. and Joe, Helen and Tony,
George, Pat, Peggy, and Fred

– "gladnesse of the best"

CONTENTS

Foreword   ix
Acknowledgements   x v
A note on sources and spelling   xvii

1 Irremediably Donne   1

2 Ben Jonson and the art of inclusion   23

3 Patriotic and popular poets   54

4 Caroline amusements   91

5 Substance and style in George Herbert's *The Temple*   135

6 The once and future poet: Milton in the 1645 *Poems*   156

7 Arenas of retreat: blood, bread, and poetry in Henry
   Vaughan   190

8 From Wroth to Philips: women poets of the earlier
   seventeenth century   210

9 Andrew Marvell: "Here at the Fountain's Sliding Foot"   253

Notes   287
Index   310

FOREWORD

Literary histories are supposed to be things of the past. This is especially true of histories of poetry – that most literary of genres – and truer still of poetry of the distant past, like the lyric poetry of the early seventeenth century: the subject of this book. What more can be said? And need anything more be said about Herrick or Donne when there is so much to say today about their "culture"? And to whom is one to speak? To other specialists? To people seeking to enter the profession? To university or college students? To readers who want to know more about poetry in general? To readers and practitioners of contemporary verse who feel the need, say, to know something about Herbert if they wish to understand that most nuanced of his many descendants, Elizabeth Bishop? I raise these as concerns at the outset because they are part of the present climate of literary studies and, tonally at least, are one way of differentiating the present inquiry from previous literary histories and the judgments they contain. But I raise them as questions since the purpose of this study is not to produce another lament that literature has been kidnapped for "other" purposes, but to indicate a belief that, partly in response to the scholarly and critical work produced during the last two decades, the poetry of the earlier seventeenth century – an awkward period designation if there ever was one – continues to be immensely rewarding for those who wish to read not only between the lines but the lines themselves, and who prefer individual poets to overarching themes and genres.

In making this claim, I plead guilty in advance to enjoying thoroughly much of the verse of the period. I would rather have written a line by Marvell than by Marx; and a few poems by Herbert are worth many late nights with Calvin. Of course there is no reason, except for time, to read exclusively, and the appearance in these pages of John Taylor, the Water Poet, serves as a warning that not every bit of verse in the seventeenth century was written with a Jonsonian design to escape the ages. And yet Taylor is such an odd duck, publishing his *Works* (numbering "three and sixty") halfway through his literary life, that it's difficult to refuse him notice for a lifetime of versifying. I do not mean to sound flippant about matters of inclusion or exclusion, although scholars have sometimes been too heated or solemn on this subject. (I regret, rather than applaud, the absence of Crashaw and Traherne in these pages.) And another critic would no doubt develop a different angle on the poetry of this period – indeed, probably questioning the notion of the earlier seventeenth century as a discrete literary period, except by default, as a time in between "the Renaissance" and "the Restoration" – as Dryden would have wished. But my concern has been less to challenge the notion of historical periods in general than to structure an account of the period that allows room for the particular to emerge in the process of "reading": the particularity of an author, of a poem, of a group of poems. ("Authors to themselves," as Milton might have said – did say – with the emphasis in the phrase falling on both the solitary and the collective, or shared, nature of the literary.)

One way of speaking generally about the first sixty or so years of the seventeenth century is simply to say that, for whatever complicated historical reasons, it produced a sufficient number of exceptional poets and poems that invite sustained analysis. Another, less judicious way, is to hail it as a great age of lyric experimentation, a period that saw not only a continued interest in the formal invention that marked the last decades of the sixteenth century, especially in the hands of Sidney and Spenser, but also a further emphasis on variety and compression, of saying much in little, and an increasing recognition later in the century, as the antiquarian John Aubrey understood, that their many "brief lives" were ripe for collecting: that poets had become a named part of what historians today would call Early Modern Britain – and women poets too. The appended nature of that remark indicates the tentative place they were beginning to be accorded at the end of a work like Edward Phillips's *Theatrum Poetarum* (1675).

In its earliest phase, I had in mind an even broader survey than the one that appears here, one that might have included a place for *Paradise Lost*, even if Cowley's *Davideis* or Davenant's *Gondibert* might not have garnered much commentary along the way. But, increasingly, problems of space loomed larger and larger, along with a concern as to the usefulness of such a book, and in the end I elected to pitch the study more in the direction of lyric and attempt to give familiar and less-familiar authors a fuller hearing than they might have otherwise received. Poets largely popular in their own day only are interesting for the light they shed on contemporary reading habits and for the context they provide for understanding a Donne or a Jonson, a Herbert or a Milton, and for reminding us again of their greater achievements: the varieties of invention and imagined realities that distinguish poetry at its most accomplished. Poets barely known in their own day, or not at all, like Martha Moulsworth, interest us now because of who we have become. The final decision to allot individual chapters to the authors most deserving of attention seems scarcely novel, nor does the notion of grouping other poets loosely together according to a few familiar trends or movements. The method of apportionment belongs to an earlier version of literary history, although I have for the most part dispensed with speaking of "schools," even if the idea of a coterie or "tribe" of writers is, along with authorship, one of the distinctive trademarks of the early seventeenth century.

In the interest of general or first-time readers, I have risked, at times, redescribing or redrawing lines of continuity and change familiar to specialists: those sometimes connecting poet with poet, those occasionally differentiating one generation from another. The remarkable shift in generic emphasis and the poetic line that accompanies the beginning of the seventeenth century still seems worth observing in some detail, although it is surely possible to minimize the element of change associated with the death of a particular monarch like Elizabeth if, for instance, one maximizes a "Republican" view of the Renaissance that sees the English Civil War and the new government as the culmination of events and practices initiated with Henrician reform.[1] (Donne and Jonson, of course, were not Republican sympathizers; indeed, notions of monarchy were crucial to their authoritative – some would say "authoritarian" – conception of poetry; and Marvell and Milton are interesting in part because of the Caroline rule they left behind.)

On occasion, too, I have not been able to resist the temptation of analyzing in detail some of the century's better known as well as some of its less familiar lyrics. Slowing down the pace allows for a more sustained engagement with other critical points of view. It also interrupts the temporal flow of literary histories that often succeed at finding compartments for poems but sometimes at the expense of exploring the verbal nooks and crannies of a particular stanza or poem – the box "where sweets compacted lie," to adapt Herbert's playful phrase from "Vertue." But it would be wrong to deny another motive operating as well, one that could be extended into a partial rationale for having originally agreed to write this study as part of the Routledge History of Poetry before the series was disbanded. Lyric poetry frequently invites intimate engagement, an opportunity to "converse" across time and across cultures, as well as within a particular culture. The observation is so common that it has almost disappeared from sight, especially in the criticism of poetry in the early fields (and the discourse of literary studies more generally.) But in this regard Helen Vendler's recent reminder, or rather "defense," of the lyric as the genre in which "the soul" speaks – in contrast to a more "socially specified self" – tells an important, if not the whole, truth about lyric: that it invites immediate identification with the speaker. "If a poet was a castaway, I too was a castaway; if a poet regretted Fern Hill, I too had a house I regretted," writes Vendler, with disarming candor, of her early encounters with poetry. "Everything said in a poem was a metaphor for something in my inner life, and I learned about future possibilities within my inner life from the poetry I read with such eagerness."[2]

Like many potential readers of verse, Vendler is especially drawn to lyric as personal utterance, and it is not surprising that her own substantial criticism of the lyric should date back to the poetry of the earlier seventeenth century, or that her most involved interpretations should center on Shakespeare's sonnets and George Herbert's poetry – those sweetly compacted, complicated, passionate declarations of amorous subjectivity. But if she is right to draw our attention to the intimacy of "soul speak" as being different in kind from the language of the "socially specified self" that she finds best exemplified in the novel – and therefore understood primarily through "changing registers of diction, contrastive rhythms, and varieties of tone," what she calls the "destiny" of words – it is also the case that in the Renaissance and early seventeenth century "lyric" was a generally more inclusive genre than her intensely perceived valuation of the "private" implies. A poet like Jonson, who has been nearly "rediscovered" in the aftermath of New Criticism, is difficult to hear if we don't attend to the ways a "self" becomes "socially specified" through talking in verse with another. And a poem like Marvell's "An Horatian Ode upon Cromwell's Return from Ireland" requires at the outset an even more radical trimming of the private as the privileged domain of the lyric.

My point is not that Vendler's preference for lyric as private utterance is partial when it comes to understanding seventeenth-century poetry more generally, let alone to deny, in the name of sophistication, the process of learning that comes with the experience of identifying with the speaker of a lyric or the poet. Rather, it is to take her principal point about lyric identification one step further, as Marvell himself did, and urge that it also includes gaining tempting access to, if not exactly permitting easy identification with, a world different from the one we think we know around us. In this context, it is worth recalling Jorge Luis Borges's enticing description of what happens between the poem and the reader, as told by Seamus Heaney in "The Redress of Poetry," for it helps to illuminate a reading process as potentially true for Jonson's "To Penshurst" as for Herbert's "Affliction":

> The taste of the apple (states Berkeley) lies in the contact of the fruit with the palate, not in the fruit itself; in a similar way (I would say) poetry lies in the meeting of poem and reader, not in the lines of symbols printed on pages of a book. What is essential is … the thrill, the almost physical emotion that comes with each reading.[3]

Where Borges differs from most reader-response theorists of a decade ago is in his emphasis on the palpable "thrill" of the encounter, "the fluid, exhilarating moment which lies at the heart of any memorable reading," which Heaney, widening the frame a bit, sees as fulfilling "the continual need we experience to 'recover a past or prefigure a future.'" Not every poem will supply the "thrill" of which Borges and Heaney speak, but a history of poetry that does not, at some level, signal the precipitous attraction of verse as "possessing" a different kind of knowledge from what is won in reading a novel or a diary is also not quite doing its work. To press this point a little further, by way of attempting to fuse Vendler's weighty sense of the "destiny" of words as a special prerogative of poetry with a Borgesian emphasis on the heady rush, "the almost physical emotion that comes with each reading," I would emphasize that an encounter with the literary (aesthetic) provides, as Heaney suggests, an encounter with history (politics) at an experiential level. "In the contact of the fruit with the palate," it is possible to taste, to be more specific still, events as distant from us and as disparate from each other, for instance, as the "royalist" politics governing Lovelace's "Grasse-hopper" ode and the "puritan" energies embodied in Marvell's Cromwell marching "indefatigably on" – to say nothing about Jonson's "blushing apricot and woolly peach" in "To Penshurst."

ACKNOWLEDGEMENTS

In thinking and writing about seventeenth-century poetry, I have happily acquired many debts. The longest standing are to Anthony Hecht and Joseph Summers, former teachers, valued friends, and continual influences in my own attempt to redress the balance between past and present understandings of poetry written in this period. Over the years, Annabel Patterson has offered many models and much encouragement for thinking about the seventeenth century, especially about the relationship between literature and politics. I owe, as well, more immediate debts to my Renaissance colleagues at UCLA: Michael Allen, A.R. Braunmuller, Christopher Grose, Gordon Kipling, Claire McEachern, Debora Shuger, and Robert Watson; to Anne Mellor, who helped shape some of my thoughts about women poets in the period, although the decision to include Anne Bradstreet is my own; and to the many students who have been teaching me over the last decade and who are now themselves teachers. I think especially of Marlin Blaine, Thad Bower, Margaret Cunningham, Peter Goldstein, Lisa Gordis, Robin Grey, Gary Hall, Marge Kingsley, Grainne McEvoy, Esther Gilman Richey, and Curtis Whitaker. I am equally grateful to the students in my undergraduate courses on poetry for continuing to give the lie to the notion that poetry is somehow in decline at the end of the century.

Portions of this study have benefited significantly from specific occasions and individuals. The late Georgia Christopher afforded me the opportunity as a speaker at the 1992 Southeastern Renaissance Conference, held at the University of South Carolina, to rethink the relationship between Herrick, lyric, and history. Thomas Corns, after inviting me to extend my understanding of Vaughan in an essay originally written for *The Cambridge Companion to English Poetry: Donne to Marvell*, helped to improve the final version. Much of the Herrick portion of Chapter 4 and all of Chapter 5 have appeared in *The George Herbert Journal*; along the way, they profited from intelligent commentary by Anne Coiro, Donald Friedman, Sidney Gottlieb, and Michael Schoenfeldt. A special note of thanks goes to Reg Foakes, who got me started on this project; to Joseph Summers, Robert Watson, and Curtis Whitaker, who, along with Professor Foakes, read – and improved – large sections of the manuscript; and to Professor John Richetti and the anonymous second reader for the press for their many helpful suggestions, small and large. Without the encouragement of my colleague, Stephen Yenser, and his fine eye for the phrase, this study might never have had a chance of being "finished." That it has been completed is owing, once again, to my wife, Susan: "What other help could yet be meet!"

Although this is a book more about verse than the institutions which created the conditions for poetry in the earlier seventeenth century, I am grateful for the fortunate circumstances that currently exist at UCLA and in Los Angeles for ongoing engagements with poetry present and past. The splendid program of readings, most recently at the UCLA Hammer Museum, offers frequent reminders of how earlier poets and their verse continue to surface in unexpected ways among many of today's authors. With their rich repositories of seventeenth-century materials, The Clark Library, the Huntington Library, and the University Research Library are a scholar's haven; I want to express my appreciation to the librarians and staffs of each for the many courtesies extended over the years, and to Lynda Tolly, true guardian of the departmental English Reading Room. It is a pleasure to acknowledge as well the UCLA Center for Seventeenth- and Eighteenth-Century Studies, under the direction of Peter Reill, and the Council on Research of the Academic Senate of the Los Angeles Division of the University of California, for generously funding my research, and the Center, again, for continuing to host academic programs pertinent to this study. Finally, I am grateful for the continued encouragement offered by Talia Rogers and Jason Arthur at Routledge. I want to thank them for their patience, and Morgen Witzel for his help in preparing the manuscript for publication.

A NOTE ON SOURCES AND SPELLING

A sizeable amount of quoted poetry appears in this book. For convenience of reference, I have quoted from the Oxford Clarendon editions of individual authors whenever possible, or from another "standard" work widely available, as in the case of Jonson or Milton. Although in some instances the spelling has already been "modernized" by an editor, I have chosen to quote the texts in the editions cited and not to embark on a practice of silently modernizing spelling. I have, however, followed the usual orthographical practice of rendering *i* as *j* and *v* as *u*. Quotations from classical authors are taken from the Loeb Classical Library.

1

IRREMEDIABLY DONNE

> My name engrav'd herein,
> Doth contribute my firmenesse to this glasse.
> Donne, "A Valediction: Of my Name in the Window"

In one of the most stunningly determining moments in his life, John Donne married Anne More in a clandestine wedding in December of 1601. Donne had been employed as secretary to Thomas Egerton, Lord Keeper of the Great Seal. Anne was a member of Egerton's household and the daughter of Sir George More, a wealthy squire who had served on the Continent with the Earl of Leicester and perhaps Sir Philip Sidney. Their marriage eventually produced some twelve children, but its immediate effect on Donne's career as an aspiring courtier was disastrous; the resulting quick plummet from his employer's grace was given proverbial shape in the contemporary quip: "John Donne, Anne Donne, Un-done."[1] In the highly awkward negotiations that succeeded the marriage, Donne sought to smooth matters over with his irate father-in-law and wrote the following, which he had delivered by no less a person than the Earl of Northumberland:

> I know this letter shall find you full of passion; but I know no passion can alter your reason and wisdome, to which I adventure to commend these particulars; that it is irremediably donne; that if you incense my Lord you destroy her and me; that it is easy to give us happines, and that my endeavours and industrie, if it please you to prosper them, may soone make me somewhat worthier of her.[2]

The letter is surely one of the more astonishing flops in the history of familial correspondences. Sir George subsequently pressed for both an annulment of the marriage, which he failed to get, and Donne's dismissal from Egerton's service, which he did accomplish. But the letter is also – and this could only have added further fuel to the fire – "irremediably donne": that is, a statement asserting not just that an action is past and therefore a "fait

1

accompli" that must be accepted by all parties concerned, but that it has been done by Donne, as if the special signature gave it a final stamp of authority and thereby removed the dispute from the realm of worldly contention. Donne has spoken; Donne has done – with the pun sounding in the final stress position of what turns out to be the one indisputably pentameter line in the paragraph.

The episode suggests in small much about the person whom Jonson esteemed "the first poet in the world in some things":[3] both the supercilious side that helped to shipwreck his career at court (and, incidentally, sent him drifting in the direction of the church), and the special concern, manifested in writing, with exploring new ranges of thought, especially as they reflect, and reflect upon, his own unique status, his individuality. Donne was the poet who preached his own funeral sermon before the king. And at his death, he was the preacher-poet eulogized by contemporaries as "the Prince of wits," the "Copernicus of poets." "To have liv'd eminent, in a degree / Beyond our lofty'st flights, that is, like Thee, / Or t'have had too much merit, is not safe," wrote Henry King, Donne's executor.[4] "Not safe," in fact, is exactly the response of Dudley North, the genteel poetaster of the earlier seventeenth century who, without ever naming Donne, seemed to have Donne and his coterie in mind when he objected to those "who thinke nothing good that is easie, nor any thing beccomming passion that is not exprest with an hyperbole above reason … [but] … Like ill ranging Spaniells they spring figures, and ravished with their extravagant fancies, pursue them in long excursions, neglecting their true game and pretended affection." North preferred "his Magesties mind [King James's], that the best eloquence is to make our selves clearly understood," and his stated model was Sir Philip Sidney, appropriate enough on one level since it was to Sidney's niece, Mary Wroth, that he was writing and, on another, because North assumed poetry "unsophisticated by Art" and "possessing a free puritie of unadulterated wit" was what women wanted.[5]

Whatever Donne's critical fortunes have been among later generations of readers – and few reputations have fluctuated more dramatically – he was perceived by approving and disapproving contemporaries alike as thoroughly novel, a kind of Hieronimo or Hamlet of verse (or a Tamburlaine, as John Carey might have it).[6] Difficulty was one of his hallmarks. Jonson, whose eye rarely strayed far from posterity, thought Donne would perish for want of being understood, and the 1633 posthumous edition of Donne's poems – the first attempt to collect and publish his verse – was accompanied by an epistle addressed to the "understanders," not to the general reader, an epistle that remained in place until the fourth edition (second issue) was published in 1650. It was then only to be replaced by a polemic from the poet's royalist son, who sought to preserve his father from the "leveling" understanding of indifferent pretenders to the "chair of wit."

But difficulty in Donne, as North recognized, was really not the source of the poet's novelty, only a feature of it. Rather, it was the hyperbolic quality of Donne's imagination, it was the "figures" that seemed to spring from the mind in an act of poetic self-ravishment that identified this other, apparently alien, mode of writing and, for North, challenged the domain of the traditionally poetic.[7] Samuel Johnson would make a similar point in a famous essay written in the next century. Speaking of a "race of writers" appearing at the beginning of the seventeenth century, he remarked with no small displeasure that "their wish was only to say what they hoped had been never said before."[8]

Johnson crowned this group with the problematic title of the "metaphysical poets" when his initial notion of a "race of writers" better conveyed a sense of their otherness, their strangeness, especially to the mind deeply anchored in literary decorum; for it was precisely the undecorous – the shocking – that Donne cultivated and that so struck his contemporaries. "The flame / Of thy brave soul," wrote the Caroline court poet, Thomas Carew, "Committed holy Rapes upon our Will," a point which he then elaborated upon in an act of purposefully strenuous imitation, transparent only in celebrating what today would be called, with no less obliquity, Donne's phallocentric "hardness":

> thy imperious wit
> Our stubborne language bends, made only fit
> With her tough-thick-rib'd hoopes to gird about
> Thy Giant phansie, which had prov'd too stout
> For their soft melting Phrases.[9]

Carew made these observations about Donne's "Giant phansie" in his elegy on the author written in the early 1630s, probably soon after Donne's death in 1631, when the late Dean of St. Paul's was at the height of his popularity. But they also describe a language, voice, and attitude – especially an attitude – whose principal effects were forged nearly forty years earlier and did not undergo significant change in either idiom or utterance. Even if we resist agreeing completely with Ben Jonson's view that Donne wrote all his best poetry before he was twenty-five, there is almost every reason to believe that he wrote much of the poetry that survives by that age, which means by the late 1590s. At this point, Donne was in his early to mid-twenties. He had been born in 1572, the child of a well-to-do citizen ironmonger of the same name and Elizabeth Heywood, the youngest daughter of John Heywood, epigrammatist, writer of interludes, musician, and Catholic recusant descended from Sir Thomas More. He had already seen something of the world: Oxford, from 1583–7(?), perhaps Cambridge for another two years, and the Inns of Court in London, probably from 1591–4, where he studied law. As the Marshall engraving of Donne in 1591 reveals, he also had military aspirations that were realized in 1596–7, if not earlier, when he joined the Earl of Essex in the campaign against the Spanish and sailed to the Azores.[10]

In many regards, Donne's was a typical career of a late Elizabethan courtier.

A great frequenter of the theater and the ladies, he was educated in the arts and law, a path designed to produce scholar-courtiers to serve the state in some official capacity. Writing poetry was thus not simply an art of "recreation"[11] (to choose the description Donne's first biographer, Izaak Walton, applies to Donne's early verse); it was economically and socially purposeful recreation, as a number of recent scholars have emphasized.[12] Crucial to the courtier's vocation, verse was a way to advertise one's wares in front of a selective audience. The literary credo of the Inns of Court, as presented by Donne's acquaintance, John Hoskins, in his *Directions for Speech and Style* (1599?), makes explicit the common humanist assumption connecting skillful writing and state service: "Were it an honor to a prince," Hoskins asks, "to have the majesty of his embassage spoiled by a careless ambassador?" The rhetorical question prepares the way for a second and hence the rationale for the *Directions* with its epistolary emphasis: "How shall you look for wit from him whose leisure and whose head (assisted with the examination of his eyes) could yield you no life and sharpness in his writings?"[13]

Donne, satire, and the 1590s

But it is also clear that for a late Elizabethan the modes of self-presentation were in considerable, if not radical, flux. The generation of poets immediately preceding Donne – the generation of Sidney and Spenser, who came of age in the 1580s – was primarily one searching for an ideal: a golden world of pastoral romance and heroic action was central to their vision, a vision, moreover, that was pre-eminently courtly if not court-centered, as was the case with the greatest Elizabethan poem, *The Faerie Queene*. The work of these two was made available in print in the early 1590s, and though there was to be only one *Faerie Queene* (in two parts, however), the idealizing legacy was continued in the early 1590s in the spate of sonnet sequences that began to appear shortly after the publication of Sidney's *Astrophil and Stella* in 1591. Samuel Daniel's *Delia* was one of the first to arrive (1592). It was quickly joined by Drayton's *Ideas Mirrour* (1594, tellingly named), Spenser's *Amoretti* (1596), and the works of lesser lights like Bartholomew Griffin (*Fidessa*, 1596) and William Smith (*Chloris*, 1596). All were attempting to use the form to establish their poetic authority with a particular patron or patroness. And for all, the idealizing mode of the Petrarchan poem ensured that the poet remained apparently subservient to his mistress, his *noli me tangere* whom he pursued in sonnet after sonnet by performing endless variations on fire and ice, military imagery, sleepless nights, blazons, and radiant eyes, to say nothing about the odd postures he might assume that signaled his devotion, whether it was Barnabe Barnes's wish to be turned into a glove so that he might range freely over his mistress's body, or Drayton's complaint that unrequited love produced the same pain as an anatomy lesson performed on a still-breathing criminal.

When Donne began writing in the early 1590s, it was not in but against this context. Nor was it just against it in the sense of favoring or helping to inaugurate the newer fashions of verse that were emerging in the mid-1590s and were associated especially with urban reality: satire, epigram, elegy, and the verse epistle. It is surely right to put Donne in the company of the new breed of authors that chose to "discover" these demonstrably Roman genres, authors like Thomas Lodge, John Marston, Joseph Hall, John Davies, and Ben Jonson. But with the exception of Jonson, it was only Donne who was able to redetermine the expansive energies of his predecessors into a radically different idiom.

Donne established in England the "lyric of insistent talk,"[14] and he did so on something approaching a grand scale. Although there had been earlier examples of courtly poetry moving in the direction of speech, most notably in the "manly" lyrics of Sir Thomas Wyatt, who had also experimented with Horatian satire, no poet had so charged verse with the searching, colloquial immediacy that Donne brought to all his poetry, whether it was the early satires and elegies, the *Anniversaries*, the more private love poetry of the *Songs and Sonnets*, the still more private devotional poems, the verse epistles, or the divine hymns. The claim, "I sing not, Siren-like, to tempt; for I / Am harsh"[15] becomes, in Donne, the standard by which he insists that we judge the poetic. The registers of speech, not song, are what the poet puts in motion with his opening utterances: "Sir; though (I thanke God for it) I do hate / Perfectly all this towne," "I wonder by my troth, what thou and I / Did, till we lov'd?" Or, "Marke but this flea, and mark in this, / How little that which thou deny'st me is." Or, "Stand still, and I will read to thee / A Lecture, Love, in loves philosophy." And again, and perhaps most famously: "For Godsake hold your tongue, and let me love."

How deeply Donne's imagination was affected by the quotidian in all its mutability, how deeply he pursued the prosaic in verse can be partially glimpsed by reading any one of his satires, generally thought to be among his earliest poems, against those of another late Elizabethan, Joseph Hall. Hall was born within two years of Donne, in 1574. Like Donne, though more quickly, he was to find preferment in the church, eventually succeeding in his unusually full life to the bishoprics of Exeter and then Norwich, before being sequestered by the Puritans in the Civil War. Much earlier, though, he had presented himself to the public as the "first English Satirist" with the publication of *Virgidemiarum* (A Harvest of Rods) in 1598. Hall was attempting to capitalize on the new fashion for strong lines, and in A *Post-script to the Reader* he defended his bristly project: "It is not for every one to rellish a true and naturall Satyre, being of it selfe besides the native and in-bred bitternes and tartnes of particulers, both hard of conceipt, and harsh of stile, and therefore cannot but be unpleasing both to the unskilfull, and over Musicall eare, the one being affected with onely a shallow and easie matter, the other with a smoth and currant disposition."[16] Toughness of thought and feigned irascibility, "hard of conceipt [idea], and harsh of stile": this was the new image of a generation of malcontents who seemed to follow the disgruntled Jaques out of the Elizabethan forest to challenge its woodnotes wild, its pastoralizing, courtly forms: a cultural shift that

Spenser, too, reluctantly acknowledged in the figure of the Blatant Beast careening among the courteous in Book 6 of *The Faerie Queene*, published in 1596. And in the six books that make up the *Virgidemiarum*, Hall seems even to provide a convenient index for changing tastes. The first three books are designated, politely, as "Tooth-lesse"; the last three are called "byting Satyres."

But despite the bravado of the postscript, as well as the tonal shift between the two parts and the real and constant use made of Roman models of satire, Hall is in many ways only a transitional figure. He rejects romance as the proper subject of poetry, but his verse is still studded with archaisms. In his own way, his vision is nearly as nostalgic as Spenser's: "Ye Antique *Satyres*, how I blesse your daies, / That brook'd your bolder stile, their owne dispraise" (V, iii). Although he has substituted individual satirical portraits for the legends of British history, the legendary nonetheless continues on in the primarily narrative, rather than dramatic, presentation of types. Hall's is a poetry of the heavily accented, regular, end-stopped pentameter line, a historically fascinating though poetically uncertain blend of the medieval complaint and the modernized urban muse. Years later, Milton was to seize on the unacknowledged native origins of Hall's satires when, in the charged polemical context immediately preceding the Civil War, he unceremoniously referred the Bishop to the earlier and better *Piers Plowman*.[17]

With Donne, however, the newness of tart particularity is not advertised; it is embodied. Or rather, it is advertised by being embodied, as Donne, with characteristic diffidence over appearing in print, has left it to others to proclaim his satires as the first "sustained 'imitation' of a Latin genre" in English.[18] Like Hall, he found in the writings of Horace, Juvenal, and Persius a stylistic alternative to the musicality of court verse; and like Hall, he seems to have appreciated general differences among the models: Horace's association with urbane laughter and moderation, Juvenal's with vituperation, and Persius's with moral seriousness and obscurity.[19] But in Donne, the medievalisms vanish; the urban landscape takes over, and with it a new language emerges, perhaps inspired by a visit to the theater but seemingly cut from the jagged edges of reality itself:

> Now leaps he upright, joggs me,'and cryes, 'Do'you see
> Yonder well favour'd youth?' 'Which?' 'Oh, 'tis hee
> That dances so divinely.' 'Oh,' said I,
> 'Stand still, must you dance here for company?'
> Hee droopt, wee went, till one (which did excell
> Th' Indians, in drinking his Tobacco well)
> Met us; they talk'd; I whisper'd, 'Let us goe,
> 'T may be you smell him not, truely I doe.'
> He heares not mee, but, on the other side
> A many-colour'd Peacock having spide,
> Leaves him and mee; I for my lost sheep stay;
> He followes, overtakes, goes on the way,

Saying, 'Him whom I last left, all repute
For his device, in hansoming a sute,
To judge of lace, pinke, panes, print, cut, and plight,
Of all the Court, to have the best conceit.'

(Satyre I, ll. 83–97)

This snippet of interpolated dialogue is taken from one of the more Horatian satires in which the speaker, a naif of sorts, is accosted by a pretentious bore on his walk through the city. (See Horace's Satire I.9, "Ibam forte Via Sacra, sicut meus est mos.") Among other things, it is meant to convey the city's seaminess: its smells, its licentiousness, its strange sights, including the silly sartorial habits of a stray fop. But it is also meant to convey the poet's extraordinary agility, not just in his momentary asides and triumphs over his boorish companion, but in his thorough flouting of poetic convention: in the interpolated "dance" of dialogue. Part of the challenge of this passage (and in Donne in general) is simply keeping up with it; here the game involves seeing how many different kinds of speech acts can be compressed into a short space. How far can poetry go in the direction of gossipy prose before it is no longer verse? Where is the vanishing point?

Jonson, of course, thought Donne deserved hanging for not properly counting his accents,[20] a judgment not necessarily occasioned by the satires but certainly appropriate to them. There is really nothing in the verse of the period to compete either with the radically shifting point of view expressed in the quoted passage or with the accentuation of the shifts through a relentless wrenching of stress patterns. (The staccato of "To judge of lace, pinke, panes, print, cut, and plight" is, metrically speaking, only slightly less daring than Milton's more famous "Rocks, Caves, Lakes, Fens, Bogs, Dens, and shades of death.") But Jonson's wish to "hang" Donne for his metrical liberties seems appropriate in another sense since it recognizes the potential iconoclasm in this verbal "gesture." Donne's posture here as well as in the second and fourth satires is consciously anti-courtly; and his best-known satire, the third, is at pains – and perhaps considerable risk – to prize the mind that continually seeks after true religion, that refuses to rest on the surface or to settle for one fashion or another, even the fashion of scorning surfaces, and that questions the absolute authority of kings: "men do not stand / In so'ill case here, that God hath with his hand / Sign'd Kings blanck-charters to kill whom they hate" (III, ll. 89–91).[21] Whether these gestures are more than gestures, that is, whether the authorizing of verse satire in the late 1590s constitutes something more than a shift in generic paradigms and is responsive to the larger issue of political succession, is difficult to determine. But the fashion for verse satire, set in the more turbulent context of the "war of the theaters," a war that included the younger Jonson himself, was certainly perceived by contemporary authorities as subversive. Even Hall's satires, toothless as they might have appeared to a zealous reformist like Milton, were considered sufficiently dangerous to warrant censoring in 1599. Along with Marston's satires, Marlowe's Ovid, and Davies's epigrams, the extant copies were called in to be burnt.

Amorous Donne: the elegies and the songs and sonnets

To most modern readers, however, the "essential Donne" is not the Donne of the satires, with their often bulky topicality and grotesque gesturing – "Thus He with home-meats tries me; I belch, spue, spit, / Looke pale, and sickly, like a Patient" (IV, 108–10) – but the amatory and devotional Donne: the Donne who seemingly stemmed the Petrarchan tide in England, who re-wrote Sidney and "got," more often than not, the food of desire; and the Donne who anticipated George Herbert by making religious verse not just an acceptable part of the canon of seventeenth-century poetry but a central constituent of it. Donne the priest and Donne the love poet: these were the initial images projected in the respective engravings of each of the first two editions. But even so, we ought to remember that at least one later author, Alexander Pope, thought the satires and verse epistles to be Donne's "best" productions, and though it is easy to account for this preference on personal and historical grounds, it reminds us that the satirical in Donne was not a surface interest. Not only were the five satires apparently made ready as a kind of "book" to be passed along to that favorite patroness of Jacobean poets, Lucy Harrington, Countess of Bedford, sometime around 1607, with a covering poem by Jonson, but the anatomizing habits, the demystified view of language, the authorial bravado, the keenly real-ized vision of corruption, all are at the core of all of Donne's poetry, secular and religious alike. The satirist who dissects court and city in the 1590s anatomizes the world in the *The First and Second Anniversaries* in 1611 and 1612. And in the 1620s, he presents his body as yet another site for the scalpel, this time bearing witness to the hand of God. There are important shifts in Donne's poetry, shifts dictated in part by circumstances, but Donne never departed from a language spiked with the bits and pieces of human speech.

What Donne did for love poetry was give it a complicating significance. This meant not simply providing a critique of Petrarchan clichés, as in "The Canonization," or articulating an anachronistic view of innocence ("Love's not so pure, and abstract, as they use / To say, which have no Mistresse but their Muse" ("Loves Growth")), or even boasting that "I can love both faire and browne" ("The Indifferent") instead of the usual "faire" *or* "browne." By the early 1590s, these "anti-Petrarchan" responses were already part of the stock in trade of English Petrarchists. It meant, rather, re-imagining for a private audi-ence the situation of amatory verse itself, which Donne accomplished through one simple but comprehensive and destabilizing move: by wresting from the female the kind of autonomy and referential control she "possessed" in the Petrarchan system (to say nothing about her actual presence on the English throne). The real as well as imagined hierarchy not only exercised severe limits on the kinds of address possible within a courtly poem – a compromising situation that even a court poet like Spenser felt[22] – but also worked to constrain the significance of the individual lyric encounter by frequently placing it within a sequence or cycle of other poems, one that ended either "happily" (*Amoretti*) or, as is more often the case, with the poet graveled.

In Donne's love poetry, the principal point of reference is always "I," as in "I can love both faire and browne," not *she* is "both faire and browne." A simple comparison of the sonnets of Spenser and Sidney with those of Donne shows how reluctant they were to begin a poem with an authorizing first-person pronoun. But Donne's "I" is also never stable (as in, again, "I can love both faire *and* browne" [my italics]). Nor is the "I" part of a continuous sequence: the "order" of the *Songs and Sonnets* as first published in 1633 and then rearranged and identified as a group in 1635 is editorially determined, as is the case with the *Elegies*, and nothing survives in the manuscripts to indicate a preferred placement by Donne. And, of course, the poetic forms in the *Songs and Sonnets* are extraordinarily varied, each seemingly invented for the specific experience.

Donne's love poetry consequently asks us to imagine a fuller range of attitudes and expressions than previous amatory verse had acknowledged. But even this way of conceiving the poems on a behavioral spectrum seems inadequate: partly because the pressure on the reader in moving from poem to poem is to reconceive anew not just the "situation" but the speaker himself, or more exactly, his and sometimes (as in "Sapho to Philaenis")[23] her character as defined in relation to a shifting and no longer idealized "other"; and partly because the pressure of Donne's dramatizing intelligence – his relentless arguing, his penchant for graphic detail, his hyperbolic imagination – demands an altogether more strenuous kind of involvement than is usually requested by the sonneteer. The poet of "insistent talk" always threatens to overwhelm all but the most entrenched reader.

This is especially true of the elegies, that genre of erotic love poetry stemming from Tibullus, Propertius, and Ovid and misdescribed by George Puttenham, the courtly rhetorician, in the *Arte of English Poesie* (1589) as "certain piteous verse" in which lovers "sought the favor of faire Ladies, and coveted to bemone their estates at large & the perplexities of love."[24] Puttenham was perpetuating a notion of the love elegy as erroneously described by Horace in the *Ars Poetica* (ll. 75–8), a definition that also later failed to distinguish it adequately from the Petrarchan poem; and the blurring continues into the early 1590s when the elegy became a popular genre and the term first began to appear on the title pages of amorous verse, though always in the company of the sonnet and always, in order of appearance, subordinated to it, as is suggested by the title of Thomas Lodge's *Phillis: Honoured with Pastorell Sonnets, Elegies, and amorous delights* (1593).[25]

Donne, however, seems to have conceived of the genre as an opportunity to drive a wedge between these two kinds of amatory experiences and their discursive models. His elegies have nothing to do with "pastorall sonnets," even less to do with honoring an imaginary "Phillis." His women change with each poem (they are occasionally married and frequently cunning), and sometimes change within a single poem ("Natures lay Ideot"); and Donne's attitude, although occasionally intimate, is anything but revering. Not only do the elegies, like the satires, smack of the city in their material view of sex, but the speakers are most surely "men" of the world: explorers and exploiters alike, verbal conjurers ("The Anagram," "On his Mistris") as well as sexual creationists ("Natures lay Ideot"). The most infamous of the elegies, in fact, combines the frank eroticism of Ovid (I, v) and Propertius (II, xv) with contemporary expansionist discourse. The poem, "To his Mistris Going to Bed," is too good, and too representative, not to quote in full:

> Come, Madame, come, all rest my powers defie,
> Until I labour, I in labour lye.
> The foe oft-times, having the foe in sight,
> Is tir'd with standing, though they never fight.
> Off with that girdle, like heavens zone glistering
> But a farre fairer world encompassing.
> Unpin that spangled brest-plate, which you weare
> That th'eyes of busy fooles may be stopt there:
> Unlace your selfe, for that harmonious chime
> Tells me from you that now 'tis your bed time.
> Off with that happy buske, whom I envye
> That still can be, and still can stand so nigh.
> Your gownes going off such beauteous state reveales
> As when from flowery meades, th'hills shadow steales.
> Off with your wyrie coronet and showe
> The hairy dyadem which on you doth growe.
> Off with those shoes: and then safely tread
> In this loves hallow'd temple, this soft bed.
> In such white robes heavens Angels us'd to bee
> Receiv'd by men; Thou Angel bring'st with thee
> A heaven like Mahomets Paradise; and though
> Ill Spirits walk in white, we easily know
> By this these Angels from an evill sprite:
> They set our haires, but these the flesh upright.
>   Licence my roving hands, and let them goe
> Behind, before, above, between, below.
> Oh my America, my new found lande,
> My Kingdome, safeliest when with one man man'd,
> My myne of precious stones, my Empiree,
> How blest am I in this discovering thee.
> As soules unbodied, bodies uncloth'd must bee
> To taste whole joyes. Gems which you women use
> Are as Atlanta's balls, cast in mens viewes,

That when a fooles eye lighteth on a gem
His earthly soule may covet theirs not them.
Like pictures, or like bookes gay coverings made
For laymen, are all women thus arraid;
Themselves are mystique bookes, which only wee
Whom their imputed grace will dignify
Must see reveal'd. Then since I may knowe,
As liberally as to a midwife showe
Thy selfe; cast all, yea this white linnen hence.
Here is no pennance, much less innocence.
    To teach thee, I am naked first: Why than
What need'st thou have more covering than a man.

As we might expect, this elegy, popular in the miscellanies of the period, especially at Oxford, seems destined for controversy, which it has inspired beginning with initial acts of censorship (the poem was not printed until the Restoration edition of Donne's poems in 1669) and continuing into the present with critical worrying over the speaker's moral and physical posture. Is he a cad? A colonizer? A dominator of women? (By the poem's end, Carey imagines the woman cowering under a bedsheet.)[26] Or is he a radical libertine and liberator? Indeed, the reference to "Licence my roving hands" seems designed to call attention to the daring bravado of writing licentious poetry in general, and in addition, to the daring politics of a poetic act that a woman has the power to approve. We, and perhaps more significantly, Donne's earlier audience might remember that Marlowe's limp translation of Ovid's *Elegies* was among the works censored in 1599, and this poem is anything but limply written.

In any event, from the opening command ("Come, Madame, come") to the closing query ("What need'st thou have more covering than a man"), Donne plays fast and loose with sexual puns, wittily blasphemous allusions, hyperbole, mock worship, and, most of all, with the underlying conceit of the speaker as a kind of indecent Sir Walter Raleigh of the bedroom attempting to display, in private, the full extent of his male identity: his "masculine, persuasive force." As commentary testifies, Elegy 19 is clever, shocking, outrageously male, easily insulting to women and to king alike. And yet Donne is so enthusiastic over the prospect of sex – "Oh my America, my new found lande" – that the poem also possesses a kind of radical innocence justifying, in the minds of some, the variant reading of the crucial line 46: "There is no pennance *due to* innocence" (my italics). If this poem has long been read as the quintessential Donne elegy, and furthermore, if it helped to enable more consciously artful poems like Carew's "The Rapture" and Marvell's "To His Coy Mistress," it is not because it is less indecent than some of Donne's other attempts in this genre. It is because the intoxicating power of promiscuity is central to the (male) imaginative experience of the poem, where it is figured on something approaching a grand scale. ("Behind, before, above, between, below," we might be tempted to say.)

11

Whatever moral or political value we assign to the speaker (and recent critics emphasizing only the colonizing urges of the poet usually forget that Donne's final gesture of authority is made "deshabille"), the poem is a triumph of *licence*. It is a boundary stretcher: generic, geographical, and sexual. And in these dilations, it testifies to a powerful fantasy of the male English Renaissance: the yearning for more that is Donne's and his era's, a desire perhaps best epitomized in the poem's concluding line: "Why than / What need'st thou have more covering than a man," as if man could cover everything. When Marvell begins his great poem more than fifty years later with the haunting line "Had we but world enough and time," we know that the bloom of exploration is partly off the rose. Three hundred years later, in 1955, when the Australian poet A.D. Hope writes a poem called "The Elegy, Variations on a Theme of the Seventeenth Century," the suave, Augustan tone and elegiac shadows of that poem's post-coital, post-colonial setting place Donne's in another era altogether.

In important ways, the stylistic and rhetorical battles waged in the *Satires* and *Elegies* were won in the *Songs and Sonnets* and in the divine poems, particularly the hymns. That, at least, has been the judgment of most modern readers from Eliot onwards. We do not have to accept the view that Eliot was being only self-serving in pressing the case for Donne's "undissociated sensibility" to recognize that Donne's genius was for argument, especially arguing himself into and out of small corners and tight places, for generating bold leaps of thought that seem only the more spectacular because of the apparent constraints of the topic. In a broad sense, this kind of formal athleticism is going on throughout the *Songs and Sonnets* when love poetry is suddenly made to "entertain" new, often marginalized perspectives: the poet writing from the point of view of a sexually active woman in "Breake of Day" and "Confined Love" (women were generally imagined as speakers of laments only), or from beyond the grave in "The Legacie," "The Dampe," and "The Relique" (rather than merely claiming to be killed by his mistress). Donne's persona can be a tortured Petrarchist triply vexed by his own "whining Poetry" ("The Triple Foole"), a possibly seedy scholastic explicating the apparent difference between men and women ("Aire and Angels"), or a Mark Antony incarnate: "She'is all States, and all Princes, I" ("The Sunne Rising").

But this athletic activity is also going on within the poetry. "The Flea," placed first in the 1635 edition, has long seemed vintage Donne because the corner out of which he writes seems doubly barred. What does one say about a flea as a subject for erotic poetry, first of all? And what does one say when a rage for flea poetry in the early 1580s has already produced "a collection of over fifty poems on fleas in French, Spanish, Italian, Latin, and Greek"?[27] Jonson, by way of calling attention to the decorum required in writing about small things – in this case an epitaph commemorating a girl bearing only a first name – remarked "Wouldst thou hear what man can say / In a little"; and his poem on "Elizabeth, L.H." is a model of compression. Donne's response, on this occasion as well as others (see, especially, *The First and Second Anniversaries*, which Jonson thought "profane and full of blasphemies"),[28] is to see how *much* one can say. In the space of twenty-seven lines, he makes his flea an emblem of sexual tumescence, of the marriage bed, of marriage itself, and of martyrdom: it is killed by the lady between the second and third stanzas (one is tempted to say acts). And finally (though one hesitates to say "finally"), it is an emblem of the honor that the lady will lose in giving herself to the speaker. "The Flea" is not a model of compression only; it is a model of expansion and compression, collapsing with a bang of the fist and concluding where so many of the love poems conclude: with a persuasion to love.

With a poetry of this kind of explosive wit, there is always the danger of under- or overvaluing its effects. Some of the poems seem little more than sophistical squibs, syntactically complicated pirouettes, that disappear from memory once figured out. (Nothing has so worked against Donne as the modern assumption that everything he wrote is canonical.) And the desire to outwit the imagined females who serve as "objects" of address, to have the final, sometimes nasty last word, as in the concluding dig at the end of "Loves Alchemie" – "Hope not for minde in women" – shows a misogynist Donne participating fully in the culture's stereotypical attitudes toward women. (The best response to these moments may be simply to admit into this "dialogue of one" a later female poet like Edna St. Vincent Millay who, in a sonnet like "I, being born a woman," clearly and coolly expresses her fatigue with the whole idea of being ardently wooed.)[29] But it is not easy to forget – and surely this is a motivating concern as well as a professed problem for the "devout" Donne – a great number of the lyrics, which seem to have been written with the intention of commemorating a private moment of two-as-one by turning it into an occasion that extends into the farthest reaches of the universe. Chatty, rustic immediacy in "The Good-morrow," for instance, is made to include a vision of love that "all love of other sights controules," right down, one feels, to the last, splendidly measured alexandrine in each stanza:

> And now good morrow to our waking soules,
>   Which watch not one another out of feare;
> For love, all love of other sights controules,
>   And makes one little roome, an every where.
> Let sea-discoverers to new worlds have gone,
> Let Maps to others, worlds on worlds have showne,
> Let us possesse our world, each hath one, and is one.
>
> (ll. 8–14)

In a similar vein, "The Sunne Rising" presents the lovers in bed on the morning after, the poet wrestling with the daybreak until the moment of his heroically generous compromise:

> Thine age askes ease, and since thy duties bee
> > To warme the world, that's done in warming us.
> Shine here to us, and thou art every where;
> This bed thy center is, these walls, thy spheare.

And in "The Anniversarie," celebrated commitment sounds throughout, from the resonant crescendo of:

> All Kings, and all their favorites,
> All glory'of honors, beauties, wits,
> The Sun it selfe, which makes times, as they passe,
> Is elder by a yeare, now, then it was
> When thou and I first one another saw:
> All other things, to their destruction draw,
> Only our love hath no decay;

> > > > > > (ll. 1–7)

to the regally punctuated pledge at the end:

> Let us love nobly, and live, and adde againe
> Yeares and yeares unto yeares, till we attaine
> To write threescore: this is the second of our raigne.

Making "one little room, an everywhere," claiming "This bed thy center is, these walls, thy spheare," constantly placing love above the social hierarchy: this august, expansive, and authoritative idiom marks the high flight of Donne's love poetry, a flight controlled by rigorous argument and sometimes interpreted by biographical critics as either the cause of, or compensation for, the career actually sacrificed by his clandestine marriage. The preferred alternative depends on whether one wants to emphasize the romantic or conservative temper of Donne's mind; but given the problem of dating many of the lyrics with any certainty, either view can become dangerously circular when pressed very hard. It also goes without saying that the transcendental claims being made for a love that includes sexuality provide a significant revision of the Petrarchan, Neoplatonic tradition. Both "aubades" and "The Anniversarie" celebrate mutuality in the present – a pervasive intertwining of "I" and "thou" into a persuasive "us" – and consciously set that experience against "the rags of time," as Donne asks his audience to imagine the possibility of a momentous victory within a moment of human love.

By the same token, parting in Donne is never simply sweet sorrow, even in the unusually tender song "Sweetest love, I do not goe." The four valedictions and the magnificently dour "A Nocturnall upon S. Lucies Day" take a minor mode within the amatory tradition – the occasion of parting – and orchestrate it into a major strain in the *Songs and Sonnets*. It simply will not do, for instance, to call "A Valediction: of Weeping" by the kind of generic title often supplied in the miscellanies to describe the occasion of lovers separating. When Donne weeps, he weeps as no other has done, a pun that might seem strained were the poem or Donne in general less eagerly committed to "conceits," including the possibility here that amid the many kinds of mirrorings the poet has encoded his wife Anne's maiden name (More) within the body of the poem. It might, too, be easy to arraign Donne on charges of mere cleverness if the concluding heptameter, in its cadenced reach, did not season the wit so absolutely:

> Let me powre forth
> My teares before thy face, whil'st I stay here,
> For thy face coines them, and thy stampe they beare,
> And by this Mintage they are something worth,
>   For thus they bee
>   Pregnant of thee;
> Fruits of much griefe they are, emblemes of more,
> When a teare falls, that thou falls which it bore,
> So thou and I are nothing then, when on a divers shore.
>
>   (ll.1–9)

Parting *and* departing, separation *and* death, division *and* dissolution, something then nothing: Donne's imagination slides relentlessly, and precariously, between these related realities in all his love poetry but especially in the Valedictions, where the thread linking the two lovers receives perhaps its finest – in both senses of that word – spinning in "A Valediction: forbidding Mourning."[30] And when Donne is the one who is left, as in "A Nocturnall upon S. Lucies Day," grief knows no bottom:

> 'Tis the yeares midnight, and it is the dayes,
> *Lucies*, who scarce seaven houres herself unmaskes,
>   The Sunne is spent, and now his flasks
>   Send forth light squibs, no constant rayes;
>   The world's whole sap is sunke:
> The generall balme th'hydroptique earth hath drunk,
> Whither, as to the beds-feet, life is shrunke,
>   Dead and enterr'd; yet all these seeme to laugh,
>   Compar'd with mee, who am their Epitaph.
>
>   (ll. 1–9)

Donne does not paint death into some tidy corner. For this carnival of grief, this doubly darkened festival of midnight mourning – St. Lucy's Day falls on the shortest day of the year in the old calendar (December 12th) – Donne pulls out all the stops. The somber musicality and "spent" imagery of the opening stanza set the mood for the bleak, witty paradoxes that follow. All attempt, and in some measure fail, to define the experience of absolute emptiness, of Donne as the nadir of nothingness. Whether appearing, as he does above, in the last line of the stanza – but then only as the epitome of death, a speaking epitaph – or emphatically admitting that, in his grief, he cannot even be an "ordinary nothing," a shadow (for to be a shadow is to have a body), Donne turns the upwardly spiralling wit of amatory mutuality into a sharply delineated descent into deprivation: "Of absence, darknesse, death; things which are not." "All others, from all things, draw all that's good," but not Donne, the exception who proves the rule; and in the moving final stanza, he invites us to listen to a voice on the brink of extinction:

> But I am None; nor will my Sunne renew.
> You lovers, for whose sake, the lesser Sunne
>   At this time to the Goat is runne
>   To fetch new lust, and give it you,
>   Enjoy your summer all;
> Since shee enjoyes her long nights festivall,
> Let mee prepare towards her, and let mee call
> This houre her Vigill, and her Eve, since this
> Both the yeares, and the dayes deep midnight is.

The plain admission that "my Sunne" will not "renew" allows a bittersweet salute for others to "Enjoy your summer all," while Donne will "prepare towards her," the deceased and sometimes thought to be his wife. And though the imagery of the concluding line recollects the beginning of the poem, it does so with a difference. The final trail of stressed words ("dayes deep midnight is") leads us only deeper into the surrounding darkness and leaves us perhaps a little short of breath as well.

Donne, the divine

The problems and effects analyzed so far reappear, though sometimes in a more concentrated light, in the "religious" poetry. I use the quotation marks to signal the difficulty in making an absolutely clear distinction, as Walton tried to do, between the "Jack Donne" who wrote amorous poetry and the Dr. Donne who, having taken orders in 1615, reportedly wrote "many divine Sonnets, and other high, holy, and harmonious composures."[31] In so far as dates can be determined with any degree of certainty, a good many of the "Holy Sonnets" are thought to have been written before Donne took orders, and at least one hymn, "Goodfriday, 1613: Riding Westward," clearly preceded that event. There are also questions about how narrowly we should construe the notion of "religious" verse. The Third "Satire" is concerned with the vexing problem of determining the "true" church, although we hardly think of it as especially pious. The *First*

and Second Anniversaries, published in 1611 and 1612 respectively and interpreted often as religious meditations, have also been read in the context of
Donne's other occasional verse as appeals for patronage. "A Nocturnall upon S.
Lucies Day" helps to make the point: clearly a vigil, it is often read as an occasional poem but almost always appears in editions of the *Songs and Sonnets*.

But the idea of a "devotional" Donne certainly has validity so long as the
devotional in Donne is not made to exclude the effects we have so far encountered: the disturbing particularity of a scene ("Oh my blacke Soule! now thou
art summoned / By sicknesse"), the sudden extension of the concentrated
moment into the universe ("What if this present were the worlds last night"),
the tortured exhibitionism ("Spit in my face yee Jewes, and pierce my side"),
intellectual complexity ("Oh, to vex me, contaryes meete in one"), and an
idiom characterized by passionate exhortation, though now turned against the
self ("Batter my heart, three person'd God"). But there is another reason not to
overvalue the pious in Donne, since it is precisely the problem of impiety – the
problem of subordinating the "I" in all of its materiality to the "eye" of God –
that determines the kind of response we most often find in the devotional
poetry: the fear of being forgotten, of failing in the ultimate sense of not getting
to the other shore. Whether the source of such anxiety lies in the deeper
reaches of Donne's religious biography as an isolated Catholic who ultimately
accepted the creeds and codes of Protestantism, or whether it resides in more
immediate worries of employment, or whether the answer is in the heterodox-
ical nature of Donne's mind – its refusal ever to be at rest – or even in his guilt
over his earlier "idolatries," the disturbance was sufficiently seismic not only to
be explicitly realized in the most private of his divine poems, the *Holy Sonnets*;
it was also to be given a kind of public exorcism in "A Hymne to God, the
Father," that extraordinary poem filled with puns on the poet's name, which
Donne reportedly caused "to be set to a most grave and solemn tune, and to be
often sung to the organ by the Choristers of St. Paul's Church, in his own
hearing."[32]

After generally refusing to write formal sonnets during the decade of the
sonnet, Donne's decision to reanimate the form in his *Holy Sonnets* might be
explained as another instance of his working against the grain. The religious
sonnet, while receiving some attention in the 1590s from the likes of Henry
Lok (*Sundry Christian Passions Contained in Two Hundred Sonnets*, 1593, 1597)
and Barnabe Barnes (*A Divine Centurie of Spirituall Sonnets*, 1595) went under-
ground in the early years of James's reign. But it was still the form most suitable
to a poet who might imagine himself now in the position of unrequited lover,
suffering in his alienation spiritually as well as vocationally, and seeking some
sign of recognition from a God frequently and hopefully figured as a jealous,
sometimes violent, lover. This posture is only barely developed in the "La
Corona" sequence, a series of linked sonnets on the principal events of Jesus's
life in which the last line of one becomes the first in the next until finally
completing a circle or "*crowne of prayer and praise*." In this most ritualized of

poems, second only to "A Litanie" in this regard, Donne's speaker begins in a mood of "low devout melancholie" and gradually, over the course of the seven meditations, weaves himself out of this condition, sustained by the larger – and one is tempted to say residual Catholic – claim that "*Salvation to all that will is nigh.*"

For the *Holy Sonnets*, however, we might also be tempted to rewrite that claim as "salvation to me is well-nigh denied." At least, that is the perspective from which many of these poems are conceived, a perspective that has encouraged some critics to view the sonnets as substantially informed by Protestant worries over individual election.[33] As in the moving lament, "O might those sighes and teares returne againe," devout melancholy now borders on despair. The desire to be touched can be imagined in only the most sexually paradoxical and violent of terms: "Take mee to you, imprison mee, for I / Except you'en-thrall mee, never shall be free, / Nor ever chast, except you ravish mee." Even when Donne writes of receiving a sign of election, as in the curiously poignant sonnet on his wife's death ("Since she whome I lovd, hath payd her last debt"), it fails to satisfy him. "Why should I begg more love," is the note of insecurity frequently and sometimes feverishly sounded in these sonnets, one that can become irritating in its self-pity – "Weaker I am, woe is mee, and worse then you" – and threaten the formal integrity of the poem with a facile turn after the octave. A discourse of ingratiation never came easily to Donne. One sometimes feels that, as with his own prolonged delays in joining the Church, he needed more room than that provided by the sonnet to work out the turn in a convincing fashion.

We might find evidence to support this view in two great, though greatly differing, places: "Goodfriday, 1613: Riding Westward," written two years before his ordination, and the three hymns, all written well after that event, two perhaps as late as or later than 1623. In "Goodfriday," the religious "turn" is everything: the center and circumference of the universe as well as the poem, with its vision of the sacrificed Christ, either tuning or turning the spheres, placed at the exact center of the poem: "Could I behold those hands which span the Poles, / And tune [turne] all spheares at once, peirc'd with those holes?" (The editorial dispute surrounding the choice here has been resolved only in so far as "tune" has been offered as including "turne.")[34] That feared but desired vision also provides a focal point for the meditation, the gravity of which requires the full forty-two lines for Donne to sort through the many conflicting layers of his devotion on this day of sacrifices: "Hence is't, that I am carryed towards the West / This day, when my Soules forme bends toward the East." To read "Goodfriday" is to witness an imagination deepening, in successive stages, its devotional potential, drawn inevitably to the thing it initially attempted to resist, as if the very notion of setting out westward instigated a counteracting, greater plot from the East, one that gradually inhabits the speaker's entire being and all his thinking.[35]

The climax begins in line 33, perhaps as numerologically significant as the number of lines in the poem, forty-two. (Donne was in his forty-second year in 1613.) But these mathematical nuances would matter little if the felt logic of the poem were less strong, if our sense of Donne's earlier reluctance to be a witness of the sacrifice beginning as far back as line 11 were not so thoroughly turned and eventually trumped by the functioning memory; functioning, that is, by finally remembering the spiritual significance of Christ's sacrifice, the act of God turning into man to save mankind, to save even the guilt-ridden speaker riding westward in 1613:

> Though these things, as I ride, be from mine eye,
> They'are present yet unto my memory,
> For that looks towards them; and thou look'st towards mee,
> O Saviour, as thou hang'st upon the tree.

On their own, these lines are almost disturbingly casual, at least until the emerging trinity of memory and "things" is suddenly completed in the second half of line 35 and the speaker sees himself at the center of Christ's gaze. In the turn (or is it a leap?) to the apostrophe beginning the next line, moreover, if we sense another voice taking over, that voice is made to sound all the more resonant to the reader who has come to this poem from the *Holy Sonnets*. Christ goes by many titles there but is never called "Saviour," let alone "O Saviour." Eyed by this Jesus, Donne can now make a concluding, though not ultimately final, turn as he offers up his back in a purposeful act of penance:

> I turne my backe to thee, but to receive
> Corrections, till thy mercies bid thee leave.
> O thinke mee worth thine anger, punish mee,
> Burne off my rusts, and my deformity,
> Restore thine Image, so much, by thy grace,
> That thou may'st know mee, and I'll turne my face.

"Goodfriday" is a fully persuasive poem, a powerful dramatization of the irresistibility of divine grace operating on the will of the speaker. It might even be tempting to think of it as a "conversion" poem; but if we resist the pleasantly Walton-like desire to assign it a pivotal place in Donne's career story, it is because we know Donne still had a few cards left to play in his quest for secular preferment. (As late as 1614, Donne was seeking the ambassadorship to Venice.) But "Goodfriday" does suggest, as the sonnets do not, how the turn could be both imagined and enacted, how a deferral of choice (riding westward) could be fashioned into a desire for the East, a desire made stronger by the very nature of its delay. And that dimension of the poem does accord with what we know of Donne's career as a divine. Once ordained, he was a fully committed servant of the Church, rising quickly to become Dean of St. Paul's in 1622 and one of England's most famous preachers.

To readers approaching the later poetry, it is also that story, in several versions, that Donne kept remaking in verse. In the three great hymns, the face has turned and all that seems to remain is the fine tuning, the turning of phrases to celebrate a choice as having been made and as having been the right one. Although Donne wrote very little poetry after being ordained, these poems, in their assured seriousness, lend support from a different quarter to the idea that he did not want to be known as a "pleasant poetical" dean.[36] The tuning here is of a canonical kind. The poems have a public, ritualized dimension that is not present in the *Holy Sonnets*, but they are not so communal as to erase all traces of the speaker's identity from the text. If anything, one feels that the effort in these hymns is to define and place the personal in a wide, divinely determined, arena. In "A Hymne to Christ, at the Authors last going into Germany," the Protestant divine and possible martyr sets forth, but not before re-presenting himself in the final stanza as the fully converted, former love poet:

Seale then this bill of my Divorce to All,
On whom those fainter beames of love did fall;
Marry those loves, which in youth scattered bee
On Fame, Wit, Hopes (false mistresses) to thee.
Churches are best for Prayer, that have least light:
To see God only, I goe out of sight:
        And to scape stormy dayes, I chuse
        An Everlasting night.

In the "Hymne to God my God, in my sicknesse," the elected preacher gives himself the opportunity for one final divertissement before joining "thy Quire of Saints for evermore." The poem concludes by producing a text from a sermon to underscore the Augustinian turn in his life, which he now turns authoritatively, climactically, into an emblem for others: "Be this my Text, my Sermon to mine owne, / Therefore that he may raise the Lord throws down." And in "A Hymne to God the Father," the pun on his name comes dizzyingly and, initially at least, arrogantly to the fore as a sign of his own egocentricity and mortality until the final stanza when the friction between God and Donne, represented in the first two stanzas in the conflicting senses of "done," is imagined as being erased by a heavenly sign that helps to stabilize the referents through a careful subordination of meaning:

I have a sinne of feare, that when I have spunne
    My last thred, I shall perish on the shore;
Sweare by thy selfe, that at my death thy Sunne
    Shall shine as it shines now, and heretofore;
        And, having done that, Thou hast done,
            I have no more.

Donne's language here remains richly polysemous, but the several puns now point toward a single, overarching reading: overcoming death. "I have no more," with the pun for death in Latin (mors) helping to cinch the note of closure.

In all three poems, too, one feels their force as hymns, poems that, if actually problematic to sing, nonetheless invite the reader into their stanzaic folds by virtue of the simple imperatives or ritualized acts of interrogation performed by the speaker: "In what torne ship soever I embarke, / That ship shall be my embleme of thy Arke." The wit remains, but its intricacies are directed more toward revealing a dominant register of worship than toward displaying a self only vexed by contraries, a register whose tonal range is controlled by the significant preposition in the title of each: "to." For all their purported immediacy, the *Holy Sonnets* are rarely intimate; but in the hymns, the modulations of speech develop out of a seasoned colloquy with God:

> Since I am comming to that Holy roome,
>> Where, with thy Quire of Saints for evermore,
> I shall be made thy Musique; As I come
>> I tune the Instrument here at the dore,
>> And what I must doe then, thinke now before.

Part of what pleases here is our sense of the chatty love poet returning to his work on a more consciously respectful, elevated plane. Although we can only speculate about the trafficking that went on between Donne and the Herberts, perhaps the note was also heard by the future author of *The Temple*, George Herbert, who was getting ready to "step foot" into divinity shortly after this last hymn was written, probably in December, 1623. In the context of the unprecedented public celebration of English poets as authors in the early seventeenth century, a celebration that began with the publication of the 1616 Jonson Folio and continued with the 1617 Spenser Folio, and the 1623 Shakespeare and Daniel Folios, Donne's hymns, themselves perhaps a partial response to this situation, as well as Donne's example made it possible for both a culture and an individual to conceive of not just the traditional Spenserian poet-priest but the priest who could also be a serious poet. Herbert, of course, is only the most brilliant instance in the seventeenth century of an author whose achievement is not possible to comprehend without also understanding the poet whose verse was transcribed more often than that of "any other British poet of the 16th and 17th centuries."[37]

* * *

In this chapter, I have been attempting to read Donne in large part from the perspective of his best contemporary interpreter, Thomas Carew, who, borrowing from the language of political discourse in his elegy on Donne, elevated him to "The universall Monarchy of Wit" and then, for good measure, placed him in another poem in the company of Virgil, Lucan, and Tasso.[38] That idealizing but responsive reading has been considerably complicated since then, and recent critiques of Donne have generally sought, sometimes explicitly, to downplay his originality from a variety of angles: by attempting to view him within an emerging tradition of Protestant poetics in which concern with the self is set in the larger context of methods and practices that govern Reformed habits of meditation; by interpreting Donne's language as already contained within a contemporary politics of absolutist discourse; or by defining the specific community of poets – the gentlemen amateurs of the earlier seventeenth century – with whom Donne frequently affiliated, minor versifiers like Everard Guilpen or Christopher Brooke, or more able but still marginal and self-professed amateurs like Sir Henry Wotton and Edward, Lord Herbert of Cherbury, whose poetry, once gathered, might add a retrospective grace note to a career already distinguished by other accomplishments.[39] In many respects, these recent revaluations seem as necessary as they are inevitable in their response to problems initiated by several generations of critics who either resisted historical readings or, operating in the afterglow of Eliot, consistently made Donne the originator of a "school" of poets. Donne was not so original as Eliot wanted him (what poet could be?), and he certainly did not think of poetry as a kind of Yeatsian "artifice of eternity" into which the aching soul could be gathered. We do not know the occasions motivating all his poems, but we do know that enough were produced in hopes of personal advancement to question a fully romanticized view of the creating poet serving his muse in solitude.

But, however we contextualize Donne, it must also be said that he sounds very little like anyone else. A bit like Jonson perhaps in a few of the elegies, but surely not much like the other coterie poets with whom he associated; and he certainly does not sound at all like James or even a good meditating Protestant like Joseph Hall. Though we can credit his full emergence as a poet-priest to the efforts of friends, publishers, kin, and hagiographers like Walton, we ought to recognize that to a great degree Walton, for one, was only amplifying what Donne had already written. The poet who was obsessed with his own signature on a pane of glass had reason to be. It was original in the way all discourse is original, not by claiming to be first, but by claiming to be different from what came before and then demonstrating that difference within the text. If Donne can weary us, it is only on this score.

2

BEN JONSON AND THE ART OF INCLUSION

I know to whom I write.

Jonson, "An Epistle to Master John Selden"

It is always astonishing to read the thumbnail sketch provided by William Drummond of the poet who has generally come to be recognized as England's first great Neoclassicist: Ben Jonson – without the "h." His grandfather, so the Dickensian sounding narrative begins,

> came from Carlisle, and he thought from Annandale to it; he served Henry VIII, and was a gentleman. His father lost all his estate under Queen Mary; having been cast in prison and forfeited, at last turned minister. ... He himself was posthumous born a month after his father's decease; brought up poorly, put to school by a friend (his master Camden), after taken from it, and put to another craft (I think was to be a wright [workman] or bricklayer), which he could not endure. Then went he to the Low Countries, but returning soon he betook himself to his wonted studies. In his service in the Low Countries he had, in the face of both the camps, killed an enemy and taken *opima spolia* from him; and since his coming to England, being appealed to the fields, he had killed his adversary, which had hurt him in the arm, and whose sword was ten inches longer than his; for the which he was imprisoned, and almost at the gallows. Then took he his religion by trust of a priest who visited him in prison. Thereafter he was twelve years a papist.[1]

This depicts anything but serenity incarnate – hardly what we expect of the author of such supremely finished and thoroughly enchanting lines as the following:

Queen and huntress, chaste and fair,
Now the sun is laid to sleep,

Seated in thy silver chair,
State in wonted manner keep:
    Hesperus entreats thy light,
    Goddess excellently bright.

(p. 482, ll. 1–6)

Anyone turning to this frequently anthologized lyric taken from *Cynthia's Revels* (1601) after reading Donne could probably immediately begin producing a list of opposites to account for differences in tone, theme, and subject matter; and until recently this list would probably have worked against Jonson. It might identify a poetry of vigorous invention (Donne) versus a poetry of stated elegance (Jonson); a poetry that constantly violates decorum, sexual as well as verbal, versus a poetry that emphasizes chasteness of diction and phrase and celebrates love with cool reserve; a poetry that banished, in Carew's phrase, the "traine / Of gods and goddesses"[2] in favor of mythologizing self-expression versus a poetry that seems to subordinate self-expression to the timeless constellations of ancient myths: in short, a poetry of conscious excess versus a poetry of conscious limitation. Or, as psychoanalytically inclined critics might argue, the repressed aristocrat exercising his fantasies in poetry versus the displaced gentleman attempting to recuperate his authority in print.

On the basis of these observations, we might also wish to pry these authors even further apart from another angle and for a different reason, by invoking Roman Jakobson's distinction between metaphor and metonymy to describe the fundamental semantic habit that governs the different poetics of each.[3] Donne, the master of metaphor whose yoking of opposites has long been seen as his special trademark, searches as few poets ever have to find resemblance amid difference. Jonson, the poet of metonymy for whom listing, not yoking, is at the core of his distinctly ethical vision, seeks to identify, to define, and frequently to rank individuals and objects in relation to one another in this world. If "The Good-morrow," with its taut dialectics of body and soul, time and eternity, and its allusively symbolic language positing worlds within worlds is central to Donne's art, then "Inviting a Friend to Supper" lies at the heart of Jonson's. The various foods described – or rather presented and named – in his imaginary menu exist in casually arranged relation to each other:

It is the fair acceptance, sir, creates
    The entertainment perfect, not the cates.
Yet shall you have, to rectify your palate,
    An olive, capers, or some better salad
Ushering the mutton; with a short-legged hen,
    If we can get her, full of eggs, and then
Lemons, and wine for sauce; to these, a coney
    Is not to be despaired of, for our money.

(ll. 7–14)

Donne, we are continually reminded, wrote for a private audience. Jonson, as the above poem suggests, wrote from a deliberately social and socializing perspective: "It is the fair acceptance, sir, creates / The entertainment perfect, not the cates."

Seventeenth-century poetry owes much of its character and variety to these alternative models – the densely metaphoric and the richly metonymic, the metaphysical and the social – and the kinds of significant extension and refinement they received from later poets. But it is also dangerous (and the word is deliberately chosen) to view Jonson in too sharp an opposition to Donne. Both poets were born in the same decade – within a year of each other, in fact – and in their choice of genre and idiom, favoring the "newer" urban modes of satire, epigram, and verse epistle and emphasizing a language of matter over manner, the concise utterance over the display of copia, both set themselves in deliberate opposition to their fully Elizabethan predecessors – Spenser and Sidney – and not to each other. And both were writers of unusual lexical and imaginative strength. If it is one measure of a poet's stature to have greatly influenced others, then Donne and Jonson can lay equal claim to this palm. Both have been routinely accorded their own schools, Jonson even in his own time.

Donne's immediate fame as a poet was due in part to his fame as a preacher – to the institution of the church. Much of Jonson's reputation as an author came from the simple fact that no one, not even Spenser, worked harder to establish it. "A good poet's made, as well as born," he observed with august inclusiveness in his eulogy to Shakespeare,[4] and for Jonson, this meant making as well as making it on a number of different fronts: in the roguish world of the theater, in the more refined world of the court, at country estates of the wealthy, at the university, with the printing press – the principal institutions in the early seventeenth century by which a resourceful poet, with serious pretensions to artistry but who survived on the basis of his writings, might gain recognition. Beginning essentially with *Every Man in his Humour*, first acted in 1598 – I say "essentially" because Jonson deliberately chose not to remember a number of other "Elizabethan" productions including the Shakespearean sounding *Richard Crookback* – and continuing at least through *Bartholomew Fair* in 1614, Jonson put himself at the center of stage history by his continuous attempts to reform the Elizabethan and Jacobean theater: to purge it of its popular vices (especially sentimentalizing romantic comedy) as well as its medieval heritage by insisting on a return to Classical models, Plautine as well as Aristophanic, and not simply in the interest of serving the Aristotelian unities of time, place, and action, but also in order to recover for the playwright the role of moral judge and lawmaker. Horace is how he represented himself on stage in *Poetaster* in 1601. The poet who was to translate the *Ars Poetica* not once but twice rarely strayed from that pose in his later works.

As a partial outgrowth of his success in the theater and with comparable revisionary gusto, Jonson also became the principal maker of masques under James, a position he helped to secure with *The Masque of Blackness*, presented in the second year of the king's reign (1605). Jonson's reach extended now into the court and stretched, artistically speaking, in a more deliberately allegorical and Neoplatonic direction. For a while, it also included a productive collaboration with Inigo Jones, England's first Neoclassical architect and inventor of elaborate stage machinery, who managed the difficult task of pleasing two kings, James and Charles. And, as a writer of masques and entertainments, Jonson served some of the most powerful families in England. He did so sometimes on their estates, as with the early pastoral entertainment presented at Althorpe in 1603 for that most artistically patronizing of families, the Spencers (Spenser claimed them for kin; Shakespeare and later Milton wrote for some of the family members, and they remain in the news today); and occasionally at court when James chose to honor one of his favorites. Throughout his long career, moreover, a career that extended into the 1630s, the poet who never went to university but was a student of the most famous historian of the period, William Camden, and who came of age under a monarch who took special pride in appearing wise; the poet who, according to Drummond, "in his merry humour … was wont to name himself The Poet,"[5] was busy presenting himself as the most learned author of his day. It seems only fair that the author who dedicated *Volpone* to the two universities in England should receive an honorary degree from at least one (Oxford, 1619).

Individually, these literary acts or occasions were often impressive as well as expensive. Collectively, they helped to constitute a new version of poetic authority, which Jonson invites us to witness in that audacious and notorious "miscellany" of his published in 1616 when the poet had reached middle age, his *Workes* (fig. 1).[6] By the end of the sixteenth century, it had become common enough for aspiring poets to publish their verse in individual editions (usually quartos), although aristocrats like Sidney and those wishing to preserve their aristocratic connections like Donne generally disdained the medium of print in favor of circulating their poems in private manuscripts. Indeed, by the early seventeenth century it was even possible for a veteran poet like Jonson's occasional rival, Samuel Daniel, to attempt to advance his cause by putting out a large-page edition of his *Workes* in 1601. But Jonson improved on both of these precedents by extending to himself a privilege that so far in English literary history had been allowed only to canonical writers of the past, usually of the distant classical past. He collected, edited, and published his *oeuvre*, or to use the Latin term everywhere begged by Jonson's massive folio but not by Daniel's collection, his *opera*. When T.S. Eliot remarked some three hundred years later that a true understanding of Jonson begins with "intelligent saturation in his work as a whole,"[7] Jonson would not have wished it otherwise.

To set Daniel's *Workes* momentarily alongside Jonson's is also to glimpse a significant dimension of the shift in taste that occurred, if not immediately then gradually and profoundly, in the transition from Elizabeth to James, a shift that Jonson helped both to inaugurate and to confirm. Coming at the end of Elizabeth's reign, Daniel's *Workes* functions, in many regards, as a Masque of

Retrospection: an act of poetic homage to literary interests that dominated the late Elizabethan imagination. The Tudor concern or obsession with England's national past, for instance, the same dynastic interests motivating Shakespeare's history plays in the early 1590s, appears at the outset in the six books of *The Civile Warres betweene the two houses of Lancaster and York* (begun in 1594), all written in that chosen Renaissance form for epic, the canto. Then appears the much briefer and more recent philosophical poem *Musophilus* (1599), dedicated to Sidney's friend and future biographer Fulke Greville, in which the humanist ideal of the courtier poet is enacted once more. After that come two Neoclassical exercises, *A Letter from Octavia* (1599), in ottava rima, and the unactable *Cleopatra* (1594), produced at the request of Sidney's sister, the Countess of Pembroke; and after that appear Daniel's earliest productions, *The Complaint of Rosamond* (1592), linked to the still earlier *Mirror for Magistrates* tradition in both subject matter and form, and his *Sonnets to Delia* (1592). The whole is curiously circular in shape and nostalgic: the product of a Petrarchan courtier with one foot in the Sidney circle, responsive to "our Spenser," seeking patronesses by writing frequently about women and still serving, in her twilight, his sovereign queen, to whom the volume is dedicated.

Although Jonson thought Daniel "no poet" and was "at jealousies with him,"[8] we ought not to view the publication of his *Workes* as in any way a direct retort. If Daniel is a better poet than Jonson allowed, Jonson's sense of his own artistic superiority was sufficiently grounded that he could still allow Daniel the compliment of being a "good man" – not an empty gesture in Jonson's ethically conscious lexicon. But Daniel's *Workes* does pale, literally and metaphorically, against the thoroughgoing self- (one is tempted to say shelf-) consciousness of the Jonson folio. Published only fifteen years later, Jonson's seemingly belongs to a different culture altogether, one less interested in pressing dynastic claims than in pursuing the rewards of peace: those of learning, art, and entertainment, as now epitomized in the figure on the throne, the Solomonic king who claimed to unite England, Scotland and Wales under the common banner of "Britain," who placed the twin allegorical figures of Religion and Peace on the frontispiece of his own *Workes*, and who spent lavish sums of money on court entertainment.

Not because of size alone, however, does Jonson's folio ask to be housed with those other, prodigiously Jacobean literary productions contemporary with his: the Authorized Version of the Bible (1611), Raleigh's *History of the World* (1614), and, of course, *The Workes of King James*, published in the same year as Jonson's. Jonson's folio overlaps in illuminating ways with each. It delivers a newly authorized version of canonical genres, plays and masques (previously considered ephemera); it shares, with Raleigh's, a resourceful publisher in William Stansby, whose interest in producing two works of this scope and size allowed Jonson an extended opportunity to be actively involved in the production of his own book;[9] and it is a work that, while showing deference to the king on a number of particular occasions, nonetheless claims its own autonomous status. James is everywhere present within the text; nothing could be clearer than Jonson's presentation of himself as James's poet: but the king is absent where we might most expect to find him, in the dedication.

Jonson's *Workes* is the work of an author, not a poetaster. It represents a conscious and conscientious "advancement of learning," to borrow Bacon's title and apply it to his friend. The thousand-plus, large-size pages gather together all Jonson's significant publications to date, placing them in chronological order within their appropriate genres and introducing the whole with a lavishly engraved title page that spells out the thoroughly artistic concerns of the contents. A Roman theater appears in the central cartouche, flanked by allegorical figures representing Satire and Pastoral, with Tragi-comedy above. Directly below, framed between Tragedy and Comedy and further set off by Corinthian pillars, is the announcement, *The Workes of Benjamin Jonson*, accompanied by the motto from Horace: "neque, me ut miretur turba, / laboro: / Contentus paucis lectoribus" (I do not work so that the crowd may admire me: I am contented with a few readers).[10] Some of Jonson's "few readers" are then made manifest in the Table of Contents, or "The Catalogue," where the list of dedications is as impressive as the list of individual texts. The horizontal pairing, in fact, of text and dedicatee presumes a kind of easy reciprocity existing between author and patron, as if to say, here at last is an English poet finally at home in a variety of distinguished settings; here at last is a poet who has earned his keep.

The volume then proceeds to historicize, without mummifying, the poet and his literary productions as it attempts to reinforce the shift in cultural values and generic hierarchy that Jonson himself sought to determine on separate occasions. The individual plays no longer appear as shoddy quartos but have been transformed into dramatic artifacts, part of theater history, and yet done so with the intention of preserving, through careful punctuation, their performative features: "their dramatic and rhetorical effects."[11] Each is introduced by a separate title page, with the one constant amid the changing descriptions being the recurring imprint, "The Author B.J." Each is also framed by a concluding page that lists the players (*Every Man in His Humor* includes the name "Will Shakespeare") and gives, once again, the year in which the play was first acted. The masques and entertainments are likewise enrolled in a permanent hall of records. Treated now as cultural documents, they are presented as fully capable of existing on the strength of the text alone and some detailed notes by Jonson describing scenic particularities and allusions. Only the two volumes of poetry – *The Epigrams* and *The Forest* – evade, to a degree, this historicizing process; but they make their mark in other ways. Calling *The Epigrams*, as Jonson does, his "ripest studies," is akin to preserving ephemera like plays and masques, at least in that it consciously dignifies a traditionally lowly form of poetry (Puttenham called epigrams "privy nips, or witty scoffes");[12] while *The Forest*, after Jonson coyly separates it from a vast tradition in the Renaissance with a brief apology about "why I write not of love," offers itself as the first miscellany in English patterned on classical forms – perhaps even the first collection of verse in

Figure 1 The Workes of Benjamin Jonson. Printed by William Stansby, 1616, title page
   engraved by William Hole.
(Reproduced by permission of the William Andrews Clark Memorial Library.)

29

English to use a title with both a thematic and generic focus. (After Jonson, it became common for lyric poets like Herbert and Herrick to signal major organizing concerns through their choice of title.) In the context of the claims being made about art by the poet, both his own and the high Jacobean culture that supposedly helped to produce it, it seems only right that the folio should conclude with a masque entitled *The Golden Age Restored*. Or rather, Jonson made it seem only right by departing, on this one occasion, from the normal chronological scheme in order to place this masque last. The volume might now be read without a hitch as progressing from low to high, "from public forum, through select private readership to the aristocratic patrons, Court and King,"[13] where it could finally end by embracing the age. It could also be read as a new kind of epic, with "The Poet" – the high fashioner of *opima spolia* – its hero.

Poetry, marked off and near the center: 1616

Were Jonson merely an antiquarian with a large ego and some polish, it might be possible to get around him as Suckling and others have tried to do: by turning him into a caricature of ambition, a kind of sotted Sejanus, or into one of his own humor characters, as Edmund Wilson did in a famous essay entitled "Morose Ben Jonson." If there is an element of truth in both responses – and Wilson's is drawn almost exclusively from the drama – the exaggeration seems inevitably the result of the gentleman amateur or "man of letters" (or now Foucauldian critic) sizing up the thoroughly entrenched and frequently embattled professional.[14] But Jonson is also too significantly craggy, too variously and deeply shaded, as his picture in the National Portrait Gallery suggests, indeed too unpredictably hospitable to be routed from the canon with ease; and if as a poet he does not quite stand with Milton, "Like Teneriff or Atlas unremov'd," neither does he sit with other poetasters of the period in the shadow of Apollo's tree. Although Jonson's verse, of particular interest to us here, forms only a small part of his output, it is an essential part, as the placement of the two volumes between the plays and the masques and near the center of the *Workes* indicates; as too does the fact that writing verse was a lifelong habit. And it continues to make its mark, partly for the same reasons that Jonson turned to his muse increasingly in later age when, after the death of James in 1625, his fortunes at court declined: not because of its polish alone – how it embodies convictions Jonson set down in his *Discoveries* valuing a perspicacious style – but because of the grain underlying the polish, the kind of measured resilience that makes ancients and moderns seem, at times, as if they were tracking him. Few have ever taken poetry more seriously, in the best sense of that word. Even fewer have had Jonson's effect on the course of poetry.

With the exception of the songs from the plays and masques, Jonson's poetry falls into three kinds, all rooted in the classics: the epigram, with its resources in Martial and the Greek Anthology; the epistle, especially as practiced by Horace; and the ode, whether Anacreontic, Horatian, or Pindaric. There were precedents for each in English and on the Continent, but by the time Jonson finished writing they had become his special property although in remarkably different ways. By contrast, his one designated attempt at writing a sonnet (to Sidney's niece, the poet Mary Wroth) is clearly an attempt. (I mention "designated" because scholarly sleuthing will eventually uncover five other sonnets in the canon.)[15] The poem is so deliberately and comically left-footed, rhyming "poet" with "show it," "know it," and "owe it" for starters – Jonson used nearly the identical scheme in the burlesque on "Sir William Burlase, The Painter to the Poet" – that its placement next to "A Fit of Rhyme against Rhyme" can hardly be accidental. It is, in kind, an "anti-sonnet,"[16] though the poem manages to smooth out in the sestet in part as a graceful gesture signaling Mary Wroth's apparently beneficial influence: her worth. But one also suspects that however much we might think of this poem as a partial anticipation of *Hudibras*, Jonson's own pride as a poet would never allow him to appear only in a comical light. Even if he disliked the Procrustean constrictions imposed by the sonnet – Drummond reported Jonson's cursing Petrarch for "redacting verses to sonnets, which he said were like that tyrant's bed"[17] – he was too much the master of forms ever to be fully its victim. Hence in the next poem we get the formal paradox fully sounded of writing a fit of rhyme against rhyme.

Jonson's "fits" of stanzaic complexity, though done often with virtuosic grace in the later poetry ("My Picture Left in Scotland," "The Hour-Glass," "A Celebration of Charis, Her Triumph") when the established poet was clearly willing to *play* the courtier, are exceptions that seem designed to help prove the Jonsonian "rule" on another front: that couplets are "the bravest sort of verses, especially when they are broken, like hexameters; and that cross-rhymes and stanzas – because the purpose would lead [the poet] beyond eight lines to conclude – were all forced." Jonson was speaking here specifically about heroic poetry in the double context of his own "intention to perfect an epic poem, entitled *Heroologia*, of the worthies of his country roused by fame"[18] and of the long-standing Renaissance controversy over the propriety of rhyme in verse that had been recently rekindled in the dispute between the Latinizing Campion and the patriotic Daniel. But the general point is not lost, even if both *Heroologia* and Jonson's discourse, in which he (predictably) disagreed with both Campion and Daniel, were among the works that perished when his library burned in 1623. For the pressure of the couplet pervades his poetry from beginning to end. "He detesteth," reported Drummond in 1619, "all other rhymes."[19]

The Epigrams, in fact, the first collection of poetry a reader of the folio meets (or is it confronts?), is virtually a *tour de force* of the form. Cut and chiseled into a variety of lengths ranging from two to 196 lines (the majority are of a block-like, twelve-line length), all but nine of the 133 poems are in couplets. A look, moreover, at one of Jonson's contemporaries like Everard Guilpen – one could make a similar point with Sir John Davies's *Epigrammes* (1599) – will quickly disabuse us of the belief that books of epigrams published at the turn of the seventeenth century were necessarily concise or what we think of as "epigrammatic." Less than half of Guilpen's sixty-nine epigrams are in couplets. Many are simply cross-rhymed stanzas. Jonson's, on the other hand, seem fully *written*, doubly set down. If in their weightiness they inevitably call to mind the poet's early apprenticeship as a bricklayer, they also seem designed to recollect their formal origins as inscriptions. The meticulously observed pauses, for instance, of his opening address to the reader, "Pray thee take care, that tak'st my book in hand, / To read it well; that is, to understand,"[20] help to mark a close that is absolutely essential to the measured note of moral authority that Jonson sought to reinstill in a genre too often praised then (as well as now) with regard to either its pointed wit only – its salt – or else thought of, as was the case with Davies, almost exclusively in conjunction with knock-about-town trivia like "Buckministers Almanacke."[21]

This situation differs only slightly from that in his other collections. Although containing far fewer poems – a total of fifteen – *The Forest* is generically and formally more diverse, something we might expect from a volume whose title has been seen as consciously alluding to the sylva tradition descending from Statius, in which different kinds of matter are deliberately crowded into a single volume.[22] And as a feature of its variety, Jonson unveils a surprising array of speakers and situations, modes and moods: from the epigrammatic confession of a poet too old to love in a romantic way, to more weighty moral epistles; from slender songs of seduction to women, to impressively severe acts of female ventriloquism; from epode to ode to psalm. But for all its metrical and modal variety – and few poems in English successfully employ a more sophisticated rhyme scheme than "Drink to me only with thine eyes," Jonson's much anthologized nugget extracted from Philostratus – the controlling form remains the couplet. In all but three poems, it is the chosen rhyme scheme. Whether appearing in the suave octosyllabics of "Come My Celia" or the more sedate pentameters of "To Penshurst" and "To Heaven" (the two "framing" poems of the volume), the couplet shores up *The Forest*, helping to differentiate its timber from the many flowers of dainty device produced by Jonson's "amateur" contemporaries and pastoralizing forebears. Much the same might be said of its cousin, *The Underwood*, Jonson's largest and most generically diverse collection of poetry, which he was apparently getting ready to publish as part of a second folio at the time of his death in 1637. The couplet gradually exerts its pressure, reappearing even where we might least expect it, in the great Pindaric Ode: "To the Immortal Memory and Friendship of That Noble Pair, Sir Lucius Cary and Sir H. Morison."

In a sense, Jonson's decisive preference for this form might be seen as his version of Donne's "masculine, persuasive force." It was a way to give his poetry a kind of architectural solidity without necessarily hampering the movement of thought: a way to write works – finished products – without denying the workings of the mind, the performative aspect of the utterance; a way to be, in effect, both formal and familiar, a poet of the printed page and of the parlor. To speak of the couplet in light of its potentially liberating, rather than restricting, qualities might seem strange at first to modern readers who look back at Jonson from a distant, post-Augustan prospect that has come to place special value on free verse. But the desire for greater personal expressiveness is part of the rationale underlying Jonson's criticisms of cross-rhymes and stanzas as forcing the author's purpose. In these distinctly Elizabethan forms, the thought does not appear natural, plain, or downright, especially when set against the urbane ruminations of a Horace. It does not appear to be one's own, in the richly complicated sense in Jonson in which ownership and originality, possessing property, especially literary property, and individual identity, are mutually defining activities. Taking over the couplet was clearly one way for a poet to say "here is my place," both within the individual poem and in literary history.[23]

We can see a number of these characteristic Jonsonian features uniting in a fully meditated epigram like "To William Camden." The poem appears fourteenth in the collection, but in the mini-canon of poems written to "real" people (as opposed to fictional types and declared non-entities like "Sir Annual Tilter" and "Brain-Hardy"), it comes second, after the poem "To King James," Jonson's other "head":

> Camden, most reverend head, to whom I owe
>   All that I am in arts, all that I know,
> (How nothing's that?) to whom my country owes
>   The great renown and name wherewith she goes;
> Than thee the age sees not that thing more grave,
>   More high, more holy, that she more would crave.
> What name, what skill, what faith hast thou in things!
>   What sight in searching the most antique springs!
> What weight, and what authority in thy speech!
>   Man scarce can make that doubt, but thou canst teach.
> Pardon free truth, and let thy modesty,
>   Which conquers all, be once overcome by thee.
> Many of thine this better could than I;
>   But for their powers accept my piety.

The poem might be read as a discreet revision of that other kind of poem also in fourteen lines, the sonnet. Instead of neat divisions appearing between quatrains or between the octave and sestet, shifts usually signaling significant alterations in thought, tone, and emotional range, the epigram progresses forward in carefully measured increments, with the couplets firmly overriding these traditional formal divisions. The triple symmetries of "what name," "what sight," "what weight" in lines 7–9, in fact, ensure that no break or even significant pause happens at this juncture in the poem. The act of homage simply continues – as if Jonson were making one long bow – although the poem finally does not feel simple.

Where, one may ask, does it acquire its resonances, its weight and authority of speech, its ripeness? Surely part comes from little effects, like Jonson's judicious maneuvering with enjambment and medial pauses, his constant but varied markings that prevent couplets from jingling and draw the sense out, as in "to whom I owe / all that I am in arts." The reach across the line ending is a crucial indicator of the vastness of his debt to Camden, a debt re-emphasized and remeasured in the echoing rumination, "all that I know," and then refigured on a national scale, "to whom my country owes / The great renown and name wherewith she goes." And in line with this observation, much, too, is owing to the actual placement of words, especially (as is often the case with Jonson), the last word, in this instance, "piety." With its fine Virgilian shadings, sustained by the perfectly managed imperfect closure of half rhyme, it rescues the convoluted glibness of the preceding line ("Many of thine this better could than I") and asks us to imagine a fully Roman backdrop to the poem, one that gathers past and present into its folds in the Aeneas-like vision of the individual sacrificing himself for his country. The act of homage is not simply between pupil and teacher; it is cast in a familiar language that belongs to each but that also asks to be seen as a common language, a language that binds Camden, poet, country, and history together.

But even these qualities, though they point to it, do not quite explain (or explain away) the mastery here, for mastery is surely the ultimate effect the poem seeks to convey: the sense of Camden as the absolute authority in his field and Jonson, notwithstanding his deft touches of modesty, the comparable master, judge, and teacher in his; the one, an historian who helped to rediscover Britain for his countrymen by recovering the many place names that combine to form *Britannia* (1586), the other, a poet who, through the precise use of diction and syntax, "discovers" the particular features of Camden, charts his moral and intellectual geography, his "reverend head," and articulates a new standard of praise in doing so. However flattering the portrait might be, the great illusion Jonson presents is the illusion of immediate truthfulness. Camden is not part of a Spenserian allegory; he does not belong in some remote, courtly fairy land, vaguely related to a legendary British history. Nor is he part of an elaborate Donnean panegyric. Heroic in his vocation, Camden belongs fully to the present.

Names and places

To be mythologized as one's self, moreover, as an individual (as, in this case, "William Camden") on the basis of one's merit rather than one's social position alone, and at a particular moment in history when, because of the unprecedented inflation of honors that began under James, having a title did not necessarily mean being worthy in any other than a financial sense; to be celebrated, furthermore, by a poet who knows all the rules of the game (how nothing is that?) and yet still comes across as both discriminating and sincere: this is the promise so many of the poems hold out. This is especially so in *The*

Epigrams, that "theater" or "gallery" of nobles and knaves in which Jonson asks us to know good by knowing evil: to reckon the true from the false, the substantial from the airy, the established from the *arrivistes*, the Sir John Roes, John Donnes, and Lucy Harringtons, from the Don Surlys, poet-apes, and Lady Would-be's, the Ben Jonsons from the John Weevers. Jonson's is not, in the poetry at least, a complicating or even a complicated moral vision, as Milton's is. But it is deeply held, layered by years of reading the classics in a Christian setting, particularly the writings of the Stoic philosophers, Cicero and Seneca, with their emphasis on cultivating the self; and as a number of critics have recently stressed, it is fully responsive to the complex pressures of Jacobean culture, pressures of patronage that could make a poet, dependent on those whom he praised, even regard his muse on occasion as a mere prostitute ("To My Muse").

In this "theater" or "gallery" – and Jonson uses both dramatic and pictorial metaphors to describe his book – the epigrams to fools ask that we see them as such at the outset (and even from a distance because of the titles) and then mark off the boundaries separating them from the living, with compass-like firmness. Typical is the brilliant trifle, with its hobbled and disabling title, "On Something that Walks Somewhere":

> At court I met it, in clothes brave enough
>   To be a courtier, and looks grave enough
> To seem a statesman. As I near it came,
>   It made me a great face; I asked the name;
> A lord, it cried, buried in flesh and blood,
>   And such from whom let no man hope least good,
> For I will do none; and as little ill,
>   For I will dare none. Good lord, walk dead still.

"Walk dead still": Jonson's fools are all of one kind – spiritual somnambulists buried in flesh and blood and without a personal identity. Like Lieutenant Shift or Don Surly they move and talk as if on automatic pilot, repeating tag ends of speech, blurting out oaths, until Jonson turns off the switch. Or they metamorphose, like Court-Worm, but are never seen to move up the chain of being to where they might possess an individual identity, a specific name. When he chooses, Jonson can be crushingly off-handed, as in this thoroughly unsentimentalized rendition of the *sic vitae* trope:

> All men are worms: but this no man. In silk
>   'Twas brought to court first wrapped, and white as milk;
> Where afterwards it grew a butterfly,
>   Which was a caterpillar. So 'twill die.

If it were not for their role as foils for the worthy many in *The Epigrams*, these squibs might well belong in an almanac; but deliberately insubstantial as they are, their presence heightens our sense of the value of naming as a distinguishing human act and, in a further act of discrimination, they help to enshrine the named community with whom Jonson affiliated: past and present poets, his children, actors, patrons and patronesses, musicians, fellow soldiers; individuals who, whether they were or not, in fact appear to be at the center of the poet's life. In deliberate contrast to contemporary epigrammatists, Jonson insisted that his book follow Martial by being richly peopled and encomiastic and not just salty and ill-tempered.

He makes this point with characteristic directness in "To My Mere English Censurer" (emphasis on "Mere English") when he remarks how "To thee my way in epigrams seems new / When both it is the old way and the true."[24] What is both old and true is the significant element of "admiration" in the collection. (Jonson uses "admire" here in its quasi-religious Latin sense of expressing wonder or astonishment.) The many poems of praise – approximately one-third of the collection, as in Martial – not only serve to set the author off from the new wave. They combine to give the volume a feeling of substantial quality, a sense of depth, balance, and emotional richness, a sense of being worth something in the vision of a poet willing to honor others, to receive and in turn to be received. And in at least one respect Jonson achieved what he set out to do, since this group of encomia and eulogies includes a number of his most "admired" performances: the four epitaphs, particularly the two on his children, the several poems to Lucy, Countess of Bedford, the two to Donne, the poem to Camden, and the several to the Roes, especially the one to Sir Thomas beginning "Thou hast begun well, Roe" and concluding with a proverbial sentiment that identifies one of Jonson's keenest ideals:

> Be always to thy gathered self the same,
>   And study conscience more than thou wouldst fame.
> Though both be good, the latter yet is worst,
>   And ever is ill-got without the first.

In all of these poems, having a name is consequential. It provides the stamp of individual being, a sign that differentiates one person from another and yet also links that individual to a greater and firmer reality, which the epigram in turn consecrates, although it does so in no single or simple way. "On Lucy, Countess of Bedford," for instance, hangs graciously but firmly on a regal summoning of a place name in the last line, one that confirms Lucy's position – and independence – in an otherwise dominantly male society:

> Only a learned and a manly soul
>   I purposed her, that should, with even powers,
> The rock, the spindle and the shears control
>   Of destiny, and spin her own free hours.

Such when I meant to feign and wished to see,
My muse bade, *Bedford* write, and that was she.

As the poem makes luminously clear, *"Bedford"* ensures that Lucy is perceived as no ordinary "spinster." Nor is the poet. In this rich revision of the Petrarchan tradition (one hears the opening sonnet of Sidney's *Astrophel and Stella* in the background), he partakes in a similar act of prestidigitation with the abrupt, final spinning: "and that was she." And perhaps no poem in English makes a more exquisite adjustment to the signifying registers of a Christian name than "On My First Daughter," short enough to quote in full:

Here lies, to each her parents' ruth,
Mary, the daughter of their youth;
Yet, all heaven's gifts being heaven's due,
It makes the father less to rue.
At six months' end she parted hence
With safety of her innocence;
Whose soul heaven's Queen (whose name she bears),
In comfort of her mother's tears,
Hath placed amongst her virgin train;
Where, while that severed doth remain,
This grave partakes the fleshly birth;
Which cover lightly, gentle earth.

Although practically formulaic, the epitaph is anything but impersonal, and along with his even better known eulogy to his first son, it reminds us that the collection Jonson designated as his "ripest" comes bearing his autograph, as if helping to authenticate the accounts of praise and blame meted out elsewhere as well as to add a touch of value, or worth, to the book so as to make it into something of a collector's item. Not even Martial, whose epitaph on Erotion (V. 34) lies behind this poem, can be seen grieving for his own children.

Jonson's most celebrated and comprehensive act of naming, however, does not occur in *The Epigrams*, a volume that, with the notable exception of the scatological "On the Famous Voyage" – that 196-line mock epic that ridicules so many distinctly "Elizabethan" devices – generally restricts itself to poems of not more than thirty lines. It happens in *The Forest*, and not to a person but to a place. "To Penshurst" celebrates the ancestral home of the Sidneys in Kent, the original construction of which dated as far back as the mid-fourteenth century; but the building had been improved and extended at various times since then, especially in the mid-sixteenth century when it came into the possession of Sir William Sidney during the reign of Edward VI as a gift for service done to the crown. When Jonson composed his poem, it was owned and occupied by Robert Sidney, the younger brother of Sir Philip, and his wife, Barbara Gamage.

That Jonson should choose to write this poem seems, in retrospect, almost inevitable. He had already explored the subject of hospitality on a more limited scale in "Inviting a Friend to Supper" – if indeed it predates "To Penshurst"; and as someone who provided entertainments for the wealthy, he was familiar with country estates, their symbolic value as expressions of power and munificence as well as their practical workings, the general system of economy that put food onto the table and into the mouths of host and guest alike, although sometimes in different amounts and servings.[25] That Jonson should choose to celebrate the Sidney household seems also right. England's first defender of poetry and Neoclassicism, the courtier, soldier, scholar, and his descendants were still very much in the public eye in the first decade of the seventeenth century, especially among those concerned with literary traditions and dependent upon patronage for support, a category that obviously included Jonson. With its twin dedications to Sidney's nephew, William Herbert (*Catiline* and *The Epigrams*), and niece, Mary Wroth (*The Alchemist*), the folio announces up front, in fact, what the poems in *The Forest* and most elaborately "To Penshurst" reveal in more detail in private: how deeply ensconced their author was in the Sidney household. And yet for all its apparent predictability (and our sense of inevitability is perhaps only increased if we recall that Jonson's father reportedly lost "all his estate under Queen Mary"), "To Penshurst" was also, if not the first, certainly the most influential country house poem in English and much imitated thereafter.[26]

So familiar has the poem become to readers of English verse that it is also easy to forget that the poem represents a novel solution to a specifically English – indeed Jacobean – literary problem with powerful social implications. "To Penshurst" extends the patronage poem beyond the narrow boundaries of the epigram; and it does so, moreover, without simply returning to the Spenserian formula of writing an extended allegory, an "endlesse worke" of "mirrors more than one" set in a distant landscape that ultimately celebrated the queen on the throne. For his solution, Jonson went his usual route: to the past. Three epigrams by Martial help to create the substructure of the poem: IX, 61, beginning "In Tartesiacis domus est notissima terris" (a house renowned stands in the land of Tartessus); X, 30, "O Temperatae dulce Formiae litus" (O temperate Formiae, darling shore!); and most significantly III, 58, "Baiana nostri villa, Basse, Faustini" (The Baian villa, Bassus, of our friend Faustinus). Details from each as well as the general notion of celebrating a particular, historical place clearly influence Jonson's vision; but finally what is so impressive about "To Penshurst" is how fully it escapes its literary roots in the past; how thoroughly it transplants a classical ideal onto English soil. "To Penshurst" is not the Baian villa updated; it represents, without an ounce of nostalgia, an idealized view of English society, from toe to top, from peasant to king, all paying tribute, even along with the "fat aged carp" in the pond, to the beneficence of the Sidney family, a beneficence, moreover, represented as anchored in nature itself. So thoroughly translated is the classical past that it seems merely accidental for the sum of Martial's three epigrams to equal exactly the number of lines of Jonson's poem.

"To Penshurst" is probably the best thank-you note in English (and resisted sometimes for being so). Praising the grounds and the house enables Jonson to celebrate the Sidney family, to record his gratitude for their patronage and a visit, itself memorably (and characteristically) recorded in a vignette near the center of the poem where a hungry and self-conscious Jonson describes their hospitality as such that it even allowed the well-fed poet to retire for the evening and momentarily fantasize that he "reigned here." But the poem also represents something of a triumph of the pentameter line in the service of a wider social vision that values modesty and generosity, order and liberality. "Penshurst" would not be "Penshurst" if it were a foot shorter, that is, if the poem were written in the tetrameter couplets that Marvell was to exploit so brilliantly in "Upon Appleton House." Think of what would happen to the familiar but authoritative opening of:

> Thou art not, Penshurst, built to envious show
> > Of touch or marble, nor canst boast a row
> Of polished pillars, or a roof of gold;
> > Thou hast no lantern whereof tales are told,

if it were written as follows:

> Thou art not built to envious show
> Of marble, nor canst boast a row
> Of pillars, or a roof of gold,
> No lantern whereof tales are told.

The latter, of course, is weak tea and most certainly not Jonson (nor Marvell, for that matter); but it helps to show the uncanny link between the proper name and the pentameter line in the poem, with "Penshurst" giving weight and ballast to the opening line in much the same way that – to switch metaphors – a keystone gives strength to the arch. And, of course, not only is the slimmed down version without the substantive and adjectival heft of the original (soon to be put to morally descriptive purpose by Jonson once we enter the estate), but without the gaudy alliteration of "polished pillars," it foregoes one of the means that Jonson uses to distinguish Penshurst from what it is not: another Jacobean prodigy like the enormously expensive house being constructed at Hatfield by James's unpopular treasurer, Robert Cecil.

To rewrite "Penshurst" in anything but pentameter is to see again the understated art of the poem Jonson wrote. Veering at times toward the ludic, it never abandons the leisurely, as Jonson's rhymically varied, sure-footed couplets convey us through the landscape, which is always paying honor to the family Jonson is celebrating:

> And if the high-swoll'n Medway fail thy dish,
> > Thou hast thy ponds that pay thee tribute fish:

Fat, aged carps, that run into thy net;
   And pikes, now weary their own kind to eat,
As loath the second draught or cast to stay,
   Officiously, at first, themselves betray;
Bright eels, that emulate them, and leap on land
   Before the fisher, or into his hand.
Then hath thy orchard fruit, thy garden flowers,
   Fresh as the air and new as are the hours:
The early cherry, with the later plum,
   Fig, grape and quince, each in his time doth come;
The blushing apricot and woolly peach
   Hang on thy walls, that every child may reach.

(ll. 31–41)

We do not need to trim these verses to see that to change the line is to change the place, and to change the place is to begin to spoil the estate. In Penshurst place, everything in its time doth come: the "blushing apricot and woolly peach," the farmer and the clown, the poet and the king, lord, lady, and children, as the poem goes on to reveal through a vision of household economy that includes some modestly politicized court critique.[27] Jonson's is a conservative view of the social order, but the vision is not a static one, with the poet simply reciting a catalog of riches. Nor is it without warmth. "What (great, I will not say, but) sudden cheer" (l. 82) is Jonson's carefully modulated phrasing used to describe the hospitality exhibited by Barbara Gamage when she welcomes the king. In the face of authority, this ideal of controlled spontaneity is also what best characterizes the movement of the poem: the Jonsonian line, as it were, celebrating the Sidneyan line, and yet maintaining a dignified distance on the object of praise. Indeed, so exemplary of cultural "life" in England is Penshurst, says Jonson in closing, that any attempt by others to "proportion thee" (and the poem, as we have seen) will be destructive of the original; a deviation from a perfect living mean:

Now, Penshurst, they that will proportion thee
   With other edifices, when they see
Those proud, ambitious heaps, and nothing else,
   May say, their lords have built, but thy lord dwells.

(ll. 99–102)

Jonson on Shakespeare

To speak of Jonson in "To Penshurst" as fully transporting a classical ideal of moderation on to English soil – to identify him, in other words, as a Neoclassicist – is not to suggest that the act of transposing, of receiving, assimilating, and revaluing the significant prestige attached to antiquity was necessarily a simple one. The most recent of a long line of critics on this subject, Thomas Greene, has eloquently traced both the cultural impediments to an easy transcription – or as Greene would say, invention – of a classical idiom in England and the complex moral and artistic dynamic within Jonson that enabled him to receive the past into the present, to think not anachronistically about Horace, Martial, or Catullus, but to respond to them as contemporaries with the kind of easy hospitality he rarely accorded contemporary poets.[28] When, for instance, Jonson presents his (now) famous English version of Catullus' "Vivamus, mea Lesbia" in *The Forest* ("Come, my Celia"), he invites us not only to admire the splendidly wrought octosyllabic line but to chart the line of descent itself, from the poem's origins in Catullus, through its appearance in *Volpone* (1606), where it was first sung in English, to its present anthologized place in a volume that might, at first, cause us to puzzle over the principle of selection. (Is the poem somehow not about love?) And in another lyric from *The Forest*, suggestively entitled "To the Same," the author invites us to witness even more precisely the actual process of naturalizing a text from the past, of creating, in effect, a small classic. The pleasure of counting kisses in Catullus, kisses whose numbers are said to equal the "Libyan sand that lies on silphium-bearing Cyrene, between the oracle of sultry Jove and the sacred tomb of old Battus; or as many as are the stars, when night is silent," finds a no less exotic system of measurement in the English landscape:

> First give a hundred,
> Then a thousand, then another
> Hundred, then unto the t'other
> Add a thousand, and so more,
> Till you equal with the store
> All the grass that Romney yields,
> Or the sands in Chelsea fields,
> Or the drops in silver Thames,
> Or the stars that gild his streams
> In the silent summer nights,
> When youths ply their stol'n delights.

The idea of conscious selectivity, so evident here in the careful disposition of place names, goes to the heart of Jonson's art, and it is nowhere more evident than in his penchant for judging contemporary authors according to strenuously held standards of decorum, to place them in careful relation to himself and within the literary culture of the early seventeenth century. Jonson's remarks about other poets in his *Conversations With Drummond* have achieved legendary status for their acuity and severity: "Drayton feared him, and he esteemed not of him," "That Donne, for not keeping of accent, deserved hanging," and so on.[29] But more to the point, because more public, is the considerable number of commendatory poems he wrote for specific literary occasions – enough, in fact, to make another separate volume of poetry. They read like a literary *Who's Who* of the early seventeenth century. George Chapman, the translator of Homer, is there, along with the popular Nicholas Breton, the prolific Michael Drayton, Sir Walter Raleigh, William Browne, and, of course, that other William, Shakespeare. Present, too, are minor writers and acquaintances like Donne's friend Christopher Brooke, John Beaumont, brother of Francis the dramatist, commended in *The Epigrams*, and Jonson's apprentice from the stage, Richard Brome. Little of significance, in fact, was published that did not come bearing Jonson's seal; and from the many commendatory poems to the actual creation of a Tribe of Ben, it was only a small step.

Until recently, and with a few notable exceptions, commendatory poetry has almost always been read as marginal verse, so much puff produced by the author's friends. But we ought to recognize that it was also the place in the earlier seventeenth century where poets often practiced what today goes by the name of literary criticism. Before the advent of the critical essay at the end of the century, commendatory verse was one of the principal sites where literary – as well as political – values were contested and out of which a canon of authors emerged; a site, furthermore, that in its significant growth during the course of the seventeenth century testifies to a general cultural shift in which poetry moved part way out of the salon and onto the streets, from manuscript into print.

Jonson's place in effecting this transition is crucial, and not just because as an author of note he made it his business to be frequently engaged in this task. In his hands, the commendatory poem acquired a critical weight and mass it simply had not had before in English. With Jonson, the commendatory sonnet that had prefaced the late Elizabethan poem – the sonnet of praise, of which a vestigial example is his early poem to Nicholas Breton – gave way to the literary epistle, that spaciously Horatian form in which judgments could be enacted and in which an estimation, in the double sense of both esteeming and measuring, could be "performed," a word that also helps to mark off the Jonsonian commendatory mode from that of its immediate predecessors. And it was in the form of the epistle, not the sonnet, that subsequent authors like Carew and Marvell, building on Jonson's example, produced some of the most important acts of literary criticism in the century; including, as the law of literary inheritance would have it, Carew's of Jonson.

Jonson's most famous – and controversial – commendatory act is, of course, his eulogy to Shakespeare that prefaced the 1623 folio edition of the dramatist's works, which Jonson might have had a hand in producing. (The folio also includes a brief epigram by Jonson, "To the Reader.") As the reigning literary authority of the day as well as sometime rival and friend of Shakespeare, Jonson was an obvious choice for this occasional task, and something of the complexity of his response, or rather something of the complexity of the situation in which the author of the 1616 *Workes* found himself, is indicated by the full title, "To the Memory of My Beloved, The Author, Mr. William Shakespeare: And What

He Hath Left Us." Friend, author, and authority – these different and potentially conflicting perceptions run through a poem that, since the days of Dryden
and Pope, has inspired powerfully conflicting views from its readers: some, like
Dryden, dismissing the poem as an "insolent, sparing and invidious panegyric,"
others, like Pope, praising it for its unstinting humanity, and still others
assessing these critical perspectives in light of classical theories of praise, especially those enunciated by Horace in the *Ars Poetica* and *Satires* (I.4 and I.10).[30]

Wherever we eventually land in this debate – and a poem as complex as this
ought to make us wary about choosing sides too quickly – a fair place to begin is
with the recognition that probably no one had a keener idea about what was at
stake in commemorating Shakespeare than Jonson. Whether or not tales of
their rivalry as told by near contemporaries like Thomas Fuller are apocryphal,
it is clear that none of Jonson's other commendatory poems so seriously engaged
his attention. (Although longer and initially troubled by issues of friendship,
the poem to Drayton is so uncharacteristically accommodating in its enthusiastic survey of Drayton's writings as to prompt suspicion that it is a send-up.)
The problem facing Jonson was not simply how to praise a living contemporary
but how to estimate an author of Shakespeare's amplitude who is already a part
of history. And Jonson's response, one that betrays both generosity and anxiety
– "Am I thus ample to thy book and fame" reads the second line – is to do unto
Shakespeare what Jonson, in effect, had already attempted to do unto himself in
the 1616 *Workes*: to make Shakespeare into a canonical author, to preside over
the act of coronation itself, an act, however, that inevitably and paradoxically
only further underscores significant individual and historical differences
between the authors.

In fact, of the many commendatory poems that grew up around the four folio
editions of Shakespeare's works in the seventeenth century (1623, 1632, 1664,
and 1685), only Jonson's is thoroughly motivated to define Shakespeare's place
in the full panorama of literary history. After the opening sixteen lines in which
Jonson elaborately prepares himself to receive Shakespeare in his fullness, he
arrives at the moment of summoning:

> I therefore will begin. Soul of the age!
>   The applause, delight, the wonder of our stage!
> My Shakespeare, rise.

He also arrives at his subject – where he will put Shakespeare – and it is not in
the place already prepared by the minor poet, William Basse. Basse's popular
elegy to Shakespeare, which Jonson must have seen in manuscript, begins with
the apparent assumption that Shakespeare is to be buried in Westminster
Abbey:

> Renowned Spencer lye a thought more nye
> To learned Chaucer, and rare Beaumond lye

A little neerer Spenser, to make roome
For Shakespeare in your threefold, fowerfold Tombe.[31]

In a pointed correction, Jonson vastly extends the field of reference, and in doing so helps to lay the groundwork for our modern view of Shakespeare as not only England's pre-eminent author but, as a rival of the great Classical dramatists, a symbol of England's cultural dominance as well:

> My Shakespeare, rise: I will not lodge thee by
>   Chaucer or Spenser, or bid Beaumont lie
> A little further, to make thee a room;
>   Thou art a monument without a tomb,
> And art alive still while thy book doth live,
>   And we have wits to read, and praise to give.
> That I not mix thee so, my brain excuses:
>   I mean with great, but disproportioned, muses;
> For if I thought my judgement were of years
>   I should commit thee surely with thy peers:
> And tell how far thou didst our Lyly outshine,
>   Or sporting Kyd, or Marlowe's mighty line.
> And though thou hadst small Latin, and less Greek,
>   From thence to honour thee I would not seek
> For names, but call forth thundering Aeschylus,
>   Euripides, and Sophocles to us,
> Pacuvius, Accius, him of Cordova dead,
>   To life again, to hear thy buskin tread
> And shake a stage; or, when thy socks were on,
>   Leave thee alone for the comparison
> Of all that insolent Greece or haughty Rome
>   Sent forth, or since did from their ashes come.
> Triumph, my Britain, thou hast one to show
>   To whom all scenes of Europe homage owe.
>
> (ll. 19–42)

"Triumph my Britain": Jonson never played the role of James with greater vigor; but there is also more than a touch of the Shakespearean thaumaturge here. In his commendatory verse to poets, Jonson frequently used stylistic imitation as an honorific device, and his promise in these lines to call forth spirits from the vasty deep ought to call forth a host of Shakespearean ghosts as well, especially that last playwright as magician, Prospero himself. Along with their mutual concern with summoning and name magic – and surely part of Jonson's interest in the more obscure "Pacuvius, Accius, [and] him of Cordova dead" (Seneca) is the opportunity to perform a bit of verbal prestidigitation on the nearly forgotten – Jonson's apparently graceless pun on Shakespeare's name ("shake a stage") plays allusively but not gratuitously with this act of overlapping, as it returns us to the scene of Prospero's farewell to magic itself, in which one sign of his power involved how "The strong-bas'd promontory / Have I made shake" (*The Tempest*, V, i, 46–7).

Jonson's reminiscence here might be said to attempt to catch the spirit of amplitude itself in order to do full justice to this new canonical author. But if there is some irony in the fact that when scholars refer to the "first folio" today, they mean Shakespeare's, not Jonson's, the twist does not seem to have been lost on Jonson either: for the remainder of the poem seeks a more contained, sober, and intimate estimation of Shakespeare's art along peculiarly Jonsonian lines. The dramatist celebrated in the first half of the poem as "not of an age, but for all time" is historicized in the second half as a fellow-laborer in the muse's vineyard ("he / Who casts to write a living line must sweat" (ll. 58–9)); and the features Jonson finds to praise – Shakespeare's "well-turned and true-filed lines" – are precisely what Jonson, not Shakespeare, brought to English poetry.

There is insolence as well as honor in holding another to the standards one most cherishes; but there is a fall of another sort recorded in this poem as well, a fall into art from nature, from a necromantic view of language spoken when "all the muses still were in their prime" (l. 44) to a view of language as pounded out "Upon the muses' anvil." In the poem, Jonson attributes both qualities to Shakespeare, but the latter art is Jonson's and the former his only by imitation. Whether Jonson was making a virtue out of a necessity here is probably impossible to tell, but the revaluing does not seem so much "insolent and sparing" as inevitable: the powerful reflex of a poet who, perhaps in spite of himself, knows that he has helped to give away the store that he has also helped to create:

> But stay, I see thee in the hemisphere
>   Advanced, and made a constellation there!
> Shine forth, thou star of poets, and with rage
>   Or influence chide or cheer the drooping stage;
> Which, since thy flight from hence, hath mourned like night,
>   And despairs day, but for thy volume's light.
>
> (ll. 75–80)

Finding the center again: late "Ben / Jonson"

If in the 1623 poem to Shakespeare, Jonson is as much the focal point as Shakespeare, the problem with Jonson's later career was one of attempting to remain near the center of English culture. Shakespeare's "advancement" was a matter of history, Jonson's an increasingly precarious venture. With the death of James in 1625, this defining Jacobean poet fell out of favor at court: after having averaged nearly a masque per year from 1605 to 1625, Jonson produced only two more during his remaining twelve years, both in 1630. Well before the ascension of James's son, Charles, he had all but stopped writing for the theater. Between 1614, the date of his last large-scale performance (*Bartholomew Fair*, played both in the public theater and at court) and 1629, when he tried disastrously to renew his fortunes on the stage with *The New Inn*, Jonson wrote only two plays. In 1629, he also suffered a partially paralyzing stroke from which he never fully recovered.

Wherever critics have traditionally located the zenith of Jonson's dramatic career – Carew identified it with *The Alchemist* in 1611, and Dryden, in a phrase with which modern critics of the dramatic Jonson have since been wrestling, pronounced all the later plays "dotages" – few have felt compelled to chart a similar line of descent with the poetry, despite Jonson's own wish to characterize his final collection of verse entitled *The Underwood* as "lesser poems of later growth." That critics have not is owing in part to the sheer generic diversity of the volume, its resourceful mix of old and new. Three poems of devotion, suggesting a productive reading of Herbert's *The Temple* (1633), mark the entrance. Then appear, in only approximate order, a number of elegies, both Ovidian and funerary, perhaps the earliest "suite" in the language, as Hugh Kenner aptly called the ten amatory lyrics entitled "A Celebration of Charis";[32] one pastoral dialogue; a handful of courtly love lyrics of the witty, Donnean kind (several read as if they were "answer" poems); "An Execration, Upon Vulcan"; "A Speech according to Horace"; "A Fit of Rhyme against Rhyme"; one sonnet, a handful of odes (Anacreontic, Horatian, and Pindaric), one epitaph, several eulogies, an epithalamion, several birthday poems, back-to-back verses on the theme of the poet versus the painter, some satirical squibs and occasional epigrams, one funeral sequence lamenting the death of Venetia Digby, and a few translations including Horace's second epode, "The Praises of a Country Life," and the brilliant fragment misattributed in the Renaissance to Petronius, "Doing a filthy pleasure is, and short." Last of all, and appropriately last because it seems to sum up almost everything *missing* from Jonson's later years and poems, is a translation of Martial's famous epigram "Vitam quae faciunt beatiorem," or in Jonson's rendition of the opening line, "The things that make the happier life are these." Most of the genres and subjects represented here were to be of major concern to the generation of poets immediately following Jonson.

There is also nothing lesser about some of the individual performances. The epitaph on Vincent Corbet and the Epistle to John Selden are fully persuasive poems, characteristically Jonsonian in sounding the depths of male friendship; and "A Celebration of Charis," along with being the most adeptly self-indulgent and the funniest poem Jonson ever wrote, includes one of the most serious and elegant distillations in English of current Neoplatonic views of love in the section marking Charis's "Triumph":

> See the chariot at hand here of Love,
>   Wherein my lady rideth!

Each that draws is a swan or a dove,
    And well the car Love guideth.
As she goes, all hearts do duty
    Unto her beauty;
And enamoured, do wish, so they might
    But enjoy such a sight,
    That they still were to run by her side,
Through swords, through seas, whither she would ride.

The inspiration for representing Charis riding triumphantly in a chariot – with the pun suggesting the inevitable appropriateness of the seat – is surely owing to Jonson's work with the masque. (The 1608 Haddington masque is usually cited.) But the stanza also pays homage in a different direction. "Spenser, in affecting the ancients, writ no language; yet I would have him read for his matter." [33] The double-edged nature of Jonson's famous comment in *Discoveries* is borne out in the celebration here, with the Spenserian notes recollected from "An Hymne in Honour of Love" ("Thou art his god, thou art his mightie guyde … / Through seas, through flames, through thousand swords and speares"), though in a finer key – more fully modern, intricate, and triumphant sounding, as if Jonson were writing a Spenserian Alexandrine but in only nine syllables: "That they still were to run by her side, / Through swords, through seas, whither she would ride." The final triumph in this section, however, belongs even more definitively to Jonson, and not merely because it initially appeared in one of his plays (*The Devil is an Ass*). When has a catalogue of the senses been more exquisitely presented and to the one sense not represented in the stanza: the ear?

Have you seen but a bright lily grow,
    Before rude hands have touched it?
Have you marked but the fall o' the snow,
    Before the soil hath smutched it?
Have you felt the wool o' the beaver?
    Or swan's down ever?
Or have smelled o'the bud o' the briar?
    Or the nard i' the fire?
Or have tasted the bag o' the bee?
O so white! O so soft! O so sweet is she!

                          (ll. 21–30)

Suckling's parody of the stanza in his play, *The Sad One*, makes explicit how another review of the senses can only produce crudeness. In Charis, a jovial ripeness is all.

Or nearly all: the other principal reason against discounting Jonson's later poetry is its significant "growth" in the nearly opposite direction. Although a number of poems in *The Underwood* describe an author painfully aware of his financial dependency on others, including the king, the recognition of his being a lesser figure on one front helped also to create the conditions for his later growth on another. Jonson's Pindaric Ode, "To the Immortal Memory and Friendship of That Noble Pair, Sir Lucius Cary and Sir H. Morison," is very much a late achievement, both within Jonson's canon and in the history of its reception. Indeed, were it not for the fact that it is still possible to find the poem represented in teaching anthologies by only a single stanza, the amount of recent criticism on the poem would seem to guarantee the ode the kind of canonical stature Jonson so much desired.

From one perspective, the ode ought to be read as a powerful revision of the poem to Shakespeare. Jonson's spectacular division of himself in the famous enjambment near the middle responds to the problematic act of "advancement" in the earlier eulogy, with Jonson now imagining a portion of himself ("Ben") as already among the celebrated and transcendent dead and the poem, as "a bright asterism," playing a complex mediating role between heaven and earth. At the same time, however, the decision to write not just an ode but a full-blown Pindaric provides an allegory of a kind of Jonson's waning authority. From the time of his first attempt with the Pindaric ode – the exceptionally murky "Ode to James, Earl of Desmond. Writ in Queen Elizabeth's Time, Since Lost, and Recovered" – Jonson had associated the genre not only with the high flight of lyric but, as Desmond's situation required, with an oppositional politics. Under Elizabeth, the Earl had been in prison from 1579–1600, first in Dublin Castle, then in the Tower of London; and in the ode, Jonson, whose attitude to Elizabeth remains characteristically ambivalent, promises an imagined release:

> Then shall my verses, like strong charms,
> Break the knit circle of her stony arms
> That hold[s] your spirit
> And keeps your merit
> Locked in her cold embraces.
>
> (ll. 18–22)

Although both the situation and promise look forward to the use made of the ode by Cavalier poets like Lovelace in "To Althea, from Prison," Jonson's response here is resolutely iconoclastic, not elegantly transcendent; and when he returned to Pindar some thirty years later, something he did only when he was once more on the outskirts of power, the genre retained for him the same militant associations.

Both the Cary–Morison ode and the ode on the failure of *The New Inn* were written in 1629, with the Pindaric almost surely being the later of the two. (Morison died in July or August of that year, whereas the debacle involving the play belongs to February and March.) Whatever differences, moreover, that have traditionally been perceived as distinguishing one kind of ode from another – Jonson's contemporary, Michael Drayton, for instance, associated Pindar with the "high dialect" of heroic poetry, Anacreon with the amatory muse, and Horace with a "mixed kinde" – they were alike in Jonson's mind in one regard. They represented a notion of the lyric as elevated, highly wrought, and bold, a celebration of significance; a celebration, that is, not only of a significant occasion but of a signifying presence as well:

> Leave things so prostitute,
> And take the Alcaic lute,
> Or thine own Horace, or Anacreon's lyre;
> Warm thee by Pindar's fire:
> And though thy nerves be shrunk and blood be cold
> Ere years have made thee old,
> Strike that disdainful heat
> Throughout, to their defeat:
> As curious fools, and envious of thy strain,
> May, blushing, swear no palsy's in thy brain.
> ("Come, leave the loathed stage," ll. 41–50.)

The ode on the failure of *The New Inn*, however, may well be one of the most painfully embarrassing poems in English and not just because, in blaming everyone but himself for the debacle, Jonson committed a lapse in taste and caused a scandal among the Sons of Ben. It is painful for the same reason that Lear's "Reason not the need" speech is; for its sputtering helplessness. Jonson might have helped here to inaugurate a loyalist association of the ode with Charles that was to become the hallmark of later Cavaliers like Lovelace, but his pledge to reinvest himself as the king's poet by "tuning forth the acts of his sweet reign: / And raising Charles's chariot 'bove his wain" was so much whistling in the dark. As far as revenge was concerned, Jonson might just as well have said with Lear "I'll do such things – / What they are yet I know not, but they shall be the terrors of the Earth."

Except, of course, for the revenge to be won from art. In the Cary–Morison ode, Jonson converted or turned the "simple fury" and "disdainful heat" of "Come, leave the loathed stage" into a profound act of imitation, into a profound act of reconfirming his significance as a poet (literally spelled out in the enjambment, "Ben / Jonson"); and he did so in the full classicizing sense rather than as a poet only of Charles's reign. "Observe how the best writers have imitated, and follow them," Jonson wrote in *Discoveries* in a key discussion of the requisites of a poet: "how Virgil and Statius have imitated Homer, how Horace, Archilochus; how Alcaeus, and the other lyrics; and so of the rest."[34] And to this line, one is tempted to say, add Pindar and Jonson. Although the poem might not be, technically speaking, the first attempt to imitate Pindar in English, Jonson's thorough assimilation of specifically Pindaric features involving form and subject has made other candidates for this laurel a matter of academic debate. As has been observed of Jonson's immediate audience, "even those who did not know Pindar in Greek could have recognized certain stylistic features that commentators had often remarked: his brilliant opening figures (imitated by Jonson in the opening "Infant of *Saguntum*"), his abrupt shifts in subject, his sudden leaps to the sublime,"[35] as well as more generalized resemblances like the choral form of the strophes, designated by Jonson as "The Turn," "The Counter-Turn," and "The Stand," and the use of the ode to commemorate victories by noble warriors and athletes. If Jonson was beginning to hark back to Elizabethan times in the theater when he wrote *The New Inn*[36] – and part of what lies behind Jonson's rage in "Come, leave the loathed stage" is surely the humiliation of having capitulated to popular taste and failed – the Cary–Morison ode insists that he be judged by other standards altogether. This is not a poem for "My Meere English Censurers."

The 128-line ode combines and heightens most of the features we generally think of as characteristically Jonsonian. In well-filed lines that insist on the essential relatedness of art and life, Jonson celebrates the immortal values of poetry and friendship. But under the reactive pressure of the commemorative occasion, these features achieve a new level of significance. There is a great deal of "Ben Jonson" in the poem, a Jonson for whom the brave infant of Saguntum (who at the sight of Hannibal razing the town returned to his mother's womb) represents a tempting alternative to the horrors of life. (It is difficult to imagine Jonson earlier entertaining a notion of childhood retreat in precisely this manner.) And the "stirrer" who did nothing but "die late" (with the pun on "dilate") represents another unacceptable version of life that was obviously worrying the poet, a version that becomes more painfully self-referential in the charge:

> Go now, and tell out days summed up with fears;
> And make them years;
> Produce thy mass of miseries on the stage,
> To swell thine age.
>
> (ll. 53–6)

Both of these alternatives are invoked by Jonson to serve as foils for Morison, who died young at age 21. But they also represent challenges reckoned by the poet himself, who is as much at the center of this poem as either Cary or Morison:

> *The Counter-Turn*
>
> Call, noble Lucius, then for wine,
> And let thy looks with gladness shine;
> Accept this garland, plant it on thy head;
> And think, nay know, thy Morison's not dead.

He leaped the present age,
Possessed with holy rage
To see that bright eternal day,
Of which we priests and poets say
Such truths as we expect for happy men;
And there he lives with memory, and Ben

The Stand

Jonson, who sung this of him, ere he went
Himself to rest,
Or taste a part of that full joy he meant
To have expressed
In this bright asterism;
Where it were friendship's schism
(Were not his Lucius long with us to tarry)
To separate these twi-
Lights, the Dioscuri;
And keep the one half from his Harry.
But fate doth so alternate the design,
Whilst that in heaven, this light on earth must shine.

This portion of the poem has been interpreted so often of late that it is tempting to see the giant enjambment as an intentional rupture – a sign in which the signifying poet opens himself up for interpretation, halves himself, as it were, for inspection, and in doing so controls the interpretive act. No matter how we read the poem, we are aware of "Ben Jonson," in some relation to the author, powerfully turning our thoughts. But a reading of this kind would be merely acrobatic – indeed, in the same way that Jonson's attempt to recuperate his authority would be only a grand "act" – if we were not meant to see the leap itself rooted in the poem's argument and the beliefs and creed at the center of Jonson's art. In the stanza that concludes at the exact center of the poem, we are asked to witness the author taking a stand against himself that is also, by the end of the stanza, a stand for himself, for everything he has stood for as a poet: exactness of phrasing, decorum, the essential connection of art to life; a stand, moreover, that turns the subsequent stanza ("The Turn") into both a celebration and an embodiment of that ideal:

The Stand

Go now, and tell out days summed up with fears;
And make them years;
Produce thy mass of miseries on the stage,
To swell thine age;
Repeat of things a throng,

To show thou hast been long,
Not lived; for life doth her great actions spell
By what was done and wrought
In season, and so brought
To light: her measures are, how well
Each syllabe answered, and was formed, how fair;
These make the lines of life, and that's her air.

The Turn

It is not growing like a tree
In bulk, doth make man better be;
Or standing long an oak, three hundred year,
To fall a log at last, dry, bald, and sere:
A lily of a day
Is fairer far, in May,
Although it fall and die that night;
It was the plant and flower of light.
In small proportions we just beauty see,
And in short measures life may perfect be.

"The Turn" here has always been admired, sometimes to the exclusion of the rest of the poem and sometimes for the wrong reasons. It is undeniably judicious in its phrasing. The precise whittling away of the ungainly beginning in order to produce the line at the center neatly corresponds to the shift to praising small things; and the sentiments that emerge draw on Biblical and classical precedents in evaluating Morison's accomplishment. (Good men "flourish as a lily" and accomplish God's commands "in due season," writes Ecclesiasticus, while Seneca observes, "just as one of small stature can be a perfect man, so a life of small compass can be a perfect life.")[37] But what is remarkable, I believe, about "The Turn" is not simply its intricate allusions and mimetic quality but the pressure the stanza is asked to bear within the consolatory arc of the elegy. "Lycidas," a no less artful poem, turns on a much vexed phrase that includes nothing less than a reference to divine intervention: "Look homeward Angel now, and melt with ruth: / And, O ye Dolphins, waft the hapless youth." Jonson's poem pivots on its own axis. "In small proportions we just beauty see / And in short measures life may perfect be." The full weight of the Pindaric seems momentarily to rest on a single couplet, the "bravest" form of verse, as Drummond reported Jonson saying.

I doubt whether any poet in the seventeenth century, even Milton, asks more from his art than does Jonson at this moment. Perhaps it is too much. But perhaps, too, the ultimate fascination of the Pindaric and of Jonson's career in general cannot be measured by the ideal of perfecting "small proportions," nor even in how these might "great actions spell," as if poetry could serve Jonson as a hieroglyph for some other, greater reality. The fascination lies, rather, in the new authority Jonson gave to poetry in the early seventeenth century. No longer the exclusive property of either the rich or the inspired, of either a Sidney or a Spenser, it belonged also to the individual willing to "strike the second heat / Upon the muses' anvil" and claim the work as his own.

3

PATRIOTIC AND POPULAR
POETS

In publishing this Essay of my Poeme, there is this great disadvan-
tage against me; that it commeth out at this time, when Verses
are wholly deduc't to Chambers, and nothing esteem'd in this
lunatique Age, but what is kept in Cabinets, and must only passe
by Transcription.

Michael Drayton, *Poly-Olbion*, 1612, "To The Generall Reader"

Donne and Jonson were the most important and influential poets writing in the
first quarter of the seventeenth century. They were the new voices, as the last
two chapters have attempted to show. But their poetry was hardly "popular," if
we mean by that word a poetry either conceived with a large population of
readers in mind or concerned with exploring issues that might be described as of
broadly public or national interest. Donne's poetry circulated widely but in
manuscript and, initially at least, among a highly select group of aristocrats and
educated friends. He saved his preaching for the pulpit and for prose. When
financial circumstances forced him finally and for the only time to publish some
verse, it is significant that the "First and Second Anniversaries," the work he
entitled *An Anatomie of the World*, appeared without his name on the title page
and that the world he chose to anatomize has little to do with the particularities
of daily life. In this regard, Eliot's famous description of Donne as possessing the
kind of mind that amalgamates experiences as disparate as falling in love and the
smell of cooking is misleading.[1] Indeed, were it not for the fact that in his poetry,
at least, Jonson wrote for an audience similar (in some cases identical) to
Donne's, the description might apply better to him, where there is more cooking
and more of the world. But except when Jonson's purpose is satirical, his sense of
"society," like Donne's, does not extend very far downward; and though his route
into print was very different from Donne's, both ultimately sought to disguise the
vulgar connections binding them to booksellers and stationers and ultimately to
the public. It is not mere flattery that inspired Jonson to depict Donne as his
ideal judge and reader in Epigram 96. "A man should seek great glory, and not
broad" defines a credo the two men held in common.

54

The following chapter seeks to enlarge and complicate our view of the earlier seventeenth century by exploring a group of poets who, if they occasionally did seek great glory, nonetheless generally conceived of the role of poetry in a broader cultural context than did either Donne or Jonson. Most of the writers discussed here usually appear in literary histories under the general heading of "Spenserians"; indeed, some owe the most recent publications of their works – and not very recent at that – to the efforts of the Spenser Society in the later nineteenth century.[2] And most are generally placed by modern scholars and anthologists in the second, sometimes third rank of poets of the period, their diminutive status often indicated, in fact, by a rubric that locates their collective place on the literary map through a common parent. We do not regard Donne or Jonson as "Sidneyans," although Sidney's amatory, religious, and Neoclassical concerns anticipate some of the major interests developed by each poet.

As with all labels, the Spenserian tag is useful up to a point. It reminds us, for one thing, that although political fortunes in Renaissance England could change with the breath of kings or queens, imaginative works of literature and the use to which they were put by later writers did not necessarily die with their authors. The variegated strain of Elizabethan poetry, especially pastoral and mythological, survived well into the first three decades of the seventeenth century, as the frequent reprintings of Marlowe's *Hero and Leander* testify, and its currency helps to explain how authors as fundamentally different from each other as Milton and Herrick could tap its resources for very different purposes. So too, nostalgia for the apparently greater, simpler, golden age of Elizabeth could be summoned, as often happened, in moments of acute political crisis to offer poets and readers some crumbs of comfort or platforms for criticism. When the staunch royalist, Izaak Walton, suffering under Cromwell's government, recalled Marlowe's famous shepherd's song, "Come live with me, and be my love," in *The Compleat Angler* in 1653, it was only one example, albeit a late one, in a long history of Elizabethan "revivals" in the early seventeenth century, not all of which identified the pastoral with the peaceful.

But if the Spenserian label is useful as a way to delineate an alternative tradition to Donne and Jonson, it also should not prevent us from seeing how different those generally grouped under the heading of Spenserians – Michael Drayton, William Browne, George Wither, Francis Quarles and John Taylor – are from each other (as well as from Spenser), or from recognizing their own popularity in their time. With the exception of George Herbert's *The Temple* (1633), none of the poetry of their now better-known contemporaries appeared in print with anything approaching the frequency of some of the works produced by these men. Although only John Taylor, the Sculler, might qualify as a "popular" poet – that is, as someone who deliberately cultivated his position as a poet of and for tradesmen – the others sought frequently to engage a broader readership, often on matters of national interest, in styles that ranged from the bardic prophecy of Drayton to the combative journalism of Wither, from the bald didacticism of Quarles to the picaresque reports of the Water Poet. And with the exception of Browne, all had more than a moment in the sun.

Michael Drayton (1563–1631)

Michael Drayton would certainly have been proud to be called a Spenserian, but he would just as surely have winced at having his name mentioned in the same chapter as John Taylor's. His more usual companion in literary history has been the respectable Samuel Daniel, and in some ways this pairing is appropriate. The two authors were born within a year of each other, Daniel in 1562 and Drayton in 1563, which means they were born not just in the decade of Shakespeare but in the decade between Sidney and Spenser (1550s) on the one hand and Donne and Jonson on the other (1570s). Both are usually regarded as transitional figures, twin Januses, each bearing an Elizabethan and a Jacobean face; but it is probably more accurate to think of them as not quite belonging to either, as representing something of a "lost" generation. At least this situation is certainly true of Drayton, if not for the poet Spenser consciously designated as his heir in *Colin Clouts Come Home Again* (1595). For if the fortunes of the two poets were intertwined in typically Elizabethan ways in the 1590s, with Daniel's *Complaint of Rosamond* (1592) serving, for instance, as inspiration for Drayton's *Piers Gaveston* (1593) and *Matilda* (1593) – an intertwining that testifies in each case to a life-long interest in British history (the first four books of Daniel's *The Civil Wars* were first published in 1595) – and with both paying homage to Sidney's *Astrophil* in their respective sonnet sequences, *Delia* (1592) and *Ideas Mirrour* (1594), as well as hovering around Lady Bedford, Daniel redirected his energies under James toward writing masques and his prose history of England, the first part of which was published in 1613. Drayton's career as a poet, on the other hand, was only just getting underway; but he never really became a Jacobean.

The crucial turning point involved his failure to become for James what he assumed Spenser had been to Elizabeth: the poet of the realm. That Drayton harbored such ambitions is clear from several remarks he made later in his career, most publicly in the epistle to the "General Reader" of *Poly-Olbion* (1612) – a form of address that by itself distinguishes Drayton's sense of audience from either Donne's or Jonson's – in which he complains of how he saw his "long nourisht hopes" for advancement from the king "buried alive before my face"; and then again in his epistle entitled "To Master George Sandys, Treasurer for the English Colony in Virginia," written probably in 1621 or 1622, where he laments how "it was my hap before all other men / To suffer shipwrack by my forward pen."[3]

It is not entirely clear what offense Drayton committed. His modern editors suggest that his problems stemmed from a failure to mourn properly the death of Elizabeth when he celebrated the arrival of the new king in 1603 (V, 53); but his own allusion in the epistle to Sandys to his "forward pen" suggests that the impropriety ought not to be regarded as only a sin of omission. In the years immediately preceding James's succession, Drayton had received considerable recognition for the publication of his *Heroical Epistles* (modeled loosely on Ovid's *Heroides*), a collection of grandly imagined dramatic monologues delivered by English nobility from the past that ran through five editions between 1597 and 1602. If nothing else – and echoes from "Matilda" were soon to be heard in contemporary works like Aemilia Lanyer's *Salve Deus Rex Judaeorum* (1611) – the popularity Drayton won from the publication inspired him to assume the more boldly Spenserian mantle of the prophet-poet in *The Owle*; written apparently before James's accession, it was first published in 1604 when it went through four editions in that year. In the poem, in the guise of a popular beast fable reminiscent of Spenser's *Mother Hubbard's Tale*, Drayton takes it upon himself to advise James of the manifold problems in the realm – the enclosure of common land, religious deceit, legal mischief, court treachery (as epitomized even in the "gallant Oke" figuring as Essex), and a weak foreign policy, especially after the death of the Protestant hero of "Elegance and Act," Sir Philip Sidney.

Again, we do not know of any specific response James made to this poem, but it is not really necessary that we have this information in order to realize that the king and Drayton were already moving in diametrically opposite directions. For one thing, the kind of freedom Drayton exhibited in making veiled references to contemporary events and persons was not likely to win favor from a king who, a few years earlier, thought Spenser ought to be punished for slandering (as contemporaries, including James, interpreted it) Mary Queen of Scots, James's mother, as the evil Duessa in *The Faerie Queene*. For another, even if *The Owle* represents a pledge of loyalty by the poet to the new king, the poet's sympathies for an older kind of militancy, as represented in the lament for Sidney and embodied in the visionary mode of address, run clearly counter to the king's peaceful wishes in matters involving both domestic and foreign policy but especially the latter, in which James's pursuit of peace with Spain represented a radical departure from the more aggressive, globally-conceived, anti-Spanish activities carried out under Elizabeth. James often behaved foolishly in appointing court favorites to positions of power, in contrast to the shrewd use Elizabeth made of her advisors; but he handled his poets very well. Jonson's gifts were more suitable to James's needs at court, just as it was worth his waiting for Donne to take orders and officially defend the faith. Drayton was not for the new king.

Nor was James really for Drayton. It would be a mistake to think of Drayton, like the later Milton, as a participant in an extended and sometimes glorious struggle with the monarchy. Even if he occasionally voiced veiled criticisms of the king (who appears unflatteringly as "Olcon" in the eighth eclogue of the 1606 *Poems Lyrick and Pastorall*) and also included among his friends Protestant militants like John Reynolds, who actively opposed royal policy by advocating England's intervention in the Thirty Years War on behalf of the Protestant cause (and spent time in prison for having done so), Drayton does not register suspicion over the institution of kingship, only concern for the way James was conducting domestic and foreign affairs. As he remarks to George Sandys, "I dare not speake of the *Palatinate*"; but once a new king was on the throne in 1625, Drayton seems to have quickly rekindled his hopes for preferment. If recent scholarship has reshaped an earlier image of Drayton as a belated Elizabethan into a more sharply etched portrait of him as a trenchant critic of Jacobean policy, then even more recent scholarship has qualified that view by pointing to the local constraints and interests often influencing Drayton's ventures.[4] Drayton is the classic case not simply of a poet in need of an England that no longer (if ever) was. He was also a poet continually searching for patrons to support his needs.

And yet in retrospect (the word is almost unavoidable with Drayton), it is also a little difficult to imagine how his "forward pen" could ever have adapted itself to the narrow confines of the Jacobean court. Drayton was, above all, a poet who needed room. He needed room to celebrate the heroic achievements of English legends; room to celebrate the English landscape with its customs and traditions; room to speak out; room to experiment with different genres – besides composing sonnets and historical legends, he also wrote many versions of pastoral through his long career, attempted several kinds of odes, practiced his hand at ballads, beast fables, verse epistles, and elegies, and produced the longest "chorographical" poem in English;[5] room to revise – no poet of the period reworked his canon in so many different ways. Drayton needed room, in short, to be an English poet of the heroic vein and in the process to continue the native line of poetry extending from Chaucer into the present – a tradition, as he emphasizes in his verse epistle to Henry Reynolds, that equates the grave and noble with the native and home-spun (III, 226–31). Reading Drayton reminds us how significantly Donne and Jonson deviated from their immediate predecessors, how much, in effect, they shrunk the scope of poetry in order to enlarge it in a different direction.

It is also difficult to conceive of Drayton, bred in the country and a life-long critic of deforestation, as being very courtly in manner. (In *The Worthies of England* (1662), Fuller describes Drayton as "slow of speech, and inoffensive in company.")[6] Except for the early sonnets, his verse is marked by plain speaking and sturdy sentiments, not elegance, wordplay, and wit. Very early on, in fact, he seems to have disdained anything that might smack of "foreign inventions" – "foreign," in his case, includes sartorial or sexual innovations as well as linguistic ones. Drayton characteristically reserved his most courtly touches for his pastorals, something that might have pleased Elizabeth but not James; and when he fully refined this art, to the point of miniaturizing it as he did under Charles and Henrietta Maria in his most elegantly "Elizabethan" poems – the often praised song to Sirena that begins "Nearer to the Silver Trent," *Nymphidia, the Court of Fayrie* (1627), and *The Muses Elizium* (1630) – Drayton was easily the oldest living poet in England and hardly an obvious candidate for preferment. And even then, he still bore some rough edges. As much as the new king and his

French queen might have wished to purge the Jacobean court of its notorious excesses, they were probably not ready to hear, along with *Nymphidia*, the kind of pulpit-pounding denunciations Drayton leveled against the "Sons of Belial" in *The Moon-Calfe*, written perhaps under James but first published in 1627. Drayton's "conscience," Fuller notes, had "always the command of his fancy."[7]

Not surprisingly, Drayton's best moments as a poet rarely involve fine psychological, emotional, or social discriminations, qualities we associate particularly with either a Donne or Jonson. His special penchant was for the rugged and the heroic, even the primitive. "Since there's no help, come let us kiss and part," his most frequently anthologized poem, testifies to both his unusual resolve as a poet (it is the reward of years of working with the sonnet) and his ability to present, in remarkably precise and direct language reminiscent of Wyatt, a fully persuasive posture of resolution and independence – at least until the beginning of the sestet, when the posture suddenly and melodramatically expires with a deliberate flourish of passionate abstractions:

> Since ther's no helpe, Come let us kisse and part,
> Nay, I have done: you get no more of Me,
> And I am glad, yea glad withall my heart,
> That thus so cleanly, I my Selfe can free,
> Shake hands for ever, Cancell all our Vowes,
> And when We meet at any time againe,
> Be it not seene in either of our Browes,
> That We one jot of former Love reteyne;
> Now at the last gaspe, of Loves latest Breath,
> When his Pulse fayling, Passion speechlesse lies,
> When Faith is kneeling by his bed of Death,
> And Innocence is closing up his Eyes,
> Now if thou would'st, when all have given him over,
> From Death to Life, thou might'st him yet recover.

(II, 341)

Not published until 1619 as part of *Idea*, this sonnet is generally assumed to epitomize the virtues of Drayton's revisionary habits, and so it does. One has only to read through his effete first attempt at the sonnet form in the 1594 *Ideas Mirrour* (bearing the French subtitle "Amours in Quatorzains" no less) to realize how much paring and cutting has gone into producing the spare, high drama of the later version, a toughening that reflects a general shift away from the florid toward the epigrammatic that was part of the complex exchange in literary values and taste that marked the 1590s. (Drayton's early sonnets were themselves the objects of attack by satirists.) But however thorough the purge – and the weak final rhyme is perhaps all that remains of the "sonneteer" of the 1590s – Drayton's revisions stop short of providing a radical critique of the genre in the manner of Donne. The drama is stark but still Petrarchan – evidence of a better poet for sure, but one born too deeply in the reign of Elizabeth to give over his roots completely.

Drayton's most innovative and interesting single collection of verse marks his conservative, syncretistic habits from a different angle. His odes are usually regarded as having a significant, though slightly suspect, place in histories of the genre: significant because their publication in 1606 as part of *Poems Lyricke and Pastorall* (they came to have their own title page in 1619) allows them some claim as the first "genuine" odes in English, but suspect because Drayton obviously did not reconceive the genre with a Jonsonian emphasis on recovering the original in all its formal, classical purity.[8] However this may be – and one feels the prescriptive weight of Jonson in these histories – Drayton was working a different, more popular vein than Jonson, one distinctly reminiscent of Sidney in *The Defense of Poesie* when that poet notoriously confessed his own "barbarousness" by praising "the old song of Percy and Douglas," the ballad of Chevy Chase, and placing it in the company of Pindar:

> I never heard the old song of Percy and Douglas that I found not my heart moved more than with a trumpet; and yet is it sung but by some blind crowder [fiddler], with no rougher voice than rude style; which, being so evil apparelled in the dust and cobwebs of that uncivil age, what would it work trimmed in the gorgeous eloquence of Pindar?[9]

Sidney's praise of the popular ballad is thoroughly aristocratic and clearly done with the purpose of defending the lyric against Puritan attacks on poetry for its supposed enervating effects, but it also justifies linking, if not equating, the ballad with the ode, the low with the high, the native with the imported. Both were heroic songs of old, twin forms of patriotic lore.

Drayton's odes were conceived in a Sidneyan light. They stress the continuity between classical and native traditions, an attitude made explicit in the modestly learned preface to the reader in which Drayton identifies the specific attributes of the ode associated with its various practitioners – Pindar, Anacreon, and Horace – which he, in turn, associates with the medieval ballad as practiced by "our Chaucer" and reincarnated by himself in the "old English Garbe" of "The Ballad of Agincourt" (II, 345–46). That generically inclusive vision is further emphasized in the historical sweep of the introductory ode "To Himselfe, and the Harpe," as well as in the volume as a whole. Both become progressively more British: in the description of the "skilfull Bard" who plays the harp; in the gradual concentration on decidedly English subjects (Drayton even includes "A Skeltoniad"); and in the final mutation of the ode into the ballad that marks the end of the collection.

Drayton's scheme is hardly that of a purist, and he readily admits in the preface that he barely attempted the "high dialect" of Pindar. Whatever features we might designate as most Horatian or Anacreontic had also to await a later generation of poets before they were to be fully "Englished." (In his use of the short-line stanza, Drayton more often stumbles than soars.) But if he is rarely more than a fledgling Neoclassicist in this volume, the reason in part is simply that his voice took its greatest energies from below, from his native soil and the popular themes associated with it. In recasting himself as one of the old Bards of Britain, whose principal concern, like Sidney's "blind crowder," was to stir the hearts of his fellow countrymen, Drayton wrote some of his most persuasive verse.

"To the Virginian Voyage," "The Ballad of Agincourt" (dedicated "to the Cambro-Britans"), and "An Ode Written in the Peake" are decidedly patriotic, fully imagined addresses, and among his best known poems. The first, prompted by the 1606 patent that authorized further explorations of the New World and led to the founding of Jamestown, celebrates a wished-for return to the seafaring exploits under Elizabeth; urges, in fact, a rereading of "industrious HAKLUIT" and, along with offering the usual material enticements "to get the Pearle and Gold," shows an exuberant familiarity with reported "golden age" flora and fauna including the "use-full Sassafras." The abbreviated line and occasionally inverted syntax seem part and parcel of the bard's rough voice and rude style:

You brave Heroique Minds,
Worthy your Countries Name,
  That Honour still pursue,
  Goe, and subdue,
Whilst loyt'ring Hinds
Lurke here at home, with shame.

(II, 363)

As the reference in the first line of the poem to "You brave Heroique Minds" suggests, Drayton is less interested in inspiring others to bring home booty from abroad than he is in figuring anew British identity as a feature of going forth and subduing. The same might be said of the poem commemorating that most heroic of English battles and kings, Henry V's victory over the French at Agincourt. It makes use of all the resources of the popular ballad – simple plot, plain diction, grand action, famous names – in an effort to make the legendary past bear intensely, and critically, on the present.[10] The poem concludes with a question-begging apostrophe that is also the volume's last word:

Upon Saint CRISPIN's day
Fought was this Noble Fray,
Which Fame did not delay,
  To *England* to carry;
O, when shall *English* Men
With such Acts fill a Pen,
Or *England* breed againe,
  Such a King HARRY?

(II, 378)

The unspoken answer for Drayton, as for many English Protestants in 1606, lay not with the present king but with his son, another "Harry": the chivalric Prince Henry (to whom the first part of *Poly-Olbion* is dedicated). And the third ode or ballad might well be the most satisfying regional poem written in English before Denham's "Cooper's Hill" (1642). Despite the "breeme Winters scathes" ("breeme" was a characteristically Spenserian use of the northern dialect for "bitter" or "chilly"), the poet shows not the slightest remorse for his absence from London, the court, and "the Princely *Thames*":

> Though in the utmost *Peake*,
>   A while we doe remaine,
> Amongst the Mountaines bleake
>   Expos'd to Sleet and Raine,
> No Sport our Houres shall breake,
>   To exercise our Vaine.
>
> What though bright PHOEBUS Beames
>   Refresh the Southerne Ground,
> And though the Princely *Thames*
>   With beautious Nymphs abound,
> And by old *Camber's* streames
> Be many Wonders found;
>
> Yet many Rivers cleare
>   Here glide in Silver Swathes,
> And what of all most deare,
>   *Buckston's* delicious Bathes,
> Strong Ale and Noble Cheare,
>   T'asswage breeme Winters scathes.

> (II, 365)

"Strong Ale and Noble Cheare" by "*Buckston's* delicious Bathes": the difference between drinking in Drayton and in Jonson points up precise differences between them as poets. In Jonson, the "we" is always a particular "you" and "I": a Cary or a Morison, a member of the Sidney family, or at its most indefinite, "a friend" who shares similar culinary and literary interests with the poet, an "I" who is or pretends to be always the same "Ben Jonson." Jonson's poetry, at its very best, manages to convey a subtle regard for the complexities involved in social interchange at many levels. In Drayton, the "we" is a collective "we," rarely specifically identified and, as in this instance, often thoroughly subordinated to the landscape of England, with its customs and natural "wonders." His subjects almost always border on the mythic, his persons are personifications. At its best, Drayton's poetry manages to convey a sense of gusto, a sense of the heart fully stirred by its native subject:

This while we are abroad,
   Shall we not touch our Lyre?
Shall we not sing an Ode?
   Shall that holy Fire,
In us that strongly glow'd,
   In this cold Ayre expire?

                           (II, 365)

Love of land and country was never taken to greater lengths than in *Poly-Olbion* (1612, 1622). Drayton's "Herculean labor" and great debacle – the second and final installment in 1622 was ruefully dedicated "To Any that Will Read It," a challenge that remains rarely answered today – was intended to fuse Spenser with Camden, a general interest in pastoral mythology with a specific concern for historical detail, legendary and factual alike – all done in alexandrines that total nearly 15,000 lines (14,716 to be exact, though many have thought it longer, including Henry Hallam who fostered the still current rumor that it is around 30,000).[11] Drayton's organizing strategy, such as it is, follows Camden's in *Britannia* by giving precedence to individual regions, corresponding in many cases to individual counties, although the patriotic sweep of British history is preserved, at least in the first part, by beginning in the west with Cornwall and the legend of Brute and working toward an eventual celebration in the seventeenth song of England's most recent monarch, Elizabeth. (James is conspicuous by his absence from the roll call.) The second part concentrates on the east and north of England. A promise to explore Scotland in a third installment was never realized.

Drayton was not the first to call on the muse to deliver a capsule view of England in verse. He was succeeded – and partially inspired – by the all-but-forgotten William Warner whose popular *Albions England* (1586, books 1–6; 1596, 7–12; 1602, 13) uses a not-so-trim mixture of prose and verse (fourteeners) to detail a largely classicized history of Britain. (Apart from its stated impatience in 1586 with Elizabethan habits of "running on the letter," the work is of interest for revealing through the additions an evolving sense of national consciousness.) And there was also Thomas Churchyard's popular *The Worthies of Wales* (1586), with its partial celebration of the British landscape. Nor was Drayton's the last travelogue of its time: Milton's landscape-happy "L'Allegro" is a neater but not-so-distant offshoot. But *Poly-Olbion* will always be the great curiosity of chorographical poems and not merely because of its matter – its "intermixture of the most Remarkable Stories, Antiquities, Wonders, Rarities, Pleasures, and Commodities" with the more usual topographical reports. Its epic scale (the work initially appeared as a folio), sumptuous title page (Albion is presented as the most fertile and beautiful of women), elaborate notes to the first part by the learned antiquarian, John Selden (they make E.K.'s gloss of *The Shepheardes Calendar* seem like schoolboy scribblings), engraved maps of the individual regions by the great Elizabethan cartographer, Christopher Saxton, and the author's indefatigable commitment to the device of prosopopoeia (in the poem, the landscape is represented as doing most of the talking): all help to make *Poly-Olbion* into something more than the vast sum of its many parts, although just what that something is continues to be a matter of scholarly headscratching. (The most persuasive and sympathetic reading of late connects the poem's pervasive regionalism to debates over the legal and political origins of England prompted by the possible annexation of Scotland under James.)[12] Indeed, its untraversable pathways would seem to underlie Jonson's tongue-in-cheek praise of Drayton's "universal circumduction" in the odd poem he wrote for the 1627 publication of *The Battle of Agincourt*. "Circumduction" meant both "round about" and, in legal parlance, "annulling" or "canceling."

Certainly, its roundaboutness has made *Poly-Olbion* difficult to read except piece by piece, locale by locale, and then not always with pleasure. Sir Thomas Browne, who was not one to be easily intimidated by arcane matter, thought the verse "smooth" and the sea nymph's song in the second page worth quoting to his son who was setting out to Jersey.[13] Pope was characteristically less generous in his praise of Drayton ("a very mediocre poet"), but significantly indebted in "Windsor Forest" to portions of the poem (songs XIII, XV, and xvii);[14] and modern critics, looking for an entry into the poem, often choose to concentrate on the section describing the poet's native Warwickshire (again, song xiii). But the difficulty the poem presents is that it really does not make much difference where one begins: it all begins to sound alike. As a polyphonic hymn to the particular, there is no "plot" to *Poly-Olbion*, other than to stage singing matches in praise of each region for its local attributes, antiquities, and wonders; but the more individualized the specific locale, the more it also seems to resemble other locales in its celebration of wonders and curiosities. Every region, in effect, makes a bid to be exceptional in a poem whose "long verses" – to adopt Jonson's stigmatizing description of them – gradually insist on sameness, that "all local claims are equal – not that they are identical or interchangeable, but that each particular pride of place must concede that its own sovereignty coexists with many others, and may indeed, in time, become transformed into another."[15] One has only to read the portion on the Peake district to see the poetic consequences of Drayton's syncretist habits mightily at work. What he gives up in height, he gains in length:

> Yet for her Caves, and Holes, *Peake* onely not excells,
> But that I can againe produce those wondrous Wells
> Of *Buckston*, as I have, that most delicious Fount,
> Which men the second Bath of *England* doe account,
> Which in the primer raignes, when first this well began
> To have her vertues knowne unto the blest *Saint Anne*,
> Was consecrated then, which the same temper hath,
> As that most daintie Spring, which at the famous *Bath*,

Is by the Crosse enstild, whose fame I much preferre,
In that I doe compare my daintiest Spring to her.

(Song XXVI, ll. 453–62)

In the flow of hexameters, the English countryside is awash in particulars that defy time and space: one "bath" calls up a "second," which recalls the consecration of the first by "the blest Saint Anne" and then invites a further comparison of sorts with "that most daintie Spring." One can understand why Selden, although never more needed, annotated only the first part of the poem.

An author less committed to an heroic vision of poetry and the poet might well have closed shop with *Poly-Olbion*. The publishers of the first part, in fact, attempted to do just that to Drayton when they refused to bring out the second installment.[16] But with Drayton, the will to continue to write was itself material for legends or lampoons, as the remarks of contemporaries diversely testify; and if in his final years he consciously limited the scope of his muse, he was still capable of unfurling the banner when the moment seemed right, as it apparently did in the early years of Charles's reign when preparations for war with both Spain and France occurred on a scale unknown since Elizabeth. In 1627, the year of Buckingham's disastrous assault on La Rochelle, Drayton's recuperative powers as well as his rekindled patriotism were again fully on display in a 2500-line epic version of *The Battle of Agincourt*. The collection in which it appeared was dedicated to "those Noblest of Gentlemen, of these Renowned Kingdomes of Great *Britaine*: who in these declining times, have yet in your brave bosomes the sparkes of that sprightly fire, of your couragious Ancestors" (III, 2), and along with the jingoistic gore of the title poem – the French come off very badly – the volume included a mixture of consciously folksy Elizabethan poetry (*Nymphidia, the Court of Fayrie* pulls heavily on Shakespeare) with more up-to-date verse epistles that reveal a poet out of sorts with the previous king's attitude of military and maritime caution. Three years later, with the political climate significantly quieter, Drayton, at sixty-eight, published his final collection, *The Muses Elizium* (1630), a partial concession to the Caroline habit of pastoral refinement that, in its delicate spinning, anticipates Herrick and Marvell more than it recollects Spenser. There is not much to say about these ten wistful "Nymphalls," Drayton's coinage for "A meeting or Feast of Nymphs" (*Poly-Olbion*, XX, 4); but C.S. Lewis's remark that "nothing more Golden had ever been produced. They teach nothing, assert nothing, depict almost nothing"[17] needs to be updated to include the possibility that they were originally written for a performance for the Sackville family at Knole. Drayton had dedicated *The Muses Elizium* to the 4th Earl of Dorset – the great-grandson of the author of *Gorbudoc* – and included verse paraphrases from the Bible for his wife, Mary, Countess of Dorset, who was soon to be responsible for the monument of Drayton in Westminster Abbey.[18] A court culture harking back to Elizabeth had caught up to Drayton at last.

William Browne (1590/1?–1643/5?) and George Wither (1588–1667)

Drayton was too consciously respectful of the English literary traditions ever to imagine originating and sealing a tribe of poets about him in the manner of Jonson, even if he had had anything like the latter's personal and poetic power. All the same he became, by accident as well as design, both mentor and magnet for a succeeding generation of writers who, though conversant with courtly traditions, were, like Drayton, never of the court and thought the proper subject of poetry was the larger matter of the "country," in both the pastoral and political sense of the word. Of these – and the group would include Abraham Holland, the son of the great Elizabethan translator, Philemon Holland – the most interesting are William Browne and George Wither. Both expressed their allegiance to Drayton by being among the very few to supply commendatory poems for the second part of *Poly-Olbion* in 1622. (In turn, Drayton commiserated with Browne about the world being "All arsey varsey" in a late verse epistle where he criticizes the sudden rise of the undeserved (III, 209).) But the story of Browne's and Wither's affiliation goes back at least ten years earlier when both poets, born in rural England fairly late in Elizabeth's reign (Wither in Hampshire in 1588, Browne in Devonshire in 1591) and having attended Oxford, came on the literary scene with elegies to Prince Henry, who had died suddenly in November, 1612. This act alone hardly separated them from the many who mourned the death of England's first heir to the throne in some eighty years; their subsequent publications, however, did.

Browne's *Britannia's Pastoral* (Book I, 1613; II, 1616; a third book lay in manuscript until 1851) is the most sustained attempt to write a version of Spenserian epic romance in the early part of the seventeenth century. To a small degree, the poem draws on Drayton's version of Spenser in *Poly-Olbion*, that is, the dynastic poet who celebrates Britain's mythic past and its legendary founder, Brute, and some of its actual heroes of the more recent, Elizabethan present, especially those associated with great maritime exploits such as Sir Francis Drake and Sir Richard Grenville. (Hailing from Devon, Browne was especially partial to Drake.) To a much greater extent he exploited other recognizably Spenserian devices: archaic diction, pictorial imagery, allegory, romantic episodes in a landscape that can be alternately comforting and threatening. But in Browne, the epic vision has been folded fully within the pastoral, at least with regard to the action or plot. There is no presiding figure, no Gloriana, toward which all things point; there is no hero on a quest, no gentleman to be fashioned into a knight. Browne's skills, particularly in the first two books, are essentially those of a lyricist, a Colin Clout of the Tavy River who has mastered a number of shorter forms. Anagrams, elegies, echo poems, singing contests, topographical description – he occasionally produces them with anthology-like elegance:

Never more let holy *Dee*
   O're other Rivers brave,
Or boast how (in his jollitie)
   Kings row'd upon his wave.
But silent be, and ever know
That *Neptune* for my Fare would row.[19]

With such sweet sounds – and the lyric is sung by a shepherd timing it with his oar (in anticipation of Marvell's gospel voyagers in "Bermudas") – it is only right that one of the few lyrics added to the 1614 edition of *Englands Helicon* (1600) would be his ("Thirsis' Praise of His Mistress").

What distinguishes Browne, however, from other turn of the century pastoralists like the immensely prolific Nicholas Breton is the "higher strain" found in *Britannia*. (Alastair Fowler speaks of the inspiration Browne discovered in Virgil's *Georgics*.)[20] We do not automatically have to subscribe to the long tradition, dating back to the eighteenth century, that Milton owned and heavily marked up a copy of the poem to sense a poet capable of some graver or greater subject. Without ever being an historical poem, *Britannia's Pastorals* is a poem that keeps opening out into history: sometimes to lament the nation's fortunes (he interpolates the elegy on the death of Prince Henry into the end of the first book); sometimes to satirize, in prophetic fashion, the country's ills and its poor leadership on both foreign and domestic fronts (the Cave of Famine represents, in this regard, a significant adjustment away from Spenser's Cave of Mammon); and occasionally to deliver short stretches of pure, unbridled patriotism that reveal a poet of significant imaginative reach:

Haile, thou my native soile! thou blessed plot
Whose equall all the world affordeth not!
Shew me who can so many crystall Rils,
Such sweet-cloath'd Vallies or aspiring Hils:
Such Wood-ground, Pastures, Quarries, welthy Mines:
Such Rocks in whom the Diamond fairely shines:
And if the earth can shew the like agen,
Yet will she faile in her Sea-ruling men.

(II, 43)

As Browne's contemporaries recognized – and the first two editions included commendatory poems by no fewer than twenty-six authors, mostly from the Inns of Court and Exeter College, Oxford – *Britannia's Pastorals* was a poem that promised much. "Drive forth thy Flock, young Pastor, to that Plaine, / Where our old Shepheards wont their flocks to feed," is how Drayton expressed his hopes for a pastoral renaissance (I, 7).

But promise in this case did not lead to fulfillment. The enthusiastic send-off by a coterie audience points to the power of nostalgia for things

Elizabethan in the early years of the second decade, a nostalgia made acute by the death of Prince Henry in 1612 (for many, including Browne, Henry was perceived as the direct link to Elizabethan chivalry and maritime exploration) and the subsequent marriage of Elizabeth to the Elector Palatine in 1613. But Browne was still too much the gentleman amateur to do more than either refine what he had already received or call for something he could only intermittently produce.

In 1614, as part of the short-lived resurgence of pastoral, Browne "drove forth" once again in a sort of generic stutter step with *The Shepheard's Pipe*. The seven eclogues, on diverse topics, seek to create a larger poetic moment for their author and themselves by turning pastoral into a community mode as Browne (Willy) incorporates his friends, George Wither (Roget) and Christopher Brooke (Cutty), into several of the eclogues. There is also a small attempt to resuscitate a native tradition of poetry: Browne translates the Tale of Jonathas by Chaucer's contemporary Thomas Hoccleve in the first eclogue, and the third eclogue is meant to stir our sympathies for Old Neddy (Drayton?), who because of deceit and treachery, finds a receptive audience only in "The Farmer's house" – hardly a Penshurst Place. But how significant can the moment be or become when the poet urged to exchange the oaten reed for a trumpet is Christopher Brooke? How deep is Browne's commitment to the native past when Skelton is summoned as the epitome of the bad poet (Eclogue 1)? In the pastoral revival of 1613–16, it is surely possible to witness its thinning as an imaginative resource, and the fact that Browne never published the third part of *Britannia's Pastorals*, with its trenchant criticisms of the Spanish,[21] suggests how marginal the pastoral had become as a way of voicing national themes. It could still serve as an opportunity for self-presentation, and Browne would be occasionally echoed by later regionalists like the Welsh poet of the Usk, Henry Vaughan. But beyond that, Spenserian pastoral, with its complex relation to national destiny, needed to be forgotten before it could be fully reactivated, as Milton was to do beginning in 1629 with his ode "On the Morning of Christ's Nativity."

Browne's was a literary career – if "career" is even the right word – that became increasingly less visible. Many of his later years were spent either at Oxford or with the Herbert family at Wilton, the same location where Sidney had composed portions of the *New Arcadia* in the 1580s. The latter was surely an appropriate retreat for the poet who praised Drayton in *Poly-Olbion* by associating him with "Immortall *Sydney*" and who also wrote one of the century's best epitaphs, if one reads only the first six lines, on Mary Sidney, the Countess of Pembroke, who died in 1621:

Underneath this sable Herse
Lyes the subject of all verse:
Sydneys sister, Pembroke's Mother:
Death, ere thou hast slaine another,

Faire, & Learn'd, & good as she,
Tyme shall throw a dart at thee.

(II, 342)

With its combination of fine finish and gradually deepening sentiments, it is not surprising that the poem routinely appeared in early collections of Jonson's poetry (although one suspects Jonson would have made something of her name); but the problem of assigning authorship, in this case at least,[22] also points to the larger issue of Browne's near anonymity as a poet.

Anonymity was never an issue with George Wither. A Spenserian by affinity, not by imitation, and then only in the early part of his career, Wither was one of the most colorfully busy poets of the century. "He would make verses as fast as he could write them," wrote John Aubrey. "And though he was an easie rymer, and no good poet, he was a good vates. He had a strange sagacity and foresight into mundane affaires."[23] Aubrey's comment points accurately to Wither's entrepreneurial energies, especially with print, energies that accounted for his publishing over one hundred books or pamphlets in his lifetime (mostly poetry), got him into repeated trouble with authorities (he was frequently imprisoned, perhaps as many as five times),[24] and made him the apparent enemy of those poets who valued propriety and form in verse. Jonson satirized him in the figure of Chronomastix in his 1622 masque, *Time Vindicated*, and around mid-century Sir John Denham conferred immortality of a sort upon Wither in one of the period's more famous anecdotes. According to Aubrey, Denham "went to the king, and desired his majestie not to hang [Wither], for that whilest G.W. lived, he [Denham] should not be the worst Poet in England."[25]

Despite the drubbing Wither has received at the hands of Neoclassicists – and he inevitably makes an appearance in Pope's *Dunciad* – Wither was one of the most read poets of the early seventeenth century. His *Abuses Stript and Whipt* went through five editions alone in the year of its publication (1613) and another three by 1617; and in conjunction with *The Shepherd's Hunting* (three editions in 1615) and his *Motto* (seven in 1621), it catapulted him into the public eye, where he remained for nearly half a century until his death in 1667. To be "the very *Withers* of the City" was, in Dryden's *Essay of Dramatic Poesy* (1668), to be the ultimate popular poet: the multitudes "have bought more Editions of his Works than would serve to lay under all their Pies at the Lord Mayor's *Christmass*."[26]

Much of Wither's extraordinary success must be ascribed to the initial notoriety he received from *Abuses*, notoriety that included being thrown in Marshalsea Prison. (In Charles Lamb's apt phrase, Wither was "for ever anticipating persecution and martyrdom; fingering, as it were, the flames, to try how he can bear them.")[27] The offended party was in all likelihood Henry Howard, Earl of Northampton, a staunch Catholic who had long been attempting to secure an alliance with Spain and one of the most unscrupulous and powerful men in the Jacobean court. He had also probably been led to mark Wither because of the zealously Protestant attitude the poet had already expressed in *Prince Henries Obsequies* (1612) and his *Epithalamion* (1612) celebrating the marriage of Elizabeth – "another Terror to the Whore of Rome" – to the Elector Palatine.[28]

On the surface, or at least apart from its abrasive title, the work seems innocent enough. It is mild Marston: a collection of satirical verse essays on various human passions like love, lust, envy, revenge, and so on, topped off by a whimsical dedication to the author and an apparently autobiographical verse introduction in which Wither plays the melancholic truth seeker. But there is also more than a little of Webster's crafty and suspicious Bosola in Wither, and whether or not he actually reveals many "secret villanies" of state, his constant insinuating pose of "worldly sagacity" at least promises much. In the unstable political circumstances of 1613, when court factions, responding to the death of Henry and the marriage of Elizabeth to the Elector Palatine, were vying over the role England might play in international politics (1613, it will be remembered, was also the year in which Browne first "went forth" in *Britannia's Pastorals*) and doing so, moreover, in the unfolding context of one of the great domestic scandals of James's court (the highly suspicious annulment of the marriage between the Earl of Essex and Lady Frances – Howard's niece – in order to allow her to marry the king's favorite, Robert Carr), *Abuses Stript and Whipt* struck home, especially as far as Howard was concerned.

Wither was also never one to let an opportunity for advancement pass. Although he spent only four months in prison, from March to July of 1614, he managed through the publication of *The Shepherds Hunting* to make it seem as if all England were sharing his drama. Subtitled "Certaine Eclogs written during the time of the Authors Imprisonment in the *Marshalsey*" and bearing a double dedication "To those honoured, noble, and right vertuous friends, my visitants in the Marshalsey: And to all other my unknowne favourers, who either privately, or publickly wished me well in my imprisonment" (I, p. 3), the work reverses the formula for Spenserian pastoral in which, as Drayton remarked, "the most High, and most Noble Matters of the World may bee shaddowed" in this lowly form (II, 517). In Wither, the background is the foreground. The political and historical have become the occasion for the poetic, as interlocutors like Willy (William Browne) and Alexis (William Ferrar, brother to Nicholas of Little Gidding and adventurer) visit their friend Philarete (Wither) in jail, who alternately proclaims his innocence – "I suffer 'cause I wish'd my country well; / And what I more must bear I cannot tell"[29] – and the efficient power of his song. In the latter case, Wither commemorates not simply his "transcendent" virtuosity as a pastoralist but his previous role as a scourge in *Abuses*.

A penchant for the pyre and a desire to self-dramatize were essential to Wither's early popularity. (In 1622, he was back in jail, this time for publishing his *Motto*.) But Wither also had a keen eye for the literary marketplace, and in 1623, he secured from the king, perhaps with aid from the Earl of Pembroke, a potentially highly lucrative grant, one requesting that a copy of his most recent work, *The Hymns and Songs of the Church,* be bound and sold with each copy of the popular Sternhold and Hopkins Psalter. Had the patent remained uncontested by the Stationers, Wither might have realized sales in the range of 90,000 copies over the next ten years. As it turned out, however, the booksellers not only persuaded Parliament to have the patent repealed, but they initiated a boycott against Wither that prevented normal publication of any new works of his for nearly ten years.[30] After 1623, Wither never again managed to command the kind of readership for individual works that he had had early in his career, despite his attempt to write for an increasingly broad segment of the population. But his impulse to write was only partly a condition of the marketplace, and though many, including Wither himself, have pointed to his evident decline as a "poet," there was no decline in his productivity.

However one attempts to describe Wither's popularity in circumstantial terms – and one jaundiced contemporary thought his poetry had life only because it was forbidden – Wither commanded an individual idiom that lent itself more fully to the "common reader" than did that of the other Spenserians. At their most inclusive, Drayton and Browne wrote about topics of national concern, about matters of Britain; but they still conceived of the poet not only as a privileged sage (for Drayton, this view was practically self-defining) but also as still writing for a highly select audience of aristocrats and fellow poets alike – indeed, one not substantially different from the audiences of Donne or Jonson. Wither, too, could write the occasional courtly poem. His frequently anthologized "Shall I, wasting in despair / Die because a woman's fair" reveals in miniature what *Fair Virtue, The Mistresse of Phil'arete* seems consciously designed to show at no small length: that Wither could woo with the best. But even in this mode, his idiom has an easy geniality and saucy immediacy that go well beyond a simple attempt at a kind of Sidneyan *sprezzatura,* the use of art to hide art:

> Pedants shall not tie my strains
> To our antique poets' veins;
> As if we, in latter days,
> Knew to love, but not to praise.
> Being born as free as these,
> I will sing as I shall please,
> Who as well new paths may run,
> As the best before have done.
> I disdain to make my song
> For their pleasures short or long.
> If I please I'll end it here;
> If I list I'll sing this year.
> And, though none regard of it,
> By myself I pleas'd can sit,

And with that contentment cheer me,
As if half the world did hear me.

(II, 27–8)

It might seem a large step between Lamb's acutely registered praise of Wither, made in connection with *Fair Virtue*, as the first English poet to celebrate the power of poetry "at home," and Jonson's scornful representation of Wither in *Time Vindicated* as the poet-hero of the barely literate, but both critics are responding to the same feature in Wither: the free-born, self-generated and generating element in his verse. It feels fully home-spun, not just native, a response to the personal moment, not a product of tradition: "If I please I'll end it here; / If I list I'll sing this year." From the perspective of a Romantic who was pre-eminently an essayist, Wither's loose poetics, his run-on line, signaled his independence and originality.[31] But from the point of view of a Neoclassicist like Jonson, the absence of the well-licked line could spell anarchy of sorts, especially when the subject matter was of the kind to appeal immediately to a popular audience, as both *Abuses Stript and Whipt* and the *Motto* obviously were. However rebellious or libertine Donne might appear to the modern reader, he could never have said, as Jonson imagined Wither saying, "A pudding-wife, that would despise the Times / Hath utter'd frequent pen'worths, through my rimes."[32] Early Wither was a poet who could write both up and down the social register, for kings as well as commoners, as the royal imprimatur *Cum Privilegio Regis Regali* on the title page of the *Hymns and Songs of the Church*, a text for the ordinary reader, makes clear.

After 1623, however, Wither increasingly conceived of his audience in largely popular terms and his own role as that of preacher or prophet. (The transition is sharply marked by the publication of his *Juvenilia* in 1622.) To some degree, his shift from a predominantly courtly to a religious poet corresponds to the elevated status of the devotional lyric that began under James, and hence in Wither to an elevation of the pastoralist to the psalmist, with an increased emphasis on the virtues of the plain style – an emphasis on matter over manner. In 1632 Wither published his translation of *The Psalms of David*. In further didactic works like *A Collection of Emblemes, Ancient and Moderne* (1635) and *Hallelujah, or Britain's Second Remembrancer* (1641), a volume of hymns and songs apparently inspired by the recent examples of Herbert, Sandys, and Quarles but still ultimately modeled on the Sternhold and Hopkins Psalter, Wither sought consciously and with some success to make a virtue out of "affected plainness." A poem like the "Hymn LXXII, For Deliverance from Public Sickness" – one of Wither's favorite themes – still commands attention for its stark, concentrated passion:

> Lord! when a nation Thee offends,
>   And when Thou wouldst correct their lands,
> An army still on Thee attends,
>   To execute Thy just commands;

> Yea, famine, sickness, fire, and sword,
> Stand ready to fulfil Thy word.
> And here among us for our sin,
> A strong infection lately reign'd:
> Whose rage hath so malignant been,
> As that it could not be restrain'd
> By any care, or art of our,
> Or by a less than heavenly power.[33]

Famine, sickness, fire, and sword: these were also the principal subjects of Wither's later poetry. Beginning with *Britain's Remembrancer* (1628), Wither gave his earlier satiric persona a prophetic strain and made England increasingly his theme, not the England of Drayton's *Poly-Olbion*, however, an England of past and potentially future heroic deeds, but an England of the present racked by disease. While Drayton was still trying to encourage the gentry once more into the breach in *The Battle of Agincourt* (1627), Wither was reminding England of the recent ravages of the 1625 plague (in which some 41,000 perished) by becoming its voice of conscience:

> Yea, mark, mark *London*, and confesse with me,
> That God hath justly, thus afflicted thee,
> And that in ev'ry point this *Plague* hath been
> According to the nature of thy sin.
> In thy prosperity, such was thy pride
> That thou the *Countries* plainnesse didst deride
> Thy wanton children would oft straggle out,
> At honest husbandman to jeere and flout.
> Their homely garments, did offend thine eyes:
> They did their rurall Dialects despise.[34]

As the quotation suggests, Wither's six-canto Jeremiad is never theologically or stylistically subtle. "In plaine expressions, and in words, that show / We love not, in affected paths, to goe"[35] might well serve as the motto of this and much of his later writings. And, indeed, it is the unaffected paths that make portions of *Britain's Remembrancer* still worth remembering – its low Dantesque moments in which the voices generally excluded from modern appreciations of seventeenth-century poetry make their appearance:

> Of these, and of their households, daily dy'd
> Twice more then did of all sorts else beside;
> An hungry *Poverty* (without reliefes)
> Did much inrage and [multiply] their griefes.
> The *Rich* could flye; or, if they staid, they had
> Such meanes that their disease the lesse was made,

Yea, those poor aged folkes that make a show
Of greatest need, did boldly come and goe,
To aske mens Almes; or what their Parish granted;
And nothing at this time those people wanted,
But thankfulnesse, lesse malice to each other;
And grace to live more quietly together.
Their bodies, dry'd with age, were seldome struck
By this *Disease*. Their neighbors notice took
Of all their wants. Among them, were not many
That had full families. Or if that any
Of these had children sick; some good supplies
Were sent them from the generall Charities.[36]

Wither's later poetry is dauntingly topical and repetitious, and a fully satis-factory assessment of his "musings," as he often called them, is only beginning to emerge.[37] The very "openness" of his verse (his continually evolving perspec-tive on contemporary events and frequent maneuvers in the face of criticism), in conjunction with the seismic shifts in the political landscape in the 1640s and 1650s, makes an overview difficult to hold in focus. In the words of his most resourceful critic, "Wither would keep edging toward a radical position and then withdrawing, and yet radical elements were never quite erased."[38] The Wither, for instance, who defended his decision to side with Parliament in *Campo-Musae* (1643), the first of several lengthy prophetic poems written during the war, assumed the posture of a moderate in *Vox Pacifica* (1645) but also questioned the sacrosanct authority of kingship and admitted a rhetoric of democratic inclusiveness into his vision of the state. The Wither who pleaded for unity and toleration could therefore be read sympathetically by John Lilburne, the Leveller. And yet, a believer in monarchy, Wither also resisted regicide right down to the final hour, only to aid in the sale of the royal estate; and though he supported Cromwell, he eventually became critical of the Protector's imperialistic schemes, although not because he thought conquering abroad was of itself a bad thing. The master of "a loose poetics" slipped and slid among powerful ideas and people; always claiming to be his own person, he spoke in a voice said to be inspired by God.

In one sense, however, Wither's long career forms a huge continuum. His verse participates in the revolutionary energies of his age, even performing, Norbrook argues, a critique of the politically conservative, closed couplets of a John Denham or Edmund Waller. (Certainly Wither always bridled when in the company of either man.) In a culture now openly admitting competing kinds of allegiances and authorities, those not only identified with the political order – king, Parliament, or the people (the last mentioned is a named body that looms large in Wither's later verse) – but those also associated with potentially competing epistemologies, the moral and the scientific,[39] Wither's poetry seems almost made to order, a visible commentary on, or allegory of, the multiplicity it seeks to understand.

That metacritical overview of his "art" may offer little comfort to non-specialists or those simply wishing for a better controlled poetic line, but in short stretches Wither's later poetry can be powerfully eclectic. A poem like *Westrow Revived, a Funeral Poem Without Fiction* (1653), for instance, will never satisfy on the basis of strict poetic merit; but as a work that reflects – and recirculates – problems of discursive instability more generally, an instability only fully exploited when it seemed to disappear into the creation of that new genre, the novel, *Westrow Revived* can make a strong claim on our attention. The poet's ultimate allegiance is to a professed Spenserian ideal of poetry: "what shall that *Musing* profit, which affords / Nothing but bare *Relations*, or mere *Words*."[40] And Wither identifies the muse's proper or idealized home with the prince or king, a vision sustained generically, at least, in the formal division of the poem into cantos, each replete with a rhyming argument. But the claim is in many ways vestigial. Not merely the specificity of detail, but the continual admission by Wither that he is writing "truth" and not some *"poetick strain*,"[41] and doing so, moreover, from his own parlor in which casual dialogue is an enduring feature: these elements suggest a poet feeling his way to the outer edges of the lyric, someone who, without taking the final step of either a Bunyan or Defoe and abandoning verse, nonetheless has begun to take the peripheral into the center:

> The foll'wing *evening*, after I had heard
> That verifide, whereof I was afeard
> The *night* before, I, then afresh inspir'd,
> To give my *Musings* utterance, retir'd:
> And, that no *interruptions* I might find,
> Put all my own *concernments*, out of mind:
> For, he, that honestly *one work*, would do,
> Must not, the same time, be imploy'd on *two*.
> But, on the paper, ere I fixt my pen,
> Such things, as possibly by other men
> Might be objected, question'd, or alleadg'd,
> To hinder that, wherein I was ingag'd,
> Rush'd in upon me; and, *delaies*, had wrought,
> Had I not on a sudden kickt them out;
> And given some of them, (ere they would go;)
> A reasonable civell answer too.[42]

Placed against Sidney's description of writer's block in the opening sonnet of *Astrophel and Stella*, this passage not only reveals vast differences separating Wither from the courtly ideal of careful invention; it also charts the descent of the muse into the marketplace in which the need to get the work into print is now set against the demands for accurate representation: "for, he, that honestly *one work*, would do, / Must not, the same time, be imploy'd on *two*."

Francis Quarles (1592–1644)

Wither's name and Francis Quarles's have been coupled at least since Anthony à Wood's misleading remark that these two "Puritanical Poets" were especially patronized by the Earl of Essex, Robert Devereux, only son of the beheaded earl and the eventual commander of the Parliament forces in the Civil War.[43] How much a patron Essex was to either poet is a matter of considerable uncertainty. Only Wither in *Campo-Musae* (1643) dedicated a work to the earl, and according to the *Dictionary of National Biography*, Quarles died supporting the crown, but it is easy to see superficial resemblances between the two men. Both were Protestant sympathizers, with associations with the Palatine court of Elizabeth and Frederick; both were admirers of Drayton – Aubrey attributed the verses on Drayton's monument in Westminster Abbey to Quarles, "his great Freind";[44] both wrote much didactic poetry of a narrowly pietistic sort; both tapped into the new vogue for emblem poetry and brought out separate volumes in the same year, 1635; and both were remarkably popular although for very different reasons. If Wither's fame is inseparable from his notoriety – his knack at making "George Wither" into a public event and capitalizing on, to the point of parody, seventeenth-century notions of authorship – Quarles's success stemmed from precisely the opposite effect: from his willingness to efface himself before the authority of others. "He faithfully discharged the place of cup-bearer to the Queen of Bohemia," wrote his wife, Ursula, in a brief memoir attached to his posthumously published *Solomon's Recantation* (1645), and the image of Quarles as a faithful cup-bearer is a telling one. For although he was to hold other employment – he served for a time in Ireland as a secretary to Archbishop Ussher, and later he inherited the post, held separately by Jonson and Middleton, of "Chronologer" to the City of London – he was as a poet constantly going to the well and making even more palatable what was already fully respectable, if not always familiar, to most English readers of the early seventeenth century. Quarles was the paraphraser *par excellence* of his time.

Versifying exemplary "histories" from the Old Testament was how Quarles began, and his thirst for reproducing canonical texts – whether sacred or secular – was never really quenched. By the time of his death in 1645, in fact, he had rendered into workable couplets the heroical exploits of Jonah (*A Feast for Wormes*, 1621), Esther (1621), Job (1624), and Samson (1630), interlining the arguments of each with meditations suitable to an educated Protestant audience – Quarles was to supply a commendatory poem to Thomas Hyne's 1641 translation of *The Life and Death of Dr. Martin Luther* – and spiced with topical allusions, usually of a moderately conservative sort. To these Biblically centered efforts, he added versified paraphrases from Jeremiah (*Sions Elegies*, 1624) and Solomon (*Sions Sonets*, 1625). He also experimented with some of the usual shorter forms in *Divine Fancies* (1632), epigrams, meditations, and observations, among others; produced the requisite number of elegies to important people; and during the early phase of the Civil War made use of Spenserian pastoral in *The Shepheardes Oracle* (published posthumously in 1646) to defend his loyalty to the ancient British church.

The Biblical histories and poems were reprinted often in Quarles's lifetime under the general rubric of *Divine Poems* (five editions by 1642 and frequently thereafter), and the *Divine Fancies* were hardly less popular.[45] But the Quarles who, according to a bemused Walpole, made Milton "wait till the world had done admiring" him,[46] was rather the less severe Quarles, the Quarles who moved out from underneath the canonical weight of Scripture and busied himself with artful presentations of contemporary texts: the Quarles of *Argalus and Parthenia* (1629) and the *Emblems* (1635). Again, both were acts of "translations," or to use the author's organic metaphor, "graft[ings],"[47] not original compositions; and both were astonishingly successful ventures. The first was taken from that most popular of prose romances in the seventeenth century, Sidney's *Arcadia*, but it is questionable whose version was the better known since by the end of the century, *Argalus and Parthenia* had gone through twenty-one editions as against seventeen for the original.[48] Quarles's also generated graftings of its own, as the anonymous *Unfortunate Lovers* (1700) reveals upon close inspection. As for the *Emblems*, although there was English precedent of a sort for the genre in Geoffrey Whitney's *A Choice of Emblemes and Other Devises* (1586) and Henry Peacham's *Minerva Britanna* (1612) – the latter serving in the 1620s as the design for the magnificent ceiling at Blickling Hall – and although there were soon to be contemporary rivals besides the collection produced by Withers, it was Quarles who brought the art doubly "home" to English readers by domesticating a genre with a long history of popularity on the Continent that dated back to the 1531 *Emblemata* of Andrea Alciati and by producing a text that could be "read" by a full household, adults and children alike. "His visible poetry (I mean his *Emblems*), is excellent," observed his contemporary, Thomas Fuller, in his *Worthies of England*, "catching therein the eye and fancy at one draught, so that he hath *out-Alciated* therein, in some men's judgment."[49] For Christmas, 1634, the Countess of Derby, the honored patron and subject of Milton's *Arcades*, gave what must have been a first-run copy of Quarles's *Emblems* to her twelve-year old grandson, William Brydges.[50]

What was Quarles's appeal, especially as reflected in these works? For one thing, even if he conscientiously dedicated his work to aristocrats, he rarely attempted a complex thought. In the preface to *Argalus and Parthenia*, for instance, he makes explicit his distaste for "strong lines" (III, p. 240) – a position he shared, paradoxically, with his massively learned employer – precisely because, in Quarles's view, they are "made for the third *Generation* to make use of," and not for the reader's immediate pleasure and benefit. The final poem in *Argalus*, in fact, reinforces this point exactly where we might expect. Quarles produces a much straighter version of Donne's knotty and reflexive "A Hymn to God the

Father." (In 1629, the Dean of St. Paul's was now fully on the scene, approaching canonical status and, like Sidney, good fare for imitation.) The third and last stanza of "The Author's Dream" reads as if Quarles were trying to release what Coleridge later thought of in Donne as "meaning's press and screw." As happens over and over in his poetry, Quarles eschews metaphor in favor of simile, the imaginatively daring in favor of the predictably timid, the unique experience of a particular identity in favor of general equation that underscores a common (and usually commonplace) attitude. In Quarles, there is nothing special in a name:

> My sinnes are like the Starres within the skies,
> In view, in number even as bright, as great:
> In this they differ: These doe set and rise:
> But ah! my sinnes doe rise, but never set.
>> Shine, Sunne of glory, and my sinnes are gone
>> Like twinckling Starres before the rising Sunne.
>
> (III, p. 285)

At the same time, however, Quarles's aversion to "strong lines" does not mean his poetry is altogether without substance or art. His conscious moralizing even in *Argalus and Parthenia* gives a certain pith and drama – or rather melo-drama – to his verse, and his poetry is rhetorically knowing in a way that Wither's rarely is. An admittedly formulaic passage like the following, for instance, is not intellectually demanding. It matters little whether one understands the allusion to Erra Pater, the supposed author of A *Prognostycacion for Ever* (1563), but neither is it dull:

> Have you beheld when fresh *Aurora's* eye
> Sends forth her early beames, and by and by
> Withdrawes the glory of her face, and shrouds
> Her cheekes behind a ruddy maske of clouds,
> Which, who beleeve in *Erra Pater*, say
> Presages winde, and blustry stormes that day,
> Such were *Partheniaes'* lookes; in whose faire face,
> *Roses* and *Lillies*, late had equall place.
> But now, twixt mayden bashfulnesse, and spleene,
> *Roses* appear'd, and *Lillies* were not seene:
> She paus'd a while, till at the last, she breakes
> Her long kept angry silence, thus; and speakes.
>
> (III, p. 243)

The passage has a quick and easy pace, something essential for a successful narrative poem in the exuberant manner of Marlowe's *Hero and Leander*, and it certainly attempts to be highly sensuous. Like a good deal of Quarles, including the "silken Frontispiece" to the book, it seeks to titillate without ever becoming erotic or disturbing. Quarles gives us the frills – literally, in the frontispiece – the set speeches, the swell of grand passions, the extended pictorialism associated with Sidney or Spenser, the sense that something significant is occurring; and so the poem served those without either the leisure, inclination, or energy for the original.

Initially at least, *Argalus and Parthenia* capitalized on a flair for romance that accompanied the coronation of Charles and his marriage to Henrietta Maria – the king and queen who elaborately presented themselves as if they belonged to the ideal order of courtly art, not to the hurly-burly of political reality, a role Charles continued to play until the very end when, in Marvell's phrase, he mounted "the tragic scaffold high" in 1649 and bowed his comely head to the executioner's axe. The immediate success of the *Emblems*, on the other hand, ought to be traced to a slightly different source: to a convergence between high and low forms of art, pictures and scripture.

Under the Stuarts in general, but especially under Charles and following the lead of nobility like the Duke of Buckingham and the Earl of Arundel, England witnessed an extraordinary increase in interest in the visual arts among the well-to-do.[51] With Van Dyck and Rubens making extended visits, the Caroline court was instrumental in effecting this shift in cultural focus; indeed, the king and queen amassed the finest collection of art yet by any English ruler, with works by many of the greatest European artists being represented in their rooms and halls. There were paintings by Leonardo, Raphael, Titian, Caravaggio, Holbein, Dürer, Cranach, and others, including, of course, van Dyck and Rubens. England was clearly no longer the home of miniaturists only. At the same time, testifying to the diffusion of interest in the visual arts was a substantial increase in the number of treatises published during the first half of the century. A theoretical work like that by the Dutch humanist Franciscus Junius the Younger, *De pictura veterum* (1637), was now quickly brought out in an English version (1638). (Until Junius's work, the only other broad assessment of the arts available in English had been Richard Haydocke's 1598 translation of Gian Paolo Lomazzo's *Trattato dell' arte de la pittura*, 1584). Over the same period, more specialized essays on architecture and the arts also began to appear. Sir Henry Wotton's *The Elements of Architecture* (1624) and Sir William Sanderson's *Graphice, or The Use of the Pen and Pensil* (1658) are among the best known today, while prints and drawings by contemporary artists like Wenceslaus Hollar – the gifted Dutch engraver who served England's greatest private collector of the period, Thomas Howard, Earl of Arundel – could be purchased with increasing ease from London booksellers. A "complete gentleman," noted Henry Peacham in the 1622 work of that title dedicated to Howard's second son, ought to know how to both paint and draw. So, too, he should possess a knowledge of "the Lives of the Famous Italian Painters." And in the example of Nathaniel Bacon of Suffolk, a still widely respected portraitist and the son of England's premier baronet, Sir Nicholas Bacon, Peacham found reason to celebrate an exalted, native connection with the arts.

The popularity of Quarles's *Emblems* belongs as much to the gentrification of the fine arts in England as it does to the enduring enthusiasm for works of devotional piety. In fact, the immediate personal inspiration behind the *Emblems* – the individual whom Quarles, in a bow to the sister arts, credited as having "put the Theorboe into my hand" – was none other than Edward Benlowes, the wealthy and eccentric country gentleman from Brent Hall, Essex, who was to take the art of the book to new and extravagant heights by producing one of the century's most lavishly illustrated texts in *Theophila, or Love's Sacrifice* (1652).[52] (The text includes illustrations by England's first great engraver, Francis Barlow.) In the late 1620s, this sometime poet and lifelong patron of the arts made his grand tour of the Continent. Besides putting himself in touch with much that was current in the arts in both the Netherlands and Italy, he also encountered two recently published, skillfully engraved, Jesuit emblem books: the *Pia Desideria* by Hermann Hugo (1624) and the *Typus Mundi* (1627). These were to serve as Quarles's sources.

In sharp contrast to *Theophila*, however, or even Wither's *Collection of Emblems* – both folio texts – Quarles's book is conceived on a thoroughly modest scale. If not the only reason, this is surely an important one for its huge success. Whereas both Benlowes and Wither drew on the visual as a partial sign of their desire to associate with high culture – whether conceived in learnedly esoteric or courtly terms – and produced enormously expensive texts, Quarles's octavo is meant to be cradled in the hand, to be held by the reader, who can readily take in both picture and text, placed as they are on facing pages: it is a book designed, that is, to be used and not merely admired; and it could be purchased for perhaps a little more than the price of a quart of sack.[53] As for the book's rationale (and by the early seventeenth century, thanks largely to the work of Italian humanists like Alciati and Palazzi, there was a significant body of material associated with emblems and related tropes like enigmas, symbols, and devices), Quarles's preface to the reader is positively anti-Jonsonian in its general appeal: succinct, courteous, and invitingly simple. It begins by rehearsing Simonides's familiar argument that painting is mute poetry; by the passage's end, author and reader exist in a happily reciprocal relationship.

> An *Embleme* is but a silent Parable. Let not the tender Eye check, to see the allusion to our blessed Savior figured in these Types. In holy Scripture he is sometimes called a sower; sometimes, a Fisher, sometimes a Physician. And why not presented so as well to the eye as to the eare? Before the knowledge of letters God was known by *Hieroglyphicks*: and, indeed, what are the Heavens, the Earth, nay every Creature but *Hieroglyphicks* and *Emblemes* of His Glory? I have no more to say. I wish thee as much pleasure in the reading, as I had in the writing. Farewell, Reader.
>
> (III, p. 45)

As Wither understood but failed to enact, emblems were a way of appealing to "the common reader." Enigmas, by contrast, wrote Henri Estienne in a passage that calls to mind important differences between Donne and Quarles, "may very well be used at merryments and in Princes Courts," but emblems ought to "declare the matter more plainly."[54]

The matter plainly declared is divine worship. The five books, essentially stitched together from the *Typus Mundi* (largely underlying Books I and II) and the *Pia Desideria* (Books III–V),[55] unite illustrated text, Biblical inscription, poetry, relevant quotations from the Fathers, and a four-line epigram – always in that order – to give a collaborate perspective on a familiar topos: the fall of man, Job suffering, Paul in prison, the soul anticipating its welcome by the New Jerusalem, and so on. The most significant alteration Quarles performed on the originals, whittling down the patristic commentary, gives the lyric – and hence the individual, private experience – greater prominence. The shift is appropriately Protestant, but the private utterance is also itself framed and thereby partly contained by a generalizing epigram. On doctrinal and artistic grounds, the emblems were intended to appeal to a wide audience.

Pope thought, rather nastily in *The Dunciad*, that "the pictures for the page attone / And Quarles is sav'd by Beauties not his own";[56] and few critics have since seriously attempted to challenge this view of the verse. Coleridge made a half-hearted stab at doing so, and in his still "standard" edition Grosart made a full but finally ineffective lunge by constantly comparing Quarles to Milton, Wordsworth, and Tennyson. Grosart was even sufficiently persuaded by Quarles's lyrical qualities that he saw no need to re-create the original engraving for the poems but printed instead the mawkish illustrations by Charles Bennett and W. Harry Rogers. He then proceeded to sever completely the relationship between visual and verbal texts by placing the engravings as a group after the poems.

However well intended, Grosart's editorial decision points unwittingly to the truth of Pope's quip: that the poems need the engravings if they are to be enjoyed at all. But there is a further truth, I think, beyond observing the essential dependency of text upon image, one that helps to account for the special distinction of Quarles's book, regardless of whether it serves to explain its original popularity. Through a variety of allusive techniques within the verse, Quarles insists that we have the illustrations in front of us while reading the poetry. As a recent critic has argued with considerable acuity, the poems are constantly dramatizing issues having to do with vision, even sometimes pointing to the deceptive and potentially idolatrous nature of sight itself and the dangers graven images might pose to the Protestant reader.[57]

Whether or not Quarles is as puritanical as this line of argument suggests is open to debate; if so, it would surely lend a further level of irony to Pope's notion of the word being saved by the picture. But it does point to the integral and generative relationship between image and text beyond the didactic function the poems perform when they gloss a given illustration. An occasionally anthologized poem, for instance, like the one on the lines from Job 14: 13 ("O that Thou wouldst hide me in the grave, that Thou wouldst keep me in secret until Thy wrath be past!") seems as much interested in expressing a sense of the experience conveyed in the illustration as it does in providing the appropriate moral. Both engraving and verse keenly register a dramatized moment of spiritual anxiety and fear that is neither present in the Scriptural gloss nor registered so emphatically in the original Latin verse in the *Pia Desidera*:

> O Whither shall I fly? what path untrod
> Shall I seek out to escape the flaming rod
> Of my offended, of my angry God?
>
> Where shall I sojourn? what kind sea will hide
> My head from Thunder? where shall I abide
> Untill his flames be quench'd or laid aside?
>
> (III, p. 75)

And Quarles's best-known emblem poem, "Will't ne'r be morning", is finely adjusted to capture, and to improve upon, the central experience represented in Marshall's crude picture – the quiet of nocturnal prayer:

> Will 't ne'r be morning? Will that promis'd light
>   Ne'r break, and clear these clouds of night?
> Sweet *Phospher*, bring the day,
>   Whose conqu'ring ray
> May chase these fogs; Sweet *Phospher*, bring the day.
>
> (III, p. 55)

In sharp contrast to Wither yet again, whose response to the excellent engravings by Crispin van Pass is strictly utilitarian, Quarles shows signs of worrying over aesthetic detail in his verse: of trying to establish in the poetry a tone and mood appropriate to the pictures, of trying not to set the pen at odds with the pencil in the manner of the usual paragone between poet and painter so common in the seventeenth century, but to strike a chord between the two in the interest of aiding worship. In this regard, perhaps the most unusual feature of the *Emblems* is not Quarles's commonplace definition of the emblem itself as a "silent parable," but the eerie way picture and poem dovetail to form a "speaking picture." To meditate, for instance, on the virgins depicted in the engraving at the beginning of the fifth book is to mark a threshold separating viewer from illustration, to observe the mystery of silence imposed by the icon (Fig. 2). But to read the accompanying poem, even if it is not great verse, is to cross the threshold of silence and to enter abruptly into the religious scene itself, now as one of its participants:

Figure 2 *Emblemes*, by Francis Quarles, 1669. Engraving for Book V, I.
(Reproduced by permission of the William Andrews Clark Memorial Library.)

You holy Virgins, that so oft surround
   The citie's Saphire walls; whose snowy feet
Measure the pearly paths of sacred ground,
   And trace the new Jerus'lem's Jasper street;
Ah, you whose care-forsaken hearts are crown'd
   With your best wishes; that enjoy the sweet
      Of all your hopes; If e'r you chance to spie
      My absent Love, O tell him that I lie
Deep-wounded with the flames that furnac'd from his eye.

(III, p. 90)

Plaintive and sweetly effete, the voice is not one we can listen to for long, even if it is energized by the closing alexandrine and the slightly unusual use of "furnace" as a transitive verb (this usage was briefly in vogue in the early seventeenth century); and in its characteristic appeal to sentiment rather than argument, one can see Quarles's limitations. When not paraphrasing others, he was paraphrasing himself, modulating only the phrase and accent as he went. But there is still the slightly mysterious shock at the outset that comes from our sense of being suddenly drawn into a drama greater than any poet's making. The appeal is immediate, if not lasting, enabled in part by the illustrated engraving and by the paradoxically simple fact that Quarles is not himself a poet of strong lines.

John Taylor (1580–1653)

An altogether more roguish spirit belonged to John Taylor, the Water Poet, who from Jonson's lofty perspective seemed the very epitome of the popular poet. "If it were put to the question of the water-rhymer's works against Spenser's," wrote Jonson with evident distaste in *The Discoveries*, "I doubt not but [Taylor's] would find more suffrages."[58] For almost every one of his more than forty years as an "author," Taylor had something in the public eye; and usually more than one piece at that, whether prose or verse: "thumb" Bibles, epigrams, satires, nonsense verse, first-person travel accounts, lowbrow encomia like "The Praise of Hemp-seed," reports of strange wonders, biographies (the Virgin Mary and Thomas Parr, "the old, old, very old man" from Shropshire, are among his subjects), pamphlets against cursing, guidebooks to London taverns, the odd elegy including one to Jonson, "A Memoriall of All the English Monarchs" with woodcuts of each, a tiny version of Foxe's *Book of Martyrs* measuring four centimeters, and so on, including a host of royalist writings during the Civil War – one involving a full-scale repudiation of George Wither. At mid-career when, like Jonson, he brought out a Folio edition of his *Works*, his writings already numbered "sixty-three" – something announced with comic exactitude on the title page, as if quantity alone were now the principal determiner of an author's oeuvre; and at his death in 1653, the number had expanded to an even heftier 141.[59]

In an important sense, the attention on the title page to quantity tells a large part of Taylor's story as a poet. Instead of the usual allusion to genre – a gesture often made to link an author to a classically derived tradition that might elevate him above the commonplace – Taylor's "sixty-three" signals at the outset the material concerns that run throughout his writings (when, why, and for how much he undertook a project), their frequently practical bent, and the rather astonishing fact that someone as lowly as a sculler could be visited so frequently by the muse. Taylor is in many ways the citizen hero of seventeenth-century verse, a cross between Shakespeare's Bottom and Deloney's Jack of Newbury. A Gloucestershire boatman with a minimal education who exchanged rowing for a most rare vision of himself as the "King's poet" when business on the Thames slackened because of a rerouted theater traffic and the invention of the carriage, Taylor never attempted (in contrast to Jonson) to hide his lowly feet in the tracks of the ancients. He sought instead to peregrinate around England in plain view to all and to record his thoughts in simple and often unabashedly clumsy verse:

> Thus have I been imployd, besides my trade is,
> To write some Pamphlets, to please Lords and Ladies,
> With Gentleman or others that will read them,
> Whose wits (I hope) not over much will heed them.
> To all these services I am immediate
> Obedient, willing, at occasions ready at,
> My riches is my Lame Legge, let the blame lye
> Upon that Legge, because I have writ Lamelye.
>
> (W, II: 8)

This epilogue from his *Mad Verse, Sad Verse, Glad Verse, and Bad Verse* (1644) sounds as if it could have been spoken by any one of Shakespeare's mechanicals in *A Midsummer Night's Dream*, but it is doubtful how many lords and ladies would have actually suffered their way through Taylor's works, or for that matter, how many of the gentry either. Taylor's primary audience of "others," despite the usual references and dedications to nobility, were fellow sailors, tradesmen, and craftsmen – that segment of England's population who experienced the greatest rise in literacy at the end of the sixteenth century and who might be most amused by a sculler swatting out anagrams on the spot, sparring with the likes of William Fennor over the right to be called "his majesties Riming Poet," and otherwise intruding into the domain of the privileged. Taylor was quick to add a groat's worth of wit to an already infamous occasion, as in the case of the coterie brouhaha surrounding the 1611 publication of Thomas Coryat's *Crudities* (Taylor mimicked the whole production in a sequence beginning with *Laugh and be Fat*), and made it a frequent point to sit down to supper with the well-to-do on his many journeys around England.[60]

From more than one perspective, too, Taylor was the great literary sponge of the period. Not only was poetry the vehicle that helped propel him around the countryside where he usually made a point of staying in inns and taverns for free (Taylor initiated the idea of subscription verse as a means of supporting himself), but his muse readily soaked up the writings of others: portions of Dubartas (his *Works* begins with an extended prayer to Urania), Spenser (in his many river celebrations), Drayton of *Poly-Olbion*, Wither (especially of *Abuses Stript and Whipt* and *The Motto*, whose meaning Taylor precisely reversed in giving his own), Donne of *The Anniversaries* (in *The Fearful Summer, or London's Calamitie*), Thomas Nashe (particularly *Piers Penniless*), and most of all Ben Jonson, who was convinced that Taylor's journey to Scotland in the same year was undertaken in order "to scorn him."[61] It was not, at least if we believe Taylor's account of the warm meeting between the two in his *Pennilesse Pilgrimage to Scotland* (FW, I: 138); but had the poet of "Inviting a Friend to Supper" read any of Taylor's many renditions of feasting, like the following, he might well have been only further convinced that literary foul play was brewing:

> Our beere was bravely boyl'd and strongly malted,
> Our Pidgeon Pie was pepper'd well and salted,
> Most tender Chickins, Pullet, and a Capon,
> We (in our fury) did commit a rape on.
>
> (*Taylor on Thames Isis*, in *W*, I: 23)

The repeated dangling eleventh syllable – to say nothing about rhyming "capon" with "rape on" – was just the kind of artistic slovenliness to put Jonson's teeth on edge.

And yet, it would surely be a mistake to think of Taylor as having been deeply influenced by any single group of authors or a particular literary tradition. (He is easily the least Spenserian poet to be published by the Spenser Society.) Despite many allusions to ancients and moderns alike, his is a poetry of the surface, albeit a rough one: a record of the sights and sounds, preferences and prejudices emanating from what he refers to in *The description of naturall English Poetry* (FW, II: 387) as "the home-spun medley of my mottley braines." A quick nod to another writer might generate an entire poem, as happens when he delivers his own *Motto*, but his verse, mostly in couplets, rarely engages authors on generic, stylistic, or lexical grounds, or on what we might think of as "poetic" issues.

Taylor sought instead to be novel by making a virtue out of a necessity: "My skil's as good to write, to sweate, or row, / As any Taylors is to steale or sow" (FW, II: 386). Or, to phrase it in more sociological terms, his claim to originality lies in the novel way in which the literary "high" culture is constantly being absorbed into and played off against low forms or popular topics. When, for instance, he published his pamphlet poem *A Dogge of Warre* (FW, II: 364), he prefaced it with the remark that he was not going to write in the usual heroic or iambic meter – "I deale with no such Traffique" – and then urges his reader to be content with sapphics, no less. But this turns out to be a false promise (presumably generated by the joke that Sappho was wedded to the waterman named Phaon referred to in his *Motto* (FW, I: 215)) when he writes the poem in "doggerall rhyme" (the pun is typically Taylor's) in response to an apparently higher law of decorum.

Here and elsewhere, the game in part is for his presumably motley audience to watch the Water Poet appropriate sophisticated forms for his own lowly purpose – to watch him bring into the common realm what is usually regarded as being the exclusive property of the sophisticated and learned. Hence, Taylor gives us many parodies and mock encomia – praises of Hemp-seed and clean linen – in turning an Erasmian tradition with purported antecedents in Homer and Virgil in a direction that might appeal to drapers and clothiers. He even drags the idea of the book itself into the streets (he likens it to both a whore and a thief in works with these titles) but does so without registering a jot of Jonsonian outrage over its becoming common property. The sculler might have read his Homer or Ovid, and he certainly attempted a purple passage or two, often of a storm scene, but he never sought to erase from his work (as Spenser, Jonson, and Drayton did), the signs associating him with trade. As he notes in his *Motto*, when he heard the muses sing, it was while rowing on the Thames.

If one strand of Taylor's art anchors him in the popular and propels him toward parody and travesty, the other binds him firmly to king and country. (However "carnivalesque" some of his poetry might seem, Taylor was entirely respectful of hierarchy.) If he conceived of himself as a "popular" poet in more particular terms than any of the other authors discussed in this chapter and on a grander scale than any other rhymester in the early seventeenth century, he also conceived of the country, England and Scotland, in more particular terms too. A great deal of Taylor's writings – prose and verse alike and sometimes a mixture of each – falls into the general category of travel narratives, that vaguely conceived and variously executed genre which had been recently reinvigorated by voyages to the New World and the increasingly frequent grand tour of the Continent made by well-to-do Englishmen of the early seventeenth century. Witty and eccentric, *Coryat's Crudities* played especially to the latter crowd, as did later, domestic versions of travel given by Richard Brathwait (*Barnabees Journall*, in both English and Latin) and Richard Corbett (*Iter Boreale*). The frequent reprinting throughout the century of George Sandys's *Relation of a Journey begun in 1610 containing a description of the Turkish Empire etc.* testifies further to a more general lure of the exotic that Richard Hakluyt had helped to initiate at the end of the sixteenth century in his *Principall Navigations* (1589).

Taylor's travel narratives divide roughly into two kinds. Some, like *Sir Gregory Nonsense, His Newes from No Place* (1622), are purely fantastic – a gallimaufry of nonsequiturs that, like anamorphic paintings popular in the day (or, more appropriately, the rhymes of Edward Lear, which they are sometimes said to anticipate), are meant to amuse by consciously distorting our perspective:

> It was in June the eight and thirtieth day,
> That I imbarked was on Highgate Hill,
> After discourteous friendly taking leave:
> Of my young Father *Madge* and Mother *John*.
>
> (*FW*, I: 161)

Others are more deliberately "realistic," although a work like A *Voyage in a Paper-boat from London to Quinborough* shows him exploiting the gray area between these modes. In their own way, the poems are as self-consciously ephemeral as nonsense verse:

> A Pamphlet (Reader,) from the Presse is hurld,
> That hath not many fellowes in the world:
> The manner's common, though the matter's shallow,
> And 'tis all true, which makes it want a fellow.
>
> (*Taylor's Travels to Prague in Bohemia* in *FW*, III: 574)

Of this kind, the great majority involve his many jaunts around England – something that presumably would appeal to the local and less affluent reader: his *Pennilesse Pilgrimage to Scotland* (1618), A *Very Merrie Wherrie-Fery Voyage, or Yorke for my Money* (1622), *Taylor on Thames Isis* (1632), and *Part of This Summers Travel* (1639) – to name only those published before the outbreak of the Civil War.

These are very much steak-and-kidney-pie accounts of Britain, close-up reports of food and drink, spiced with the occasional anecdote and recorded acts of hospitality. However much Taylor was enabled in these literary ventures by the works of Camden, Speed, Holinshed, and Drayton – "his painfull *Polyolbyon*, / Whose fame shall live, despight oblivion" (in *Thames Isis*, he gives explicit credit to them as his guides) – his focus is on the immediate and real, not the mythic or legendary: taverns and their signs, like the Saracen's head at Whetstone or the Nobody in the Barbican; names of friends visited and made, from joiners like John Piddack in Lichfield to the Laird of Gasford in Scotland (*Pennilesse Pilgrimage*); customs, proverbs, and stories related to specific locales.

Taylor's travel narratives teem with people, not nymphs or vistas. On occasion, they also deliver a refreshingly practical perspective on seventeenth-century life. No one would want to exchange Spenser's *Prothalamion* for Taylor on *Thames Isis* (1632), dedicated as it is to Thomas Howard, Earl of Arundel and Surrey, and other members of the privy council and "commissioners for the navigation and fishing of the famous Rivers of Thames and Medway"; but it is hard not to be impressed by the latter's sturdy ecological sense and concern over the economic life of the country and countryside:

> Shall *Thames* be barr'd its course with stops and locks,
> With Mils, and hils, with gravell beds, and rocks:
> With weares, and weeds, and forced Ilands made,
> To spoile a publike for a private Trade?
>
> (*Taylor on Thames Isis*, in W, I: 26)

This is *Poly-Olbion* with a fully Baconian slant to it – a vision of England potentially unified not by articulating a common ancestral myth but through a pragmatic effort to clean up its waterways:

> In common reason, all men must agree
> That if the river were made cleane and free,
> One Barge, with eight poore mens industrious paines,
> Would carry more than forty carts or waines.
> And every waine to draw them horses five,
> And each two men or boyes to guide or drive,
> Charge of an hundred horse and 80 men
> With eight mens labour would be served then,
> Thus men would be employed, and horse preserv'd,
> And all the Countrey at cheape rates be serv'd.

At the same time, however, it would be a desperate act of literary criticism to set a very high mark on any of Taylor's writings, however direct and pleasantly earthy many of them are. If the travel narratives remain his most appealing works, it is partly because, as Samuel Johnson noted in another context and with a different emphasis,[62] traveling performs a valuable regulating service on the imagination. The general shapelessness of so much of Taylor's writing, purposeful in the hands of great satirists like Burton or Swift, rarely seems more than the product of failing to exercise any restraint on speech; and Taylor is not, like Burton, a brilliant talker. (Aubrey remarked that "his conversation was incomparable for three or four morning's draughts. But afterwards you were entertained with *crambe bis cocta*.")[63] But in the travel narratives, the appeal is archetypal, the effect on the reader is almost mythic.[64] The hero sets forth (and by advertising the journey in advance in which certain conditions had to be met and obstacles overcome, Taylor cast himself in that role); he encounters various trials along the road, which often consist of his winning over strangers; and he returns, ideally to meet generous compensation from his sponsors, and often with a symbolic allusion to something happening in London, like his attending a production of *Guy of Warwick*. There is only a little suspense within the narrative; the tone is usually comic and the countryside described as usually only too willing to welcome the traveler, who seems more often on a progress than a pilgrimage. But in the later travels, especially those undertaken during the Civil War and after, Taylor's accounts acquire almost a mythic burden to them – the kind of burden, in fact, a mythological poet like Milton can capture in speaking of the good angels' tireless dedication to the cause in the War in Heaven – when he sets out on one of several journeys west, including one to Land's End. Their appeal has little to do with whether they are written in prose or verse, and they are still undertaken with the purpose of getting money; but both the traveler and the journey have come to acquire a symbolic dimension in the mind of its author:

> Like to the stone of Sisiphus, I roule
> From place to place, through weather faire and foule,
> And yet I every day must wander still
> To vent my Bookes, and father friends good will;
> I must confesse this worke is frivalowse,
> And he that (for it) daignes to give a lowse,
> Doth give as much for't as 'tis worth, I know;
> Yet meerly merily I this jaunt did goe
> In imitation of a mighty King,
> Whose warlike acts, good fellowes often sing,
> *The King of France and twenty thousand men,*
> *Went up the Hill, and so came downe agen.*
> So I this travell past, with cost and paine,
> And (as I wisely went) came home againe.

In one of the few attempts to rescue Taylor from the oblivion into which he fell as soon as he stopped writing, Robert Southey suggested that the Water-Poet had been neglected partly because, in contrast to a poet like Herrick (whom Southey regarded for the most part as "a coarse-minded and beastly writer"), he never wrote any "anthology" poems.[65] This one might qualify, not, however, because the verse is unusually meritorious, but because it captures so succinctly the sense of endless movement (and exhaustion) that comes from, as it were, flogging one's wares, even if one is doing it as "his majesty's" poet.

4

CAROLINE AMUSEMENTS

But thou art gone, and thy strict lawes will be
Too hard for Libertines in Poetrie.
                    Thomas Carew, "An Elegie upon the death of the
                                    Dean of Pauls, Dr. John Donne"

For most readers of seventeenth-century verse, Caroline poetry immediately conjures up a set of adjectives, and almost all have to do with some aspect of courtly artifice: precious (containing echoes of the French "précieuse" to denote the literary and intellectual fashions that arrived from France with Charles I's bride, Henrietta Maria); decorative (to suggest concern with surface detail, like the flow of a gown); conservative, even effete in its celebration of the king and the ceremonialism of the English church as it emerged under Archbishop Laud. Caroline poetry, we learn, is pre-eminently graceful and lyrical, conceived at a moment in history when singing and "musing" kept especially close company, but not a poetry of great intellectual substance. The Romantic critic, William Hazlitt, gave this view a conveniently precise formulation when he located Caroline verse within a larger narrative recording the decline and fall of English poetry from the Renaissance to the late eighteenth century. Poetry written under Elizabeth, Hazlitt urged, was a poetry of the "imagination." Poetry written in the time of Charles, he noted, invoking the other half of a dialectic nearly sacred to the Romantics, was a poetry of "fancy." And for Hazlitt, the slide only continued, through the "wit" of the Restoration to the "mere common places" of the eighteenth century.[1]

Fewer readers today would overtly subscribe to Hazlitt's general scheme, although influential versions can still be found even among recent literary historians.[2] The presence of Milton alone must give us pause, we are often reminded, to say nothing about either Herbert, whose *Temple* (1633) was published while Charles was on the throne, or Marvell, who began as a late Caroline. But other than a zealous Puritan perhaps – a not insignificant "other" as Caroline England especially came to understand – who would want to deny

91

altogether the metrically mesmerizing, utterly fanciful effects of the following stanza, usually attributed to the royalist poet, John Cleveland:

> Mysticall Grammer of amorous glances,
> Feeling of pulses, the Physicke of Love,
> Rhetoricall courtings, and Musicall Dances;
> Numbring of kisses Arithmeticke prove.
>> Eyes like Astronomy,
>> Streight limbs Geometry,
>> In her arts ingeny
>>> Never Marke Anthony
>>> Dallied more wantonly
>> With the faire Egyptian Queen.[3]

Everything shimmers and sways here, touched with a sense of the exotic, the erotic. From the dancing dactylic meter, to the suave reach into the trivium and quadrivium for amatory analogies, to the climactic trumping of Anthony and Cleopatra (the sudden shift to anapestic meter in the last line places a further stress on the "fairness" of the "Egyptian Queen") – this is a poem that "courts" its own fantastic grammar, that seems to have little reason to exist beyond airing its alluring rhythms, its "amorous glances." "Never Marke Anthony / Dallied more wantonly" than the author of these lines, so the poem seems to say, and points in a direction much explored of late by New Historicists: the centrality of the trivial – or the trifle – to the conception of the aristocratic self in late Renaissance England.[4] It is also difficult to imagine this poem belonging to another moment in literary history. The combative, amatory heroics of Donne – "She'is all States, and all Princes, I" – are readily assumed; so too is Donne's fusion of scholastic discourse with images of physical love. And lying immediately behind the discovery of double and quadruple dactyls are Jonson's prosodic experiments, most notably those in "A Celebration of Charis." The poem is surely an afterglow, as Hazlitt would say, but it is also a triumph of the fancy and written, we might add, when passions were not yet tempered in advance by ideal notions of verbal fluidity and witty repartee.

To shift from the world of either a Taylor or a Wither to the world circumscribing "Never Marke Anthony" is to move from the rough-hewn to the finely polished, from the country to the court. It is to mark a return, too, to the traditions and genres favored by Donne and Jonson, but with a difference. Amatory poems and verse epistles abound, as do epigrams, epitaphs, and brief translations from classical authors, especially those of late antiquity; and no poet worth his salt was without a song. But the range of the Caroline lyricist (and there were many) was distinctly narrower, decidedly less ambitious, both enabled and yet contained by the genteel culture for which dallying wantonly with words – and women – was almost *de rigueur*. One book, or at most two, was usually all that appeared by a given author – often posthumously – and the topics were frequently of the most incidental order. Thomas Randolph, a declared Son of Ben, lamented the loss of his little finger in what we might call a parody of imitative form (one line, he complains, is now a foot too short). Charles's favorite court poet, Thomas Carew, joined others in spotting a mole on his mistress's bosom; and following the way though (with the exception of the extravagantly conceited John Cleveland) rarely the wit of Donne's "The Flea," writers assembled errant bees, grasshoppers, and glowworms in collections that now began to reflect a Baconian interest in the natural world – indeed, that began to reflect the "collecting" habits going on at home and abroad in a culture that was soon to witness the birth of the museum in Oxford in 1677. When Thomas Stanley and Abraham Cowley published separate translations of Anacreon around mid-century, the rage for the incidental had clearly achieved canonical status, as Herrick's *Hesperides* beautifully shows.

Virtuosic accomplishment was the order of the day, an order that even Milton to some degree observed in *Poems* (1645), without, of course, fully obeying. And yet, it is also a peculiar historical feature of the period that rarely have so many poets produced more than a few poems worth admiring, and occasionally imitating. Eliot made this point long ago when he retrieved Henry King's "The Exequy," and though the particular features of Eliot's argument are less compelling today, the elegy, in its daring conceits and intimate tone, still resonating with modern poets, stands as remarkable proof against King's own eulogistic claim that Donne was always "Beyond our loftyst flights."[5] Indeed, we need only remember that the elegantly plangent dirge by James Shirley (a minor poet if there ever was one) beginning,

> The glories of our blood and state
>   Are shadows, not substantial things;
> There is no armor against fate;
>   Death lays his icy hand on kings;
>   Scepter and crown
>   Must tumble down,
> And in the dust be equals made
> With the poor crooked scythe and spade,[6]

was omitted from Saintsbury's three-volume *Minor Caroline Poets* (1905–21) to realize how much easier it often is to talk about Caroline modes and moods than it is to circumscribe the period's poetic wealth or to single out simple details that contribute to the success of an utterance like the one above. In the latter case, for instance, Shirley's "poor" is crucial to the adjustment away from Death's "icy hand" since it is with the wielders of scythes and spades and not with some abstract emblem of death – like Time – that the heroic must sleep. And on a smaller plane entirely typical of Caroline poetry, that adjustment is also crucial if the dimeter rhyme of "Scepter and crown / Must tumble down" is to possess its full human and historical force. As with so many poems of the period, it is difficult to escape the shadow cast by Charles himself, whether on or off the throne.

Part of what is at work here might be simply chalked up to the law of averages. With a very active manuscript culture,[7] and with so many more poets now willing to let their works appear in print – despite protests to the contrary – the harvest is bound to be richer. But we should not underestimate the productive model of artistic seriousness that accompanied Jonson's legacy or the standard of "difficulty" established by Donne. Even if Caroline lyricists wrote on a smaller scale, they wrote within a now identifiable tradition that specifically encouraged equating an author with his work, that is, not with the work's craft but with its "author," as in Jonson's Cary–Morison ode. Nothing points out this heightened – or rather specialized – sense of authorship more clearly than the case of Suckling, who spent a good part of his energies debunking Jonson's presence – Jonson's authority – but never relinquished a Jonsonian commitment to naming himself, Suckling, as the principal player in his own creations. Caroline poets tended to wear their badges in view; and even if they were not big ones, they still signaled a sense of difference from each other at the same time that they established a clear affinity with one or another major poet, Donne or Jonson, or in Carew's case, with both. Being "original," or in Hazlitt's phrase, being imaginative and not fanciful, was a distinction of little interest to Caroline poets. (The example of Drayton alone might have been sufficient to steer them away from an Elizabethan reach of the imagination.) But being different from an elder poet was of great importance. In this regard, the story of Caroline poetry is not Oedipal but fraternal; and if it is a story that at times makes us think refreshingly of a Drayton or a Taylor, if it seems at times too cozy, too concerned with who you know rather than what you write, it is also true that the pressure toward refinement, with its generating impulse coming from the most refined monarchy England had yet seen, was not incidentally precious. In the hands of Lovelace, a grasshopper could signal great things.

Thomas Carew (1594/5–1639)

Carew deserves to be at the center of Caroline verse – sometimes subversively so – simply because he achieved what so many desired in Renaissance England: a place at court. By 1630, Carew had secured the post of Sewer-in-Ordinary to the king himself (against the wishes of the whole Scottish nation if Clarendon is to be believed),[8] an appointment that had been preceded by service abroad (Italy in 1614–15 and the Netherlands in 1616, under Sir Dudley Carleton; Paris in 1619 with Sir Edward Herbert), and by some notorious living. Like Donne, Carew managed to offend his employer Carleton; for reasons yet to be fully understood, he was dismissed from his service in 1616. He also possibly paid for his libertine ways by eventually dying from a case of syphilis. In another sense, though, appointments to the king's household, while demanding loyalty, were hardly dependent upon poetic acumen, but that is exactly what Carew possessed in abundant measure. With the kind of alert intelligence that challenges easy discriminations between "creative" and "critical" faculties – an intelligence that was itself a legacy from the poets he most admired – Carew mediated the individual achievements of Donne and Jonson for a succeeding generation of courtly readers. No Caroline poet who made his immediate debts so apparent made the act of assimilation so complete. In the process, Carew also created a significant if not substantial corpus of verse. When published shortly after his death in 1640, his *Poems* became a kind of model for other Caroline poets by yoking together some "songs and sonnets," to quote from the title page of the "fourth" edition (1670), a number of verse epistles, several "country house" poems, a few epitaphs, and a longer poem, in this case a lengthy masque entitled *Coelum Britannicum*. (In the 1640s, poets as different from each other as Milton and Vaughan were to vary this formula.)

In performing this task, Carew took more seriously than any of the other "Sons of Ben" or disciples of Donne his sense of vocational responsibility – what Jonson (following Sidney and earlier classical authors) had in mind when he identified imitation as the principal ingredient in "making" and urged, along with "exactness of study and multiplicity of reading," the Horatian ideal of drawing honey from the "choicest flowers," and not from a single stalk.[9] To this end, Carew merged a genteel eclecticism with a demanding ideal of poetry, a seriousness of purpose that serves to pry him loose from those designated by Pope as the "mob of gentlemen who wrote with ease"[10] and to place him with one foot at least in the company of his near contemporaries, Herbert and Milton. Carew did not feel as Herbert so powerfully did that he owed his gifts ultimately to God; nor did he view, like Milton, his talents as part of a larger, intensely personal drama of election. He wrote, instead, for his more worldly contemporaries: fellow poets and patrons, male and female alike, at court and in the country.[11] But had he felt his responsibility to this group any less keenly, he would not have put into his verse so much thought – so much thinking – and so much pleasure.

That sense of vocational responsibility is most fully evident in the poems Carew wrote on Donne and Jonson. Both are powerfully, not incidentally, occasional. It was a common coterie act to write a poem to one or the other, slightly less so to write to both. (The two events in the early 1630s that most stirred fellow poets, including Carew here, were the publication of Donne's *Poems* (1633, 1635) and the debacle involving Jonson and the failure of *The New Inn*.) But Carew clearly viewed these separate occasions as opportunities to make important statements about the present situation of poetry and the responsibilities of the poet (with a small "p"), and each has been generally recognized in this century as the most significant act of criticism in verse either poet has received. The poem to Donne is surely the more expressive in its passionate celebration and imitation of its subject, and among elegies to poets written in the seventeenth century, only "Lycidas" has a greater imaginative reach:

Can we not force from widdowed Poetry,
Now thou art dead (Great Donne) one Elegie
To crowne thy Hearse? Why yet dare we not trust
Though with unkneaded dowe-bak't prose thy dust,
Such as the uncisor'd Churchman from the flower
Of fading Rhetorique, short liv'd as his houre,
Dry as the sand that measures it, should lay
Upon thy Ashes, on the funerall day?
Have we no voice, no tune? Did'st thou dispense
Through all our language, both the words and sense?

The Donnean idiom is fully sounded, in the abrupt beginning (forcing the muse, no less), its wrenched syntax, and its relentless interrogation. But it is also important to emphasize that Carew's estimation of Donne's art – his profound attention to both stylistic and canonical matters, to Donne's "line / Of masculine expression" as well as to the swerve Donne created in the line of English poetry – not only separates Carew from the many who celebrate Donne primarily as a priest and for politically controversial reasons;[12] Carew's testimonial also powerfully recalls Jonson in his poem on Shakespeare and reminds us that the desire motivating the verse is a generational one. "Have *we* no voice, no tune? Did'st thou dispense / Through all *our* language, both the words and sense?" (my italics).

It is a hoary cliché of funeral verse to say that all the arts died with the poet. (Donne's other mourners often utter and prove this sentiment.) But Carew makes this challenge a central constituent of the poem, actually braves a comparison with Donne; and in the marvelous conclusion to the poem, we are asked to meditate on the moment of revered silence imposed by Donne's departure and the obvious disparity between this "dumb eloquence" and the loud elegy itself, and then to imagine something different: the wheel turning again, the diminished but definite sound of the elegist,

And so whil'st I cast on thy funerall pile
Thy crowne of Bayes, Oh, let it crack a while,
And spit disdaine, till the devouring flashes
Suck all the moysture up, then turn to ashes,

and then the definitive utterance:

Here lies a King, that rul'd as hee thought fit
The universall Monarchy of wit;
Here lie two Flamens, and both those, the best,
Apollo's first, at last, the true Gods Priest.

"Have we no voice, no tune?" The answer can only be "yes" – a complex blend of Donne and Jonson, with a crowning touch of Stuart absolutism.

The poem to Jonson is decidedly less revering. "Great Donne" has been replaced by "deare *Ben*," and the poem is concerned with another issue involving literary inheritance and poetic responsibility: not generational belatedness but the right to differ with a parent, especially with a parent who has behaved badly in public. Carew reminds his audience, both Jonson and his followers, that imitation need not require servility, a point demonstrated with elegant tact and precision:

> Tis true (deare *Ben*:) thy just chastizing hand
> Hath fixt upon the sotted Age a brand
> To their swolne pride, and empty scribbling due,
> It can nor judge, nor write, and yet 'tis true
> Thy commique Muse from the exalted line
> Toucht by thy *Alchymist*, doth since decline
> From that her Zenith, and foretells a red
> And blushing evening, when she goes to bed,
> Yet such, as shall out-shine the glimmering light
> With which all stars shall guild the following night.

"'Tis true … and yet … [and] yet": the ease with which Carew spells out his difference here must have appeared a little unnerving to Jonson, whose career is summed up by someone who has clearly mastered the form that Jonson himself was responsible for establishing when he addressed other authors. (Carew understands exactly how to maneuver the caesura and how to enjamb so that his line, even if more regular than Jonson's, is never predictable.) In a bid for an authority comparable to Jonson's, Carew further anchors his judicious phrasing and the right to differ (as well as to differentiate) in Anglo-Saxon law itself:

> but if thou bind
> By Citie-custome, or by *Gavell-kind*,
> In equall shares thy love on all thy race,
> We may distinguish of their sexe, and place;
> Though one hand form them, & though one brain strike
> Soules into all, they are not all alike.

Carew also delivers a concluding verdict as tough-minded (and Jonsonian) as any great poet would ever wish to receive from an admirer:

> Thy labour'd workes shall live, when Time devoures
> Th'abortive off-spring of their hastie houres.
> Thou are not of their ranke, the quarrell lyes
> Within thine own Virge, then let this suffice,

The wiser world doth greater Thee confesse
Then all men else, then Thy selfe onely lesse.

The assessment, with its compact, subtle qualification at the end, seems nearly perfect. Great as he is, only Jonson would call himself greater than the wiser world, and in doing so he manifests the self-love that also limits his judgment.

The poems to Donne and Jonson show Carew at his most serious. As for pleasure, here is Carew operating within the suave confines of the courtly lyric:

Give me more love, or more disdaine;
    The Torrid, or the frozen Zone,
Bring equall ease unto my paine;
    The temperate affords me none:
Either extreame, of love, or hate,
Is sweeter than a calme estate.

Give me a storme; if it be love,
    Like Danae in that golden showre
I swimme in pleasure; if it prove
    Disdaine, that torrent will devoure
My Vulture-hopes; and he's possest
Of Heaven, that's but from Hell releast:
    Then crowne my joyes, or cure my paine;
    Give me more love, or more disdaine.

The theme of "Mediocritie in love rejected" is not quite the commonplace of amatory poetry that we are sometimes told, at least not until Carew worked out the parallels and antitheses so explicitly and was later echoed by more minor Caroline songsters like Sidney Godolphin. The emphasis in Petrarch's "Ite, caldi sospiri, al freddo core" ("Go, hot sighs, to her cold heart") is resolutely plaintive. That of Jonson in "The Dreame" ("Or Scorn, or pity on me take") is on the disturbance love has suddenly created in the heart of the speaker and on the poet's need to make a "true relation" of it, that is, on the speech performance itself. (Jonson seems fully aware that he might be playing the part of the fool in Donne's "The Triple Fool.")

The brilliance of Carew's song lies in a different direction – in the diffident balancing act itself: the coolly measured alternatives neatly chiseled in language Jonson surely would have admired. Where a Donne would have tipped his anti-Petrarchan hand at the end, moreover, by graveling the lady because she might finally choose to remain indifferent to his ploys, Carew merely (and deftly) ends where he begins, by posing the alternatives once again: "Give me more love, or more disdain." "Glittering Icicles" is how one nineteenth-century reader described Carew's poetry.[13] But that description isn't altogether accurate either. For however brilliant the surface, something also opens up in the momentary extension of the simile and the relaxed space it creates in the poem: "If it be love, / Like Danae in that golden showre / I swimme in pleasure." For a moment Carew imagines – and his original courtly audience is encouraged to imagine – surrendering to sexual passion in a way that, however un-Petrarchan each might be, neither Jonson nor Donne (even in the Elegies) ever could.

With a performance like this one, it is easy to see why a contemporary could observe that Carew's "Sonnets were more in request than any poet's of his time, that is between 1630 & 1640."[14] The studied poise was perfectly suited to a court audience, some of whose members were learning to pose for Van Dyck, and even perhaps to think of themselves in a slightly classicized setting. (The much celebrated Lucy, Countess of Carlisle, whom Carew addressed in "A New-Years Sacrifice," had her portrait painted no fewer than four times by Van Dyck; in company with the Caroline dramatist, Thomas Killigrew, Carew is the possible subject of another Van Dyck.) And the significant place Carew allots in his verse to scene-painting of one kind or another gives it an added touch of finish. Whether describing nature or art, as seen in the change of seasons in "The Spring" or a musical performance in "Caelia Singing," or giving one of his many accounts of female beauty, Carew's is a poetry of high craftsmanship – "mannerist," as one critic suggests,[15] but distinguishable at the very least from that of a Quarles because of the serious attention given to surface. Exactness of phrasing, the careful elaboration of a conceit often found in Donne with a touch more delicate than Jonson's, is Carew's special trademark:

> This silken wreath, which circles in mine arme,
> Is but an Emblem of that mystique charme,
> Wherewith the magique of your beauties binds
> My captive soule, and round about it winds
> Fetters of lasting love; This hath entwind
> My flesh alone, That hath empalde my mind:
> Time may weare out These soft weak bands; but Those
> Strong chaines of brasse, Fate shall not discompose.
> This holy relique may preserve my wrist,
> But my whole frame doth by That power subsist ...

And so "Upon a Ribbon" unwinds. A near "still life" in verse generated by a line from Donne's "The Funerall" ("That subtile wreath of haire, which crownes my arme"), it impresses precisely because the poet, who seems to know all the moves in advance, executes the turns so perfectly. We might well find it difficult in this context to dismiss as inauthentic a contemporary anecdote involving Carew (even if on the same page occurs the statement that "Milton, the poet, died a Papist"): "Queen Henrietta Maria – Thomas Carew, Gentleman of the Privy Chamber, going to light King Charles into her chamber, saw Jermyn Lord St. Albans with his arm round her neck; – he stumbled and put out the light; – Jermyn escaped; Carew never told the King, and the King never knew it. The

Queen heaped favours on Carew."[16] Artfulness, in the Caroline court, had its rewards.

Perhaps too many: Carew has never been entirely free of charges of decadence of one kind or another. Initially, at least, these were levied by moralizing, anti-courtly contemporaries (perhaps George Wither) who were offended by the presumed illicit sexuality expressed in "The Rapture," Carew's most notorious libertine poem. (It was not admitted into the Norton Anthology of English Literature until the fourth edition.) As the author of the 1646 Assises Holden in Parnassus remarked, indicating the foreign nature of Carew's corruption, "this fellow / In Helicon had reared the first Burdello";[17] and, indeed, in Carew's "Neroesque" fantasy spun in part from Donne's Elegy 19, with appropriate strands twisted out of Spenser ("Be bold and wise"), artfulness is all, even perhaps a knowledge of the (porno)graphic arts, as has been recently urged.[18] Carew is nothing if not a connoisseur of poses:

> The Roman Lucrece there, reades the divine
> Lecture of Loves great master, Aretine,
> And knowes as well as Lais, how to move
> Her plyant body in the act of love.
> To quench the burning Ravisher, she hurles
> Her limbs into a thousand winding curles,
> And studies artful postures.

The enjambments involving "move" and "hurles" are neatly calculated to emphasize the sway of bodily pliancy itself. And in his marvelously intricate reversal of the old Apollo/Daphne myth, we can readily understand why from Wither to Courthope male critics have nervously chosen to brand Carew's art "effeminate" and why, at the same time, it has not been embraced by feminists either:

> Daphne hath broke her barke, and that swift foot,
> Which th'angry Gods had fastned with a root
> To the fixt earth, doth now unfetter'd run,
> To meet th'embraces of the youthfull Sun:
> She hangs upon him, like his Delphique Lyre,
> Her kisses blow the old, and breath new fire:
> Full of her God, she sings inspired Layes,
> Sweet odes of love, such as deserve the Bayes,
> Which she her selfe was.

As Daphne's seductively creative meeting with Apollo illustrates, Carew preferred making love to making war; or better yet, he preferred to celebrate the intertwining of Eros and art rather than to record the loud bellow of the drum, as he makes clear in his lengthy response to Aurelian Townsend, where he refuses to comply with Townsend's request for an elegy commemorating the death of the Protestant Swedish king Gustavus Adolphus. Drayton, were he still alive, yes, but Carew most certainly not. He greets the request as if struggling with a hangover:

> Why dost thou sound, my deare *Aurelian*,
> In so shrill accents, from thy *Barbican*,
> A loude allarum to my drowsie eyes,
> Bidding them wake in teares and Elegies
> For mightie *Swedens* fall? Alas! how may
> My Lyrique feet, that of the smooth soft way
> Of Love, and Beautie, onely know the tread.

One purpose of the courtly poet, in Carew's view and developed in the remainder of the poem, was to celebrate the court, however narrowly it construed itself; even, if necessary, to defend its insular policies, however much this action has disappointed some of Carew's modern readers.[19] Later, Carew's anti-imperializing, sybaritic sentiments would lead him to praise, after Charles's disastrous attempt to tame the Scots in 1639,

> the temperate ayre of *Wrest*
> Where I no more with raging stormes opprest,
> Weare the cold nights out by the bankes of Tweed,
> On the bleake Mountains, where fierce tempests breed,
> And everlasting Winter dwells.

Had Carew's desire to make everything artful – even when claiming to be celebrating nature – not issued from a deeper concern for stasis (in his revision of the Daphne/Apollo myth, the two impulses seem mutually defining), we might think his poems to be too many beads of amber. (A great many Caroline poems do not escape this fate.) But with Carew, waywardness is a way of being, a poignant and at times powerful counterpoint to the predictable. His celebrations of art and artifice are almost always set against a wider horizon of loss and disorder: "the temperate ayre of Wrest," with its obvious pun, against "everlasting winter"; the idealized landscape of the female body in "The Rapture" against the double standard of sexual practices at court (of which Carew himself is not free); or the light in "To Saxham" perceived from afar, in which "Those cheerful beames send forth their light, / To all that wander in the night." Carew is rarely as settled or cozy as Herrick, nor is he ever led to rage against the night, which is one way of characterizing his limitations. But the note of potential vulnerability and exile that runs, for instance, through "To Saxham" profoundly differentiates the poem from its Jonsonian model. The abundance of Penshurst is seen largely, strenuously, from within its secure walls. By contrast, Saxham is more a hospice for the poor, a refuge for people who are otherwise beyond the pale, as Carew adjusts his angle of vision to include a range of terms otherwise excluded from Jonson's poem:

> thy gates have bin
> Made onely to let strangers in;
> Untaught to shut, they do not feare
> To stand wide open all the year;
> Carelesse who enters, for they know,
> Thou never didst deserve a foe;
> And as for theeves, thy bountie's such,
> They cannot steale, thou giv'st so much.

"Strangers," "foe," "theeves": Carew's discursive modulations can probably be traced to worsening economic conditions during James's later years and the evident failure of the Elizabethan Poor Laws to provide adequate relief for the many who "wander in the night."[20] But the difference is temperamental as well. The sexual libertine was also the potential exile, spiritually and therefore culturally, a point given legendary significance by contemporary interest in Carew on his deathbed. Izaak Walton insisted that because of his licentious ways, Carew was refused the final sacraments, while Clarendon, evading the issue of last rites, reported more happily that Carew "died with the greatest Remorse for that Licence, and with the greatest Manifestation of Christianity, that his best Friends could desire."[21]

Which of these reports is closer to the truth is impossible to determine, and in a late verse epistle entitled "To my worthy friend Master Geo. Sands, on his translation of the Psalmes," Carew would seem to have authorized both interpretations. The poem has obvious revisionist affinities to Donne's "A Hymn to God, My God in My Sickness," insisting, as it does, on the space separating the poet from "thy holy room" and on the possibility of making a potential virtue out of an evident necessity:

> I presse not to the Quire, nor dare I greet
> The holy place with my unhallowed feet;
> My unwasht Muse, polutes not things Divine,
> Nor mingles her prophaner notes with thine;
> Here, humbly at the porch she listning stayes,
> And with glad eares sucks in thy sacred layes.
> So, devout penitents of Old were wont,
> Some without dore, and some beneath the Font,
> To stand and heare the Churches Liturgies,
> Yet not assist the solemne exercise.

Carew is conspicuously an auditor, not a singer here, but the reflective capacity of the verse epistle also gives him room to consider subjects otherwise inappropriate to the hymnist, the kind of longing stimulated, not stabilized, by the appeal of liturgy. "Who knows," writes Carew of his muse,

> but that her wandring eyes that run,
> Now hunting Glow-wormes, may adore the Sun,
> A pure flame may, shot by Almighty power
> Into her brest, the earthy flame devoure.

Who knows? The longer Carew contemplates his answer, the more delphic the question becomes, until it is difficult to imagine a more controlling and moving "perhaps" than the one that wistfully directs his closing utterance:

> My eyes, in penitentiall dew may steepe
> That brine, which they for sensuall love did weepe.
> So (though 'gainst Natures course) fire may be quencht
> With fire, and water be with water drencht.
> Perhaps my restless soule, tyr'de with persuit
> Of mortall beauty, seeking without fruit
> Contentment there, which hath not, when enjoy'd,
> Quencht all her thirst, nor satisfied, though cloy'd;
> Weary of her vaine search below, Above
> In the first Faire may find th'immortall Love.
> Prompted by thy example then, no more
> In moulds of clay will I my God adore;
> But teare those Idols from my heart, and write
> What his blest Sprit, not fond Love shall indite;
> Then, I no more shall court the verdant Bay,
> But the dry leavelesse Trunke on *Golgotha*;
> And rather strive to gaine from thence one Thorne,
> Then all the flourishing wreathes by Laureats worne.

Perhaps Carew's "Perhaps" flirts with another great moment of hesitation by a contemporary: the moment when George Herbert, writing from within *The Temple* in "The Forerunners," reaffirms his total commitment to God's service but does so in a context that also accounts for all that must be sacrificed, including "Beauty and beauteous words," in this act of resignation:

> Yet if you go, I passe not; take your way:
> For, *Thou art still my God*, is all that ye
> Perhaps with more embellishment can say.
> Go birds of spring: let winter have his fee;
>> Let a bleak paleness chalk the door,
> So all within be livelier than before.

Carew's response is less certain, more fully ambivalent than Herbert's, but it does have its own peculiar integrity, for the pursuit of mortal beauty never proceeded on a more oracular, mesmerizing level in the seventeenth century than in his celebrated song "Aske me no more." How could an author who repeats with exquisite variation the plaintive request, "aske me no more," and responds with ever increasing desire, imagine the turn to religious verse to be anything but a turn away from "the verdant bay" to "the dry leavelesse Trunke on *Golgotha*":

Aske me no more where Jove bestowes,
When June is past, the fading rose:
For in your beauties orient deepe,
These flowers as in their causes, sleepe.

Aske me no more wh[i]ther doth stray,
The Golden Atomes of the day:
For in pure love heaven did prepare
Those powders to inrich your haire.

Aske me no more wh[i]ther doth hast,
The Nightingale when May is past:
For in your sweet dividing throat,
She winters and keepes warme her note.

Aske me no more where those starres light,
That downewards fall in dead of night:
For in your eyes they sit, and there,
Fixe become as in their sphere.

Aske me no more if East or West,
The Phenix builds her spicy nest:
For unto you at last shee flies,
And in your fragrant bosome dyes.

If Carew will always be remembered as a poet who gave renewed expression to the voice of physical desire, who saw his later identity as a poet largely constituted in this light (and that is one way of reading the poem to Sandys), it is so in part because this song seems to be a definitive act, a last word on the subject of beauty itself. Whether or not this lyric marks an end to a tradition of Petrarchan love poetry in English – Tennyson has an answer poem of sorts in "The Princess" – it presumes to exhaust its subject. All the conceits of Petrarchan poetry are here, as John Hollander has pointed out in a remarkable reading of the poem: rosy cheeks, sunny hair, starry eyes, sweet voice, and fragrant bosom.[22] But these are now exotically crossed with the *ubi sunt* tradition, and the crossing produces its own ripe answer, different from either the Petrarchist's celebration of ideal beauty or the lover's sweet melancholy over time's passing. All things have not, like the ladies of yesteryear, melted away with the snow. In Carew's response, beauty has its elemental origins in a lady who is, at once, their preserver and their generator: their author, as Hollander notes, but also their final resting place. If we read the 1640 printed text, moreover, against the several extant versions of the song, probably earlier drafts as Carew's editor suggests,[23] we can measure even more exactly the originary value Carew places on his mistress as a storehouse of beauty. The revisions are done not merely to make the already aureate even more resplendent. To exchange, as Carew does, "damask" for "fading" (as in "When June is past, the fading rose"), "dark" for "dead" (of night), and "lies" for "dyes" (as in the final line "And in your fragrant bosome dyes") is to raise the epistemological stakes a few notches, to heighten the worth of the question that is not supposed to be asked; and in doing so to deepen the mystery surrounding the object of Carew's praise and the subject of beauty itself: its association with beginnings and endings, with the place of ultimate rest, with even the potential source of regeneration. As the "answer" poems to Carew's answer suggest, the only way forward is downward – toward parody.

John Suckling (1609–42?)

With a poet of Carew's talent, questions almost always arise as to why he did not write a "major" poem, and there are nearly as many answers given as there are theories of inspiration. (Carew has anticipated most in his "Answer" to Townsend.) With John Suckling, it is significant that the question does not even arise. Some fourteen or fifteen years younger than Carew, Suckling (whose name derives from "socage," denoting a person holding an estate by "terms of the plow")[24] was, in many regards, the Caroline Oscar Wilde:[25] a flamboyant personality and a brilliant conversationalist, although hardly an "aesthete," as we shall see. Suckling, wrote Aubrey, was "the greatest gallant of his time, and the greatest Gamester, both for Bowling and Cards, so that no Shopkeeper would trust him for 6d, as today, for instance, he might, by winning, be worth 200 pounds, and the next day he might not be worth half so much, or perhaps sometimes be *minus nihilo*."[26]

Here today, gone tomorrow: so, too, with Suckling, the author of, among other things, two poems entitled "Against Fruition." He was probably dead at thirty-two: "Obyt anno attatis sue 28," reads the slightly erroneous inscription above the Marshall engraving of Suckling, in turn set within a sumptuous laurel wreath, that accompanied the first edition of his writings in 1646 entitled *Fragmenta Aurea* (golden fragments) and augmented in 1659 with *The Last Remaines*. During his short life, Suckling had posed for Van Dyck in full Caroline dress – with a copy of the Shakespeare folio opened to *Hamlet*, no less. He had wooed for money and lost; been a soldier at home and abroad; written plays (four in all); scuffled at the theater with the likes of Sir John Digby, brother to that "absolutely, complete Gentleman," Sir Kenelm Digby; penned a brief *Account of Religion by Reason*; fled overseas to Paris once his conspiratorial involvement in the First Army Plot came to light; and died, unmarried, probably no later than early 1642, from either a violent fever or suicide. "They that convers'd with him alive," runs the note to the reader of the 1646 *Fragmenta Aurea*, "will honour these posthume Idea's of their friend: And if any have liv'd in so much darknesse, as not to have knowne so great an Ornament of our Age, by looking upon these Remaines with Civility and Understanding, they may timely yet repent, and be forgiven." *Fragmenta Aurea* also included, for display, Suckling's "Letters to divers Eminent Personages."[27]

"So great an Ornament of our Age" might seem like a bizarre appellation for Suckling, although perhaps no more bizarre than the occasional comparisons made at the time between him and Sidney. (Suckling would seem to have had almost nothing in common with Sidney except a literary sister and an extreme case of *sprezzatura*.) But the emphasis on the reader's "conversing" with Suckling – on remembering his talk and him as a talker – points to the reason why Suckling, "natural, easy Suckling" in Millamant's phrase from Congreve's *The Way of the World*, was, almost more than any other Caroline poet, the favorite of the Restoration. At the moment when Carew's star was beginning to fade – 1671 marks the date of the last edition of his poems for more than one hundred years – Suckling's was on the rise; and it was so in part because Suckling set his sights so low: at the point where poetry and gossip – a major constituent of Restoration and eighteenth-century literature[28] – would seem to converge, but not as in Donne, in the urban streetlife of London, or as in Wither, in the rhyming journalese that comments on contemporary history, but in a setting that still savored of the genteel. "They can produce nothing so courtly writ, or which expresses so much the Conversation of a Gentleman, as Sir *John Suckling*," spoke Eugenius in Dryden's 1667 *Essay of Dramatic Poesy*.[29] "They" were the poets of the English past; and Suckling, who heads a list that includes Waller, Denham, and Cowley, is called on to help mediate what has sometimes been regarded by modern critics as "the burden of the past" felt by post-Renaissance English poets beginning with Dryden and Congreve.

Suckling, naturally, had nothing so epochal in mind for himself. "Faith comes by hearsay," he remarked, proleptically, in "Upon St. Thomas his unbeliefe," one of his earliest poems. The ease of his verse has more to do with the way he "slides off" the voices of the past and present, and changes gospel to gossip. This has more to do with various acts of impersonation, with the nudge in the side, with the casual extension of syntax, than with any desire to mold a specific literary credo involving the proper relationship of sound to sense, rhyme to reason. When, for instance, Suckling begins a song,

> Out upon it, I have lov'd
>   Three whole days together;
> And am like to love three more,
>   If it hold fair weather,

it is difficult not to smile over the ballet-like plummet into the commonplace in the fourth line, a comic release that would be slightly less amusing (and complex too) if we were not meant to hear, somewhere in the background, the muffled wit of Donne's urgent "Now thou hast lov'd me one whole day, / Tomorrow when thou leav'st, what wilt thou say." Donne's hard-driven line seems almost sentimental next to Suckling's calculated wave of indifference in the off-hand rhyme of "together" and "weather," despite the fact that it is Suckling, not Donne, who proves on this occasion to be less of a rake.

But Donne, or for that matter Jonson, is hardly essential to Suckling's poetry in the way that each is to Carew's. (Drayton would have been altogether beyond the pale.) When Carew writes, he writes, as Leavis emphasized, in a direct line of wit; indeed, as someone central to the formation of the line itself.[30] When Suckling writes, it is from the margins, as someone who has overheard much but who refuses to authorize any special school or tradition, not even one of his own. His game – and it is difficult not to use this metaphor in speaking about his poetry – is to offer something else, a frank behind-the-scenes glimpse of the great, a Lucy, Countess of Carlisle, walking in Hampton Court gardens in the poem of that title:

> 'Troth in her face I could descry
> No danger, no divinity.
> But since the pillars were so good
> On which the lovely fountain stood,
> Being once come so near, I think
> I should have ventur'd hard to drink.

Or of the not-so-great:

> Wat Montague now stood forth to his tryal,
> And did not so much as suspect a denial;
> Wise Apollo then asked him first of all
> If he understood his own Pastoral.
> For
> If he could do it, 'twould plainly appear
> He understood more than any man there,
> And did merit the Bayes above all the rest,
> But the Monsieur was modest, and silence confest.
> ("A Sessions of the Poets")

Or it is to take that most traditional of subjects among court poets – love – and give it a demystifying twist, as if the speaker were the very incarnation of indifference and not merely playing the part in the hope of winning the "lady":

> Of thee (kind boy) I ask no red and white
> to make up my delight,

no odd becomming graces,
Black eyes, or little know-not-whats, in faces;
Make me but mad enough, give me good store
Of Love, for her I court,
       I ask no more,
'Tis love in love that makes the sport.

For Suckling, women and poetry alike are not objects of desire, as they are for Carew, something to be wooed and possibly won, but the opportunity for witty conversation itself – and preferably a conversation that oscillates between mock fastidiousness ("the Monsieur was modest") and the shockingly blunt:

'Tis not the meat, but 'tis the appetite
    makes eating a delight,
      and if I like one dish
More than another, that a Pheasant is;
What in our watches, that in us is found,
So to the height and nick
      We up be wound,
No matter by what hand or trick.

                       ("Sonnet II")

The typical Suckling gesture is that of the highborn nay-sayer; he is beyond love but not beyond speculating about the fortunes of passion in a disinterested, humorously condescending way – "Do'st see how unregarded now / that piece of beauty passes?" – or about how others, caught in love's throes, might behave, as in his much celebrated song that begins

Why so pale and wan fond Lover?
      Prithee why so pale?
Will, when looking well can't move her,
      Looking ill prevaile?
      Prithee why so pale?

For a moment, thanks to the repetitions, he seems almost interested in the situation, at least long enough for the final jettisoning to have some force:

Quit, quit, for shame, this will not move,
      This cannot take her;
If of her selfe shee will not Love,
      Nothing can make her,
      The Devill take her.

Suckling even seems indifferent about that most masculinist of aristocratic assumptions, continuing the genealogical line: "But since there are enough / Born to the drudgery, what need we plough?" The debonair wave seems exactly right. Procreative sex, like difficult poetry, is just too much work to be enjoyable:

> Fruition's dull, and spoils the Play much more
> Than if one read or knew the plot before:
> 'Tis expectation makes a blessing dear:
> It were not heaven, if we knew what it were.
>
> ("Against Fruition")

And in all of these situations, too, we are most struck by Suckling the talker, the amusing and sometimes shocking conversationalist, the raconteur: "J.S." in dialogue with "T.C.," in the case of "Upon My Lady Carliles Walking in Hampton Gardens," a poem whose principal energies, like those underlying much of Suckling's verse, derive in part from a larger courtly dialogue between platonic and antiplatonic strains.

Suckling's best known and much imitated "A Sessions of the Poets," in fact, is a series of set-ups:

> A sessions was held the other day
> And Apollo himself was at it (they say);
> The laurel that had been so long reserved,
> Was now to be given to him best deserved.

The "poets" come to town like country gulls ("'Twas strange to see how they flocked together"), pure grist for Suckling's anecdotal mill, with the bastardized bob-and-wheel quatrains churning out caricature after caricature. First wine-laden Jonson appears proclaiming his "Works," then Carew, "hard-bound" (constipated) muse and all, and many lesser lights, although not necessarily so in their own day. But Suckling's intentions are clearly comical, not canonical:

> Will Davenant, ashamed of a foolish mischance
> That he had got lately travelling in France,
> Modestly hoped the handsomeness of's Muse
> Might any deformity about him excuse.
>   And
> Surely the Company would have been content,
> If they could have found any President [precedent];
> But in all their Records, either in Verse or Prose,
> There was not one Laureate without a nose.

All but one makes a bid for the laurel crown:

Suckling next was call'd, but did not appear,
But straight one whispered Apollo in's ear,
That of all men living he cared not for't,
He loved not the Muses so well as his sport.

The loose syntax and casual rhymes are part of the undoing here. (Suckling's trick is partly to remove the heavily invested caesura Jonson put into the English line, and he is almost as good as Molière's Célimène at opening and shutting doors.) It also seems just right that not only should Suckling signal his presence in the poem and thereby mark his absence at the sessions (improving upon the inevitably fashionable guest who comes late to a party) but also that his absence should itself be marked by the buzz of gossip. At this session, busyness and the business of poetry are two sides of the same coin and not even Apollo, it turns out, is above taking a bribe. He bequeaths the laurel crown to the Alderman, with a single, vatically deflationary phrase: "'twas the best signe / Of good store of wit to have a good store of coyne."

As a prototype of sorts for *The Dunciad*, "A Sessions" helps to explain why Suckling remained popular throughout the eighteenth century. Without ever doing very much, he seems to have anticipated, in remarkable ways, a number of significant stylistic and intellectual trends that became prominent in the Restoration, including, in his frequent use of the image of man as a clock, a Hobbesian materialism. But it is important to emphasize that the marginal posture represented in his verse was still a courtly one. Suckling was the *enfant terrible* of an increasingly narrow circle and limited to a great degree by the few attitudes he chose to subvert. When it came to imagining what went on elsewhere – in the country, for instance – he was hardly more persuasive than Alceste, as his "Ballad upon a Wedding" makes clear.

This, Suckling's other generic innovation, has been much admired. Even so notably "radical" a critic as Hazlitt liked the ballad's "voluptuous delicacy of the sentiments and luxuriant richness of the images" and its "Shakespearean grace."[31] But the poem has not been happily received in all quarters, and mainly because its rusticity seems of the most suspicious sort: that contrived by one court wit for the amusement of another, West Country accent and all.

I tell thee, *Dick*, where I have been,
  Where I the rarest things have seen,
    Oh, things without compare!
Such sights again cannot be found
In any place on English ground,
    Be it at Wake, or Fair.

The poem need not necessarily remind us why theories involving the polarization between "court" and "country" as well as Marxist accounts of incipient class struggle have been offered as alternative explanations for the cause of the

English Civil War, but the distance registered here between urban poet and rustic speaker, elite and popular culture, the distance between Suckling's notion of a ballad and Drayton's, is striking.

> Her fingers were so small, the Ring
> Would not stay on which they did bring,
>> It was too wide [by] a Peck:
> And to say truth (for out it must)
> It lookt like the great Collar (just)
>> About our young Colts neck.

> Her feet beneath her petticoat
> Like little mice stole in and out,
>> As if they feared the light;
> But oh! she dances such a way,
> No sun upon an Easter day
>> Is half so fine a sight.

The jokes just don't seem very funny, despite the colloquializing "wots" and parenthetical nudges. Suckling made his niche as a versifying poet by playing himself off against Caroline high culture, with its aureate phrases and elaborate poses. But the game of caricature does not work the other way around, not at least when the speaker proclaims himself to be one of them.

Robert Herrick (1591–1674)

Robert Herrick, by contrast, wished to belong fully, not just politically, to the *ancien régime*. Born into a family of goldsmiths and later apprenticed to one, then educated at Cambridge before being ordained a priest and settling down as a parson in Devon (only to be later ejected from his living during the Civil War), he found it difficult to be anything but revering: of English customs and rustic charms, of proverbs and tag ends of speech, of sack, ceremony, and the country life (particularly its flora), of friends, of his household, of his king, and most of all, of poetry: poetry as it descended to him from classical lyricists like "Anacreon" (in one of Henri Estienne's frequently reprinted editions of the *Carminum*),[32] Horace, Martial, and Tibullus; as it appeared in contemporaries like Drayton and Jonson ("Saint Ben"); and even, or rather, especially as it was written by "Robert" or, as he further naturalized it, "Robin" Herrick himself.

Herrick packed all these sentiments and then some into the 1,130 poems that make up his *Hesperides*, an often beautiful but also baffling collection of lyrics and epigrams: beautiful because few poets in English have seemed to be so triumphantly and naturally lyrical as Herrick, whose name, he reminds us, even rhymes with lyric; but baffling, too, because despite Herrick's profound concern with ceremony in its many forms, it is still nearly impossible to determine how "seriously" we are meant to take him as a poet:

> Give me a Cell
> To dwell
> Where no foot hath
> A path:
> There will I spend
> And end
> My wearied yeares
> In Teares.

("His Wish to privacie")[33]

Even by the nugatory standards of much Caroline verse, this poem – and there are literally hundreds like it in *Hesperides* – is something of a collector's item. (In fact, the Kentucky publisher Robert Barth has made a souvenir postcard of this poem.) Too slight for a Carew, too sentimental for a Suckling, too slender for even the "Anacreontic" Stanley, it seems to survive as a vestige of the monastic spirit itself, a twenty-three word prayer rendered into rhyming dimeter and monometer lines: a curiosity of sorts, as if Herrick had jotted it down in an off moment and then quietly disregarded his own wish for privacy.

Given Herrick's generous sense of inclusiveness – and there are another three hundred or so poems in the accompanying, less celebrated *Noble Numbers* – it is hardly surprising that sorting the wheat from the chaff in *Hesperides* has been a major critical operation at least since the end of the nineteenth century, when Swinburne proclaimed Herrick the greatest songwriter in English and thereby implicitly excluded much that did not fall under this rubric.[34] (The numerous contemporary musical settings of his lyrics, which exceed those of other poets of his generation by a significant margin, would seem to bear out Swinburne's judgment.)[35] Herrick's most recent editor, in fact, surmised that had the poet published some 150 of his best poems only and done so in the early 1630s, then he might have "laid the foundations for a reputation that would have grown as three or four other volumes appeared at intervals."[36] *Which* 150 poems he does not say; only a few are specified by title. But the drift of the argument is clear, and it does not rely on exact numbers in any case: if Herrick had played his cards better, he could have been a major poet. He could have been a contender, a bit more like Milton.

The notion of Herrick as a "major" poet is an intriguing one and not limited to an editor's amusing fancy that someday a *"New Hesperides"* might be found. Eliot, too, wrestled with the problem in his own way, initially denying a sense of "continuous conscious *purpose*" in Herrick's poems only to relent a few sentences later by admitting, "still, there is *something* more in the whole than in the parts."[37] And a number of recent scholars have attempted to define that "something" by assigning to *Hesperides* a conscious design, usually of a political or thematic order.[38] (As has been richly documented, Herrick, of course, was a royalist.) But whether Herrick will ever answer to modernist worries about his artistic stature (or to the larger question about the status of art in modern society) is doubtful, especially since he seems to have positively luxuriated in his modest role as a latecomer:

> Ah *Ben!*
> Say how, or when
> Shall we thy Guests
> Meet at those *Lyrick* Feasts,
> Made at the *Sun,*
> The *Dog,* the triple *Tunne?*
> Where we such clusters had,
> As made us nobly wild, not mad;
> And yet each Verse of thine
> Out-did the meate, out-did the frolick wine.
>
> My *Ben*
> Or come agen:
> Or send to us,
> Thy wits great over-plus;
> But teach us yet
> Wisely to husband it;
> Lest we that Tallent spend:
> And having once brought to an end
> That precious stock; the store
> Of such a wit the world sho'd have no more.
>
> ("An Ode for him")

In an important sense, Herrick is designating here a poetry of leftovers, the "overplus" of someone else's wit; but we should recognize too that the excess, the extra, does not come without a sense of obligation attached to it, without identifying a sense of purpose for the recipient. Herrick's little parable of poetic talent performs a slight revision on Matthew; the good servant here husbands wisely, seeing that the "precious stock" is limited and therefore that the consequences of overspending are the same as not spending at all. Either way the store more than diminishes; it disappears. But Herrick's economizing does not rule out the possibility of abundance – indeed, we might think of this ode as visually a little corpulent – but abundance itself ought to be seen in light of its smaller constituents, as in the example of a volume that consists of more than a thousand particles.

Hence the presence in *Hesperides* of what Alastair Fowler has termed "microphilia,"[39] Herrick's fetish for small things: fairies and household gods, bits of clothing, daffodils, lilies in crystals, flies in amber, wisps of women (Julia,

Anthea, Sappho), himself, his pets, his maid – what we often think of as the bric-à-brac of daily life, even the making of poetry itself:

> More discontents I never had
>   Since I was born, then here;
> Where I have been, and still am sad,
>   In this dull *Devon-shire*:
> Yet justly too I must confesse;
>   I ne'r invented such
> Ennobled numbers for the Presse,
>   Then where I loath'd so much.
>
> ("Discontents in Devon")

I doubt whether anyone would confuse this lyric with a poem of Drayton's like "An Ode Written in the Peake," even though both poets are concerned with the relationship between a specific locale and poetic inspiration. But I doubt, too, whether anyone would regret the redirection for very long. Herrick has fully domesticated his subject, has shifted the emphasis toward the common-place, the manageable emotion: "Where I have been, and still am sad." At the very least, Drayton would have reversed the last two lines so the emotional trajectory would have concluded with the ennobling of numbers. But Herrick is, above all, a poet of sentiment, a poet of the familiar, not a poet of the sublime, or in his case, what would have been the hierophantic overreach. However "enchanting," his are poems to be sung or heard after supper, by the hearth ("When he would have his verses read").

As with place, so with time and the theme of "*Times trans-shifting*" signaled in "The Argument of his Book." The poet who sets a high price on the familiar naturally laments change of any sort, but especially change that involves the customary.

> Faire Daffadills, we weep to see
>   You haste away so soone:
> As yet the early-rising Sun
>   Has not attain'd his Noone.
>   Stay, stay,
>   Until the hasting day
>   Has run
>   But to the Even-song;
> And, having pray'd together, we
>   Will goe with you along.
>
> We have short time to stay, as you,
>   We have as short a Spring;
> As quick a growth to meet Decay,

As you, or any thing.
        We die,
As your hours doe, and drie
        Away,
Like to the Summers raine;
Or as the pearles of Mornings dew
        Ne'r to be found againe.

("To Daffadills")

It would be difficult to find a more exquisite response to mutability in the seventeenth century. The poem is characteristically Herrick's in its ceremonial blend of nature and religion, its refusal to risk spoiling the mood – the deliquescent moment – by oversounding the moral, and its elegantly simple diction. If the first stanza's blending of personal grief and communal prayer leads us to recollect Paul's charge, "Let all things be done decently and in order" (I Corinthians 14: 40) – itself a staple of the *Book of Common Prayer*'s defense of the use of *some* ceremonies in religious worship[40] – the reminiscence is purposefully distant. It serves as a kind of undersong to remind the reader that Herrick's "we" is indeed "real," a "we" with a collective depth to it, and that the elaboration spun here in verse is around one of the most familiar – the most common – of sentiments.

To describe Herrick as a poet of the familiar or commonplace, however, is not just to agree with but to refine upon Eliot's notion that it is the "honest *ordinariness* which gives the charm" to Herrick's poetry.[41] As someone in part indebted to the epigrammatic tradition, Herrick has a good deal of everyday stuff in *Hesperides*: salutes to friends, brief comments about his book and its readers, scurvy distichs, bits of advice; and as with "Discontent in Devon," these poems often appear with little embellishment:

Lay by the good a while; a resting field
Will, after ease, a richer harvest yeild:
Trees this year beare; next, they their wealth with-hold:
Continuall reaping makes a land wax old.

("Rest Refreshes")

Again, no one would confuse this with a Jonson epigram, in which that poet strenuously sets himself apart from the proverbial or what might be construed as the "popular" voice; Herrick seems singularly undefensive about this dimension of his art, even as he hints at making a wider statement about civil unrest. So, too, Herrick characteristically thinks of hospitality in local, household terms. No kings lodge at his "grange," but this absence hardly interferes with the pleasure he gets from taking a personal inventory of his "private wealth." Counted correctly – in this case with a ritualizing regularity that manages not to be metrically monotonous – "slight things do lightly please," as a glance at the first half of the poem suggests:

> Though Clock,
> To tell how night drawes hence, I've none,
> A Cock,
> I have, to sing how day drawes on.
> I have
> A maid (my *Prew*) by good luck sent,
> To save
> That little, Fates me gave or lent.
> A Hen
> I keep, which creeking day by day,
> Tells when
> She goes her long white egg to lay.
> A goose
> I have, which, with a jealous eare,
> Lets loose
> Her tongue, to tell what danger's neare.
>
> ("His Grange, or private wealth")

But once "honest ordinariness" gives "charm," it ceases to be "ordinary" in a meaningful sense. Or to put the matter another way: the ordinary and the unusual, the familiar and the peculiar (a favorite word with Herrick), are reciprocal activities in *Hesperides*, together constituting a basic impulse, one even inscribed in the way the gorgeously resonant title – with its rich mythological connotations, it has tempted more than one critic into allegorizing the meaning of the collection[42] – applies to a volume of poems equally concerned with incidentals:

> I saw a Flie within a Beade
> Of Amber cleanly buried:
> The Urne was little, but the room
> More rich than *Cleopatra's* Tombe.
>
> ("The Amber Bead")

Herrick's reworking of a familiar trope in Martial (IV, 32, 59; VI, 15) helps to make this point. A fly might be of little significance, but how it is set, how it is framed, can tell an altogether different story. In Herrick, moreover, there is a kind of *trompe l'oeil* effect lacking in Martial because he makes the matter of perception an issue in the poem from the beginning and because he asks us to think of "clean" and "rich" as belonging, in this instance, to the same category of experience. There is, too, the possibility of a third dimension here: that the room in which the fly in amber is viewed – a favorite object in *Wunderkammer* ("wonder cabinets") of the period – is also made richer because of its presence.

If Herrick plays wantonly with our perceptions here, he consciously thought of this activity as one of art's little (or great?) pleasures. His celebrated rewriting of Jonson's "classic" statement of "sweet neglect" in "Still to be neat" creates a space for eccentricity – for "a wild civility" in poetry:

> A sweet disorder in the dresse
> Kindles in clothes a wantonnesse:
> A Lawne about the shoulders thrown
> Into a fine distraction:
> An erring Lace, which here and there
> Enthralls the Crimson Stomacher:
> A Cuff neglectfull, and thereby
> Ribbands to flow confusedly:
> A winning wave (deserving Note)
> In the tempestuous petticote:
> A carelesse shooe-string, in whose tye
> I see a wilde civility:
> Doe more bewitch me, then when Art
> Is too precise in every part.

("Delight in Disorder")

What poet until Herrick had ever been ravished by a shoestring? (In this respect, Castiglione's courtier is a little disappointing since his attention is drawn only to the more usual velvet stockings and dainty shoes.)[43] And it is this exaggerated, quirky posture that keeps being rewritten in *Hesperides*: in the surprisingly blunt erotic fantasy of "The Vine," in the mock grandiose farewell and welcome to sack, in the bursts of passion that snake skimpily down the page, in the humorously inflated notion that poets – especially Caroline poets – are supposed to worship ladies (Herrick has more than fifty poems to Julia alone), and in his occasionally bizarre diction – Herrick's belief that producing a momentary "delight in disorder" had a lexical dimension.

On this last point, Herrick's celebrated poem "Upon Julia's Clothes" only does more exactly what a great many of the lyrics seek to do; it drops an unusual word (usually Latinate) into a commonplace description that sets off a ripple effect of suggestiveness within the text:

> When as in silks my *Julia* goes,
> Then, then (me thinks) how sweetly flowes
> That liquefaction of her clothes.
>
> Next, when I cast mine eyes and see
> That brave Vibration each way free;
> O how that glittering taketh me!

"Liquefaction" does not so much serve to crystallize a particular meaning (in the manner of a *mot juste*) as to catalyze a response in the speaker, amplified and retuned in "brave vibration," that only further accentuates the mysterious effect of Julia's shimmering silk. Part of the success of "liquefaction," too, is that Herrick's use of the word – the context in which he sets it – does not require that we choose between its material and spiritual significance, but that we see them as somehow connected. "Sweetly flowes" suggests we emphasize the watery nature of Julia's silk; but the ecstatic response by the speaker – "O how that glittering taketh me!" – keeps the spiritual association of the word in play, one that, in the hands of a Christian Neoplatonist like Sir Thomas Browne at the end of *Urn-Burial*, would be tilted fully toward the transcendental ("and if any have been so happy as truly to understand Christian annihilation, extasis, exolution [exhalation], liquefaction …")[44] but that in Herrick remains pre-eminently a source of a "wilde civility."

From "liquefaction," it is possible to move to other startling words that seek to set off the usual from the unusual: coinages like "circum-crost" and "circum-spangle" (neither is listed in the *OED*, in contrast to the apparently more common "circumspacious" that Herrick uses elsewhere); diminutives like "rubulet" for a little ruby and "thronelet" – in the company of "refulgent," no less (in both instances, Herrick's is the only usage cited in the *OED*); rare and now obsolete words like "regrediance" (regression), "repullation" (bud or sprout again), or the more earthy "bowzing" and "cup-shot" (to denote different stages of intoxication.) Most of the effects are brief, but occasionally the resonances are of a more complicated kind:

> Go I must; when I am gone,
> Write but this upon my Stone;
> Chaste I liv'd, without a wife,
> That's the Story of my life.
> Strewings need none, every flower
> Is in this word, Batchelour.

("To his Tomb-maker")

Herrick presumably means for us not just to smile over his act of compressing the meaning of his life into a single word (and therefore to outdo his prospective tomb maker who is represented as requiring a full couplet) but also to see in the word and its rhyming pun on flower/flour the happy hominess of his existence. By way of a false etymology, Herrick points to his bachelorhood as the very bread of life, even containing all its flowers and responsible for producing *Hesperides* itself. (From the middle ages through the seventeenth century, "batch" was associated with baking bread.) The joke, moreover, seems to be one he shared with his royalist patron, Mildmay Fane, the Earl of Westmoreland, who wrote in *Otia Sacra* (1648), "Those blest with the true batch [bread] of life may ever rest so satisfied," an attitude toward "bachelormania" in turn shared by a number of mid-century poets and put to the test by Marvell in "The Garden."

All is meant to be good postprandial fare: *"Jocond his Muse was; but his Life was chaste"* reads the harmless last line of *Hesperides*. But it is a fare made poignant by touches of pathos throughout:

> I have lost, and lately, these
> Many dainty Mistresses:
> Stately *Julia*, prime of all;
> *Sapho* next, a principall:
> Smooth *Anthea*, for a skin
> White, and Heaven-like Chrystalline:
> Sweet *Electra*, and the choice
> *Myrha*, for the Lute, and Voice.
> Next, *Corinna*, for her wit,
> And the graceful use of it:
> With *Perilla*: All are gone;
> Onely *Herrick's* left alone,
> For to number sorrow by
> Their departures hence, and die.
>
> ("Upon the losse of his Mistresses")

The fact that the loss has been confined to the "dainty" means, too, that the idea of loss itself is never fully plumbed and also never fully expended. The elegiac can keep being touched on, and can keep being touched up. A brother dying, a father dead, Julia with a fever, the poet forever marking his departure:

> Onely a little more
>   I have to write,
>   Then Ile give o're,
> And bid the world Good-night.
>
> ("His Poetrie his Pillar")

That sentiment occurs with more than nine hundred poems to go; if the emotional reach were more dramatic, we would accuse Herrick of bad faith.

And the elegiac can itself be expanded, too, little by little: to incorporate, for one thing, notions of exile. *Hesperides* is studded with political commentary – brief allusions to the bad times, bits of advice relating to governing – and over the course of the 1,130 poems Herrick's concern with his household, in its immediate and more extended forms, becomes a concern for his homeland. The king who does not visit his grange nonetheless comes to nearby Exeter and unfurls his banner ("To The King, Upon his coming with his Army into the West"), as does his son some seven hundred poems later ("To Prince Charles upon his coming to Exeter"). Conversely, the poet who likens his return to sack to an Odyssean homecoming (in "The Welcome to Sack") broods over his sense of placelessness when he is expelled from Devon, a brooding that deeply qualifies, as a recent critic has noted,[45] the pleasures that might be assumed to accompany a return to one's birthplace:

> London my home is: though by hard fate sent
> Into a long and irksome banishment;
> Yet since cal'd back; henceforward let me be,
> O native countrey, repossest by thee!
> For, rather then I'le to the West return,
> I'le beg of thee first here to have mine Urn.
> Weak I am grown, and must in short time fall;
> Give thou my sacred Reliques Buriall.
>
> ("His returne to London")

Herrick's anxiety is different from that of the refugee's, for his fear is that the once familiar has become strange – London, too, was in the hands of the Puritans – and there are no other ports of call. In a sense, the counter-plot, as Claude Summers designates the poem's layered irony, hinges on the possibility of a double betrayal, a double plot by history, as the poet who worries elsewhere about being abandoned by daffodils and damsels now worries about being abandoned by his mother country.

* * *

Herrick's concern for homeland becomes, at its deepest, braided into a concern for the mythic and pagan origins of England and for the old rituals that he sees as permeating and sustaining English life: celebrations of rural harvests ("The Hock-cart"), ceremonies at Christmas, May-pole and May Day dances, and the like. These qualities have long been considered among the most original and attractive features of *Hesperides*, but their full cultural import is difficult to assess. Although powerful arguments have been made to equate Herrick's mythologizing with Archbishop Laud's program for ritualizing religious worship in England as a further response to Puritan attacks on ceremony, the scheme is not without its problems when applied to a lyricist like Herrick.[46] For one thing, it assumes that policies generated out of the Star Chamber were immediately and cleanly adopted in the rural parts of England, as if it were impossible to continue to celebrate pastimes without ultimately using them for politically oppressive purposes. But the example of Drayton should remind us that not everyone who celebrated English customs and faery lore was necessarily doing so in support of the established ruling powers; and Drayton was a far more politically motivated poet than Herrick.

Neither is it clear that Herrick was as loyal a Laudian as is sometimes assumed. Even if we discount the tantalizing allegation made by Laud's secretary, William Dell, that Herrick was living in London as the father of an illegitimate child, possibly in 1640,[47] we ought still to observe that the vicar of Dean Prior was never a conscientious apologist for the church like his more visible ecclesiastical contemporary Richard Corbett, the eventual Bishop of Norwich and the author of a number of anti-Puritan poems like "The Faeries Farewell":

> Lament, lament, old Abbies,
>   The *Faries* lost Command:
> They did but change Priests *Babies*,
>   But some have changd your *land*;
> And all your children sprung from thence
>   Are now growne *Puritanes*:
> Who live as *Changelings* ever since
>   For love of your Demaines.[48]

With witty attacks like this, it is possible to see why Corbett found preferment under Laud. As the stanza indicates, Corbett saw the connection between religious magic and social control in precise sociological terms: with the dissolution of the monasteries under Henry VIII, the disappearance of (in Corbett's view) the festive sport of changing babies, is causally related to a more malevolent threat involving a shift in land ownership. His "Lament, lament" toys with a more politically charged form of lamentation, that of Jeremiah. But in Herrick, the historical (and polemical) perspective is missing; so, too, is the causal connection that might link the economic with the festive in a consistent, ideological manner. Although acutely aware of *"Times trans-shifting,"* Herrick nonetheless proceeds to celebrate ceremony and customs as if they were fully vital forces, as if the disjunction of which Corbett speaks has yet to occur:

> When I verse shall make,
> Know I have praid thee,
> For old *Religions* sake,
> Saint *Ben* to aide me.

> Make the way smooth for me,
> When I, thy *Herrick*,
> Honouring thee, on my knee
> Offer my *Lyrick*.

> Candles Ile give to thee,
> And a new Altar;
> And thou Saint *Ben*, shalt be
> Writ in my *Psalter*.

>   ("His Prayer to Ben Johnson")

It is easy to recognize in this prayer a defense of perfume and incense and to posit a noxious reception by Puritans, but it would be also a shame to limit a poem obsessed with its own flirtatious lyricism to a polemical context. The "charm" of Herrick's verse is precisely that it can trifle with solemnities – even solemnities associated, in this case, with "old *Religions* sake" – in the name of poetry. It can, in short, be a little bit political without becoming frantic or repressive. If a "book of sports" – and some of the poems reflect satirically on rural life in the manner of Dutch caricaturists like Jan Steen – it is written in the lower case by an author whose name rhymes with lyric, not Laud.

The problems with reading Herrick too defensively become especially acute with an invitational poem like "Corinna's going a Maying," Herrick's gorgeous and much anthologized Mayday celebration. As Leah Marcus among others has pointed out, the poem specifically alludes to "The Proclamation made for May," the kind of festive celebration identified in *The Book of Sports*, which Laud sought to enforce in the 1630s; and the allusion resonates, like liquefaction, with contemporary political significance. But how much is another question. It is doubtful whether Laud himself would have approved of the deeply imagined, pagan nature of Herrick's *carpe diem* poem, with its repeated enjoinders for Corinna to run off to the woods, its playful reversals of Christian notions of sin, its keen celebration of the present moment for "harmlesse follie," its indifference to the Christian afterlife. As a poem made in part smoother by Jonson's loose translation of Catullus's "Vivamus, mea Lesbia" into "Come my Celia, let us prove," the lyric is wonderfully alive to surface detail, as Herrick extends the range of reference well beyond the courtly to include the rustic chiding of "Get up, sweet-Slug-a-bed" and a Botticelli-like celebration of Corinna as Flora:

> Rise; and put on your Foliage, and be seene
> To come forth, like the Spring-time, fresh and greene;
>> And sweet as *Flora*. Take no care
>> For Jewels for your Gowne, or Haire:
>> Feare not; the leaves will strew
>> Gemms in abundance upon you:
> Besides, the childhood of the Day has kept,
> Against you come, some *Orient Pearls* unwept:
>> Come, and receive them while the light
>> Hangs on the Dew-locks of the night:
>> And *Titan* on the Eastern hill
>> Retires himselfe, or else stands still
> Till you come forth. Wash, dresse, be brief in praying:
> Few Beads are best, when once we goe a Maying.

The casual assimilation of the classical and the colloquial, the majestic and the immediate – Titan on the eastern hill retiring while the speaker hurriedly directs Corinna through her morning routine – is surely Herrick at his best; the effect is one that could have been achieved only after a poet already had the example of Jonson. And the pleasure taken in daily life in this passage, as well as the poet's pleasurable urgings, prepares the way for the poignant last stanza, when the *carpe diem* note receives its sharpest – and subtlest – shadings:

> Come, let us goe, while we are in our prime;
> And take the harmlesse follie of the time.
> > We shall grow old apace, and die
> > Before we know our liberty.
> > Our life is short; and our dayes run
> > As fast away as do's the Sunne:
> And as a vapour, or a drop of raine
> Once lost, can ne'r be found againe:
> > So when or you or I are made
> > A fable, song, or fleeting shade;
> > All love, all liking, all delight
> > Lies drown'd with us in endlesse night.
> Then while time serves, and we are but decaying;
> Come, my *Corinna*, come, let's goe a Maying.

Although the sentiments expressed here about life's evanescence are general enough to coincide with the Scriptural readings found in the liturgy for that day, Herrick's seductive invitation runs counter to the spirit of these passages, and can no more be "contained" by them than the poem can be fully explained by recourse to the Laudian Proclamation for May.[49] Herrick's age-old argument, rich in echoes from classical as well as Scriptural sources,[50] reflective of poetry's modest memorializing powers, cares little for anything but the present: for briefly arresting time in the name of "All love, all liking, all delight," a phrase that sweetens as it grows, counterpoising everything pleasurable in this life against the emptiness of the next, and stealing between the "fleeting shade" of memory and an "endlesse night" of pagan oblivion to make a hope of the final rhyme's dying fall. With sentiments like these, one can understand why Herrick never made it big in the church.

Richard Lovelace (1618–57)

Carew, Suckling, and Herrick might well be thought of as a first wave of Caroline poets. As lyricists who came of age while Charles was on the throne, they reflected only indirectly on the political concerns either anticipating or generated by the Civil War, and of these, Herrick alone lived through the Civil War itself, indeed through the Interregnum and well into the Restoration. But 1648 effectively marks the date in which he spoke and then fell silent: his two collections of verse, *Hesperides* and *Noble Numbers,* sit like small monuments against a darkened landscape, runic testimonies to what "we up-rear, / Tho kingdoms fal," as he remarks in "The Pillar of Fame."

Richard Lovelace, on the other hand, might well be regarded as the leader of a second wave.[51] Or at least of a second ripple, since the spring that had nurtured Carew's hardbound muse – his proximity to Donne and Jonson – or Herrick's miniaturized artistry was only occasionally realized and then over a conceptually narrower terrain, one to a large degree dictated by a combination of political circumstances and genteel concerns, noble gestures and flourishes from "abroad." When Lovelace gives a version of Carew's "Mediocritie in love rejected" in a lyric entitled "A la Bourbon," we know that craftsmanship is not of paramount concern:

> Divine Destroyer pitty me no more,
>   Or else more pitty me;
> Give me more Love, Ah quickly give me more,
>   Or else more Cruelty!
>   For left thus as I am
>   My Heart is Ice and Flame;
>   And languishing thus I
>   Can neither Live nor Dye![52]

The relaxation in discipline has little in common with either Herrick's delight in disorder or Suckling's calculated indifference.

Nonetheless, in the eyes of one near contemporary at least, Lovelace seemed "a fair pretender to the Title of Poet."[53] The phrase belongs to Milton's nephew, Edward Phillips, who goes on to say, after the fashion, how one may discern in Lovelace "sometimes those sparks of a Poetic fire, which had they been the main design, and not Parergon, in some work of Heroic argument, might happily have blaz'd out into the perfection of sublime Poesy." In the reference to "some work of Heroic argument," we can hear the ample voice of the uncle speaking through the nephew; and Phillips might have been further stirred toward a sympathetic reading of Lovelace because of Lovelace's friendship with Milton's friend, Andrew Marvell, acknowledged in the commendatory poem Marvell wrote for Lovelace's first collection of poems, *Lucasta* (1649). But there is also a ring of truth in the distinction Phillips draws between poetic desire and fulfillment, between the aspirations for poetic sublimity and the absence of heroic argument, for as much as lapses in craft distinguish Lovelace from his Caroline contemporaries, so too does the reach toward sublimity. Neither Carew, Herrick, nor Suckling could – or would – have claimed so much for his muse.

Phillips might have arrived at so generously qualified a judgment by taking any number of routes. Lovelace surely had an unusual ear and a good, though sometimes quirky, grasp of phrasing that went beyond mere Cavalier *sprezzatura*:

I cannot tell who loves the Skeleton
Of a poor Marmoset, nought but boan, boan.
Give me a nakednesse with her cloath's on.

("La Bella Bona Roba")

Even if the rough bravado here no longer seems quite so modern as it did to a previous generation of readers often taking their cue from Donne, the jaunty repetition of "boan, boan" neatly pinpoints the grisly image of the marmoset and sets up a paradox to be reworked in the remaining four stanzas that does shock. And though Lovelace will probably always be better remembered for uttering high-arching, (now) proverbial sentiments like "I could not Love thee (Deare) so much, / Loved I not Honour more" ("To Lucasta, Going to the Warres"), or "Stone Walls doe not a Prison make, / Nor Iron bars a Cage" ("To Althea, from Prison"), he also had a knack at capturing and fixing a lyric moment at its fullest:

See! with what constant Motion
Even, and glorious, as the Sunne,
  Gratiana steeres that Noble Frame,
Soft as her breast, sweet as her voyce
That gave each winding Law and poyze,
  And swifter then the wings of Fame.

("Gratiana dauncing and singing")

In a gesture like this, it is difficult not to think of the real sympathy that must have existed between Lovelace and Marvell, especially the Marvell of "Upon a Drop of Dew" or "A Picture of Little T.C. in a Prospect of Flowers."

At the same time, Lovelace (again like Marvell) found the pastoral mode a congenial way of writing about political circumstances – whether by using amatory figures like Lucasta or Amarantha (the latter in a poem bearing this title has been seen recently as a partial source for "Upon Appleton House,"[54] although an equally strong case can be made for its influence on Marvell's "Nymph Complaining for the Death of Her Faun"), or by employing emblems taken from nature, especially from the insect world. In "Calling Lucasta from her Retirement," for instance, Lucasta, like Marvell's Juliana, possesses apocalyptic power, although of a more comforting sort (especially to displaced royalists) in her capacity as a figure representing ultimate Truth:

Sacred Lucasta like the pow'rfull ray
Of Heavenly Truth passe this Cimmerian way,
Whilst all the Standards of your beames display.

> Arise and climbe our whitest highest Hill,
> There your sad thoughts with joy and wonder fill,
> And see Seas calme as Earth, Earth as your Will.

And scattered among his verse, especially in the second volume entitled *Lucasta: Posthume Poems* (1659), a number of poems take the Caroline fetish for small things in an overtly political direction. Without being fully Aesopian, these suggest that Lovelace's emphasis on ants and snails in the latter collection marks a further turn toward a genre already coded as subversive – Aesop himself was a slave – and exploited as such by fellow royalists like John Ogilby in his 1651 edition of *The Fables of Aesop Paraphras'd in Verse*.[55]

A willingness to spot diamonds in the rough – and few poets in the seventeenth century are as syntactically convoluted as Lovelace – and an interest in drawing connections between Lovelace and a major poet like Marvell, who seems to have made sustained imaginative works out of possibilities barely glimpsed by Lovelace, are necessary responses to his verse. So, too, is recognizing Lovelace as the epitome of the Cavalier poet: a third generation soldier (his grandfather had been knighted by Essex for his efforts in the Irish campaign, his father by James) and loyalist virtuoso whose knowledge of the sister arts – to say nothing about his quasi-scientific interest in natural lore – seemed an inevitable extension of his royalist sympathies. Van Dyck's pupil and successor at Charles's court, Peter Lely, was an intimate friend of Lovelace; both were admitted to the Freedom of the Painter's Company in 1647. Allusions to Italian masters like Raphael, Giorgione, and Titian dot the canvass of his writings. On several occasions, furthermore, Lovelace's special interest in the visual arts, besides helping to account for a hypertrophied use of imagery, shows him equating a royalist politics with an aesthetic "naturalism." In a poem that has earned the right to be called the most intensely conceived ecphrastic analysis of a painting so far produced in England,[56] the sympathetic assessment by painter and poet emerges as the only legitimate response to the current political situation. After twenty lines describing the clouded fortunes of Charles and the brave sufferings shared by the son, Lovelace insists on the acute naturalism of Lely's art, the graceful and mysterious connection between the painter and the royal sitters:

> Not as of old, when a rough hand did speake
> A strong Aspect, and a faire face, a weake;
> When only a black beard cried Villaine, and
> By *Hieroglyphicks* we could understand;
> When Chrystall typified in a white spot,
> And the bright Ruby was but one red blot;
> Thou doest the things *Orientally* the same,
> Not only paintst its colour, but its *flame*:
> Thou sorrow canst designe without a teare,
> And with the Man his very *Hope* or Feare;

So that th' amazed world shall, henceforth finde
None but my *Lilly* ever drew a *Minde*.
                    ("To my Worthy Friend Mr. Peter Lilly")

With a poet of Lovelace's self-conscious versatility, however, the risk is one of competing surfaces, or rather of competing interests that can prevent an idiom from developing that is distinctly his: a bit of this, a bit of that – some shocking images and conceits reminiscent of Donne, some distantly Jonsonian commendatory epistles (even an epithalamion of sorts in "Amyntor's Grove"), an array of Continental motifs popular among later Caroline poets, a turn in his later verse to retreat, satire, and mockery. Of the Caroline poets discussed in this chapter, it is easy to regard Lovelace as the least in control of his muse, the least capable of assimilating the different poetic strains swirling about the 1640s and 1650s, and consequently, too, the least appreciated.

But if he differs from Carew, Suckling, and Herrick in this regard, his poetry is also more profoundly (and problematically) royalist. And with this distinction in mind, I believe it is possible to take Phillips's view of Lovelace "as a fair pretender" in another, perhaps more fruitful direction, one Phillips probably did not consciously intend but that a full reading of Lovelace's two collections encourages. The first volume of *Lucasta* (1649), like Lovelace's greatest poem, urges that we subscribe to the high, compensatory value of art, especially the art of the lyric as it weaves victory out of defeat, whether by singing to an Althea from prison, to a Lucasta from beyond the seas, or by calling Lucasta from retirement (in the poem with that title), calling, that is, in the sense of a powerful controlling speech act: "See! She obeys! by all obeyed thus; / No storms, heats, Colds, no soules contentious, / Nor Civill War is found – I mean, to us." In the wake of the royalist defeat, poetry itself, in the high ceremonial forms of "Epodes, Odes, Sonnets, Songs" – to quote from the 1649 title page – becomes a "fair pretender," a fair substitute for loss. And the poem that concentrates this experience in its most distilled form is "The Grasshopper Ode: To my Noble Friend, Mr. Charles Cotton" – a miniature *Paradise Lost* (and found).

That poem inevitably calls to mind other mid-century reworkings of Anacreon's "grasshopper" by Abraham Cowley and Thomas Stanley, but the comparison is of a limited kind. The happy insect reported by Anacreon and his translators has, in more ways than one, been fully seasoned by Lovelace. The blending involves a generic upgrading of Anacreon by Horace and perhaps Pindar as recollected by Jonson in the Cary–Morison ode. And it includes a deepening of the mood of festive drinking often found in Anacreon (and celebrated by Cowley and Stanley in their grasshopper poems) by commemorating an ideal of friendship, made emphatic, as Earl Miner has remarked,[57] in the shift of address exactly midway through the poem. Here that ideal assumes – as it does not, say, in Herrick – the broader, oppositional significance Jonson attached to it in his Pindaric Ode, except that the "opposition" now no longer involves a "throng" of lesser wits but a newly empowered Puritanical culture responsible for (in the eyes of royalists) making a winter of festive celebration itself by officially abolishing the observance of Christmas by order of December 19, 1644.[58] And the seasoning is tonal as well: laudatory, elegiac, wry, spontaneous, Spartan. Beginning with the underlying Aesopic tale reported in Caxton (and elsewhere) of the aristocratic grasshopper who sings in the summer but fails to store up corn for the winter, the ode braids together a range of classical gestures and allusions to achieve a powerfully complex response to the experience of being ousted. When Lovelace begins,

> Oh thou that swing'st upon the waving haire
>   Of some well-filled Oaten Beard,
> Drunke ev'ry night with a Delicious teare
>   Dropt thee from Heav'n, where now th' art reard,

we sense in the longing apostrophe a poet who could be great without always being very good. Since the poem is not long, and, as critical commentary attests, central to any evaluation of Lovelace,[59] I quote the remaining nine stanzas:

2

> The Joyes of Earth and Ayre are thine intire,
>   That with thy feet and wings dost hop and flye;
> And when thy Poppy workes thou dost retire
>   To thy Carv'd Acorn-bed to lye.

3

> Up with the Day, the Sun thou welcomst then,
>   Sportst in the guilt-plats of his Beames,
> And all these merry dayes mak'st merry men,
>   Thy selfe, and Melancholy streames.

4

> But ah the Sickle! Golden Eares are Cropt;
>   Ceres and Bacchus bid good night;
> Sharpe frosty fingers all your Flowr's have topt,
>   And what sithes spar'd, Winds shave off quite.

5

> Poore verdant foole! and now green Ice! thy Joys
>   Large and as lasting, as thy Peirch of Grasse,
> Bid us lay in 'gainst Winter, Raine, and poize
>   Their flouds, with an o'reflowing glasse.

6

> Thou best of Men and Friends! we will create
>   A Genuine Summer in each others breast;

And spite of this cold Time and frozen Fate
    Thaw us a warme seate to our rest.

7

Our sacred harthes shall burne eternally
    As Vestall Flames, the North-wind, he
Shall strike his frost-stretch'd Winges, dissolve and flye
    This *Aetna* in Epitome.

8

Dropping *December* shall come weeping in,
    Bewayle th'usurping of his Raigne;
But when in show'rs of old Greeke we beginne,
    Shall crie, he hath his Crowne again!

9

Night as cleare *Hesper* shall our Tapers whip
    From the light Casements where we play,
And the darke Hagge from her black mantle strip,
    And sticke there everlasting Day.

10

Thus richer then untempted Kings are we,
    That asking nothing, nothing need:
Though Lord of all what Seas imbrace; yet he
    That wants himselfe, is poore indeed.

Along with some marvelous aural effects, what is striking about the poem is the sense of manifest control: the "poize" (l.19) exhibited by Lovelace, even in the way he enjambs that word against the more turbulent threat of "flouds," and so memorably represented at the outset in the image of the grasshopper swinging upon "some well-filled Oaten Beard," poised for a fall that nonetheless does not happen for several more stanzas, and then when it does, occurs with a classicizing elegance that Marvell must have admired: "But ah the Sickle! Golden Eares are Croppt." (If it could be shown that this poem was, in fact, written after the decapitation of the king, then Lovelace's "poize" must be seen as even more remarkable and more Marvellian, and the relationship between this ode and Marvell's "Horatian Ode" more interesting still.) As potentially apocalyptic as the image of the sickle is, it appears within a parable of the Fall as imagined from the perspective of someone who still believes he has a home, a place of retreat. "And what sithes spar'd, Winds shave off quite": this is a line written by a poet looking from the inside out, the melodious control verifying the comfort found in friendship and further illuminated in the pun on "harthes," a word that links the "Genuine Summer in each others breast" with their imagined Roman surroundings. As critics have observed, the image of the "sacred harthes" could have come from Herrick, except that it has more defensive bite.

To spell out more exactly the difference with Herrick is to see where Lovelace's ode begins to engage another poem that appeared in public for the first time in the mid-1640s – Milton's ode "On the Morning of Christ's Nativity." Albeit in a more modest way, Lovelace's poem returns the pagan deities banished by Milton; and it does so by calling attention to another kind of "new music," this made out of "show'rs of old Greeke" rather than prophetic or angelic song, and delivered not as inspired utterance but as communal pledge, one that simultaneously fuses the natural and the political order, religion and royalism:

> Dropping *December* shall come weeping in,
>   Bewayle th'usurping of his Raigne;
> But when in show'rs of old Greeke we beginne,
>   Shall crie, he hath his Crowne again!

As with the season, so with the king: both shall recover their crowns in this month of miracles because of the genuine summer of "harthes" that burn with eternal loyalty. So incandescent, in fact, is the warm light emanating from communal play and mutual pledge that in the penultimate stanza of the poem even the Night Hag, about whom Herrick writes as part of the inevitable and unalterably dark mythos of Nature,[60] can be stripped of her "black mantle" and made into "everlasting Day" – stripped but not disenchanted, transformed not silenced. And though an immediate engagement with another Miltonic work – *Areopagitica* – cannot be asserted with any more certainty, the closing sentiments of Lovelace's ode take the issue of temptation and trial, central to that pamphlet and to Milton's writing in general, and turn it into a proof of the necessary benefits of seasoning, in all that word has come to imply in the poem:

> Thus richer then untempted Kings are we,
>   That asking nothing, nothing need:
> Though Lord of all what Seas imbrace; yet he
>   That wants himselfe, is poore indeed.

"Poize" of the sort exemplified by the Grasshopper Ode helps to explain why this poem has been central to modern definitions of Cavalier verse. But we should emphasize, too, how this poem implicitly counters the pejorative sense of a word whose meaning, in Lovelace's day as well as ours, is associated with the off-hand gesture – the wave of the hand and the tipped glass so familiar to us from the Dutch painter, Frans Hals. Indifference has a small place in this poem. The note that sticks finally in the ear is not that of the solitary grasshopper "Drunke ev'ry night with a Delicious teare," however memorable such a line might be, but that of the moralist who measures the slight slip from "grass" to "glass" (as in Isaiah's "all flesh is grass"), and in the process manages to transform brittleness into resistance through the benefits of fellowship and the creativity reckoned on such occasions. "Golden Eares" have been cropped, but that is not the full story. The epic reach of the penultimate line plays wistfully with what was and what might be, "Though Lord of all what Seas imbrace" – Britain. But the new music is to be of a different sound, one responsive to the needs of the self, especially the royalist self, at mid-century: "yet he / That wants himselfe, is poore indeed."

To set Lovelace's second volume of verse, the more somberly entitled *Lucasta: Posthumous Poems* (1659), against the first is both to understand some of the problems of being a Cavalier poet after the execution of Charles – of continuing to fashion a royalist self by either climbing, like Lucasta, to the highest point on a white hill or turning inward in the midst of "Dropping December" – and to realize retrospectively Phillips's point about the disjunction in Lovelace between poetic fire and heroic design. If the Grasshopper ode redefines the kingly by pointing to an internalized heroics of Horatian play, the second volume points in more troubled ways to the illusory presence of the high mode as a form of representation itself. Instead of retirement, we get restlessness; instead of song, we get satire: a shift in generic emphasis that has encouraged critics to see in Lovelace an anticipation of some of the concerns of Dryden and Pope. However this may be and however much Lovelace's own personal misfortunes underlie this transition – and until more evidence to the contrary is discovered than that produced by Wilkinson, I am inclined to believe Wood's melancholic account that "after the Murther of K. *Ch.* I, *Lovelace* was set at liberty, and having by this time consumed all his Estate, grew very melancholy, (which brought him at length into a Consumption) became very poor in body and purse, was the object of charity, went in ragged Cloaths (whereas when he was in his glory he wore Cloth of gold and silver) and mostly lodged in obscure and dirty places"[61] – the prevailing mood of the 1659 *Lucasta* is one of disenchantment and dark threats, Democritean pathos and poignantly desperate reprisals.

There are no Altheas to celebrate, no stones walls to transcend, and Lucasta herself (like England) seems alien from the outset. "Her Reserved looks" is the title of the first poem; the second, "Lucasta laughing," strikes a more unsettling note:

> Heark how she laughs aloud,
>   Although the world put on its shrowd;
> Wept at by the fantastick Crowd,
>   Who cry, One drop let fall
> From her, might save the Universal Ball.
>   She laughs again
>   At our ridiculous pain;
>   And at our merry misery
>   She laughs until she cry.

As Lovelace makes clear in "Love made in the first Age: To Chloris," wooing is not merely a thing of the past, something about which to become nostalgic. The dream of a sexual golden age is material for a vengefully comic act of self-abuse along the exaggerated lines of Marvell's narcissistic mower or, in his escapist desires, the speaker of "Upon Appleton House":

> Now, Chloris! miserably crave,
> The offer'd blisse you would not have;
>   Which evermore I must deny,
> Whilst ravish'd with these Noble Dreams,
> And crowned with mine own soft Beams,
>   Injoying of my self I lye.

Here and elsewhere, the perspective ventured is meant to shock. (Is self-crowning too, one wonders, a delayed response to the current situation of political impotence?) It is not designed, as in Marvell, to facilitate continual musings on the subject of retirement; and nature, too, like Chloris, is often represented as decidedly cruel – a place in which the falcon and the crane are at war ("The Falcon"), and the fly, a "small type of great ones," must face the hungry spider; a place in which the sentiments in "A loose Sarabande" seem a necessary consequence of the complete rupture of hierarchy, not just the product of a bad night:

> See all the World how't staggers,
>   More ugly drunk then we,
> As if far gone in daggers,
>   And blood it seem'd to be:
> We drink our glass of Roses,
> Which nought but sweets discloses,
> Then in our Loyal Chamber,
> Refresh us with Loves Amber.

The second *Lucasta* has its own bleak integrity: "'Twas a blith Prince exchang'd five hundred Crowns / For a fair Turnip; Dig, Dig on, O Clowns!" We are not far from the dark wit of the gravedigger scene from *Hamlet* in these opening lines from "*On* Sanazar's *being honoured with six hundred Duckets by the* Clarissimi *of Venice.*" And as with the first volume, the wit finds its most concentrated form in the use of an Aesopic fable: the same fable in fact, but now with mocking attention to the hardworking, niggardly ant who refuses to give the grasshopper any of his store.

> Forbear thou great good Husband, little Ant;
>   A little respite from thy flood of sweat;
> Thou, thine own Horse and Cart, under this Plant
>   Thy spacious tent, fan thy prodigious heat;

> Down with thy double load of that one grain;
> It is a Granarie for all thy Train.

The whittling away of the hyperbolic in the first line strikes me as Lovelace at his near best in this volume; he performs as a kind of grim reaper whose prodigious humor stands in evident contrast to the ant's parsimonious behavior. And the taunting continues, as Lovelace develops a brief but pointed anti-Puritan fable centering on the demise of festivity during the Interregnum, a common royalist complaint during the period, and replete with darker apocalyptic ironies involving the fate of hoarders:

> Look up then miserable Ant, and spie
>   Thy fatal foes, for breaking of her Law,
> Hov'ring above thee, Madam, *Margaret Pie*,
>   And her fierce Servant, Meagre, Sir *John Daw*:
> Thy Self and Storehouse now they do store up,
> And thy whole Harvest too within their Crop.

But the poem also indicates some of the larger problems Lovelace faced in this second volume, and they involve issues of audience. In "The Ant," as with the other insect poems in the second volume, there is, in contrast to the Grasshopper Ode, no other community, no "genuine summer," no fellowship imagined by the poet, no sense really of a sustaining social order behind or beyond the poem – a point brought home on a larger scale in the belabored celebration of the marriage of Charles Cotton to Isabella Hutchinson ("The Triumphs of Philamore and Amoret"). With some poets of the period – and for different reasons both Milton and Vaughan come to mind – the experience of solitude was highly productive, an occasion for recasting the authorial self into an altogether different mode: the blind bard of *Paradise Lost* or the Job-like Singer of divine hymns in *Silex Scintillans*. But in the case of later Lovelace, it is impossible, I think, not to feel that the experience of displacement was only partially productive. It brought a new emphasis to his poetry, not a new determination of the poet's responsibilities, and the darker emphases only inscribe more deeply Lovelace's sense of isolation and his longing for a new Imperium:

> Where then when all the world pays its respect,
> Lies our transalpine barbarous Neglect?
> When the chast hands of pow'rful *Titian*,
> Had drawn the Scourges of our God and Man,
> And now the top of th' Altar did ascend,
> To crown the heav'nly piece with a bright end;
> Whilst he who to seven Languages gave Law,
> And always like the *Sun* his Subjects saw,
> Did in his Robes Imperial and gold,

The basis of the doubtful Ladder hold.
O *Charls*! A nobler monument then that,
Which thou thine own Executor wert at.

Obscure as they are, these lines from his second poem to Peter Lely, commenting in part on an unidentified painting by Titian, signal a poet who could not settle for less than a heroic view of life but who also lacked, as Phillips said, a sense of where to go in order to sustain his "argument."

In this regard, the closing, lengthy satire on Sanazarro looks forward, in formalistic and generic ways, to what literary historians are accustomed to regard as a – or *the* – Restoration mode of poetry. But in one important sense at least, the poem is deeply reactionary, deeply uncertain of its direction. The solution Lovelace imagines to what he views as the current scene of literary barbarism – "Goths in literature / Ploughman that would *Parnassus* new manure" – involves another kind of fantasized *imperium*: that of reconstituting a new order of the Sons of Ben, with Lovelace's uncle, George Sandys, and Lucius Cary among the tribe, and Jonson at its head:

Arise thou rev'rend shade, great *Johnson* rise!
Break through thy marble natural disguise;
Behold a mist of Insects, whose meer Breath,
Will melt thy hallow'd leaden house of Death.

However nostalgic Herrick was for the old order, his poetry draws strength from a knowledge of its passing: "Ah *Ben*! / Say how or when." In Lovelace, the change irrevocably determined by the fall of the axe brought gradual bewilderment.

5

SUBSTANCE AND STYLE IN GEORGE HERBERT'S *THE TEMPLE*

Poetry is the revelation of words by words.

Wallace Stevens

George Herbert might well have been an exemplary Caroline court poet: "I know the wayes of Pleasure, the sweet strains, / The lullings and the relishes of it."[1] But he became instead England's greatest devotional lyricist, and he did so in fine Caroline style, with the publication of a single, though substantial, collection of verse that appeared in print only because of the help of others. Indeed, style is very much at the heart of *The Temple*: style as it includes issues of dress, the proper mode and language of wooing, the shape of individual poems, the role of the self, even the way one might respond to courtly games and some of the symbols and devices most in fashion by courtier poets, like posies, roses, and emblems; but style, too, as it is constantly, consciously, and at times cunningly played off against substance as identified ultimately with Christ or God's word.

The authoritative nature of this shift from secular to sacred is the subject of the printer's note to the reader that appeared with the first edition of *The Temple* in 1633 and which is usually attributed to Nicholas Ferrar of Little Gidding:

> Being nobly born, and as eminently endued with gifts of the minde, and having by industrie and happy education perfected them to that great height of excellencie, whereof his fellowship of Trinitie Colledge in Cambridge, and his Orator-ship in the Universities, together with that knowledge which the Kings Court had taken of him, could make relation farre above ordinarie. Quitting both his deserts and all the opportunities that he had for worldly preferment, he betook himself to the Sanctuaries and Temple of God, choosing rather to serve at Gods Altar, then to see the honour of State-employments.
>
> (p. 3)

135

Others had proclaimed the priority of Sion Hill over Helicon: the Jesuit Martyr, Robert Southwell, most explicitly in his prefatory note to his frequently reprinted *St. Peter's Complaint* in 1595 (thereafter 1597, 1599, 1602, 1608, 1615, 1634); and Sidney, to whom Herbert was related through Sidney's sister Mary, Countess of Pembroke, had defended the subject and practice of poetry in general because of its Biblical roots, most evident in the Psalms, the Song of Songs, Job, Ecclesiastes, and Proverbs. Sidney and the Countess of Pembroke had also translated the psalter, a translation which circulated widely in manuscript in Jacobean court circles and was commended by Donne and probably read by Herbert. (It was eventually published in 1823.) But not until the publication of *The Temple* had any poet in England written so persuasively and decisively of the devotional experience.

> Ah my deare angrie Lord,
> Since thou dost love, yet strike;
> Cast down, yet help afford;
> Sure I will do the like.
>
> I will complain, yet praise;
> I will bewail, approve:
> And all my sowre-sweet dayes
> I will lament, and love.

The size of "Bitter-sweet" might remind us of Herrick; so too perhaps its subject matter. (Herrick frequently writes of being sad or discontent.) But the compressed anguish and the compulsion to particularize belong to a different register altogether, as if Herbert were wringing the sentimental out of Herrick in order to identify both the sweet and the sour as separate though related experiences that stem directly from the utterly special conditions of address. "His *measure* was eminent," wrote Henry Vaughan, the most original of Herbert's many disciples, in the 1655 Preface to his own collection of "Sacred Poems and Private Ejaculations" entitled *Silex Scintillans* and modeled to a great extent on Herbert's collection. "*Herbert* speaks *to* God like one that *really believeth a God*, and whose business in the world is most *with God*," noted Richard Baxter nearly fifty years after the publication of *The Temple*. "*Heart-work* and *Heaven work* make up his Books."[2] "My God must have my best, ev'n all I had" is how Herbert phrased the ultimate nature of his commitment in "The Forerunners."

In retrospect, it might seem almost inevitable that two of the most powerful institutions in the seventeenth century – the court and the church – should conspire to produce a devotional poet of Herbert's quality; and it might seem even less an historical accident that it should occur under James, whose interest in divine poetry led him to publish a youthful essay on the subject. But wherever the impetus originated – whether in a new cultural respectability devotional verse acquired under the king, or in auspicious family circumstances that extended to include Donne (Herbert's mother Magdalen was renowned for her piety and intelligence and is sometimes thought to lie behind the idealized personification of the British Church in the poem of that title), or in the rhetorical training Herbert received that led to his becoming university orator – and whatever the precise circumstances that caused Herbert, in Ferrar's words, to choose rather "to serve at Gods Altar, then to seek the honour of State-employments" (and explanations have ranged from long-term, organicist hypotheses to detailing specific reasons for his disenchantment with the world of secular preferment beginning in 1623),[3] *The Temple* had immediate and many readers.

That it did so is no doubt due in part to its subject matter. An increasingly literate culture that consciously linked learning and godliness as part of the legacy of the Reformation was likely to produce and consume a significant body of religious writings at many levels. In this regard, we have only to think of the phenomenal popularity enjoyed by devotional handbooks like Arthur Dent's *Plain Man's Pathway to Heaven* and Lewis Bayly's *Practice of Piety*. (With thirty-three editions in the author's lifetime, the latter was reputed to be as admired as the Bible.) If, moreover, recent historians are right in correcting the popular view of the time by identifying the 1630s as a high water mark for a literate clergy, commonly drawn from the middling and upper ranks of society,[4] then a work with a title like *The Temple* had almost a ready made audience in a way, for instance, that even Donne's religious verse, included in the more generally designated *Poems*, did not. (The editorial tinkering with the order of Donne's poems in the second edition suggests, in fact, some uncertainty about how the late Dean of St. Paul's could best be presented to his readers.) In this social and educational context, a fellow parson might take nearly as much pleasure in "The Church Porch," with its terse Solomonic attempt to rhyme a youthful (and potentially dissolute) member of the gentry to good, as he did in "The Church" proper, with its celebration of the liturgy and offices of the Church of England and its highly personal focus on the individual's relation to God – what Herbert reportedly described as "the many spiritual conflicts that have passed betwixt God and my Soul" pictured in *The Temple*.[5]

But it would be wrong to limit Herbert's audience, then and now, to fellow members of the clergy. Coleridge did remark, rather intimidatingly, that in order to appreciate *The Temple* "it is not enough that the reader possesses a cultivated judgment, classical taste, or even poetic sensibility, unless he be likewise a *Christian*, and both a zealous and an orthodox, both a devout and a *devotional* Christian … he must be [also] an affectionate and dutiful child of the Church, and from habit, conviction, and a constitutional predisposition to ceremonious-ness, in piety as in manners, find her forms and ordinances aids of religion, not sources of formality; for religion is the element in which he lives, and the region in which he moves."[6] Yet a good number of Herbert's early readers, from Baxter to Emily Dickinson, have been well outside the Church of England. And a good number continue to be so today, even if Herbert is well represented in the

Episcopal Hymnal.[7] Since the early 1950s, Herbert has been a staple of the university curriculum as well – the blue chip stock of religious poets – and the recipient of some of the best criticism of any seventeenth-century author.

"Aaron" is one reason why:

> Holinesse on the head,
> Light and perfections on the breast,
> Harmonious bells below, raising the dead
> To leade them unto life and rest:
> Thus are true Aarons drest.
>
> Profanenesse in my head,
> Defects and darknesse in my breast,
> A noise of passions ringing me for dead
> Unto a place where is no rest:
> Poore priest thus am I drest.
>
> Onely another head
> I have, another heart and breast,
> Another musick, making live not dead,
> Without whom I could have no rest:
> In him I am well drest.
>
> Christ is my onely head,
> My alone onely heart and breast,
> My onely musick, striking me ev'n dead;
> That to the old man I may rest,
> And be in him new drest.
>
> So holy in my head,
> Perfect and light in my deare breast,
> My doctrine tun'd by Christ, (who is not dead,
> But lives in me while I do rest)
> Come people; Aaron's drest.

Although less frequently anthologized than some of Herbert's poems (like "The Collar" and "Love [III]"), few poems in *The Temple* better justify Coleridge's remarks. "Aaron" is not merely concerned with a specific ceremony of the church – the priest's preparation for worship. With the recurring suite of identical rhyme words, the diastolic and systolic rhythms of each stanza (the pulse is always from trimeter to tetrameter to pentameter and back), and a further complex echoing of the number of lines by the number of stanzas (five), which, in turn, recollects the number of letters in "Aaron," the poem seems the very incarnation of religious ritual: stately and highly comforting in its returns, including especially the climactic return of holiness and light to the priest in the final stanza.

But the appeal of "Aaron" is also hardly limited to an appreciation for ceremony. As a number of readers have recently emphasized, "Aaron" combines a fascination with formalism of the most intricate kind with a concern for the most elemental of New Testament stories, especially for Protestants: the Pauline conversion of the old man to the new. If we look at only the first line of each stanza, in which the transmutation of the speaker into Christ is progressively marked, we can see this drama enacted as a kind of silhouette on the horizon. (It is typical of Herbert to signal so momentous a change by rewriting a line in which the lexical shift would seem to be so small: from "Holiness on the head" to "So Holy in my Head.") But Herbert insists, too, that the change is fully registered within – that it issues dramatically from the "inner" person, from the body and the heart, upon which the head rests. As Helen Vendler remarks, "poems are movements of hearts, as well as constructions of a pattern"[8] (or at least they should be, and most of Herbert's are); and movement in Herbert almost always begins with key words – in this case with "only," which initially carries the meaning of "except for," until this notion is magnified through the repetition of "another head," "another heart," and "another musick," and comes to signify Christ's exclusive presence identified in the fourth stanza: "Christ is my onely head / My alone onely heart and breast, / My onely musick."

I would even defend what Vendler refers to as the "strained" protestation here,[9] although not because these lines describe a state in which "the convert has now entered into a fever of self-obliteration." "Feverish" would seem to be just the wrong description of the effect achieved by the pressure of repetition. The duplications are of a more exacting sort, as if Herbert were evaluating, appropriating, and putting on (not merely trying out, as seems to be the case so often in Donne)[10] the central doctrine of Reformed theology of salvation by faith alone. His emphasis on "alone" and "only" – highlighted in the apparent redundancy – underscores exactly how an individual is supposed to reach a sense of certainty regarding salvation: through Christ, not through ceremonies. As Richard Hooker argues, in a passage that bears a remarkable resemblance to the concerns expressed here (including contesting how "only" ought to be interpreted in Luther's famous catch phrase), "Christ is the only garment, which being so put on, covereth the shame of our defiled natures, hideth the imperfections of our works, preserveth us blameless in the sight of God, before whom otherwise the very weakness of our faith were cause sufficient to make us culpable, yea, to shut us out from the kingdom of heaven, where nothing that is not absolute can enter."[11] Harmonious as it sounds, "Aaron" is a poem of absolutes.

With such a poem, it is difficult to know precisely where to draw the line between form and content. Or rather, it is difficult to know where the greater emphasis should be placed in the act of reading: on unfolding (and admiring) the intricacies of design and the pleasures they afford; or on responding (enthusiastically) to the dramatic immediacy of the conversion account. And this decision is, happily, not made easier by the ending, which, in its turn outward, from private to public, prevents us from placing an exclusive value on inward-ness. (Like Hooker, Herbert viewed "only" as a non-restrictive particle that did not rule out the need for good works.) "Come people; Aaron's drest." To find ourselves suddenly the target and the beneficiary of this elaborate preparation is both slightly disarming and enormously gratifying. The reader who has partici-pated personally in this act of self-renewal, moreover, might even feel at the end the further surprise of being introduced to his or her other, better half.

* * *

Highly civilized but persuasively simple, "Aaron" is only slightly atypical in that it asks us to see Herbert in his professional dress. Otherwise, *The Temple* is perhaps most extraordinary because it invites us to respond to a devotional temper that seemed not at all limited by its subject matter, a point made graphi-cally at least by the sheer profusion of different poetic forms visible to the eye. As one reader has remarked, Herbert seems "to include at least one example of almost every known poetic species within his microcosmic ark";[12] and the ark holds some 166 lyrics, nearly three times the number of poems in *The Songs and Sonnets*. To compare the scale of *The Temple* with that of the poetic models most immediately useful to Herbert, his book is approximately equal to the sum of *Astrophel and Stella* and *The Songs and Sonnets*, or to the Book of Psalms itself, with its 150 "poems." Among major collections of seventeenth-century lyrics, only Herrick's *Hesperides* can lay claim to greater length (by a significant margin) but not to greater variety; even if Herrick explores a number of poetic forms, the song and the epigram are clearly his dominant genres.

With Herbert, however, we might begin a summary by noting his interest in both genres and the several uses made of each. But we would quickly need to extend our frame of reference to accord a significant place for other models and traditions: the medieval liturgy for Holy Week powerfully revived in "The Sacrifice," a faint vestige of which does survive in Herrick's *Noble Numbers* ("His Saviours words, going to the Crosse"), fully renovated verse epistles like "To All Angels and Saints," a raft of lyrics that capitalize on contemporary interest in hieroglyphs ("The Altar" and "Easter-wings" are only the best known), less "sophisticated" poems that, with the help of the Bible and the metrical psalms, reveal their popular roots (like "Time" and "The Elixir"), or that participate in household literary traditions like the fable ("The Pulley") and the proverb ("Charms and knots"), or in familiar customs that mark the church calendar, urgent dramatic monologues that recall Donne ("The Temper"), and a good many poems of praise and blame, petition and complaint that remind us that Herbert both knew the psalms and lived in a world in which the patronage system was still a powerful discursive influence.

Indeed, the only form Herbert returned to with frequency was the sonnet. Seventeen in all, their combined presence points generically toward *The Temple*'s primary concern with the subject of love. (Two of his earliest poems were the pair of linked sonnets on love sent to his mother in 1609.) But even in his use of this most traditional of literary forms, Herbert is rarely slavish or dull, as a glance at "Prayer I" makes clear:

> Prayer the Churches banquet, Angels age,
>> Gods breath in man returning to his birth,
>> The soul in paraphrase, heart in pilgrimage,
> The Christian plummet sounding heav'n and earth;
> Engine against th'Almightie, sinners towre,
>> Reversed thunder, Christ-side-piercing spear,
>> The six-daies world transposing in an houre,
> A kinde of tune, which all things heare and fear;
> Softnesse, and peace, and joy, and love, and blisse,
>> Exalted Manna, gladnesse of the best,
>> Heaven in ordinarie, man well drest,
> The milkie way, the bird of Paradise,
>> Church-bels beyond the starres heard, the souls bloud,
>> The land of spices; something understood.

Unlike Calvin, who devotes some sixteen sections in the *Institutes of the Christian Religion* (3,22,1–16) to defining prayer, Herbert seems to have conceived of the occasion to describe "prayer" as an opportunity to baffle our sense of normal expectation. He gives us some of the usual sonnet features, including endstopping the lines and using a modified Shakespearean rhyme scheme; and as far as punctuation is concerned, it is possible to speak of the poem as having quatrains. But it is the departures that catch our eye: the surprising absence of the defining copula, then the splendid burst of images that seem deliberately to defy logical order (and on an individual basis, sometimes logic itself) and that range from the most graphically immediate ("Christ-side-piercing spear") to the distantly mysterious ("Church-bels beyond the starres heard") and include startling juxtapositions within a line ("Exalted Manna, gladnesse of the best") and between lines: until, of course, the final departure into "something understood" when all efforts to describe prayer are acknowledged insufficient. By the time of *The Temple*, the sonnet was hardly a novel form. Herbert's innovations here, among the boldest in the seventeenth century, ensure that the everyday need not become routine.

* * *

So much attention to formal variety and experimentation helps to explain Herbert's broad appeal: *The Temple* has something for almost everyone. As Herbert said elsewhere, "This is for you, and This is for you"[13] – something for the most sophisticated reader and the apparent bare speller as imagined in invitingly schoolish poems like "Jesu" and "Love-joy." But Herbert's reach is also hardly part of a populist program for poetry. If *The Temple* is widely habitable, it is so because in his use of subject, forms, and language, indeed in his view of devotional poetry in general, Herbert is not narrowly sectarian. Herbert worried about schism (most explicitly in the poem entitled "Church-schism"), and in "The Church Militant," he wrote with an apocalyptic, global awareness of holiness being dogged by sin in a manner that would have appealed to Wither. He was also highly sensitive to matters of church worship: the veneration traditionally but no longer accorded to all saints and angels (in the poem of that title) and the role of grace in preaching ("The Windows"), for instance. But what he said of the parson's preaching goes generally for his poetry as well: devotion, not controversy, should be its focus. In general, his engines were reserved for the Almighty. However much recent criticism has helped us to understand the circumstantial dimensions to Herbert's verse, at the climactic moment in *The Temple* when Herbert writes at the end of "Love III," "You must sit down, sayes Love, and taste my meat: / So I did sit and eat," he is not insisting that a potential doctrinal dispute about how the Eucharist ought to be taken during communion – whether kneeling or seated – be elevated over the personal drama of the soul's being cornered and finally won over by Christ's irresistible love.[14]

At the same time, if Herbert anticipates more fully than any other poet of his period Wallace Stevens's claim that "all poetry is experimental poetry" (by which Stevens meant all *good* poetry),[15] he did so in part by making the issue of language itself a subject of major concern in *The Temple*. A great deal of what feels new (and modern) about Herbert's poetry is the central place allotted to writing in *The Temple*. The two "Jordan" poems, "The Quidditie," "The Quip," "A True Hymn," and, most movingly, "The Forerunners" all ask that we attend to the nature of religious verse as a special category of poetry: the way it differs in general from other kinds of poetry ("The Quidditie"); the particular challenges it poses to an authorizing self that must remain always subordinate to the object of its praise ("Jordan [II]"); its precise relation to other generically related forms of discourse like the pastoral ("Jordan [I]"); the role of intention in producing an acceptable poem ("A True Hymn"); and the subordinate place of poetry – even devotional poetry – in the ultimate scheme of things ("The Forerunners").

Until Herbert, these issues were at best implied concerns of religious poets. Even Donne only rarely attempted to define – or as we might say today, theorize about – devotional poetry as a particular form of verse. As part of a long tradition of Petrarchists, Donne simply extended his amatory language, witty conceits and all, in the direction of God; he did not rethink the premises of language itself. But as a Protestant responding more fully to the elevated authority given to the written Word of God during the Reformation and writing with an even closer, though more circumspect eye, than Donne toward a still dominant court culture, Herbert breaks up the flow. As Milton was also to do, Herbert urges us to observe the rift – the difference – between secular and devotional language, and not from one but many angles.

Apprehended in its simplest terms, the sense of the radically special nature of religious verse could appear as a rather unexceptional list of what it is not:

My God, a verse is not a crown,
No point of honour, or gay suit,
No hawk, or banquet, or renown,
Nor a good sword, nor yet a lute:

It cannot vault, or dance, or play:
It never was in *France* or *Spaine*;
Nor can it entertain the day
With my great stable or demain:

It is no office, art, or news,
Nor the Exchange, or busie Hall;
But it is that which while I use
I am with thee, and *most take all.*

("The Quidditie")

Herbert is not worrying over measuring the divide here, although his series of thumbnail accounts is a remarkably exhaustive summary of high and low uses made of verse in his day. It is only when we reflect on the oddly utilitarian praise of religious poetry for its communicative, rather than its commercial, value that the poem acquires a slight edge to it. But it is not an edge that Herbert chooses to hew and sharpen. A poem entitled "The Quidditie" is mainly concerned with defining essences rather than developing attitudes, and the gamesmanship of "*most take all*" assures that this poem ends on a comfortable note.

On the other hand, to move from "The Quidditie" to "The Quip" is to shift from a scholastic to a rhetorical system of difference and to enter a forum in which combat thrives, in this case between "the merrie world" and the man of faith. In "The Quip," the boundary between the secular and devotional is not merely observed; it is sharply and repeatedly drawn. Against the various temptations offered – first beauty, then money, glory, and finally quick wit and conversation (all marvelously personified) – Herbert invokes at the end of each stanza the italicized refrain borrowed from the Psalms, "*But thou shalt answer, Lord, for me.*"[16] The battles are also remarkably inventive, written by someone who knows both sides of the debate, even if we have no doubt where the speaker lands at the end of each stanza and again at the end of the poem.

Then came brave Glorie puffing by
In silks that whistled, who but he?
He scarce allow'd me half an eie.
But thou shalt answer, Lord, for me.

143

There is nothing in Suckling quite as urbane as this quintessentially Caroline depiction of "brave Glorie." (Jonson's "On Something that Walks Somewhere" appears an even more deliberately clunky ancestor.) The wonderful play with the sound of whistling silk to set up the airy repetition of "who but he" provides Herbert with a perfect opportunity to introduce the Biblical refrain in all its "quiet dignity," as Chana Bloch describes its effects here and elsewhere. The contrast between shadow and substance, between gesture and statement, between a puffy redundancy and a pointed refrain, could hardly be sharper; and in the last stanza, the difference between speaking "fine things" and saying the right thing is played out conclusively:

> Yet when the houre of thy design
> To answer these fine things shall come;
> Speak not at large; say, I am thine:
> And then they have their answer home.

The two "Jordan" poems push the difference between "fine things" and "speak[ing] not at large" into the more particular literary arenas favored by the elite, indeed, into what we might even regard as the imagined homes of the Sidneys themselves: Wilton house and the kinds of literary activity centering on pastoral romance and Petrarchan sonneteering practiced there. In "Jordan [I]," speaking "not at large" now becomes identified with the kind of plain speaking Herbert associates with the original pastoral song at the nativity (further anchored in Scripture through echoes from the Psalms), in contrast to the fictitious authority accorded to fine things, including pastoral romance, found in a place like Wilton. Until the last stanza, Herbert seems to be a latitudinarian merely hoping to suggest an alternative to a dominant tradition. But the poem's ringing finish reverses this order by pointing in another direction, to the different meanings of "becoming" at the heart of the poem: "becoming" in the decorative (and for Herbert a merely mystifying) sense, and "becoming" in the sense of signaling an ultimate transformation or change in the nature of an utterance as it becomes a vow:

> Who sayes that fictions onely and false hair
> Become a verse? Is there in truth no beautie?
> Is all good structure in a winding stair?
> May no lines passe, except they do their dutie
>   Not to a true, but painted chair?
>
> Is it no verse, except enchanted groves
> And sudden arbours shadow course-spunne lines?
> Must purling streams refresh a lovers loves?
> Must all be vail'd, while he that reades, divines,
>   Catching the sense at two removes?

Shepherds are honest people; let them sing:
Riddle who list, for me, and pull for Prime:
I envie no mans nightingale or spring;
Nor let them punish me with losse of rime,
    Who plainly say, My God, My King.

That an utterance – or pledge – is plain according to a person's intentions in the act of speaking seems to be Herbert's point, not that all devotional poetry should be written in a plain style, or that language itself cannot have other uses or functions in the course of achieving this ideal moment of communication. In this regard, the surprising appearance of a miniature "defense of rhyme" in the penultimate line serves to ensure that plain speaking ought to mean not "without art" but, in the context of what has gone before, "without artifice." As has been recently suggested, it is also possible to see in this defensively stated apology ("Nor let them punish me with losse of rime") a Herbert alert to the potentially subversive nature of a general defense of devotional poetry that concludes by placing God ahead of the King.[17]

Still, radical politics is hardly what this or the second "Jordan" poem is about. If anything, "Jordan [I]" wrestles with the problem of retrieving a place for authentic devotion in a genre that had highly politicized associations in the Renaissance, while "Jordan [II]" (originally entitled "Invention" in the Williams manuscript) re-examines, even more scrupulously, matters of intention in attempting to distinguish a mistaken form of copia – narcissistic, self-involved, and showy – from true copy:

As flames do work and winde, when they ascend,
So did I weave my self into the sense.
But while I bustled, I might heare a friend
Whisper, How wide is all this long pretence!
There is in love a sweetnesse readie penn'd:
Copie out onely that, and save expense.

For a poet as conscious as Herbert of out-courting the courtly (and few critics fail to cite the Sidneyan "sources" in *Astrophel and Stella* underlying this poem), the revision of the weak final rhyme from "preparation / alteration" in the Williams manuscript to "long pretence" / "save expense," is not only typical of how Herbert pared away baggy abstractions and made his diction more emphatic and resonant; it also brings the act of re-amateurizing the lyric to its absolute genteel conclusion. For a moment one can almost imagine Suckling taking up the call.

On the other hand, expanding the linguistic and artistic boundaries of what might be acceptable poetry (and by implication, who might be an acceptable poet) was a matter of special concern to Herbert. "A True Hymn," that most consciously definitional of poems in *The Temple*, seeks to extend the possibilities for plain speaking well beyond those endorsed in the two "Jordan" poems, with their courtly setting.

> My joy, my life, my crown!
> My heart was meaning all the day,
>   Somewhat it fain would say:
> And still it runneth mutt'ring up and down
> With onely this, My joy, my life, my crown.
>
> Yet slight not these few words:
>   If truly said, they may take part
>   Among the best in art.
> The finenesse which a hymne or psalme affords,
> Is, when the soul unto the lines accords.
>
> He who craves all the minde,
>   And all the soul, and strength, and time,
>   If the words onely ryme,
> Justly complains, that somewhat is behinde
> To make his verse, or write a hymne in kinde.
>
> Whereas if th'heart be moved,
>   Although the verse be somewhat scant,
>   God doth supplie the want.
> As when th'heart sayes (sighing to be approved)
> O, could I love! and stops: God writeth, Loved.

We ought to note that it is a measure of Herbert's artistry that he can represent the barely intelligible and slightly ludicrous mutterings of the heart without slipping into mere buffoonery and thus compromise the essential message of sincerity that the poem approves. For in this poem, the primary judge of art and the only recipient imagined is God, who is represented as having not only the final word but doing so in the manner of someone supplying a final imprimatur for the poem itself.[18] But the poem is also anything but severe in either its judgments or its representations of acceptable speech – its own polyvocalism. Between the heart's mutterings and God's writing, there is, even for Herbert, an unusually wide range of verbal possibilities and different voices admitted into this poem. Subvocal sounds emerge as if part of a fully internalized musical round ("My joy, my life, my crown") rather than as separate fragments from individual psalms. Then, from humming, we move to hymning through an allusion to a more public kind of worship that is, nonetheless, part of a knowledgeable address about genres ("Yet slight not ... "). This address includes imagining God ("He")[19] as not merely demanding but "complaining" or more accurately "justly complaining," as the speaker intercedes to defend God's reaction, and asks us to hear indirectly God's thinking (which sounds like muttering, though of a slightly different order than the heart's). The final stanza then begins as if it is going to be a dictum of sorts but then quickly flattens out into a homespun proverb ("Although the verse be somewhat scant, / God doth supplie the want") on its way to a conclusion that asks us to witness a hypothetical drama ("as when"), in which we are introduced not to one but to two further modes of mediation, sighing and writing. As with "Prayer I," Herbert clearly saw "A True Hymn" as an opportunity not to delimit but to stretch our sense of the acceptable. So long as the speaker's intention is to love, then a word as prosaic as "somewhat" need not be scrubbed from the text.

* * *

"A sweetnesse ready penned," the heart's muttering, even the plain saying of "*but thou shalt answer, Lord for me*" or "*My God, My king*": these sentiments identify a poet keenly alert to spelling out the difference between being virtuous and being a virtuoso with art in the manner of the "rhetorical courtings" of a "never Mark Anthony" or an admiring Lovelace in "Gratiana dauncing and singing." "My musick shows ye have your closes" – a line from a poem often set to music ("Vertue") – points to the edifying impulse that often chastens luxury into love in *The Temple* and helps to authenticate devotion. But Herbert would be less interesting (and finally less persuasive as a religious poet) if the choices were simple or always the same. If he was conscious of the need to work *through* courtly forms, as many have argued, he did so in order to go beyond them; if he understood that the way to the simple was by way of the intricate, that beneath the pattern lies the heart, as we discover in "The Church-floor," patterns, verbal as well as visual, were still immensely important and attractive to him. No poem in the seventeenth century, perhaps no poem in English, makes a greater demand on the need for rhyme than "Deniall":

> When my devotions could not pierce
> Thy silent eares;
> Then was my heart broken, as was my verse:
> My heart was full of fears
> And disorder.

Or makes a more enchanting case for rhyme's answering call:

> O cheer and tune my heartlesse breast,
> Deferre no time;
> That so thy favours granting my request,
> They and my minde may chime,
> And mend my ryme.

And few poems can match the virtuosity of "Vertue" in creating a compact allegory of sound. The most seductive rhythms lead to the grave, but not until they are allowed to linger in the ear while the sweetness of each is seasoned in the penultimate line and refrain of each stanza, and then again at the end where the sexual connotations of "die" are absorbed into the restrained – and restraining – final line:

> Sweet day, so cool, so calm, so bright,
> The bridall of the earth and skie:
> The dew shall weep thy fall to night;
> > For thou must die.
>
> Sweet rose, whose hue angrie and brave
> Bids the rash gazer wipe his eye:
> Thy root is ever in its grave,
> > And thou must die.
>
> Sweet spring, full of sweet dayes and roses,
> A box where sweets compacted lie;
> My musick shows ye have your closes,
> > And all must die.
>
> Only a sweet and vertuous soul,
> Like season'd timber, never gives;
> But though the whole world turn to coal,
> > Then chiefly lives.

The most taxing tightrope walk with "Beauty and beauteous words" belongs, however, to the poem in which that phrase occurs. In "The Forerunners," the elegiac enters into the poem and nearly seizes the day – nearly but not quite. The poem differs from the others we have been considering in its meditative reach: the ebb and flow of passions and the comprehensive assessment of a religious poet's relation to language – "Lovely enchanting language, sugar-cane, / Honey of roses." Whereas "The Quip" and the two Jordan poems focus on drawing boundaries between secular and devotional utterances, "The Forerunners" begins by defining the difference and then turns to emphasizing the responsive, potentially trespassing heart that, like the prodigal son, wanders a bit before returning home – away from and then back to the talismanic phrase borrowed from Scripture that ultimately lights the way to a place "within livelier then before."

Although the poem has been suggestively compared to Yeats's "The Circus Animal's Desertion,"[20] the mixture in Herbert of urgent sentiment and stoic resolve does not issue from personal anxiety over what the author might or might not write in the future but from what has been already written and must now be left behind. The more relevant context is the more immediate one: Donne's several great valedictory hymns, "Upon the Author's going into

Germany" and "A Hymn to my God, my God in my Sicknesse," as sources for the grave flourish of wit on the way to God's room, and the more humanizing tradition renewed by Jonson in the epigram "On his Son" and replayed through poets as diverse as Herrick ("To his Verses") and Anne Bradstreet ("The Author to her Book"), in which poetry assumes a privileged place in the universe through its intimate, familial relation with its creator. With only some hyperbole, Helen Vendler has suggested that the poem "defies commentary";[21] it certainly bears quoting in full:

The harbingers are come. See, see their mark;
White is their colour, and behold my head.
But must they have my brain? must they dispark
Those sparkling notions, which therein were bred?
       Must dulnesse turn me to a clod?
Yet have they left me, *Thou art still my God.*

Good men ye be, to leave me my best room,
Ev'n all my heart, and what is lodged there:
I passe not, I, what of the rest become,
So *Thou art still my God,* be out of fear.
       He will be pleased with that dittie;
And if I please him, I write fine and wittie.

Farewell sweet phrases, lovely metaphors.
But will ye leave me thus? when ye before
Of stews and brothels onely knew the doores,
Then did I wash you with my tears, and more,
       Brought you to Church well drest and clad:
My God must have my best, ev'n all I had.

Lovely enchanting language, sugar-cane,
Honey of roses, whither wilt thou flie?
Hath some fond lover tic'd thee to thy bane?
And wilt thou leave the Church, and love a stie?
       Fie, thou wilt soil thy broider'd coat,
And hurt thy self, and him that sings the note.

Let foolish lovers, if they will love dung,
With canvas, not with aras, clothe their shame:
Let follie speak in her own native tongue.
True beautie dwells on him: Ours is a flame
       But borrow'd thence to light us thither.
Beautie and beauteous words should go together.

Yet if you go, I passe not; take your way:
For, *Thou art still my God,* is all that ye

149

Perhaps with more embellishment can say.
Go birds of spring: let winter have his fee;
   Let a bleak palenesse chalk the doore,
So all within be livelier then before.

Had Herbert somehow written only the first stanza, the poem would have been theologically neat, even profoundly compelling. As commentators have noted, the italicized phrase, *"Thou art still my God,"* is borrowed almost whole-sale from a line in Psalm 31, a psalm referred to in the authorized version of the Bible as "A Prayer in Calamity"; and recourse to the psalm only further rein-forces our sense of the climactic positioning of the scriptural phrase at the end of the stanza. In the psalm, the line reads as a Job-like cry of triumph amid adversities of many kind: "But I trusted in thee, O Lord: I said, Thou art my God." Herbert's addition of "still" (meaning "always") strengthens the vow. Indeed, it places the speaker in a Davidic tradition of sufferers who have resisted persecution by affirming their faith. Although Herbert has chosen to tone down the calamitous note of the psalm, he has heightened the drama – our sense of his being in imminent danger – by opening abruptly with an allusion to harbingers, who make their portentous appearance in a phrase whose verb tense is marked by the present perfect, the eternal present, we might suspect.

Whatever they signify, these servants who come before a royal progress and yet leave marks on doors reminiscent of those indicating a plague, they have come to stay. But though keen, the suspense is brief. Once the italicized line is uttered, we know that the attack on the head (and the slightly outlandish puns emanating from the speaker's sparkling wit) has not caused Herbert to lose his bearings. If he is led to think of himself as a clod – the earthen stuff of which Adam was made – that admission carries with it a recognition of his maker; and the final line emerges not so much as a defiant cry as a quiet reminder to himself of an inevitable fact: "Yet have they left me, *Thou art still my God.*" God is more than an answering rhyme for "clod," but he is that, too.

But if Herbert had written no more than the first stanza, "The Forerunners" would be also less interesting. We are used to thinking of Herbert as a poet of patterns, a master of the categories of rhetoric and dialectic so prized by Renaissance poets, but the remainder of "The Forerunners" reads more like a loose essay in verse than a rigorous argument in rhyme: a kind of trial, not in the strenuous Miltonic sense of being a trial by what is contrary (that honor is better reserved for "The Quip"), but in the essaying sense of someone who knows where he is going but still needs to settle his personal estate: "Ev'n all my heart, and what is lodged there." The "best room" that holds the image of God has room for other sentiments as well.

In the stanzas that follow, Herbert slowly disengages himself from the subject of writing through writing. The contingencies needing to be played out – exor-cized is too strong a word – and released are all emotional: tears of farewell that remind the poet of his original efforts to baptize profane language and, like a proud parent, to bring it to Church "well drest and clad"; shades of jealousy over the prospect of being abandoned ("Fie, thou wilt soil thy broider'd coat"); then a last-ditch effort to salvage what is apparently his by forcefully separating the profane from the sacred and taking the Platonic high road: "Ours is a flame / But borrow'd thence to light us thither. / Beautie and beauteous words should go together." Although highly dramatic, nothing seems staged. Herbert's emotions are too close to the surface; the subject of poetry is too much a life-long concern to be given anything less than a full hearing. But even more so is another. Way back in "The Dedication" to *The Temple*, Herbert had begun: "Lord, my first fruits present themselves to thee; / Yet not mine neither; for from thee they came, / And must return." The desire by Herbert to claim authorship is almost instinctive, and is one of the decisive trademarks of his being a poet in the early seventeenth century; but so too is Herbert's priestly admission that he is merely an agent enabling the circulation of language to honor the ultimate Creator. One recognition follows quickly upon the other in a dialectical motion that, as Stanley Fish has argued, runs deep through *The Temple*.[22]

"The Forerunners" slows down this motion. It plays with this pause, opening, as it were, the seams of a poetic career for possible inspection; but where a Jonson could not imagine saying "farewell" without leaving a sign of himself in print, where a Herrick and a Bradstreet write farewells that imagine prospective readers, Herbert's musings, unsettling and tempting as they are, yield only a closing wave: "Yet if you go, I passe not," a phrase that marks his release from the lure of a paternal, blood connection to his verse – there is only one Father in his universe – and from a parental desire to determine the future of his offspring. By the end, "lovely enchanting language" too is dismissed with a wave: "Go birds of spring"; and the "perhaps," over which so much ink has been spilt, remains the only sign of an earlier infatuation: shifting in emphasis with each reading (or reader), as a reminder of both the rewards and the sacrifices of writing devotional poetry, but ultimately irrelevant to the harbinger's call except as a fee that must be paid if all "within [is to] be livelier then before." In the end, Herbert gets off the fence on the side we knew all along that he would. What we had not anticipated is how severely he would challenge our place as readers of poetry.

* * *

By all rights, a discussion of Herbert should end with "The Forerunners." What more can be said? But Herbert did not allow this poem to be the last word. (In the next poem, he is, once again, busy defining the distance that separates himself from the world.) Nor should we. For however far Herbert takes us in the direction of silence in "The Forerunners" and elsewhere in *The Temple*, however attractive the reflexive dimension of *The Temple* has proven to be to modern readers, indeed however central Herbert made the act of writing poetry to the devotional experience, what we also remember – perhaps most remember – about *The Temple* are sounds, not merely those suggested on the title page in the respectful quotation from Psalm 29, "in his temple doth every man speak of his honour," but the uncensored sounds of the heart in full motion. Expressions of unutterable grief that still manage to get spoken:

> Oh all ye, who passe by, whose eyes and minde
> To worldly things are sharp, but to me blinde;
> To me, who took eyes that I might you finde:
> > > Was ever grief like mine?
> > > > > > ("The Sacrifice")

Of joy that seems to have no business being:

> And now in age I bud again,
> After so many deaths I live and write;
> I once more smell the dew and rain,
> And relish versing: O my onely light,
> > > It cannot be
> > > That I am he
> On whom thy tempests fell all night.
> > > > > > ("The Flower")

Of absolute rebellion that proves eventually not to be absolute:

> I struck the board, and cry'd, No more.
> > > I will abroad.
> What? shall I ever sigh and pine?
> My lines and life are free; free as the rode,
> Loose as the winde, as large as store.
> > > Shall I be still in suit?
> > > > > > ("The Collar")

Of a jingle that contains a magical tincture for all:

> All may of thee partake:
> Nothing can be so mean,
> Which with this tincture (for thy sake)
> Will not grow bright and clean.
> > > > > > ("The Elixir")

Of complete helplessness:

> Ah my deare God! though I am clean forgot,
> Let me not love thee, if I love thee not.
> > > > > > ("Affliction" [I])

And of complete happiness:

> How sweetly doth My *Master* sound! *My Master!*
>   As Amber-greese leaves a rich sent
>   Unto the taster:
>   So do these words a sweet content,
> An orientall fragrancie, *My Master*.

("The Odour")

In moments like these, we glimpse Herbert's extraordinary power as a lyricist: how in "The Sacrifice," for instance, the experience of suffering, with its excruciatingly severe ironies, never deviates into bathos, or why gratitude seems beyond feigning. Without ever trying to sound complex – in contrast to Donne, the printer does not cast the reader as an "understander" – Herbert rarely comes across as merely simple, and yet the desire for simplicity, for arriving at the core of being, is so explicit in these utterances as to be palpable. Herbert is not a philosophical poet, if we mean by that term a poet primarily interested in ideas, as Emerson perhaps wished him to be.[23] But few poets have thought more deeply about the self in relation to another, and fewer still have been able to convey that experience more directly and from as many directions. When Herbert writes at the end of "The Flower," "These are thy wonders, Lord of Love, / To make us see we are but flowers that glide," we do not doubt his sincerity, but we owe what we "see" in this poem to Herbert.

We remember, too, the narratives – the many stories in *The Temple* and their odd tellers: the afflicted but resourceful speller of "Jesu," who discovers the homonymic "ease" within the name of Jesus; the garrulous and benighted speaker of "Love Unknown," whose "long and sad" tale would appear to be a test of patience for the master himself/ and the Bottom-like tenant farmer of "Redemption" who resolves not to be left out of a scene that seems still well beyond his understanding, and yet get there he does.

> Having been tenant long to a rich Lord,
>   Not thriving, I resolved to be bold,
>   And make a suit unto him, to afford
> A new small-rented lease, and cancell th'old.
> In heaven at his manour I him sought:
>   They told me there, that he was lately gone
>   About some land, which he had dearly bought
> Long since on earth, to take possession.
> I straight return'd, and knowing his great birth,
>   Sought him accordingly in great resorts;
>   In cities, theatres, gardens, parks, and courts:
> At length I heard a ragged noise and mirth
>   Of theeves and murderers: there I him espied,
>   Who straight, *Your suit is granted*, said, & died.

Although primarily a lyricist, a poet of "private ejaculations," as the 1633 title page suggests, Herbert was also probably the finest teller of stories in verse in the seventeenth century. In "Redemption," we understand exactly why Herbert valued "stories and sayings" for their educative value: as memorial aids superior to exhortation.[24] Long after we have forgotten the particular route – bizarre as it is – that has brought this tenant farmer to Calvary, we will continue to remember the reward of resolve because the plot and the final saying are so completely punctuated: *"Your suit is granted*, said, & died." In this drastically foreshortened poem, there is no time for reflection by the speaker, no time to pause in front of the crucifixion and to meditate, no time even for a reply. Getting there then – and now – is what counts.

And, of course, we remember the final lyric of "The Church," "Love [III]": not because it is last (getting there is only just a beginning) or even because, coming after a sequence on the Four Last Things ("Death," "Dooms-day," "Judgment," and "Heaven"), it invites us to imagine the soul's reception into heaven, as astonishing as that action is; but because after so many abbreviated exchanges between Christ and the various speakers in *The Temple*, exchanges that have been rendered cryptically (as in "Redemption") or correctively (as in "Jordan [II]") or as part of a formal dialogue that is theologically unsatisfying to the speaker ("A Dialogue"), we are suddenly and finally treated to the fullest representation in language of a dialogue that has always been at the desired center of *The Temple*. In "Love [III]," the earlier "whispers" and "methoughts" give way to table talk of the most profound order:

> Love bade me welcome: yet my soul drew back,
>> Guilty of dust and sinne.
> But quick-eye'd Love, observing me grow slack
>> From my first entrance in,
> Drew nearer to me, sweetly questioning,
>> If I lack'd any thing.
>
> A guest, I answer'd, worthy to be here:
>> Love said, You shall be he.
> I the unkinde, ungratefull? Ah my deare,
>> I cannot look on thee.
> Love took my hand, and smiling did reply,
>> Who made the eyes but I?
>
> Truth Lord, but I have marr'd them: let my shame
>> Go where it doth deserve.
> And know you not, sayes Love, who bore the blame:
>> My Deare, then I will serve.
> You must sit down, sayes Love, and taste my meat:
>> So I did sit and eat.

The massive grief of "The Sacrifice" melts away like snow in May and leaves only the finest of verbal traces in the pun on "eyes" and in the breathtaking understatement regarding the consequences of the crucifixion: "And know you not, sayes Love, who bore the blame." In pointed contrast to "Love Unknown," this is a speaker who needs only to be reminded of the truth; he does not require being shocked into another zone of reality. Nor do his replies seem as potentially self-promoting as recourse to the courtesy literature of the period might suggest. If that literature helps us to understand both the process and power of social advancement as negotiated through the discursive forms and codes of behavior relevant to a highly stratified society, it falls short of being able to account for how one might respond when addressed not by a "Lord" or even "The Lord" but by "Love" – "quick-eye'd" and dextrous in every sense: "Love took my hand and smiling did reply." In this most hospitable of poems, in which as James Merrill, the most courtly of American poets, has remarked, "the two characters are being ravishingly polite to each other," Herbert is careful to establish at the outset the spontaneous response of the soul.[25] Surprised by a wave of the most casual order, it is momentarily disarmed: "Love bade me welcome; yet my soul drew back." Were it being welcomed to Penshurst Place, one can imagine that Herbert might, like Jonson, have felt free to survey the estate, to hold it in his gaze, but in "Love III" the "doxa" of God is enshrined by the hesitation and the veil is, as it were, pierced only by talk. In "Love [III]," communion is not quite holy, but nowhere in *The Temple* are we closer to thinking that speech alone has that capacity.

6

THE ONCE AND FUTURE POET
Milton in the 1645 *Poems*

Anno Domini 1619 he was ten years old, as by his picture, and was
then a poet.
>   John Aubrey, *"Brief Lives": Chiefly of his Contemporaries*

Milton never learned the art of doing little things with grace.
>   Samuel Johnson, "The Life of Milton"

The road from *The Temple* led in many directions: to Devonshire, to Wales, to
New England, eventually even to Rome itself in the person of Richard Crashaw.
But Herbert seems to have made little or no impression on the London-born poet
who, in 1645, published his first collection of verse and, though his main energies
were then going into writing prose, laid claim to being England's greatest living
poet. "As true a Birth, as the Muses have brought forth since our famous Spencer
wrote" is how the bookseller Humphrey Moseley advertised John Milton's emergence as a poet. By 1645, the thirty-six year old Milton could hardly be trumpeted
as a discovery, which the enterprising Moseley no doubt knew. Milton had
recently attracted attention (mostly negative) for his radical defense of divorce
on grounds other than adultery in four learned and passionately argued
pamphlets known collectively as "The Divorce Tracts," and these were published
during an eighteen-month spree from August 1643 to March 1645 that also
included the appearance of the now more famous *Areopagitica* in November 1644.
And before that, Milton had written a number of pamphlets denouncing the
tyrannical yoke of prelacy and urging England to bring to fruition many of the
purifying ideals of the early Reformation. The decision to publish his verse with
the innocuous, though distinctly genteel, title of *Poems* was, in Thomas Corns's
words, in part a bid for respectability amid the heated controversies.[1]

But it was more than that, too. In a peculiar but startling way, history had
caught up with some of the poems: their vatic energies now sometimes assume a
strange prophetic connection to contemporary events in a manner that the
sagacious Wither might have admired. Milton had only to add to the headnote
to "Lycidas" the phrase, "and by occasion foretells the ruin of our Corrupted

Clergy then in their height," to make a poem originally written and published in 1637 seem more pointed and relevant in 1645, more uncanny and prescient, both as a political statement and as a work of art. And even if it is difficult to prove that Lovelace's Grasshopper Ode forms a specific response to Milton's Nativity Ode by putting the pagan back into Christmas, Milton's poem, although written in 1629, could easily be read in 1645 as a commentary on, almost a brief history of, the conflicts between Puritans and Laudians, conflicts in which the episcopal clergy had been routed from their offices like the pagan deities in Milton's poem. By 1645, the kingly babe that Milton celebrates in the Nativity Ode – muscular, militant, surrounded by bright-harnessed guardian angels – would not be readily confused with the effete monarch still sitting on the English throne but unable to do anything about the doomed fate of his Archbishop preparing to be executed on January 8, 1645.

In the context of the rapidly unfolding events beginning in the late 1630s and continuing through the 1640s, it is hardly surprising that Herbert should occupy little or no place in the mind of a controversialist who spoke of himself in *The Reason of Church Government* (1642) as having been "church-outed by the Prelates."[2] On whatever side Herbert might have eventually landed in the great debates of the 1640s – he died six months before Laud was made Archbishop in 1633 – at a superficial level, at least, *The Temple* had been conscripted by Laudians in the late 1630s. Christopher Harvey's pale but partisan "imitation," entitled *The Synagogue: Or, The Shadow of The Temple,* appeared in 1641 and was frequently bound with Herbert's poems in later editions. And the high-church Crashaw was soon to publish his *Steps to the Temple* in 1646 (also brought out by Moseley in conjunction with *Delights of the Muses*). But it is the case, too, that had the younger Milton read Herbert even while at Cambridge – they missed overlapping by a little more than a year – he would not have found Herbert a congenial poetic model. Diction sometimes as spare as a stone, stanzas of dazzling intricacy and wit, a conception of subjectivity that finds fulfillment (and stability) only in God, and a view of worship that stresses the centrality of the Eucharist: these are primary religious and aesthetic values for Herbert but not for the later poet who, according to his own testimony in *Poems*, "at fifteen years old" paraphrased two Psalms (114 and 136), and, in the process of paraphrasing, recast a phrase from the authorized version like "Ye mountains that ye skipped like rams, and ye little hills, like lambs" as "the high, huge-bellied Mountains skip like Rams / Amongst their Ewes, the little Hills like Lambs."

It is not simply that the youthful, adjectival excess, the verbal expansion so characteristic of Milton's thinking more generally, would have burst the rhetorical seams of *The Temple*. Very little here would have fit into Herbert's decorous house: neither the superscription identifying the author's age at the time of composition, nor the subject of the Psalm itself celebrating Israel's triumphant deliverance out of Egypt (Herbert, characteristically, chose to paraphrase the quieter Psalm 23), nor the exuberant erotics apparent in Milton's decision to gender the landscape by adding "Ewes" to the Biblical original and then to make them the Rams' mates, their possession. High and huge-bellied, as if about to give birth, the mountain seems almost a fanciful projection of poetic expectation. And yet, of course, Milton would also become, broadly speaking, the other great religious poet of the seventeenth century, the eventual author of *Paradise Lost* (1667), *Paradise Regained* (1671), and *Samson Agonistes* (1671).

As Moseley recognized, Milton's initial collection ought to be read not in light of Herbert but Spenser, "whose Poems in these English ones are as rarely imitated, as Sweetly excell'd." There is some irony in Moseley's proclaiming a patriotic love of "our own language" as a chief reason to publish a collection of verse as conspicuously cosmopolitan as Milton's: the neo-Latin poetry constitutes an important "half" of the volume, as Stella Revard has recently emphasized, the two forming a "double book" describing Milton's sophisticated literary aspirations.[3] But Moseley's notion of Milton's imitating and excelling, indeed his notion of Milton's "sweetly" excelling the work of another English poet remembered especially for his long unfinished epic, is right on target. It points to Milton's ambitious musicality, to the varied but fruitful courtship of "Voice and Verse" – to quote from "At a Solemn Music" – that is inspirationally central to the collection as a whole and one of the chief features differentiating it from its many Caroline counterparts. Here, for instance, is Milton in the poem alluded to above. Composed when he was about twenty-five, it is short enough to quote in full and yet, in its upward phrasal sweep and grandly suspended clause, seemingly resistant to notions of closure. It is probably only right, too, that a first quotation from Milton should be from a work with "solemn" in the title. The word means both "serious" and "dignified," retaining its earlier associations with the sacred and the ceremonial but now given, in the poem, an apocalyptic emphasis, especially in the image of the saints singing around the bejeweled throne (a fusion of Ezekiel 1: 26 with Revelation 14: 3–4) and in the splendid, concluding alexandrine:

> Blest pair of *Sirens*, pledges of Heav'n's joy,
> Sphere-born harmonious Sisters, Voice and Verse,
> Wed your divine sounds, and mixt power employ
> Dead things with inbreath'd sense able to pierce,
> And to our high-rais'd fantasy present
> That undisturbed Song of pure concent,
> Aye sung before the sapphire-color'd throne
> To him that sits thereon,
> With Saintly shout and solemn Jubilee,
> Where the bright Seraphim in burning row
> Their loud uplifted Angel-trumpets blow,
> And the Cherubic host in thousand choirs
> Touch their immortal Harps of golden wires,
> With those just Spirits that wear victorious Palms,

Hymns devout and holy Psalms
Singing everlastingly;
That we on Earth with undiscording voice
May rightly answer that melodious noise;
As once we did, till disproportion'd sin
Jarr'd against nature's chime, and with harsh din
Broke the fair music that all creatures made
To their great Lord, whose love their motion sway'd
In perfect Diapason, whilst they stood
In first obedience and their state of good.
O may we soon again renew that Song,
And keep in tune with Heav'n, till God ere long
To his celestial consort us unite,
To live with him, and sing in endless morn of light.

As a verbal performance intended to capture a sense of the religious uplift associated with singing at its most sublime, the poem is a *tour de force*. Phrase seemingly grows out of phrase, sound out of sound, in the manner of a single sustained, spontaneous utterance – a poem very much composed by someone with music in his blood, not just in his head. (Milton's father, writes Aubrey, was "an ingenious man, delighted in music, [and] composed many songs now in print, especially that of Oriana.")[4] And yet, of course, the poem is highly artful in structure. The double octave of the first sixteen lines, imagined as being sung in heaven, is "answered" by a diminished half in the single octave as sung on earth, with the transition occurring when "the high-rais'd fantasy" seems, in fact, at its highest pitch: the moment when the phrase "Singing everlastingly" toys with the fantasy of the voice being released altogether from the bondage of rhyme. Rhyming "everlastingly" with "Jubilee," seven lines earlier, represents the greatest stretch in a poem otherwise written exclusively in couplets or alternating rhyme; and, to some degree, in this suspension, we can even glimpse the history of Milton's evolution as a poet: the full shift to "Singing everlastingly," or nearly so, being realized in the great blank verse of *Paradise Lost*. But even in this instance, it is difficult not to feel – and the emotive verb is deliberately chosen – the energy of the Miltonic line at work, and with it, the expressive power of voice as an efficacious means to make something happen: in this case, to bring in a future of endless singing. If "power ceases in the instant of repose," as Emerson once said, Milton concludes by imagining his way around this problem altogether.[5]

A contemporary coming upon "At a Solemn Music" in a bookstall in 1645 would not, of course, have the benefit of a "long" view of this poem or the volume as a whole and therefore would not be able to spot the acorns from which the later oaks would eventually grow: not simply the blank verse of the later epics emerging between the rhymes, but how, for instance, in "At a Solemn Music" the image of God's creatures standing in "obedience" in their state of good, able to sing in "perfect Diapason" to their "Lord," anticipates the perfect harmony of Adam and Eve before the fall in *Paradise Lost*; or even more subtly at a structural level the uncanny way in which, exactly three-quarters of the way through this poem (in line 21 of 28), the "fair music" is broken, just as in the epic paradise is lost three-quarters of the way through the poem (in book 9 of the 12 in the 1674 edition). Nor would that contemporary be in a position to chart the many concerns elsewhere in the volume as they reappear in ampli-fied form down the road: the silencing of the pagan oracles in the Nativity Ode and the expulsion of the fallen angels from heaven in *Paradise Lost*; the tempta-tion of the Lady in *A Mask* and the temptation of Jesus in *Paradise Regained*; the personal anxiety expressed over vocational direction in the sonnet written in his twenty-third year, "How soon hath time," and Samson's incessant worries over his calling in *Samson Agonistes*.

One could go on almost indefinitely reading the later verse in light of this first collection, refining points of connection, noting major and minor alterna-tions and expansions, and eventually confirming, in retrospect, a view of this volume as evidence of "The Rising Poet" – to quote the title of Louis Martz's still influential essay[6] – with "Lycidas" being accorded a climactic place in this scenario. English poetry's greatest iconoclast is also a poet of great continuity. (The repeated adjective seems unavoidable.) And a "long view" ensures, in turn, not just the lyrical Milton, but his first collection of verse, a unique place in literary history. No poet's "juvenilia" from the seventeenth century – to borrow Samuel Johnson's barely adequate description of early Milton up through *Poems*[7] – indeed, perhaps no poet's "juvenilia" in English has seemed so substantial an indication not simply of future promise (a theme Milton reiter-ated in the prose from his middle years when he was writing little poetry) but of present accomplishment as well.

In all likelihood, however, a contemporary reader's first response to Milton's *Poems* would not have been one of simple admiration but one of puzzled surprise. It might have even included irritation over a sense of entrapment by the venturesome Moseley for luring customers with a title page nearly identical in appearance to the one the publisher had just used for another Caroline look-alike: the best-selling *Poems* by Edmund Waller, which went through three editions in 1645 alone. (Copies of Milton's would remain unsold into the Restoration.) The resemblances on the title page continue in the references in each to the "Songs set in Musick by Mr. Henry Lawes Gentleman of the Kings Chappel, and one of his Majesties Private" musicians. But appearances are deceiving. Milton's "book" is no more accurately represented by its Caroline cover than the author himself by the accompanying engraving by William Marshall. (Milton ridiculed the portrait in Greek verse placed just below the engraving.) Where Waller's *Poems* follows the formula for genteel verse almost to the letter, Milton's, beginning with the truculent verse in Greek under his own portrait, questions conventional displays of geniality almost from the start. Waller's collection is nothing if not *à la mode*. One gets the news, with a strong royalist slant; occasional poems on the king abound – on his whereabouts, his activities, his escapades – and are placed first. Milton's is anything but *au courant*. The closest one comes to reportage is in a few untitled sonnets almost buried in the middle of the English poetry like "Captain or Colonel, or Knight in Arms"; and while there are two "kings" in Milton, neither bears the name of Charles, although together they form the alpha and the omega of the English verse: one celebrates the birth of Jesus, Heaven's King, the other mourns the death of Milton's friend, Edward King. For Waller, moreover, the occasion of poetry allows him to maneuver among the rich and famous, writing amatory poems and songs, including the famous "Go, lovely rose." Milton, by contrast, chooses his poetic moments carefully, even confessing, in the case of "The Passion," when a subject was "above" his years. Dedicating his verse to Lady Dorothy Sidney, Waller thought of his collection as representing his "whole vintage": "I staid till the latest Grapes were ripe, for here your ladyship hath not onely all I have done, but all I ever mean to do in this kind." Wine in itself is neither good nor bad in Milton, although it becomes the special preserve of the evil Comus. But it also hardly represents the sole source of Milton's inspiration. Inspiration comes, too, from dedicating oneself to the muse, who can be sometimes "heavenly," sometimes coy and enticing, and even sometimes "thankless," but rarely is she ever simply or easily exhausted, as the long poems in this first volume make especially clear.

The genial Waller and the budding genius Milton: both are on display in 1645, the one very much of the moment, indeed rounding off the verse with a few samples of his "speeches" before Parliament, the other concluding his English verse with the ambitious *Mask* "Presented at Ludlow Castle" and a sizable selection of Neolatin poetry that places him among an international literati. There is no evidence to sustain a view that Milton was stimulated into print in specific response to Waller, although reactive habits are elsewhere a feature of his prose and no more so than when confronting a royalist text like *Eikon Basilike*. But in publishing his *Poems* he was, at the very least, making partial payment on an implied debt in *The Reason of Church Government*, where claiming to "covenant" with "any knowing reader," he had promised some day a work not "to be raised from the heat of youth, or the vapours of wine, like that which flows at waste from the pen of some vulgar amorist." And quite possibly in making this partial payment in 1645, he was, as it were, providing a corollary proof to his argument in *The Reason of Church Government* that "no free and splendid wit can flourish" under the "impertinent yoke of prelaty." In 1645, "prelaty" was no longer, and even Milton had yet to call presbyters new priests "writ large."

* * *

"Compos'd at several times," according to the title page, Milton's early poems do not belong to a single historical moment or place. They can be courtly but

161

are not of the court, pastoral without being provincial, rooted in Protestant fervor and classical mythology alike: the work of Joanni Miltoni Londinensi who is also at home when abroad. The earliest are probably the paraphrases of the two psalms, written around 1623, when Donne was composing several of his hymns and Wither was publishing his translation of the psalter; the latest are several of the "occasional" sonnets, with their Civil War settings and allusions. At the very least, the fluid and spacious chronology makes impossible a single capsule view of the author, as does the range of subject matter and genre. If Spenser is an important influence in the early verse, he is hardly Milton's sole literary companion, a point made both with regard to individual poems selected for inclusion and within some of the poems themselves, like those remarkable twin surveys of (among other things) the poetic landscape placed midway through the English verse: "L'Allegro" and "Il Penseroso." As the scholarly literature on Milton amply indicates, there is, in the early poems, a Jonsonian Milton, especially in the finely chiseled, decorously respectful "Epitaph on the Marchioness of Winchester," which begins:

> This rich Marble doth inter
> The honor'd Wife of *Winchester*,
> A Viscount's daughter, an Earl's heir
> Besides what her virtues fair
> Addes to her noble birth,
> More than she could own from Earth.

There is a Shakespearean Milton, most evident in the sixteen-line epigram he supplied for the Second Folio (1630), indicative already of Milton's fascination with the affective power of the book:

> Thou in our wonder and astonishment
> Hast built thyself a livelong Monument.

There is a Petrarchan Milton, capable of even writing in the original Italian:

> Donna leggiadra, il cui bel nome onora
> L'erbosa val di Reno, e il nobil varco
> (Gentle and beautiful Lady, whose fair name
> honors the verdant valley of Reno and the glorious ford).

There is a pastoralist of the English country-side in the manner of William Browne:

> Hard by, a Cottage chimney smokes,
> From betwixt two aged Oaks,
> Where *Corydon* and *Thyrsis* met,

Are at their savory dinner set
Of Herbs, and other Country Messes,
Which the neat-handed *Phillis* dresses.

("L'Allegro," ll. 81–6)

And there is an epigrammatist of the familiar ("On the University Carrier") and an experimenter with short odes on sacred topics ("On Time" and "Upon the Circumcision"). The last mentioned hints at overlapping interests connecting early Milton with his slightly younger Cambridge colleague, Richard Crashaw, a link that has sometimes allowed both a place under that wide European umbrella known as the Baroque.

What keeps the collection from being strictly courtly or mannerist in its samplings is also, paradoxically, something that led Milton to abandon poetry almost altogether in his middle years: a sense of an event or occasion as more than an incident in the ongoing history of an individual life or culture. For whatever different personal reasons – later the "causes" will be more overtly public and include politically controversial issues like divorce, censorship, and regicide – the birthday of Jesus, turning twenty-three, the comparative entice-ments of the active and the contemplative lives, an opportunity to entertain nobility, the death of a Cambridge classmate: these subjects or occasions proved an irresistible challenge to Milton and were of an order quite different from those involving, say, the circumcision of Jesus or a song on a May morning. And if the poems associated with each seem almost random in the aggregate – and especially perplexing for being so – they were important in the particular, each springing from a different moment in time and set of circumstances, and requiring of Milton a different set of responses, a different kind of "song." As Michael Wilding has recently observed, registering some disappointment over the near-absence of a politically radical poet in this first collection of verse, "the dominant concern is poetry itself and the pursuit of the proper subject of poetry."[8] With another poet, this potentially narcissistic angle might signal a disabling limitation at the outset. But with Milton, it usually marks, emphati-cally, a new beginning, a new way of imagining the past and the future, and the self-balancing that accompanies sustained creative acts.

"On the Morning of Christ's Nativity"

"I am singing the starry sky and the hosts that sang high in air, and the gods that were suddenly destroyed in their own shrines," wrote Milton in the month and year of his twenty-first birthday to his friend Charles Diodati. Scholars usually associate these remarks with "The Ode on the Morning of Christ's Nativity," "compos'd 1629," as Milton notes in *Poems*. But these comments and the few others Milton made in the letter to Diodati are not adequate prepara-tion for the 244-line poem that inaugurates this first volume. A kind of sonic boom in twenty-seven stanzas (after a four-stanza proem in rhyme royal), the poem is a classic instance of Miltonic amplification at the conceptual and oral (as well as aural) level: the single event of the birth of Christ radiating outward to the Day of Judgment and beyond; the vision of the babe "all meanly wrapt" in the rude manger setting off shock waves of rapture throughout the world and time. Lyric is jubilantly calibrated to record the moment in its bold, spectral significance:

> It was the Winter wild,
> While the Heav'n-born child,
>   All meanly wrapt in the rude manger lies;
> Nature in awe to him
> Had doff't her gaudy trim,
>   With her great Master so to sympathize:
> It was no season then for her
> To wanton with the Sun, her lusty Paramour.

A new music – Spenserian sounding, the stanza is Milton's own creation – a new mood, indeed, a new mode of being accompanies the birth of the boy, perhaps even a new politics: "Yea, Truth and Justice then / Will down return to men" (ll. 141–2). Years later, Milton will represent the single action of Eve in *Paradise Lost* as the great deflationary moment of the epic: "she pluck'd, she eat." But in 1629, with youth very much on his side, the incarnation of Jesus resonates melodiously, and authoritatively, through the universe:

> But peaceful was the night
> Wherein the Prince of light
>   His reign of peace upon the earth began:
> The Winds, with wonder whist,
> Smoothly the waters kiss't,
>   Whispering new joys to the mild Ocean,
> Who now hath quite forgot to rave,
> While Birds of Calm sit brooding on the charmed wave.
>
>   (ll. 61–8)

"Charmed," a disyllable, reminds us at the end of the latent power in the new music even at its most peaceful: when "The Winds, with wonder whist." (Milton's wordplay also allows for the wondrous possibility on this occasion that the winds are both silenced – "whist" – and yet able to communicate – "whispering" – their sense of joy.)

Earlier criticism, still recollected in the Hughes edition of Milton, rightly worried about determining a "structure" for organizing these twenty-seven stanzas, with Arthur Barker's argument for a tripartite division, after the manner of "Lycidas," being the most widely accepted. "The first eight stanzas of the 'Hymn,'" writes Barker, "describe the setting of the Nativity, the next nine the angelic choir, the next nine the flight of the heathen gods. The conclusion, the last stanza, presents the scene in the stable."[9] Once this information is grasped, it seems equally important not to be bound by an overview that might prevent the manifold "signs" of sound from reverberating – the often splendid images of singing that recur, wrapped into the sonorous sweep of the metrically varied poetic line:

> Such Music (as 'tis said)
> Before was never made,
>   But when of old the sons of morning sung,
> While the Creator Great
> His constellations set,
>   And the well-balanc't world on hinges hung,
> And cast the dark foundations deep,
> And bid the welt'ring waves their oozy channel keep.
>
> (ll. 117–24)

The distinction between singing and writing keeps being blurred in this poem; the playful sounds well up in the mouth, wanting to be realized, released, through acts of speech that are sometimes more, sometimes less, than melodic. If the birth of Jesus is accompanied by a "Divinely-warbled voice / Answering the stringed noise" (ll. 96–7), then later the "trump of doom" is announced with an ear-splitting "horrid clang / As on mount *Sinai* rang" (ll. 157–8). As for the pagan gods, we only imagine their being silenced by the "Word." In the poem, Milton reveals them as disenchanted, "charmed" by a greater power but still audible, now made the subject of every strange and alluring gothic sound imaginable:

> The lonely mountains o'er,
> And the resounding shore,
>   A voice of weeping heard, and loud lament;
> From haunted spring and dale
> Edg'd with poplar pale,
>   The parting Genius is with sighing sent;
> With flow'r-inwov'n tresses torn
> The Nymphs in twilight shade of tangled thickets mourn.
>
> (ll. 181–8)

This is the parting music that Keats would remake into the "Ode to Psyche."

Such imagined acts of ventriloquism on Milton's part can be sorted into moral categories. Indeed, the poem insists that this "dividing" action – to borrow Sanford Budick's phrase – is being carried out under our eyes, with one party exiting while the other is entering.[10] But if celebration is real, cessation is also a necessary fiction, not only because the Day of Doom remains in the distance or because, as Budick points out, the alternative modes spell out "a highly specified theological reality." In 1629, Milton wants to play both parts to the verbal hilt – that of "the parting Genius" as well as the Herculean Jesus – and even to invite us to smile in the process: "Our Babe, to show his Godhead true, / Can in his swaddling bands control the damned crew." In Milton, humor almost always belongs to the triumphant; in this case it may also be free of derision.

Expressive and expansive, the Nativity Ode is marked as a double annunciation from the outset: "This is the Month, and this the happy morn" reads the first line of the poem. The birth of the Word inspires a jubilant echo some sixteen hundred years later, in what is both an act of homage and an opportunity for recognition – for visibility, as the proem makes unabashedly clear:

> See how from far upon the Eastern road
> The Star-led Wizards haste with odors sweet:
> O run, prevent them with thy humble ode,
> And lay it lowly at his blessed feet,
> Have thou the honor first, thy Lord to greet,
>   And join thy voice unto the Angel Choir,
> From out his secret Altar toucht with hallow'd fire.
>
> (ll. 22–8)

Dating the composition of the poem in 1629, as Milton does in 1645, has also encouraged scholars to widen the orbit of references beyond the boisterous autobiographical moment when a poet represents himself as a latter-day Isaiah being "toucht with hallow'd fire." The expression of Messianic sentiments in the middle of the hymn – the moment when, through the force of "holy song," Milton fancies that "Time will run back, and fetch the age of gold" – has been interpreted as part of a larger anti-papal critique running through the poem and possibly aimed at the Caroline court,[11] a criticism continued in the incipient Spenserian apocalypticism in the figure of the dragon from Revelation 12: 9 in Stanza 18. Again, Milton calculates his stanza carefully, this time to signal the threatening power of the dragon that persists into the present in the menacing sway of the alexandrine at the stanza's end:

> And then at last our bliss
> Full and perfect is,
>   But now begins; for from this happy day
> Th'old Dragon under ground,
> In straiter limits bound,
>   Not half so far casts his usurped sway,
> And wroth to see his Kingdom fail,
> Swinges the scaly Horror of his folded tail.

As the marginal gloss in the Geneva Bible makes clear, Protestants regarded the scaly dragon as a symbol of the tyrannical Catholic Church. For Milton, the bliss of a final battle is often imagined but also always deferred in favor of mastering a sense of spiritual readiness in this life, as the concluding stanza emphasizes:

> But see! the Virgin blest,
> Hath laid her Babe to rest.
> Time is our tedious Song should here have ending;
> Heav'n's youngest-teemed Star
> Hath fixt her polisht Car,
> Her sleeping Lord with Handmaid Lamp attending:
> And all about the Courtly Stable,
> Bright-harness'd Angels sit in order serviceable.

I think a poet less sure of his own talents might have risked the apology in the third line but not a final rhyme that seems so patently ordinary, so "serviceable" a finish.

"L'Allegro" and "Il Penseroso"

If the Nativity Ode aptly participates in what one historian has called "the structure of a prejudice" whereby "for many, if not most, educated Protestant English people of the period popery was an anti-religion, a perfectly symmetrical negative image of true Christianity,"[12] it would be a mistake to think of the collection in which the poem appears as a template for an emerging "Protestant" poet. (I think Milton would have resisted almost any adjective that would have narrowed his sense of the poet's office.) The psalm paraphrases that follow the ode might encourage this identification, but a little further down the line appear those marvelously elusive, undated poems "L'Allegro" and "Il Penseroso." So different in subject matter and execution than the ode, they are also substantially longer – 328 lines – if read together, and Milton has so subtly intertwined the two as to make it almost impossible to read the one and not the other. Although these "companion" poems, indebted in part to Robert Burton's recently published *Anatomy of Melancholy* (1621, 1624, 1628), are often traced to Milton's later days at Cambridge and therefore dated around 1631, Milton chose to leave this issue – and much else in these poems – debatable: a matter for speculation. "L'Allegro" and "Il Penseroso" are the only long poems in the volume to stand free and clear of any specific historical occasion.

As most readers admit, whether first-time students or seasoned scholars, these deceptively simple poems are fundamentally "resistant" to criticism, or rather, they seem endlessly open to interpretation. Indeed, in this regard, it would be difficult to get further from the Nativity Ode, their complicated inclusiveness inseparable from their temporal evasiveness. Instead of an aural explosion that fragments outward in the stellar-like burst of individual stanzas, instead of a sheep-and-goats seismic divide occurring at a particular moment in the history of mankind, we have not one but a pair of elongated poems, each written in a continuous, sinewy octosyllabic meter, each recounting an ideal "every day": two poems virtually symmetrical in appearance, nearly opposite in point of view or "content," and yet as performances equally inviting, as Milton takes some care to suggest at the end of each:

> These delights if thou canst give,
> Mirth, with thee I mean to live.
>
> ("L'Allegro")

> These pleasures *Melancholy* give,
> And I with thee will choose to live.
>
> ("Il Penseroso")

"L'Allegro" and "Il Penseroso" are "doubles" without being identical, reflections with no "Duessa," two substances or two shadows, but not, like the Nativity Ode, a substance and a shadow, at least once Milton moves beyond the archaically described, parallel acts of banishment that initiate each poem:

> Hence loathed Melancholy
>   Of *Cerberus* and blackest midnight born,
> In *Stygian* Cave forlorn
>   'Mongst horrid shapes, and shrieks, and sights unholy,
> Find out some uncouth cell ...
>
> ("L'Allegro")

> Hence vain deluding joys,
>   The brood of folly without father bred,
> How little you bested,
>   Or fill the fixed mind with all your toys;
> Dwell in some idle brain ...
>
> ("Il Penseroso")

and invokes his particular inventions in newly-minted tetrameter verse:

> But come thou Goddess fair and free
> In Heav'n yclep'd *Euphrosyne*,
> And by men, heart-easing Mirth,
> Whom lovely *Venus* at a birth
> With two sister Graces more
> To Ivy-crowned *Bacchus* bore;
>
> ("L'Allegro," ll. 11–16)

168

But hail thou Goddess, sage and holy,
Hail divinest Melancholy,
Whose Saintly visage is too bright
To hit the Sense of human sight;
And therefore to our weaker view,
O'erlaid with black, staid Wisdom's hue.

("Il Penseroso," ll. 11–16)

It is clear from these beginnings that balancing ideal (but not "idle") view-points, rather than subordinating one perspective to the other, is Milton's primary interest in these poems. He banishes from one what is only a corrupt version of the experience he celebrates in the other. "Loathed Melancholy," we discover, is not the same thing as the meditative pleasures explored in "Il Penseroso." Nor are "vain deluding joys" the equivalent of the "sweet Liberty" requested in "L'Allegro." The two "figures" or characters he chooses to create, rather, are of "far nobler shape" – to evoke a key image from *Paradise Lost* (4: 288) that hints at their eventual evolution into the first man and first woman in the epic. ("For contemplation hee and valor form'd, / For softness shee and sweet attractive Grace," Milton continues in the epic.) But in these premar-ital "companion" poems, there is no gendered difference between "L'Allegro" and "Il Penseroso," no hierarchy, no need felt by Milton to subordinate one experience to the other. Both characters are "goddesses" summoned by a fanciful male speaker-poet, who, in turn, imagines living permanently with each creation – indeed even fantasizes about being seduced by each in the separate climactic finale leading up to the Marlovian conclusion quoted above (echoing "The Passionate Shepherd to his Shepherdess"). Here is "L'Allegro":

And ever against eating Cares
Lap me in soft *Lydian* Airs,
Married to immortal verse,
Such as the meeting soul may pierce
In notes, with many a winding bout
Of linked sweetness long drawn out,
With wanton heed, and giddy cunning
The melting voice through mazes running;
Untwisting all the chains that tie
The hidden soul of harmony;
That *Orpheus'* self may heave his head
From golden slumber on a bed
Of heapt *Elysian* flow'rs, and hear
Such strains as would have won the ear
Of *Pluto*, to have quite set free
His half-regain'd *Eurydice*.

These delights if thou canst give,
Mirth, with thee I mean to live.

And here is the finale from "Il Penseroso":

And as I wake, sweet music breathe
Above, about, or underneath,
Sent by some spirit to mortals good,
Or th'unseen Genius of the Wood.
But let my due feet never fail
To walk the studious Cloister's pale,
And love the high embowed Roof,
With antic Pillars massy proof,
And storied Windows richly dight,
Casting a dim religious light.
There let the pealing Organ blow
To the full voic'd Choir below,
In Service high and Anthems clear,
As may with sweetness, through mine ear,
Dissolve me into ecstasies,
And bring all Heav'n before mine eyes,
And may at last my weary age
Find out the peaceful hermitage,
The Hairy Gown and Mossy Cell,
Where I may sit and rightly spell
Of every Star that Heav'n doth shew,
And every Herb that sips the dew;
Till old experience do attain
To something like Prophetic strain.
These pleasures *Melancholy* give,
And I with thee will choose to live.

In spite of Dr. Johnson's famous demurral that "I know not whether the characters are kept sufficiently apart" – Johnson confessed to always meeting some melancholy in "L'Allegro"'s mirth[13] – the two experiences recounted here overlap only in the exquisiteness with which Milton puts the case for each. With "L'Allegro," as Georgia Christopher remarks (unwinding Milton's elaborately imitative phrasing in the process), the speaker "wants nothing less than a poetic power so exorbitant that it will win the girl, even if she be Eurydice in Hell."[14] With "Il Penseroso" he wants, we might say with equal candor, a wisdom greater than Prospero's: not even one thought, let alone every third, is to be of the grave. As different as these requests are from each other, moreover, they also differ in even more obvious ways from the Nativity Ode. "L'Allegro" takes an erotic, if not pagan, delight in the sensuousness of the "soft *Lydian*

Airs." Suggestive phrases like "linked sweetness," "wanton heed," and "giddy cunning," following quickly on the heels of the speaker's wish to be "Married to immortal verse," draw out the linked, wanton, cunning pleasures of the poetry itself. And "Il Penseroso" expresses a form of religious ecstasy that has as little in common with the apocalyptic claims made in the Ode in 1629 as it does with the anti-prelatical Milton of 1645. Walking "the studious Cloister's pale," loving "the high embowed Roof": these are just the kind of religious habits Milton relentlessly criticizes in the prose as spiritually anemic and "superstitious."

As tricky as these poems are as single or twinned utterances – and the fluidity of Milton's tetrameter verse almost defies the best analysis[15] – they possess an equally tricky place in critical attempts aimed at delineating Milton's career along a single axis. Do they together represent what Milton left behind, much to the special regret of many eighteenth-century readers like H.J. Todd, who drew from these poems proof that "no man was ever so disqualified to turn puritan as Milton"?[16] Or are they evidence, once again, that Milton did not always practice what he preached? Or should we regard their appearance in 1645 as reinforcing a distinction Milton had recently emphasized in *The Reason of Church Government* when he memorably assigned works written in prose to the "left hand" and those written in poetry to the "right"? Or do they point to a deeper and perhaps irresolvable rift in Milton between the latitudinarian and the authoritarian: the Milton willing to think laterally and spaciously and encoding that belief in a persona who moves effortlessly across the landscape, pleased by what he sees, imagining free access to "upland Hamlets," "Tow'red Cities," and masques and pageants alike (in "L'Allegro"); or the longitudinal Milton, indifferent to the "rhubarbarians," Seamus Heaney's borrowed term for those "crying out against the mystification of art and its appropriation by the grandees of aesthetics"[17] – the Milton of "Il Penseroso" who imagines his "Lamp at midnight hour / Be[ing] seen in some high lonely Tow'r, / Where I may oft outwatch the *Bear*" (ll. 85–8)?

"How soon hath time": Sonnet 7

It is in the spirit of these "sportive" companion poems to raise more questions than they answer about the "proper" subject of poetry. They are twin products of myth making, not history, and at the very least their presence reminds the reader that there is more than one Milton even in 1645. Much of their appeal, in fact, is to keep at arm's length issues treated with utmost gravity elsewhere in Milton – and with some personal anxiety, as in the best-known sonnet from *Poems*, "How soon hath Time." Although Johnson was quick to dismiss these "little pieces ... without much anxiety"[18] – meaning all twenty-three of Milton's sonnets written over a twenty-year period, including the now canonical late ones like "Avenge O Lord," "When I Consider," and "Methought I Saw" – Milton found the sonnet hospitable for exploring a range of subjects and attitudes, not just the amatory matters of a Nightingale – a topic that might have appeared in almost any volume of Caroline poetry – but also those involving rigorous acts of self-examination, as the first quatrain of Sonnet 7 partially suggests:

> How soon hath Time, the subtle thief of youth,
> Stol'n on his wing my three and twentieth year!
> My hasting days fly on with full career,
> But my late spring no bud or blossom show'th.

Early editors of Milton's sonnets often supplied titles that made them even more pointedly – and poignantly – immediate than the dramatized settings sometimes warranted. (Warton's title for this sonnet was "On his being arrived to the age of 23.")[19] It is easy to understand this editorializing desire, for Milton's sonnets stand apart from the earlier tradition of the English sonnet through the conspicuous presence of autobiographical detail. This is not a birthday poem, as Warton's title might suggest, but the reference to "my three and twentieth year" makes "Milton" the subject of the poem in a way utterly different from how Shakespeare or even Donne represented the personal in their sonnets. Milton ensures a sense of belatedness made only more acute by the vagueness of the temporal reference. Personal as it is – and "my" is the governing pronoun at the outset – this sonnet is not a threshold poem in the manner of the Nativity Ode. Rather, it is about what comes after, or doesn't, even though the seasons keep changing.

And as the second quatrain makes clear, it is about the necessary fictions people or poets create when feeling off-track:

> Perhaps my semblance might deceive the truth,
> That I to manhood am arriv'd so near,
> And inward ripeness doth much less appear,
> That some more timely-happy spirits endu'th.

This fanciful quatrain hardly resolves the anxieties of the first. It simply offers an explanation for why Milton has no "bud" or "blossom" to show: he doesn't yet look old enough for "inward ripeness" to appear in the manner of some more "timely-happy spirits" – often glossed as referring to Spenser or Milton's Cambridge contemporary, Thomas Randolph. Worth glossing too is "endu'th," a common early form for "endowed," with perhaps a secondary sense of being "invested" or clothed with honor, from the Latin *induere*, "to put on a garment." The stanza says nothing about what might happen to Milton in the future, what "honors" or "garments" he might wear, what visible signs of recognition he might win; and in saying nothing, it leaves the problem for the sestet, where the topic of potentiality doesn't simply remain unresolved but is re-presented as remaining emphatically – one wants to say definitively – "open."

Yet be it less or more, or soon or slow,
 It shall be still in strictest measure ev'n
 To that same lot, however mean or high,
Toward which Time leads me, and the will of Heav'n;
 All is, if I have grace to use it so,
 As ever in my great task-Master's eye.

F.T. Prince's fine remark in *The Italian Element in Milton's Verse* that this sonnet reflects the poet's "new-found confidence" in his "grasp of the form" seems specifically prompted by what Prince calls the "striking outburst" of parallelisms in the sestet:[20] the feeling of gravity the measured phrasing gives to what is now no longer a poem of personal reflection but a religious meditation suddenly incorporating those Calvinist imponderables, predestination and grace. If Milton has been influenced by Italian models of phrasing, however, he has partly camouflaged that debt not only through a Protestant emphasis on grace but with a diction as monosyllabically plain in its use of English as anything Herbert ever wrote. In its sudden linguistic concentration, moreover, the sestet resonates with meaning of a higher kind. Beginning with the indefinite "it" – most scholars connect the referent to "inward ripeness" – and continuing in the expanding syntax and allusions, the sestet empties the "occasional" from the poem: the topical, the temporal, the twenty-three-year-old speaker. And in its place, it plants at more than the grammatical level the single conditional "if": the "if" of "if I have grace to use it so," then "All is."

The turn toward the conditional in the sonnet is inseparable from a turn toward a heroic conception of the self: heroic not just in the sense of the new note of resolve that suddenly saturates the sestet but also in the sense of the speaker's imagining an instrumental role for himself in the cosmic scheme of things. As *Paradise Lost* will later make explicit, Milton accepted a Calvinist emphasis on the infusion of grace as a necessary condition of election, but he also resisted the determinism underlying Calvin's notion of predestination. ("If I foreknew, / Foreknowledge had no influence on their fault," says Milton's God, addressing the fall of mankind in *Paradise Lost* 3: 117–18.) In the sonnet, from the speaker's point of view, the challenge of the conditional is everything. How to meet it remains unclear, or rather remains unspecified, but the sestet presents a future for Milton's "inward ripeness" to grow, and the future includes nothing less than "all."

By its own account, by its own strict measures of accounting, "How soon hath time" is a pivotal poem in more than a structural sense. Milton, in fact, included a copy of it in a revealing letter he wrote to a "friend" usually thought to be his former teacher at St. Paul's, the Scottish Presbyterian Thomas Young, who had apparently accused him of dreaming away his "Yeares in the armes of studious retirement like Endymion with the Moone as the tale of Latmus" goes.[21] And Milton further highlighted the sonnet's pivotal role in 1645 by placing it immediately after the amatory sonnets and before the heroic sonnet beginning "Captain or Colonel." In conjunction with the letter, I think it also helps to illuminate matters closer at hand: the kind of imposing challenges to which Milton opened himself not simply once Civil War was upon him and the nation but while he was still a young poet, though not quite so youthful as he appears in either the Nativity Ode or "L'Allegro" and "Il Penseroso." I mean, of course, the challenges presented by the occasions underlying the two "concluding" works in Poems: A Mask Presented at Ludlow Castle (often referred to as Comus) and "Lycidas."

For if the sonnet identifies a poet for whom a measured readiness is all, the letter in which it was wrapped describes an author diffident at best about fame won from hurrying into print. Indeed, in the letter to his former tutor, Milton reveals finding in the famous parable of the Talents (Matthew 25: 14–30) and the related parable of the Five Wise and Five Foolish Virgins (Matthew 25: 1–16) a strong argument for valuing watchfulness over haste. And perhaps in Matthew's injunction, "to every man according to his several ability" (25: 15), he discovered further justification to proceed at his own pace. In a sense peculiar to Milton, it is not simply the occasions themselves that are important, but the preparation as well. As a glance at the full arc of his career reminds us, Milton is a poet for whom lengthy pauses are hugely significant: Paradise Lost appeared after thirty years of his near silence as a poet.

A Mask Presented at Ludlow Castle and "Lycidas"

Both A Mask and "Lycidas" have long been viewed as possessing separate claims for pride of place among the early verse. Johnson awarded the palm to the masque, in part because he disliked "Lycidas"; modern critics, responding to Johnson, have often returned the prize to the elegy. Neither is for the faint of heart, which is one way to describe both their distance from Caroline notions of idleness and the problems they can cause for initial readers, although the masque achieves, appropriate to its genre, a lightness of touch never again attempted by Milton, and "Lycidas" remains among the most compelling poems in English: deeply unsettled – and unsettling – in the fullness of its response to personal grief. Both rank among the most complicated literary works in the early seventeenth century; and it is surely the case that no other single work in either genre has received anything approaching as much critical attention.

Chronologically, "Lycidas" is the later of the two. Begun sometime after August 10, 1637, the date Milton's Cambridge classmate, Edward King, drowned in the Irish Sea, it was probably completed in November of that year, as suggested by the canceled note in the Trinity Manuscript alongside the poem. A Mask was first performed three years earlier, on September 29, 1634. But even before appearing together in 1645, both poems had enjoyed separate publication. "Lycidas" had been brought out in 1638, as part of a Cambridge memorial volume for King and bearing the signature "J.M" at the end of the poem. A Mask had appeared in print on its own in 1637, although, as the introductory epistle by Lawes specifies, "not openly acknowledg'd by the Author." (Milton was still part of the genteel tradition, even if he was not part of the court.) And when the two works were printed together in 1645, Milton drew attention to their comparable status by allowing "Lycidas" to be the last word among the English poems but endowing A Mask with its own title page and separate identity as a literary achievement, replete with commendatory letters not only from Henry Lawes but also Sir Henry Wotton, the former ambassador to Venice and current Provost of Eton.

To some degree, it is as a "separate work" and as a "last word" that these two performances speak most powerfully (although "last" in Milton almost always includes predicating a future, and "separate" still involves interconnections with other works). "Lycidas" emerged after nearly three years of complete silence – two years and ten months to be exact. Indeed, so far as we know, except for translating Psalm 114 into Greek heroic meter – the same Psalm 114 he had paraphrased at age fifteen – Milton did not write any poetry between A Mask and "Lycidas." The usual explanation given is that during this time Milton had embarked on a program of "relentless study" at Horton, a period that saw him managing to defer a career in the clergy, against his father's wishes, while also preparing for some yet unspecified task. This preparation included voluminous reading (and note-taking in Greek, Italian, and Latin, no less) in Dante, Boccaccio, and Ariosto, but mostly in history, especially Church history and the writings of the early Fathers, whom Milton came to view with increasing distrust.[22]

Without devaluing either the importance of this extended act of self-cloistering on Milton's part (far different in spirit from Donne's forced retirement) or its significance in arming the poet for a future life as a polemicist, it seems also the case that the nearly three years of studying was enabled by the comprehensive success of A Mask, not success in a commercial sense, but in other more valuable ways for Milton, and that a significant respite was therefore at least possible if not absolutely in order. Simply receiving the commission was itself an unusual honor. The purpose of the masque was to celebrate the appointment, made several years earlier, of John Egerton, Earl of Bridgewater, as Lord President of Wales, and it allowed Milton as well the chance to collaborate with Henry Lawes, the royal musician. (Perhaps an acquaintance of Milton's father, Lawes was possibly responsible for introducing the young Milton to the world of nobility; but the precise details that might explain how Milton became connected to the Egerton household or to that of the Countess of Derby, celebrated in the fragment from Arcades, continue to elude Milton scholars.)[23]

The occasion also provided Milton with the opportunity to draw together – and to amplify – a number of themes and ideas explored in the earlier poetry. Recent scholarship has attended so thoroughly to the circumstantial dimensions potentially affecting production and subject matter, including the possible muted connections to the notorious Castlehaven scandal of 1631, in which Egerton's brother-in-law, Mervyn Touchet, Lord Audley, was tried on a number of counts of sexual perversion and executed, that it is easy to forget how well Milton turned the occasion to his advantage as a virtuoso literary adventure.[24] Before tackling the project, he had been, as we have seen, a conscientious praiser of Shakespeare in his epigram appended to the Second Folio. He had also been an enthusiastic disciple of the lyrical Spenser in the Nativity Ode and an elegant heir to Jonson on several notable occasions. But in the masque, Milton puts on something like a collective mantle of early modern English poetry by writing a Shakespearean-styled drama in a favorite Jonsonian genre on that most Spenserian of topics – chastity. If there were any lingering concerns on Milton's part over his "inward ripeness," these anxieties are fully addressed – and exorcised – in this work.

We might think of A Mask, in fact, as a place where the impending occasion itself must have served as a spur to poetic maturity, where the performed nature of the text held forth the possibility of Milton's showing in front of others the blossoms of his "late spring." No literary work of his, certainly none so far attempted, demanded greater sensitivity to immediate external circumstances – to the expectations of aristocratic entertainment: in this case, involving the three Egerton children, Alice (age 15) and her two younger brothers, John (age 11) and Thomas (age 9); to the specifics of the Ludlow locale, with its limited staging possibilities but rich mythological and pastoral associations on the banks of the Severn River between England and Wales; and to complications inherent in collaborating harmoniously with another talented artist. Yet no work to date furnished Milton with so large and potentially varied a canvas for experimentation and expression. Song, dialogue, declamation, stichomythia, incantation: the masque is a genre in which formal variety, rather than dramatic action, is the chief means of providing pace and pleasure, and Milton's is among the most formally resourceful of all masques, a genuine rival to Jonson's in this regard. As the other Johnson remarked, "a work more truly poetical is rarely found."[25] (In this respect, Carew's elaborate Coelum Britanicum, which Milton no doubt knew since the Egerton brothers had danced in it the previous year, seems practically flat-footed by comparison.)

For his audience, Milton provides not just the usual mix of narrative and lyrical modes but a wide offering of speaking parts, ranging from the octosyllabic rounds of Comus and his crew to the calculated flexibility of his principal verbal medium, blank verse – perhaps the surest of the many signs of his Shakespearean footing. (The Tempest and A Midsummer Night's Dream are the plays most frequently echoed.) Except for the river goddess Sabrina, everyone, from the younger brother to the Attendant Spirit, makes use of a pentameter line that can move from the spaciously oracular, as spoken at the outset by Lawes (playing the part of the descending Attendant Spirit):

Before the starry threshold of Jove's Court
My mansion is, where those immortal shapes
Of bright aerial Spirits live inspher'd

> In Regions mild of calm and serene Air,
> Above the smoke and stir of this dim spot,

to the dramatically immediate utterances of a thoroughly proper but momentarily confused fifteen-year old girl:

> I should be loath
> To meet the rudeness and swill'd insolence
> Of such late Wassailers; yet O where else
> Shall I inform my unacquainted feet
> In the blind mazes of this tangl'd Wood?
>
> (ll. 177–81)

to the suave commands put forward by a worldly and demanding Comus:

> Nay Lady, sit; if I but wave this wand,
> Your nerves are all chain'd up in Alabaster,
> And you a statue; or as *Daphne* was,
> Root-bound, that fled *Apollo*.
>
> (ll. 659–62)

Indeed, Milton finds even more than a single purpose, a single register of meaning, for the leaner tetrameter line. Associated initially with Comus, it is used, in allegro-like fashion, to highlight the errant, hectic movement of his midnight revels:

> Meanwhile welcome Joy and Feast,
> Midnight shout and revelry
> Tipsy dance and Jollity.
> Braid your Locks with rosy Twine
> Dropping odors, dropping Wine.
>
> (ll. 102–6)

But by the masque's end it acquires a more disciplined purpose. As part of a general chastening process, it is first used to underscore the ritual invocation spoken by the Attendant Spirit,

> Listen and appear to us
> In name of great *Oceanus*,
> By the earth-shaking *Neptune's* mace
> And *Tethys'* grave majestic pace,
>
> (ll. 867–70)

then as a charm Sabrina provides to release the ensnared Lady,

Thus I sprinkle on thy breast
Drops that from my fountain pure
I have kept of precious cure,

(ll. 911–13)

and again as a solemn tribute the Attendant Spirit pays to Sabrina,

Virgin, daughter of *Locrine*
Sprung of old *Anchises'* line,
May thy brimmed waves for this
Their full tribute never miss,

(ll. 922–5)

and finally as a way for the Spirit to announce his Ariel-like departure to the
Garden of the Hesperides,

To the Ocean now I fly,
And those happy climes that lie
Where day never shuts his eye,
Up in the broad fields of the sky.

(ll. 976–80)

As for song – central to the masque tradition and always of interest to the
poet – Milton reshaped the jubilantly archaic, rustic play of the Nativity Ode in
a more sophisticated courtly direction. For the two female parts, he invented
pastoral lyrics of exquisite beauty and color (in the imagistic sense as well):
Lady Alice's plaintive song to Echo asking help to find her brothers, beginning,

Sweet Echo, sweetest Nymph that liv'st unseen
                Within thy airy shell
        By slow *Maeander's* margent green,
And in the violet-embroider'd vale
                Where the love-lorn Nightingale
Nightly to thee her sad Song mourneth well,

(ll. 230–5)

and, much later, Sabrina's distantly answering song accompanying her entrance,

    By the rushy-fringed bank,
Where grows the Willow and the Osier dank,
    My sliding Chariot stays,
Thick set with Agate and the azurn sheen
Of Turquoise blue and Em'rald green
        That in the channel strays,

Whilst from off the waters fleet
Thus I set my printless feet
O'er the Cowslip's Velvet head,
    That bends not as I tread;
Gentle swain at thy request
    I am here.

(ll. 890–901)

Part of Milton's artistry in the masque is to connect these brief arias to larger thematic concerns articulated elsewhere in the drama. The Lady's song, for instance, while admitting her vulnerability at one level – the Attendant Spirit will refer later to her as "O poor hapless Nightingale" (l. 566) – affirms her strength at another. As a Reformation heroine in the process of emerging before our eyes – "Some Virgin sure," to borrow Comus's phrase for her in a way he doesn't altogether intend – her song is a demonstration of her "new enliv'n'd spirits" (l. 228), a way to signal the sureness of her faith in her own key. Indeed, even Comus, like Satan standing "stupidly good" in front of a beautiful and innocent Eve (*Paradise Lost* 9: 465), is momentarily moved by the higher strain he hears, although his use of the equivocal "ravishment" in the compliment indicates, too, the downward descent of his own thoughts and actions:

Can any mortal mixture of Earth's mold
Breathe such Divine enchanting ravishment?
Sure something holy lodges in that breast.

(ll. 244–6)

As for Sabrina's song, it stands as climactic proof that a power greater than Comus can be unlocked "if she be right invok't in warbled Song." For all its pastoral decoration, the simple conclusion, "Gentle swain at thy request / I am here," reverberates widely at this moment in the masque, and also in Milton; for not only does her answering song point to a more decorous – and harmonious – way of defeating the enchanter than the brothers could accomplish with their old-style heroics even with the help of a magical root, the so-called but much disputed "*Haemony*." It also validates the carefully orchestrated Spenserian moment that precedes Sabrina's appearance. The Attendant Spirit knows of the "gentle nymph" because of lore he learned from "*Meliboeus* old," – "The soothest Shepherd that e'er pip't on plains" (ll. 822–3) – usually taken as a reference to Spenser. Through Milton and the collaboration with Lawes, through, in other words, a fusion of verse and voice, the Bridgewater court is a place where Spenserian pastoral romance comes alive, where it can continue into the present. As Angus Fletcher has argued, echoing is a richly complicated device in the masque.[26] It is a way of conferring continuity at both the syntactic and symbolic level; and here, in the context of the Welsh setting, it helps form a link with a poetic past every bit as noble as the one Milton is constructing for the Bridgewater family through the elevated figure of Sabrina herself, "Sprung of old *Anchises'* line."

Still, the masque is more than a summary performance by a young poet. The heart of the work belongs to the measure-for-measure combat between the chaste Lady and the lecherous Comus: the "Tragical part," to invoke Sir Henry Wotton's description of the non-lyrical material. By "Tragical," Wotton probably meant, more specifically, the serious matter carried by the dramatic action, all conducted in blank verse: the attempt on the Lady's virginity by Comus, first by persuasion, then by force; and the related quasi-philosophical debates spoken, at some remove, by the two brothers on the subject of chastity in its manifold – and frequently heroic – representations, and the subsequent redirection of these airy debates by the Attendant Spirit in the context of the immediate, threatening situation. (By the middle of the masque, things have become dark indeed: the formerly festive Comus and his howling crew are now characterized by the Spirit as "Doing abhorred rites to *Hecate* / In their obscured haunts of inmost bow'rs" (ll. 535–6).)

Serious as it is, the conflict between good and evil at the moral center of the masque, of course, is not fully tragic in the sense that term will come to have when Milton dramatizes the fall of mankind in *Paradise Lost*, Book 9. (Throughout the masque, the Lady is protected by the Attendant Spirit.) But dramatizing conflict is still a crucial portion of Milton's "reformation" of the genre, to borrow David Norbrook's useful term for differentiating Milton's use of the form from the many masques produced at the Stuart court, whose purpose it often was to celebrate the ease with which the forces of evil – frequently represented as forces of social disturbance – were overcome by the mere appearance of a ruling authority.[27] Indeed, not just conflict but escalating scales of opposition lie at the dramatic center of Milton's work. As Comus readily exceeds, in scope and capacity, his English prototype and namesake in Jonson's *Pleasure Reconciled to Virtue* (1618), so the Lady is more than the usual chaste heroine celebrated in the court masque.[28] The one is a Circean sorcerer, whose roots go back to Homer; the other is a genuine heir to Spenser's Britomart, for whom the word, rather than the sword, is the strongest weapon. In the course of the dramatic action, and in the process of Milton's revising the masque for publication, moreover, both roles also expand in their symbolic and political significance. Comus is darkly sinister, a primitive enchanter, but also something of a Caroline libertine versed in the ways of the world: hurling his "dazzling Spells into the spongy air" (l. 154), he can change quickly into a suitor in shepherd's clothing. The Lady, in spite of the supreme value she places on chastity, on her own moral rectitude, is an impassioned defender of charity toward others: an aristocrat opposed to "lewdly-pampered Luxury," who views nature as a "good cateress" and thinks, indeed prays, in Lear-like fashion, for moderation in diet as a means for "Nature's full blessings" to be "well dispens't / In unsuperfluous even proportion" (ll. 772–3). And if Comus has a touch of the recusant about him, suddenly surfacing in the Welsh woods after "Roving the *Celtic* and

Iberian Fields" (France and Spain), the Lady shows something of the inspired preacher, calling on "the Sun-clad power of Chastity" to help her dispel Comus's magic, his "dear Wit and gay Rhetoric" as well as the physical signs of his power.

Another way of characterizing the sense of opposition is to note that in the figure of Comus lie the seeds of Satan, and in the character of the Lady a type of the Miltonic hero, whose most important line in this regard may well be "Eye me blest Providence, and square my trial / To my proportion'd strength" (ll. 329–30). Like all Milton's heroes, she understands the source of her strength to lie beyond the self (the image of the eye of Providence provides yet another gloss on "the Sun-clad power of Chastity"); and the "trial" she undergoes is, characteristically, a temptation scene, in this case quickly and unequivocally met and yet sufficient to show not simply her moral certainty but also her moral intelligence. At fifteen years old, she already knows, almost as a matter of precept, that

> none
> But such as are good men can give good things,
> And that which is not good, is not delicious
> To a well-govern'd and wise appetite.
>
> (ll. 702–5)

And in arguing for temperance, she is only further incensed by Comus's attempt to misrepresent her position when he speaks of her as "Praising the lean and sallow Abstinence." As is always true with Milton, substituting a word threatens to change the meaning, and the Lady picks up on this threat, this act of verbal juggling, in her grandly haughty denunciation of Comus beginning:

> I had not thought to have unlockt my lips
> In this unhallow'd air, but that this Juggler
> Would think to charm my judgment, as mine eyes,
> Obtruding false rules prankt in reason's garb.
>
> (ll. 756–9)

Her sense of moral outrage is acute. ("Prankt," meaning "dressed up," with a secondary sense of "tricked," is wonderfully contemptuous). And the gambit will underlie many of Milton's later outbursts in prose, including his famous retort in *The Second Defense of the English People* (1654) that "I did not insult over fallen majesty, as is pretended; I only preferred queen Truth to king Charles."[29] If at the end of this speech – much amplified in the 1637 publica-tion[30] – the Lady still requires a helping hand from Sabrina, moreover, it is equally the case that she has earned her release in true Miltonic fashion. Faced with temptation and without any intervention from the Attendant Spirit, she has exercised her will, and her reason, in the name of Truth.

As for Comus, his later fictional reworkings – all variations on the double nature of his sorcery – help to make the point that in the masque he is more than simply a "foil" for the Lady or the Egerton family more generally. It is more accurate, in terms of the genre, to think of Comus as the leader of an anti-masque who will not be readily dispelled: a master of illusion, who can be only momentarily demystified. "She fables not," Comus's response to her denunciation, is but a temporary step backward for him, almost an involuntary reaction that testifies to the power of the Lady's "sacred vehemence" at this particular moment. But a longer view of the action reminds us that to resist his wiles completely, it takes a Lady of Pauline proportions, a magical root called "Haemony," whose precise allegorical function has proven to be especially elusive, and a nymph drawn from the nearby Severn to perform a purification ritual that serves to release the Lady from the strange gummy seat to which she is stuck. It takes a strenuous effort, in other words, and though the victory is not illusory, it is also not absolute. Comus escapes from the immediate precincts, only, as it were, to prepare for longer flights in the future.

* * *

But not in "Lycidas," at least he does not appear as a single identifiable presence or counterforce to goodness. The connections between the masque and the pastoral elegy are of a more abstract kind. Wizardry continues but now as a pervasive feature of reality as seen through the eyes of the mourning elegist – in the apparent deviousness of nature and poetry for refusing to offer either help or consolation to one of its own:

> Where were ye Nymphs when the remorseless deep
> Clos'd o'er the head of your lov'd Lycidas?
> For neither were ye playing on the steep,
> Where your old *Bards*, the famous *Druids*, lie,
> Nor on the shaggy top of *Mona* high,
> Nor yet where *Deva* spreads her wizard stream:
> Ay me, I fondly dream!
> Had ye been there – for what could that have done?
> What could the Muse herself that *Orpheus* bore,
> The Muse herself, for her enchanting son,
> Whom Universal nature did lament,
> When by the rout that made the hideous roar,
> His gory visage down the stream was sent,
> Down the swift *Hebrus* to the *Lesbian* shore?

(ll. 50–63)

There is more wizardry in the delphic responses, almost amounting to a conspiracy of silence, that the poet meets when interrogating the dark forces surrounding King's death:

> He ask'd the Waves, and ask'd the Felon winds,
> What hard mishap hath doom'd this gentle swain?
> And question'd every gust of rugged wings
> That blows from off each beaked Promontory.
> They knew not of his story.
>
> (ll. 91–5)

And there is more wizardry still in the "dread voice" of St. Peter denouncing, through the arresting figure of the "Blind mouths," the false preachers who continue to "creep and intrude and climb in the fold" (l. 115), while heaven does nothing to protect the good minister or feed the "hungry sheep":

> Blind mouths! that scarce themselves know how to hold
> A Sheep-hook, or have learn'd aught else the least
> That to the faithful Herdman's art belongs!
> What recks it them? What need they? They are sped;
> And when they list, their lean and flashy songs
> Grate on their scrannel Pipes of wretched straw.
>
> (ll. 119–24)

And as "Lycidas" involves a greater reckoning of the "Tragical" in the inexplicable death of Edward King, so it produces a countervailing stress on the poet not to get lost in the night and on the medium of irregularly rhymed blank verse to explore and to exorcise the demons of doubt. "A thousand fantasies / Begin to throng into my memory / Of calling shapes and beck'ning shadows dire," remarks the Lady in *A Mask* (ll. 205–7). These fantasies are quickly quieted in the name of "pure-ey'd Faith," "white-handed Hope," and the "unblemish't form of Chastity," even if Comus continues to roam the woods. But in "Lycidas," chastity as a governing psychological condition, as an "unblemish't form" and unifying frame of reference, is already lost at the outset – a violation of innocence sounded in the violence of a poet's initial, and initiating, metaphors for writing:

> Yet once more, O ye Laurels, and once more
> Ye Myrtles brown, with Ivy never sere,
> I come to pluck your Berries harsh and crude,
> And with forc'd fingers rude,
> Shatter your leaves before the mellowing year.

The great paradox of "Lycidas" as a work of art can be glimpsed in these lines. A poet claims to be doing, once more, what he seems to be doing here for the first time, a claim that lies at the heart of most criticism of the poem, from Johnson's early attack on "Lycidas" for its artificiality ("Where there is leisure for fiction there is little grief") to the many modern defenses of the poem as an authentic act of mourning, as an original response to a "crisis," whether personal or political or some combination of the two, as the elegy eventually insists.[31]

A poem as luxurious and ecstatic as "Lycidas" will never become too familiar, in spite of its frequent appearance in the classroom or its often decried canonical status. Nor is it possible to offer here anything approaching another "full" reading. But the connections to, as well as the departures from, the masque do not often receive the emphasis they perhaps deserve. The most useful criticism of "Lycidas" from this angle tends to emphasize the prophetic connections between the masque and the elegy, the emerging sense of the poet's public "voice."[32] Audible in the Lady's "sacred vehemence," it can be heard to climb to an even sharper pitch in St. Peter's diatribe against the clergy quoted partly above, still referred to in the Hughes edition as a "digression." If a digression, it burns long with corrosive anger. Only one other verse paragraph in the poem exceeds this one in length, and it ends by sounding a catastrophic warning in one of literature's most charged images, enigmatic in the mysterious precision of its vehicle, but unmistakable in the tenor of its finality:

> Besides what the grim Wolf with privy paw
> Daily devours apace, and nothing said;
> But that two-handed engine at the door
> Stands ready to smite once, and smite no more.
>
> (ll. 128–31)

"Lycidas" rhymes irregularly, but to great effect, closing the door here on the ravenous wolves now altogether out of their sheep's clothing. The force of Milton's apocalyptic smiting at this point helps to justify the view that, among the many "sources" figuring into the poem, an important place should be allotted to one of the most notorious instances of Laud's program for ecclesiastical conformity carried out just two months before King's death: the dramatic ear-cropping (and subsequent martyrdom) in early June of the Puritans Henry Burton, John Bastwick, and William Prynne.[33] "Lycidas" is a poem of retaliation.

Casting grief in the form of a pastoral elegy allows Milton to activate the rusty machinery of political satire with greater force than Drayton ever dreamed. But the guise of a fellow pastoral singer – an "uncouth Swain" we learn at the end – also sanctions a roughness of expression, a bewailing, well beyond anything explored in the earlier poetry including A Mask, indeed far beyond anything yet written in English, if we take John Crowe Ransom's summary point that "there did not at the time anywhere exist in English, among the poems done by competent technical poets, another poem so willful and illegal in form as this one."[34] Henry Lawes, playing the part of "Thyrsis," still belongs to the decorous world of Renaissance court pastoral, in which aristocrats dress up as shepherds. Milton, in "Lycidas," does not. Or, more precisely, that world gets recollected early on in the poem – with "old *Damaetas*" now substituting for "*Meliboeus* old" – but only to be left behind:

> Together both, ere the high Lawns appear'd
> Under the opening eyelids of the morn,
> We drove afield, and both together heard
> What time the Gray-fly winds her sultry horn,
> Batt'ning our flocks with the fresh dews of night,
> Oft till the Star that rose, at Ev'ning, bright
> Toward Heav'n's descent had slop'd his westering wheel.
> Meanwhile the Rural ditties were not mute,
> Temper'd to th'Oaten Flute;
> Rough *Satyrs* danc'd, and *Fauns* with clov'n heel
> From the glad sound would not be absent long,
> And old *Damaetas* lov'd to hear our song.
>
> (ll. 25–36)

Rhyme here signals closure of a different kind than in the "two-handed" passage above. It signals the longing of pastoral song as the only music and ideal symbol for the companionship between shepherds, a desire both subtly emphasized and undone by the great refrain from Spenser's *Prothalamion* that haunts this verse paragraph ("Against the Brydale day, which is not long: / Sweete *Themmes* runne softly, till I end my Song"), and by the huge misrhyme that accompanies the sharp turn of thought when we leave this paragraph and go on to the next: "But O the heavy change, now thou art gone." "Gone" is a great near miss in more than one sense. The sudden dissonance, the "heavy change," reminds us of the generic setting for the poem, of the larger frame around the song, of the other "strains" that run against it: "In this Monody the Author bewails a learned Friend, unfortunately drown'd in his Passage from *Chester* on the *Irish* Seas, 1637." "Monody" takes us back to tragedy and the single voice of lamentation, and the notion of "bewailing" only further emphasizes the potential for an outpouring of grief not to be constrained by the classical ideal of strophes "being repeated without variation."[35] Of the eleven verse paragraphs that make up "Lycidas," in fact, only two are the same length (ll. 1–14, and ll. 50–63); and the experiences presented in each, the one an invocation to the muse, the other recounting a sense of despair over the mother muse abandoning her son, Orpheus, are almost symmetrically opposite in meaning. Otherwise, the verse paragraphs range from ten lines (ll. 15–24) to thirty-three (ll. 132–64), each further distinguished from another by the odd placement of a short line and irregular rhymes, each driven by its own emotive logic. The "uncouth Swain" may get formally identified at the end, but he has been with us all along.

Asymmetries, imbalances, weirdly dark ambiguities – what are we to make of the river "*Deva*" being described as spreading her "wizard stream"? – sharp disconnections ("But O the heavy change"; "Alas"), forced resumptions ("Return *Alpheus*, the dread voice is past"), a radically foreclosed ending before the poem has ended, and, of course, the many questions raised within the poem that are never answered: all of these aspects of the poem get pushed to the limit but only to be exhausted, not resolved. "Lycidas" is a song, a monody, without a Sabrina. No chaste figure can be elegantly summoned to smooth over the many rough edges in the poem or liberate the innocent. But it is not a poem without faith and hope, although charting the passage from lament to affirmation will probably always elude the best critical efforts because Milton represents the process of transformation itself as something of a mystery, a matter for poetry, not logic or rhetoric alone, to express.[36] In the great return of pastoral in the longest section of the poem, the speaker, in effect, pours out his heart and ends with a prayer for help, like the Lady, except in "Lycidas" prayer does not come to "the uncouth Swain" with the first motions of a "startled" thought, or a second or third for that matter, either in this passage or the poem at large. (He is "uncouth," but not unregenerate.) The passage must be quoted in full since what is important is not just where this speaker, much chastened by the sound of the "dread voice," begins, but where he ends:

> Return *Alpheus*, the dread voice is past
> That shrunk thy streams; Return *Sicilian* Muse,
> And call the Vales, and bid them hither cast
> Their Bells and Flowrets of a thousand hues.
> Ye valleys low where the mild whispers use
> Of shades and wanton winds and gushing brooks,
> On whose fresh lap the swart Star sparely looks.
> Throw hither all your quaint enamell'd eyes,
> That on the green turf suck the honied showers,
> And purple all the ground with vernal flowers.
> Bring the rathe Primrose that forsaken dies,
> The tufted Crow-toe, and pale Jessamine,
> The white Pink, and the Pansy freakt with jet,
> The glowing Violet,
> The Musk-rose, and the well-attir'd Woodbine,
> With Cowslips wan that hang the pensive head,
> And every flower that sad embroidery wears:
> Bid *Amaranthus* all his beauty shed,
> And Daffadillies fill their cups with tears,
> To strew the Laureate Hearse where *Lycid* lies.
> For so to interpose a little ease,
> Let our frail thoughts dally with false surmise.
> Ay Me! Whilst thee the shores and sounding Seas

Wash far away, where'er thy bones are hurl'd,
Whether beyond the stormy *Hebrides*,
Where thou perhaps under the whelming tide
Visit'st the bottom of the monstrous world;
Or whether thou to our moist vows denied,
Sleep'st by the fable of *Bellerus* old,
Where the great vision of the guarded Mount
Looks toward *Namancos* and *Bayona's* hold;
Look homeward Angel now, and melt with ruth:
And, O ye *Dolphins*, waft the hapless youth.

Viewed in its full arc, the point of this passage does not seem to be, as Stanley Fish suggests, that the speaker begins yet again only in order to "sing the same old song: Ay me, alas, what am I to do? What's the use? it's all so unfair."[37] Rather, it would seem to be that in spite of, or rather because of beginning again, or perhaps for no logically causal reason, beginning again as he does, he nonetheless ends up some place entirely new in the poem: with an invocation or a prayer for help, not to Sabrina but to a guardian Angel all the same. The passage challenges our understanding of just how such transformations happen, in this case to the grieving swain, who is now represented in the process of somehow bottoming out in his sorrows. We can stop the process at any particular point and ask, for instance, how psychologically important is it for him finally to confront the empty coffin for the first time in the poem? Or what is the value won from "dally[ing] with [a] false surmise"? From strewing the "Laureate Hearse" with all those sensuously described flowers (in a passage much revised in the Trinity manuscript)? How much consolation should be wrung from "the great vision of the guarded Mount," St. Michael, the dragon-slaying Watchman of England near Land's End in Cornwall looking out at Spain? How much pathos to "ruth"? How much evocative power ascribed to the amplified "whethers" and "wheres," the descent to the bottom of the sea and the reascent and the gradual relinquishing of grief? How much the whole stormy scene is meant to recall the familiar episode in St. Matthew (14: 22–33), soon to be alluded to by Milton in the vision of Jesus walking on the water, but glossed in the Genevan version as "Peter's Weake Faith": "But when he saw the wind boisterous, he was afraid; and beginning to sink, he cried, saying, Lord, save me. And immediately Jesus stretched forth *his* hand, and caught him, and said unto him O thou of little faith, wherefore didst thou doubt?" (30–1). But happen the transformation does (as it will happen to a fallen Adam and Eve in *Paradise Lost* when they "repair" to where they were judged guilty in order to begin the lengthy process of "repairing" themselves; the puns are Milton's and part of the deep fabric of regeneration in that poem.) In the resurgence of patterns coinciding with the moment of renewed energy, we are asked to witness the emergence of hope ("Look homeward Angel now"), and then to see hope further affirmed in the context of a wider expression of faith. As the grieving mourner becomes the good pastor, he offers the community what the bad ministers, caring only to fill their "blind mouths," never did, nor what Peter, in his anger and "dread voice," could not:

> Weep no more, woeful Shepherds weep no more,
> For *Lycidas* your sorrow is not dead,
> Sunk though he be beneath the wat'ry floor,
> So sinks the day-star in the Ocean bed,
> And yet anon repairs his drooping head,
> And tricks his beams, and with new-spangled Ore
> Flames in the forehead of the morning sky:
> So *Lycidas*, sunk low, but mounted high,
> Through the dear might of him that walk'd the waves,
> Where other groves, and other streams along,
> With *Nectar* pure his oozy Locks he laves,
> And hears the unexpressive nuptial Song,
> In the blest Kingdoms meek of joy and love.
> There entertain him all the Saints above,
> In solemn troops, and sweet Societies
> That sing, and singing in their glory move,
> And wipe the tears for ever from his eyes.
> Now *Lycidas*, the Shepherds weep no more;
> Henceforth thou art the Genius of the shore,
> In thy large recompense, and shalt be good
> To all that wander in that perilous flood.

(ll. 165–85)

A pastoral elegy that did not include some sort of apotheosis of the dead person was scarcely imaginable in the Renaissance, as the multiple acts of mourning in Spenser's *Astrophel* help to demonstrate. "The act of substitution," as Peter Sacks argues, and "the reattachment to a new object of love" was an integral part of the successful mourning process.[38] But readers of Renaissance elegies, whether of Christianized laments like Henry King's "The Exequy" or of classical eulogies along the lines of Jonson's testimony to Shakespeare (a poem Milton surely knew), may still not be prepared for the kind of celebration they meet in these lines, so emphatic are the similes comparing Lycidas's resurrection to the sun's rising, so sweeping is the Miltonic line on the subject of salvation ("Through the dear might of him that walk'd the waves"), and so lavish are the words of redemption: "With *Nectar* pure his oozy Locks he laves." When Milton speaks to Lycidas of "thy large recompense," he almost understates his own case. Almost, but not quite: for what also emphatically distinguishes Milton's elegy at this point from those from Virgil to Spenser and beyond is the present tense directive to Lycidas and its accompanying burden: "Now *Lycidas*, the Shepherds weep no more." The vision of joy and love described in the next world is seen to have effectively canceled the sorrows caused by the loss of Lycidas in this one. It is as if the phrase, "That sing, and singing in their glory move," flows beyond its own reflexive boundaries and "moves" the immediate audience of Shepherds, just as, in his new station as "Genius of the shore," Lycidas shall "be good / To all that wander in that perilous flood." Not even Jonson's Shakespeare could claim as much.

From the full sweep of its mourning to its triumphantly orchestrated "recompense," "Lycidas" shows "what religious, what glorious and magnificent use might be made of poetry, both in divine and human things," to use Milton's phrasing in *Of Education*.[39] One purpose of the eight-line coda is to provide some implicit limits to these claims:

> Thus sang the uncouth Swain to th'Oaks and rills,
> While the still morn went out with Sandals gray;
> He touch't the tender stops of various Quills,
> With eager thought warbling his *Doric* lay:
> And now the Sun had stretch't out all the hills,
> And now was dropt into the Western bay;
> At last he rose, and twitch't his Mantle blue:
> Tomorrow to fresh Woods, and Pastures new.
>
> (ll. 186–93)

But readers have rightly felt, too, that the formal conclusion is also Milton's characteristic way of making an ending, yet again, into a new beginning. As passions are tempered through the introduction of a single pattern of alternating rhyme and a concluding couplet, as the setting and speaker are identified, as a full day has passed, Milton drops a curtain on the performance, but only to suggest a poet thinking about "fresh Woods, and Pastures new." And few readers have resisted following Milton into the future, seeing in the figure of the "uncouth Swain" the epic poet in chrysalis, registering in the formulaic transition to "Thus sang" the distancing effect of epic narrative. Pastoral is the genre of promise, but the most suggestive connection to a future even Milton could not have known is perhaps contained in the smallest of words that also leaves almost everything potentially open. "All," as in "To all that wander in that perilous flood," permits not just the possibility of the wide reach of epic – a subject for everyone, not just for a nation[40] – but the idea of a readership restricted at the outset only by membership in the general and the knowledge of its own need of guidance. To put a different spin on Johnson's remark quoted at the outset of this chapter, "Milton never learned the art of doing little things with grace."

7

ARENAS OF RETREAT

Blood, bread, and poetry in Henry Vaughan

So in this last and lewdest age,
Thy antient love on some may shine.

Vaughan, "White Sunday"

The subtitle to this chapter is adapted from the title of an essay by the American feminist poet, Adrienne Rich. In the essay, Rich remarks how, as a student in her early twenties, she was led to believe that poetry was "the expression of a higher world view, what the critic Edward Said has termed 'a quasi-religious wonder,' instead of a human sign to be understood in secular and social terms."[1] My starting place is to remark that whatever conditions underlie Rich's sense of the opposition between poetry as transcendental expression versus poetry as a sign system to be understood in secular and social terms, the dialectic is misleading, although in interesting ways, when applied to a pre-Romantic (who is sometimes thought to be a proto-Romantic) like Vaughan, despite the fact that he is almost always remembered as the signal instance of a seventeenth-century poet who became memorable once he became a poet of transcendence: "Lord, then said I, on me one breath, / And let me dye before my death."[2]

In beginning in this way, I do not mean to suggest that the difference between secular and devotional poetry is insignificant to the seventeenth century or to Vaughan. Indeed, one of the many ironies produced by the English Civil War points in just the opposite direction. The distinction Milton drew with characteristic emphasis in *The Reason of Church Government Urged Against Prelaty* (1642), alluded to in the previous chapter, between "vulgar amorists" in verse and poets inspired by "devout prayer to that eternal spirit who can enrich with all utterance and knowledge," gets redrawn with new emphasis and force in the next decade by a royalist-turned-religious seer: a poet from Wales who, in the 1655 Preface to the completed *Silex Scintillans*, regarded himself nonetheless as a citizen of "this *Kingdom*" (my italics), rather than of the Commonwealth.

Nor do I want to suggest that the more distant reaches of the devotional experience in Vaughan – whether those associated with mystical theology or Hermetic lore – are merely imported for what are sometimes thought of as poetic occasions. Vaughan's appeal has always been the appeal of the abrupt: the vertiginous opening of "The World" ("I saw eternity the other night"), the sublime exodus of "They are all gone into the world of light," the radical telescoping of time that marks the beginning of "The Night" in which Nicodemus comes to Christ under a cover of darkness; and even when his poems seem to falter, as they are notorious for doing, their claim on us is not readily demystified. But the opposition noted by Rich is too stark, too insufficiently dialectical when applied to Vaughan for the simple reason that the further Vaughan moved toward "quasi-religious wonder," the more completely he betrayed his connections to history. Or to rephrase the issue in contemporary terms, the deeper he sounded a note of "retreat," the more deeply he entered into a discourse of "retreat" sounded by his disenfranchised royalist Anglican contemporaries. The language of devotion was also the language of debate.[3]

It is important to keep this reactive (and reactionary) paradox in mind, not because every utterance of this deeply meditative poet ought to be interpreted as a veiled political allegory, but because history in its most personally and institutionally disruptive forms – war, the loss of a younger brother William (perhaps a casualty of the fighting), the beheading of the king, and the disestablishment of the church – provided Vaughan with an imperative of the most elemental kind: to rewrite himself in relation to his immediate culture, something he did over the space of a turbulent, busy, and often sickly-spent five years, roughly from 1650 to 1655. During this time, Vaughan published no less than six separate works. He brought out three collections of original poems: Silex Scintillans, Part I (1650), Olor Iscanus (1651), and Silex Scintillans, Part II (1655), with a reissue of the poems from Part I and a substantial "Authors Preface to the Following Hymns" that, in urging a renewal of censorship, reads like a belated counter to Milton's Areopagitica. And he matched this output with three volumes of prose that included original meditations in The Mount of Olives (1652), some hefty translations of devotional works out of Latin in Flores Solitudinis (1654), and a shorter translation for medical purposes entitled Hermetical Physick (1655). During these years, too, after some time spent as a soldier in the king's army, Vaughan became a physician. Surviving in solitude is certainly one of the overarching themes in these works, a matter of his ministering to mind, body, and spirit, in prose and verse.

In pointed contrast to a number of his contemporaries (Herrick and Lovelace come readily to mind), Vaughan is the prime instance of a poet, or better yet, an "Author" who discovered his calling during the Civil War and the Interregnum. Indeed, he is perhaps the sole instance for which such a claim might be made. (His closest competitor in this regard is probably Andrew Marvell, whose most celebrated lyrics are generally assumed to belong to the same years; but the very absence of a secure chronology militates against the idea of identifying a "discovery" in the first place.) At almost the precise

191

moment when Herrick was elegiacally erecting "His Pillar of Fame" against "the Kingdom's" overthrow at the end of *Hesperides* (1648) to mark his shift into silence, Vaughan was emphatically rethinking his relationship to English poetry and to the "Kingdom" at large through the influential guiding hand of George Herbert. Herbert's "holy *life* and *verse*," Vaughan remarked in the 1655 Preface, had already "gained many pious *Converts* (of whom I am the least)" – the phrase in parentheses echoing Herbert's own motto, which was borrowed, in turn, from Jacob in Genesis 32: 10, and characteristic of the intimate bond Vaughan forged with Herbert and of the significant place the Bible held in the writings of both men. While Lovelace was seeking, uncertainly, to continue as "the Cavalier" into the 1650s, Vaughan was in the process of repudiating, publicly, any connection with "idle" verse: his own "follies" and those of his contemporaries. If Vaughan looked to France with other royalists, it was not to "naturalize" court romances – "Foreign Vanities" as he called them in the Preface. It was to translate writings from some of the "primitive" fathers of the Church once located there. If he took flight, it was as a lyricist, pure and easy; or so he wished his readers of the Preface to believe.

The urge to rewrite and the desire for the "primitive" stem from a similar wish to return blood and bread to his poetry in more ways than one; and I do not think it is at all accidental that the moment when Vaughan first identifies himself with his ancient, warlike clansman, the Silurists (on the title page of *Silex Scintillans* 1650), should coincide with his "regeneration" as a poet under Herbert's tutelage. Both involve quests for a new identity, a new authority, a new way of speaking to the present circumstances. In his earlier poetry, Vaughan had written as an outsider, as a poet on the fringe of a courtly, royalist tradition. "I knew thee not" begins his commendatory poem to Fletcher; "I did but see thee," he remarks at the outset of his verse elegy to Cartwright, although in both cases Vaughan's desire to throw in his lot and join a communal act of Royalist commendation and solidarity was sufficient to overcome these hesitations. And as a poet on the fringe, he registered his wish to belong through a tissue of echoes, especially in his early amatory verse in *Poems* (1646), from Donne, Habington, Carew, and Jonson, among others. He also came to regard himself as a regionalist. As the Swan of the Usk in *Olor Iscanus*, published in 1651 by Humphrey Moseley (but largely completed by 1647), Vaughan voiced his political views (and loyalist support) from afar as well as recorded local goings on: the death of several people killed in action, the appearance of Katherine Phillips as a poet, and of festivity and fellowship in Brecknock. If every poet had a river, Vaughan could be a tributary connected to a European and English mainstream, no less, if he had one too:

> But *Isca*, whensoe'r those *shades* I see,
> And thy *lov'd Arbours* must no more *know* me,
> When I am layd to *rest* hard by thy *streams*,
> And my *Sun sets*, where first it *sprang* in beams,

I'le leave behind me such a *large, kind light*,
As shall *redeem* thee from *oblivious night.*

("To the River *Isca*")

In the aftermath of the Civil War, however, what came west was not poetry but Puritanism.

It would be wrong to suggest that these "secular" poems (as they have come to be called) and the lyrics appearing many years later in *Thalia Rediviva* (1678) are without merit. They show evidence of literary ambition and energy beyond that of much collected in Saintsbury's three-volume edition of *Minor Caroline Poetry*:[4] an attention to odd words or conceits in contemporary usage like "*Kelder* of mists" (meaning "womb," from the Dutch for cellar and probably borrowed from Cleveland's "The King Disguised"); and an ability to extemporize at some length on an incidental topic ("Upon a Cloke lent him by Mr. J. Ridsley"). As Aubrey recognized, Vaughan could be "ingeniose." But the poetry still lacks a sustained theme or, better yet, a purposive vision, a precise register that will fully differentiate Vaughan (whom Aubrey also called "proud and humorous") from the many gentlemen poets of the period. In *Silex*, the break with the genteel tradition is decisive. In the process, however, Vaughan became not less but even more of an outsider – more of a writer on the margins, as might be said today, so long as we remember that in the tradition in which Vaughan was writing in the Renaissance, the margins, in this particular case, were also sites of textual and political power. (Recall the Geneva Bible or the role Welsh antiquity played in the formation of England's identity, to say nothing about Herbert's family lineage in nearby Montgomery.) "I am here in body but not in heart" the poetry and the prose keep repeating. I am with George Herbert, that "most glorious true *Saint*" of the British Church and "a *seer*" whose "incomparable prophetick Poems" predicted the present disasters;[5] I am with St. Paulinus of Nola (in France); I am with the Spanish Jesuit Juan Eusebius Nieremberg; I am with Christ in the Mount of Olives. I am only barely here in the body, as the penultimate paragraph to the 1655 Preface, nearly Vaughan's "final" statement, makes clear; and I am here only because of God's special mercy: "When I expected, and had (by his assistance) prepared for a *message* of *death*, then did he *answer* me with *life*."[6]

To speak of Vaughan as being only barely present in the body is to begin to see how fully he framed his role as an author in this vital but resisting light. Even if we pass quickly by his militant revision of the Book of Common Prayer (banned by the Westminster Assembly in 1645) that appeared as the first part of his *Mount of Olives* (1652), in which the Laudian practice of bowing at the name of Jesus is remembered; even if we refuse an explicitly autobiographical reading of his "Prayer in adversity, and troubles occasioned by Our Enemies" ("Thou seest, O God, how furious and Implacable mine Enemies are, they have not only rob'd me of that portion and provision which thou hadst graciously given me, but they have also washed their hands in the blood of my friends, my dearest and nearest relatives"), there is still the constant call of the wild in Vaughan: the sharp outbursts against the new Puritan authorities for propagating destruction rather than worship;[7] the pointed barbs against the apparent hypocrisy involved in sectarian sainting ("St. Mary Magdalene"); the strange mutterings about "murthered men" amid thoughts of "greenness" ("The Timber"); the frequent lashing out at lewdness ("The Daughter of *Herodias*"); even the cries against God, cries that resonate like "songs in the Night" – to borrow a phrase from the epigram from Job on the title page of the completed *Silex* – with the ubiquitous wish to be elsewhere: in the desert with St. Jerome perhaps, or walking the fields of Bethany with the raised Jesus and his disciples, or simply with the many dead, Abel or otherwise. "They are all gone into the world of light," begins Vaughan with disarming simplicity in one of his most anthologized poems, "And I alone sit lingring here."

As the above remarks will already have suggested, the calling is most acute in the devotional poetry. "More of *fashion* then *force*" is how Vaughan characterized Herbert's other followers in the Preface to the completed *Silex Scintillans*,[8] but the same cannot be said of him in his desire to be elsewhere or in the burst of stanzaic experiments that greets the reader of *Silex* Part I. Herbert had led the way in sounding the heart, but within the "daylight sanity and vigour," in Seamus Heaney's phrasing, of an ever present via media incorporating the principal events of worship.[9] *The Temple* is the story, at one level, of bringing "lovely enchanting language" to church and making it "well dressed and clad," as Herbert says in "The Forerunners." Vaughan is everywhere more woolly in *Silex Scintillans*. His is the narrative of the exile – of the person who, quickened by devotional longing, "*stole* abroad" (my italics), as he says at the outset of "Regeneration," the emphatic opening poem to the 1650 volume:

> A Ward, and still in bonds, one day
> I stole abroad,
> It was high-spring, and all the way
> *Primros'd*, and hung with shade;
> Yet, was it frost within,
> And surly winds
> Blasted my infant buds, and sinne
> Like Clouds ecclips'd my mind.

His search, amid bad inner and outer weather, is for the dazzling light of divinity, as he goes on to say, and it issues in notions of amazing radical change:

> Here, I repos'd; but scarse well set,
> A grove descryed
> Of stately height, whose branches met
> And mixt on every side:
> I entred, and once in

(Amaz'd to see't)
Found all was chang'd, and a new spring
Did all my senses greet;

The unthrift Sunne shot vitall gold
                    A thousand peeces,
And heaven its azure did unfold
            Checqur'd with snowie fleeces,
            The aire was all in spice
                    And every bush
A garland wore; Thus fed my Eyes
            But all the Eare lay hush.

(ll. 33–48)

As these remarkably energetic stanzas suggest, we are at some distance from the pastoral quietude of "To the River *Isca*."[10] With its stunningly lush version of a primitive church that resembles an episcopal cathedral, the passage reminds us that Vaughan's most brilliant verbal effects often have little to do with refashioning courtly discourse and returning it to its heavenly owner. Although there might elsewhere remain a Jonsonian dimension to his verse in his use of the pentameter line or in the smoother octosyllabics of "The Retreate," Vaughan is at his most linguistically inventive when nature (or the speaker's response to a divine quickness in nature), not the court, is the object of mimesis. Fashion disappears in favor of force, perhaps even allowing for the eruption of Welsh sounds within the pattern of English verse. As in the memorable opening of "The Water-fall," the exuberant play with liquid sounds and the shifting, cascading rhythms and abrupt enjambments present us with more than a visual hieroglyph of a waterfall (a common enough practice among emblem poets in Vaughan's day). Vaughan has heard and recirculated the "deep murmurs," as well as the chiding "call" of water, its alluring force and vital energy:

With what deep murmurs through times silent stealth
Doth thy transparent, cool and watry wealth
            Here flowing fall,
            And chide, and call,
As if his liquid, loose Retinue staid
Lingring, and were of this steep place afraid,
            The common pass
            Where, clear as glass,
            All must descend
            Not to an end:
But quickned by this deep and rocky grave,
Rise to a longer course more bright and brave.

("The Water-fall")

Given the level of linguistic intensity recorded in these passages and their evident attention to "quickness," it is perfectly understandable why scholars have not been content to locate Vaughan strictly within Renaissance conventions of the pastoral but have looked to Hermetic texts of the period, especially those produced by Thomas Vaughan, to explain the energizing potential embodied in the representation of nature in the devotional verse (as well as the presence of words with occult inflections like "ray," "seed," "dew," and "tincture," for instance). As Thomas noted, with an elitism characteristic of the Vaughans more generally, "the *Peripatetickes* [Aristotelians] look on *God*, as they do on *Carpenters*, who build with *stone* and *Timber*, without any *infusion* of *life*. But the *world*, which is *Gods building*, is full of *Spirit, quick*, and *living*."[11] "*Quick*" and "*living*" have special meaning for Henry, too, but not only as properties found in the nature identified in his verse. "*Infusions of life*," mobility of thought, characterize the very essence of "sacred ejaculations," as in the celebrated opening of "The Morning-watch":

> O Joyes! Infinite sweetnes! with what flowres,
> And shoots of glory, my soul breakes, and buds!
>> All the long houres
>> Of night, and Rest
>> Through the still shrouds
>> Of sleep, and Clouds,
>> This Dew fell on my Breast;
>> O how it *Blouds*,
> And *Spirits* all my Earth! heark! In what Rings,
> And *Hymning Circulations* the quick world
>> Awakes, and sings.

In this waking hymn, the level of identification with nature is so intense (even if Vaughan begins by way of a line from Herbert's "H. Scriptures") that it is all but impossible to distinguish internal from external: the breaking and budding of the speaker's body from nature's ("O how it *Blouds*, / and *Spirits* all my Earth"), or the "*Hymning Circulations*" in the world from those uttered by the rejuvenated speaker who forcefully twists nouns into verbs. "If *Priest*, and *People* change, keep thou thy ground," Vaughan noted in "Rules and Lessons." Here and elsewhere, the act of keeping is more than an exercise in stoic resolve, just as "ground" is more than a term in a familiar phrase. Keeping is a matter of absorbing and being absorbed by the landscape, of authoring its language in "quickening" turns.

To highlight the animated landscape in Vaughan is to underscore the non-institutionalized (or in the case of "Regeneration," the fleetingly institutionalized) opportunities for worship repeatedly "discovered" in *Silex Scintillans*, the traces of God continually glimpsed in animated things that point to their ultimate home – stones, herbs, and birds, and here especially the cock of "Cock-crowing," in singular possession of a "Sunnie seed" from above:

Father of lights! what Sunnie seed,
What glance of day has thou confin'd
Into this bird? To all the breed
This busie Ray thou hast assign'd;
      Their magnetisme works all night,
      And dreams of Paradise and light.

It is also to note the primitive, shadowy character of Vaughan's landscape to be more like that of Milton's *Mask* (originally staged in nearby Ludlow Castle) than that of the more manicured Herbert: unbounded, alluring, sometimes with odd flora in it, and occasionally overburdened with mystery and meaning. Vaughan's most moving elegy, in fact, starts off in the direction of Herbert, with a courtly reference to a "gallant flower" borrowed from Herbert's "Peace," but then shifts into a mode of deliberate inquiry more reminiscent of a mid-century naturalist like Sir Thomas Browne, in this case the Browne of *Urn-Burial* (1658), since Vaughan's wanderings lead him quickly below ground:

I walkt the other day (to spend my hour)
      Into a field
Where I sometimes had seen the soil to yield
      A gallant flowre,
But Winter now had ruffled all the bowre
      And curious store
   I knew there heretofore.

         2.
Yet I whose search lov'd not to peep and peer
      I'th' face of things
Thought with my self, there might be other springs
      Besides this here
Which, like cold friends, sees us but once a year,
      And so the flowre
  Might have some other bowre.

         3.
Then taking up what I could neerest spie
      I digg'd about
That place where I had seen him to grow out,
      And by and by
I saw the warm Recluse alone to lie
      Where fresh and green
   He lived of us unseen.

Part of the elegy's initial appeal is the leisurely address and the odd details that emerge in the process, especially in the second stanza. These help to "characterize" the speaker in retreat as a wandering recluse himself – the reference to "cold friends" further defining him in his isolation and motivating him to look elsewhere for a warmth less vulnerable to the change of seasons or the whim of social indifference. (The occult linkage between one recluse and another points toward what one critic has called "The Fellowship of the Mystery" in Vaughan.)[12] But the leisurely address is also crucial to setting up the broader drama of the poem: the personal "shock" of recognition that occurs in the middle of the poem, when after rare and intricate questions have been posed, the "warm Recluse" simply declares,

> that he now
> Did there repair
> Such losses as befel him in this air
> And would e'r long
> Come forth most fair and young.

As Stevie Davies rightly notes, the response is met with "an extraordinarily emotional outburst" at the poem's center;[13] but it is also an obscure outburst, since what the speaker "hears" is not the hopeful message of regeneration that readers often draw from the "warm Recluse's" promise to come forth " e'r long … most fair and young." Rather, it is an acute fear of his own "mortality," and the further, deepening recognition of the divided and distinguished worlds to which each "recluse" now inalterably belongs:

> 5.
> This past I threw the Clothes quite o'r his head,
> And stung with fear
> Of my own frailty dropt down many a tear
> Upon his bed,
> Then sighing whisper'd, *Happy are the dead!*
> *What Peace doth now*
> *Rock him asleep below?*

What is so striking and disconcerting (to us as well as the speaker) is the recognition that the dead, in their peaceful sleep, are better off than the living: "Such losses as befel him in this air." Vaughan never specifies what these losses might be (sickness? injury? slaughter?), but like the allusion to "cold friends," they hint at a world well left behind, an attitude amplified many times over in the great long prayer, extended over three stanzas, that concludes the poem:

> 7.
> O thou! whose spirit did at first inflame
> And warm the dead,
> And by a sacred Incubation fed
> With life this frame

Which once had neither being, forme, nor name,
Grant I may so
Thy steps track here below,

8.

That in these Masques and shadows I may see
Thy sacred way,
And by those hid ascents climb to that day
Which breaks from thee
Who art in all things, though invisibly;
Shew me thy peace,
Thy mercy, love, and ease,

9.

And from this Care, where dreams and sorrows raign
Lead me above
Where Light, Joy, Leisure, and true Comforts move
Without all pain,
There hid in thee, shew me his life again
At whose dumbe urn
Thus all the year I mourn.

Elegy, in *Silex*, rarely discovers, or in this case uncovers, a point of view that urges accommodation with an imagined community because the absence of that community is also always being lamented – right down to Vaughan's decision never even to identify by name the person whom he's lamenting. Would anybody out there really care? Or so the poem seems to say.

The wind blows where it lists in *Silex*, but rarely in one direction or for very long and often bringing a bracing sense of chill. To celebrate light – to switch metaphors – is to begin to worry over its loss: "O take it off! make no delay, / But brush me with thy light, that I / May shine unto a perfect day." To find a "gallant flowre" in the landscape is immediately to wish to see through it and eventually to view the landscape as but a "Masque" and shadow leading to a greater reality. As has been recently re-argued, *Silex* "is much more about the possibility of searching than it is about finding,"[14] or more accurately still, about the *problems* of searching, especially in the first part when, in the immediate wake of the Puritan triumph, the rhetoric of retreat is most insistent and Vaughan's sense of displacement from the present most pronounced and profound. An often anthologized poem like "Religion," for instance, begins as if an ideal devotional retreat is being envisioned:

My God, when I walke in those groves,
And leaves thy spirit doth still fan,
I see in each shade that there growes
An Angell talking with a man.

> Under a *Juniper*, some house,
> Or the coole *Mirtles* canopie,
> Others beneath an *Oakes* greene boughs,
> Or at some *fountaines* bubling Eye.

For a moment the sense of the past belongs entirely to Vaughan. The pun on "leaves" hardly diminishes the note of devotional fervor, as the idyllic description continues for another three stanzas and displays what Stephen Greenblatt might call the "marvelous possessions" of the Old Testament: figures of Jacob dreaming and wrestling with Angels, Abraham being visited by his "winged guests," and so forth.[15] But these "possessions," privately imagined and momentarily owned, also come to be seen as signs of loss ("O how familiar then was heaven"), as signs of what the recent disturbances have claimed. "Is the truce broke?" The question simply hangs there in all its glancing insinuations; then proceeds a long Spenserian allegory describing the gradual degradation of Religion until it is seen to break forth like Duessa: "And at first sight doth many please, / But drunk, is puddle, or meere slime / And 'stead of Phisick, a disease." The satire here might be chalked up to Vaughan, the physician, simply leaping into the fray, but the reference to "first sight" – ours and Vaughan's – suggests too the tenuous thread on which even mediated descriptions of faith now hang: how easily, in fact, a vision or reading is sacrificed to present events, how readily the reader is dispossessed of his or her landscape and its marvelous possessions.

The closing prayer attends to this problem. Vaughan calls for a healing that involves both a critique of Puritan worship (and therefore not a real mediation) and a revivification – a quickening – of the land that will allow Angels to talk once more to man, for retreats to be real and idylls not to be idols:

> Heale then these waters, Lord; or bring thy flock,
> Since these are troubled, to the springing rock.
> Looke down great Master of the feast; O shine,
> And turn once more our *Water* into *Wine*!

The eucharistic allusions are unmistakable; but the Biblical inscription that follows suggests, too, that renewal is also linked to the restoration of the church: "*My sister, my spouse is as a garden Inclosed, as a Spring shut up, and a fountain sealed up.*" Vaughan is not Spenser, or St. George, but he can still thrust a sword from below in an attempt to rescue the true church. Vaughan, we remember, translated Juvenal as well as Boethius.

* * *

Still, retreat is never far from Vaughan's thinking (nor is Boethius), even if the subject is often double-edged, and double-edged for more than one reason:

something eagerly desired because it has been so fully interrupted; something denied and therefore more fully desired. Based in part on Book II, Metre 5 of Boethius' *Consolation of Philosophy*, Vaughan's most famous poem, in fact, might be said to worry conventional ideas of retreat (as, say, expressed in Vaughan's own translation of Guevara's *The Praise and Happinesse of the Countrie-Life*) beyond the pale. Rather than a mere anticipation of the glories of childhood eventually perfected in Wordsworth, "The Retreate" is a poignant hymn of personal displacement:

> Happy those early dayes! when I
> Shin'd in my Angell-infancy.
> Before I understood this place
> Appointed for my second race,
> Or taught my soul to fancy ought
> But a white, Celestiall thought.

As in "Religion," the controlling scheme is relentlessly temporal: "before" (or "when," "when," "before" in the remaining paragraph). But with each restatement, the sense of bifurcation between then and now becomes only more deeply etched (as if the act of restating only made Vaughan more aware of the problem of placelessness), until the wish to retreat receives its quintessential expression in a line famously transported from one of Owen Felltham's *Resolves* ("The *Conscience*, the *Caracter* of a God stampt in it, and the apprehension of *Eternity*, doe all prove [the soul] a *shoot of everlastingnesse*"):

> My gazing soul would dwell an houre,
> And in those weaker glories spy
> Some shadows of eternity;
> Before I taught my tongue to wound
> My Conscience with a sinfull sound,
> Or had the black art to dispence
> A sev'rall sinne to ev'ry sence,
> But felt through all this fleshly dresse
> Bright *shootes* of everlastingnesse.

One is tempted to say that the simple addition of "Bright" makes all the poetic difference in the world here, especially when the "shoote" is "felt through all this fleshly dresse" and in the alliterative plural. Much of the emotive thrust of the poem, indeed of Vaughan in general, is fused in this wishful couplet. But as in many of Vaughan's most memorable lines, the brilliance leaves only a deeper yearning in the reader (and the poet) for an afterglow – in this case, if not for a vision of all going into a world of light, then for a view of a luminous past that recedes at a pace faster than the itinerant imagination, as the "O" of desire gives way to the "ah" of defeat:

O how I long to travell back
And tread again that ancient track!
That I might once more reach that plaine,
When first I left my glorious traine,
From whence th' Inlightned spirit sees
That shady City of Palme trees;
But (ah!) my soul with too much stay
Is drunk, and staggers in the way.
Some men a forward motion love,
But I by backward steps would move,
And when this dust falls to the urn
In that state I came return.

"Search well another world; who studies this, / Travels in Clouds, seeks *Manna*, where none is" ("The Search"). Peace is in another country far beyond the stars ("Peace"). Here, the flesh is weak: the soul staggers, "The sons the father kil" ("The Constellation").

If retreat is often as elusive and problematic in *Silex* as it is enchanting, there are still other responses to the difficulties of historical displacement besides melancholy lament or the kind of visionary satire only partially realized in "The World." The world that necessitates escape can also be re-turned, re-imagined as a place ripe for transformation itself: perhaps "healed," as in the end of "Religion," or more radically altered by calling for the Second Coming itself:

Ah! what time wilt thou come? When shall that crie
    The *Bridegroome's Comming*! fil the sky?
Shall it in the Evening run
When our words and works are done?
Or wil thy all-surprizing light
        Break at midnight?

("The Dawning")

In the face of such possibilities, Vaughan seems almost without defense, already transported by the cry from above and wondering now only about the hour of Christ's arrival. Like a good many writings of the 1650s, including some of Marvell's poems, *Silex* reverberates with a sense of great expectations: two Judgment Day poems, one on the Conversion of the Jews, a strange "dramatic monologue" based on an episode from Joshua ("The Stone") and a host of allusions to the day of doom, some appended in the form of Biblical inscriptions, others more loosely suggested through a kind of continuous allegory with light and darkness or an occasional reference to a phrase from Revelation itself.

Marvell might tease this theme in many directions,[16] but for Vaughan, apocalypse is most often represented as a solution to corruption, to the dark changes recently brought about, rather than as a response to belief in the impending possibility of social improvement, in a potential utopian moment:[17]

> Sin triumphs still, and man is sunk below
>   The Center, and his shrowd;
> All's in deep sleep, and night; Thick darknes lyes
>   And hatcheth o'r thy people;
> But hark! what trumpets that? What Angel cries
>   *Arise! Thrust in thy sickle.*

("Corruption")

Egypt is now; for Vaughan, there is no Psalm 114 (as there was for Milton), but the poet still has an enunciating role in the imagined cosmic drama. As Louis Martz has recently noted, "hatcheth o'r" means to close over, to form a hatch over, but "perhaps also with the suggestion of bringing to maturity a hidden process."[18] If so, it is a hidden process, like the shift from "hatch" to "sickle" (without mentioning "hatchet"), in which the speaker participates; for when he suddenly shifts from narrator to auditor to announcer ("But hark!") and recirculates in the imaginary present the blast of trumpets and the angel's cry from Revelation 14: 15, he bears witness to the moment of change itself.

That "sickle" should form a slant rhyme with "people" is perhaps the merest coincidence, a flickering sign of the antipopulism that runs fiercely at times through Vaughan's writing. Elsewhere, however, judgment scenes allow for a return of the repressed, for an opportunity to vocalize victimization beyond that hinted at in the elegies or appearing in the guise of Latin in the prefatory poem to *Olor Iscanus*, "Ad Posteros." In this regard, "Abels blood," remains one of the most restless and unsettling poems in *Silex*. As the blood of the murdered Abel emerges from the ground to protest the slaughter of innocence, so the poem protests the notion of human-sanctioned violence of any sort, including even the usurpation and amplification of Abel's voice as a justification for revenge. (Framing the case against Charles at his trial, the Republican John Cook had done precisely this in asking for justice against the king: "How long Parliament, how long Army, will ye forbear to avenge our blood?")[19]

From the beginning, Vaughan uses "still" to denote an action that is ongoing without, perhaps, ever ending – at least until the moment of Judgment itself when it will be possible, once again, to think of "still" in its other sense of meaning quiet:

> Sad, purple well! whose bubling eye
> Did first against a Murth'rer cry;
> Whose streams still vocal, still complain
>   Of bloody *Cain*,
> And now at evening are as red
> As in the morning when first shed.
>   If single thou

(Though single voices are but low,)
Could'st such a shrill and long cry rear
As speaks still in thy makers ear,
What thunders shall those men arraign
Who cannot count those they have slain,
Who bath not in a shallow flood,
But in a deep, wide sea of blood?
A sea, whose lowd waves cannot sleep,
But *Deep* still calleth upon *deep*:
Whose urgent *sound* like unto that
Of many waters, beateth
The everlasting doors above,
Where souls behinde the altar move,
And with one strong, incessant cry
Inquire *How long?* of the most high.

In Herbert, justice is a matter of balancing scales between sinner and maker, of the speaker arriving at a measured understanding of the role of "merit" at the great day. For Vaughan, it represents a supreme opportunity to speak out: not merely to "complain," but to register through the multiplying voices a sense of sheer outrage over the accumulated acts of violence, irrespective of party politics, and then to attempt to separate himself from the bloody events of Civil War:

O accept
Of his vow'd heart, whom thou hast kept
From bloody men! and grant, I may
That sworn memorial duly pay
To thy bright arm, which was my light
And leader through thick death and night.

It also represents a supreme test of patience. The passionate cry of "*How long*" runs counter to (perhaps "into," given the radical shift in argument at the poem's midpoint) the superior command of the "Almighty Judge! / At whose just laws no just men grudge," including the New Testament "law" of meekness and peace centered in the Sacrifice:

May no cries
From the low earth to high Heaven rise,
But what (like his, whose blood peace brings)
Shall (when they rise) *speak better things*,
Then *Abels* doth!

The allusion to Hebrews 12: 24, in which Jesus's blood is said to speak "better things than *that* of Abel," has Vaughan speaking "better things" than Cook did at the trial of Charles. But even here, while Vaughan can recall Hebrews and retract the thunder of voices from his poem – the "urgent *sound* like unto that / *Of many waters*" – he cannot fully "still" the exclamatory violence from his own voice:

> May *Abel* be
> Still single heard, while these agree
> With his milde blood in voice and will,
> *Who* pray'd for those that did him kill!

As the clinch of the final rhyme indicates, the deep still calls upon the deep. "Will" and "kill" are difficult to dislodge, except through a superior act of the will, indeed perhaps as difficult to dislodge, finally and absolutely for Vaughan in the early 1650s, as a "martyred" king from a crucified Jesus, both of whom are said to have prayed for "those that did him kill!"

* * *

Given the turbulent undertow in a poem like "Abels blood," it is easy to understand why Vaughan frequently prayed for "the patience of the Saints" ("The Palm-tree"). How to walk the straight and narrow ("The Ass," "The Men of War"), how to keep close counsel ("Righteousness") are frequent themes in the second part of *Silex* when the note of expectation and release is especially strong, a note that receives circumstantial grounding in the various allusions to "our sad captivity." They were also prime challenges for Vaughan, as they were for Milton, and therefore attitudes potentially ripe for fashioning into acts of heroic resistance or of sublime secrecy. In the remainder of this chapter, I want to concentrate on two of Vaughan's most impressive poems from this angle. Both are from *Silex* 1655, and in both, with their twin concerns with martyrdom and mysticism, the idea of retreat receives something approaching its ultimate expression in Vaughan.

In the case of "The Proffer," the literature of religious persecution was rich with examples of martyrdom, and the charge to remember them in times of duress was a commonplace in Renaissance England, as the illustrious printing history of Foxe's *Book of Martyrs* makes clear. Vaughan himself cited perhaps the greatest exemplar from late antiquity in his translation of *The Life of Paulinus*: "It is an observation of the Readers of Saint Cyprian, *quod in ejus scriptis singula prope verba Martyrium spirant*, that through all his writings, almost every word doth breath Martyrdome. His expressions are all Spirit and Passion, as if he had writ them with his blood, and conveyed the anguish of his sufferings into his writings."[20] Whether or not Vaughan had Cyprian in mind at the end of "The Proffer" when he exhorted himself (and others, by implication) to "keep the ancient way," he fully imagined the poem from the point of view of the body under siege – attacked by "black Parasites" and "pois'nous, subtile fowls! / The flies of hell" that are clearly associated in the poem with the "Commonwealth."

(Hutchinson plausibly suggests that Vaughan might have been made an offer to "collaborate" with the Puritan authorities.)[21] The poem begins with a powerful denunciation; then as proof of his unbending resistance to temptation, Vaughan offers in the middle a brief "character" of the holy life that he has struggled to achieve, a self-portrait in which "every word doth breath Martyrdome":

> Think you these longing eyes,
>   Though sick and spent,
> And almost famish'd, ever will consent
>   To leave those skies,
> That glass of souls and spirits, where well drest
>   They shine in white (like stars) and rest.
>
> Shall my short hour, my inch,
>   My one poor sand,
> And crum of live, now ready to disband
>   Revolt and flinch,
> And having born the burthen all the day,
>   Now cast at night my Crown away?
>
> No, No; I am not he,
>   Go seek elsewhere.
> I skill not your fine tinsel, and false hair,
>   Your Sorcery
> And smooth seducements: I'le not stuff my story
>   With your Commonwealth and glory.

We do not hear the crackle of the pyre that a recent scholar finds in Cyprian's writings, but we find a similar concern with the visceral as part of the defense of the holy way.[22] Famished as it might be, the body serves as symbol of the soul's steel-like control in the face of temptation. The eyes remain skyward to the end:

> Then keep the antient way!
>   Spit out their phlegm
> And fill thy brest with home; think on thy dream:
>   A calm, bright day!
> A Land of flowers and spices! the word given,
>   *If these be fair, O what is Heaven!*

If "The Proffer" remains undervalued (and is ripe to be further historicized), the poem that has come to seem Vaughan's richest of late "takes the ancient way" in an altogether different manner.[23] In "The Night," the potential martyr's fierce resistance melts in the dusky light of the lover's intimate and secret retreat with Christ. Dark, as it were, calls unto the dark, light unto the light. In this strange and beautiful poem, there is a welcome generosity of intent on

Vaughan's part, a desire, as Frank Kermode has suggested in a related context while revisiting this poem, "to have more of the story than was originally offered"[24] in John 3: 2 (indeed, much of John is relevant); and it produces a powerful overflow of mysterious meaning, a "dark conceit" that brings together Nicodemus and Herbert, the language of the Song of Songs and Dionysius the Areopagite, the first moments of Christianity with the last, a hallowing reverence for the quiet of prayer amid the clatter of the present, the Virgin Mary, Mary Magdalene, and the Bride of Christ, the light of midnight associated with the "Sun" and "a deep, but dazling darkness" that is God.

A poem that has stimulated so many readings need not be reinterpreted again in full, but a few oddities and points of resistance are still worth remarking on. Several appear in the crucial opening stanza:

> Through that pure *Virgin-shrine*,
> That sacred vail drawn o'r thy glorious noon
> That men might look and live as Glo-worms shine,
> And face the Moon:
> Wise *Nicodemus* saw such light
> As made him know his God by night.

On the strength of Vaughan's usual sympathy with nature, a few readers have made the opening conceit more difficult than it is by seeking to draw a parallel between the experience of Nicodemus seeing Christ at night with the habits of glowworms facing the moon.[25] But Vaughan would seem to be developing the contrast; the association of men with glowworms in the seventeenth century was often applied contemptuously, as the example (one of several cited by the *OED*) from Joseph Hall makes especially clear: "the world is full of such glow-wormes, that make some show of Spiritual Light from God." (Given the 1652 date of the work of Hall's in which this phrase appears, it is even conceivable Vaughan had this particular example in mind.)

The contrast helps to throw into sharp relief the special character of Nicodemus's "wisdom." He not only saw the light; the light illuminated him with the knowledge that it was "*his* God" (my italics). While others might continue to face the moon, kept from the light of truth by a veil, he saw through the "pure *Virgin-shrine*" of the moon, a figure that combines chaste Diana with the Virgin Mary, to this other light, "the glorious noon," the "Son" of God. The vision is both compelling and unequivocal. If it injects into the poem a conspiratorial note, moreover, involving a plot of the elect that especially sanctions secrecy, the association is one that appears frequently in Vaughan's writings, particularly later on (see "The Seed growing secretly" and *The Life of Paulinus* as well as the earlier "Love, and Discipline"). It is also a perspective inevitably and often subtly articulated by disenfranchised royalists.[26]

In focusing on Nicodemus, Vaughan stands completely apart from the other devotional poets with whom he is usually associated: Donne, Herbert, Crashaw, or even Milton have no place for Nicodemus in their poetry. And in favoring him, Vaughan goes against strong exegetical evidence to the contrary, perhaps even against Calvin's earlier condemnation of those Protestants as cowardly Nicodemites who chose to go along with Catholic formalities rather than to risk persecution.[27] Nicodemus has been always a questionable figure for the orthodox; but for Vaughan, living in a "land of darkness and blinde eyes," requiring secrecy under the threat of persecution and yet wishing regeneration, Nicodemus could readily be imagined as a "kinred" spirit. "The Night," it should be noted, is next to "Abels blood."

But something else odd happens in the poem, too, something for which, one can only guess, Vaughan's reading of Nicodemus played a pivotal role as well. *Quem quaeritis?* If Nicodemus is the exemplary believer ("Most blest believer he!") who reappears in John 19: 39 to help preserve Jesus's body, Vaughan becomes a Mary Magdalene figure looking for the Lord. "And they say unto her, Woman why weepest thou? She said unto them Because they have taken my Lord, and I know not where they had laid him" (John 20: 13):

> O who will tell me, where
> He found thee at that dead and silent hour!
> What hallow'd solitary ground did bear
>   So rare a flower,
>   Within whose sacred leafs did lie
>   The fulness of the Deity.

Mary's lament for Jesus becomes braided into Vaughan's for a vision comparable to Nicodemus's, a fusion in which the worry of loss, concentrated in the word "dead," is gradually transformed into an experience of wonder by the image of "the fulness of the Deity" emerging from "so rare a flower." There is nothing shocking here, as there is in "I walkt the other day," when the "warm Recluse" delivers its startling message of loss and renewal. Rather, the moment of solitude – Nicodemus's, Mary's, Vaughan's, the reader's – is hallowed, the ground sanctified, as it were, by a view of Jesus alone, observed only by nature and by us:

> No mercy-seat of gold,
> No dead and dusty *Cherub*, nor carv'd stone,
> But his own living works did my Lord hold
>   And lodge alone;
>   Where *trees* and *herbs* did watch and peep
>   And wonder, while the *Jews* did sleep.

"My Lord": from here, we move from one imaginary garden to another, as the voice migrates into that of the bride in the Song of Songs: "I am come into my garden … I sleep, but my heart waketh; *it is* the voice of my beloved that knocketh, *saying*, Open to me, my sister, my love, my dove, my undefiled: for my head is filled with dew, *and* my locks with the drops of the night" (5: 1–2). We might remember the bride as the church represented in "The Brittish Church" lamenting its forced separation from Christ, its head. But in this night of nights, things are different; now the body muses over an amorous return of the head in a moment of near perfect stillness:

> Dear night! this worlds defeat;
> The stop to busie fools; cares check and curb;
> The day of Spirits; my souls calm retreat
>   Which none disturb!
> *Christs* progress, and his prayer time;
> The hours to which high Heaven doth chime.
>
>   Gods silent, searching flight:
> When my Lords head is fill'd with dew, and all
> His locks are wet with the clear drops of night;
>   His still, soft call;
> His knocking time; The souls dumb watch,
> When Spirits their fair kinred catch.

In the allusion to Christ's kingly "progress, and his prayer time," we might be tempted to fantasize momentarily about the other, decapitated, king, whose habits of private prayer had been made available for all England to witness in the frontispiece to *Eikon Basilike* (1649). But the license for a lover's intimacy in this instance belongs to Scripture and to Herbert: the chime of "Prayer (I)" as part of the stanzaic "background" incorporating the "still, soft call" reminds us that the most intimate moment of communion in Vaughan could be fully realized only in company with Herbert. Still, the final enactment of "this worlds defeat" lies elsewhere – in the great concluding stanza:

>   There is in God (some say)
> A deep, but dazling darkness; As men here
> Say it is late and dusky, because they
>   See not all clear;
> O for that night! where I in him
> Might live invisible and dim.

Vaughan is not "there" yet; and were he to arrive, moreover, there would be no means of measuring his desire to be elsewhere – of defeating the world. But the wish has taken him to the farthest outpost of the imagination: to a deep but dazzling darkness so powerful and remote that all thoughts of living – whether with Herbert or Paulinus, Jesus, Nicodemus, or Mary – are willingly exchanged in favor of becoming altogether invisible in God. Here, at the end of "The Night," the distance between militancy and devotion approach zero.

8

FROM WROTH TO PHILIPS

Women poets of the earlier seventeenth century

When your faire hand receaves this Little Book,
You must not there for Prose or Verses look.
Those empty regions which within you see,
May by your self planted and peopled bee.
And though wee scarce allow your Sex to prove
Writers (unless the argument be Love)
Yet without crime or envy You have roome
Here both the Scribe and Authour to become.
　　　　　　Henry King, "Upon a Table-book presented to a Lady"

In almost all our chapters on seventeenth-century poetry, we could have dwelt on the work of women poets. The Jacobeans Mary Wroth and Aemilia Lanyer have already been briefly mentioned in connection with Jonson. Nearer mid-century, the little-known An Collins and the flamboyant Anna Trapnel continue pietistic strains, one of a personal, meditative order associated with Herbert and Vaughan, the other more radically political, with roots in prophetic literature and the popular ballad. At the same time, the poetry of Anne Bradstreet, the Puritan saint transplanted to the New World, was returning to the English shores with echoes both familiar and strange, while Margaret Cavendish was provocatively warbling her fanciful woodnotes wild. The next decade witnessed the appearance of the royalist Katherine Philips, whose lyrics responded creatively to the Caroline refinements already made on Donne and Jonson and helped to inaugurate the notion of a modern tradition of female poets.

Although questions remain about how best to represent and analyze the achievements of women writers – doesn't isolating them for reasons of gender threaten to reproduce the conditions of secondariness many were contesting? – there are practical advantages to thinking collectively about their poetry, much of which is only becoming known outside specialized scholarly circles and yet still eludes ready assessment. (The ongoing recovery and editing of primary texts has made gaining an overview especially difficult.)[1] But there are theoretical and historical reasons as well for grouping women poets together since it is frequently the case that, whatever the chosen genre or topic, the shaping perspective was self-consciously female, although in no single or simple way. And, again in no single or simple way, as this chapter will emphasize, women began to participate in the broader phenomenon of authorship that is so decisive a feature of late sixteenth- and early seventeenth-century English culture. While the sixteenth century witnessed a number of remarkably learned women, especially among the courtly elite – the names of Lady Jane Grey, Queen Elizabeth, and Mary Sidney, the Countess of Pembroke, come quickly to the lips – it is not until the early seventeenth century that independently authored volumes of verse begin to appear on the horizon as an active, if not sustained, demonstration of poetic literacy by women. To the Tudor habits of frequent paraphrase, translation, and supplementation, then, is added the occasional female venture into individual expression, sometimes, as in the case of Aemilia Lanyer, of a decidedly feminist kind.

By inviting us to think about women poets of the seventeenth century, moreover, recent scholars have helpfully laid to rest the myth of "Judith Shakespeare," Virginia Woolf's colorful but anachronistic belief that:

> any woman born with a great gift in the sixteenth century would certainly have gone crazed, shot herself, or ended her days in some lonely cottage outside the village, half witch, half wizard, feared and mocked at. For it needs little skill in psychology to be sure that the highly gifted girl who had tried to use her gift for poetry would have been so thwarted and hindered by other people, so tortured and pulled asunder by her own contrary instincts, that she must have lost her health and sanity to a certainty.[2]

As has been recently documented, over 650 first editions of works were published by women in the seventeenth century;[3] and in addition to these publicly visible signs of literary activity, one must also take into account the considerable part women played in the manuscript culture of the time as either recipient or author or both. Even if a precise reckoning of their participation is impossible to determine, we know on the basis of anecdote and inference that among some elite circles women were more active as poets than existing textual evidence will support. Jonson's tantalizing remark to Drummond that "The Countess of Rutland was nothing inferior to her father, S[ir] P. Sidney, in poesy" is well known,[4] although not a word of the countess's verse has come to light; and as the epigraph to this chapter suggests, Henry King, the Bishop of Chichester, friend of Donne, and author of "The Exequy," participated in a circle that, while recognizing wider cultural limits placed on female expression, encouraged women to think of the private "table-book" as an appropriate place to "become" both "Scribe and Authour."

In accepting the revisionist view, however, that women of the period not only wrote but wrote poetry and wrote in increasing numbers as the century progressed, we should be wary of constructing a version of female poetic authority that mirrors too closely the beliefs and assumptions available only to the dominant male writers of the period. And we should be cautious, too, of implying a counter-myth of poetic originality and technical experimentation to match what was happening in the mainstream, as varied and multiple in its tributaries as it was. For religious, social, and economic reasons, the range of activities available was far more limited for women than for men. Narrower still was a corresponding range of experience that might find expression in poetry. In a culture that rarely tired of praising women for their chastity of mind, tongue, and body – and censuring them when any of the three were thought to be absent – a good many of the "new" genres practiced at the turn of the century were simply out of bounds as acceptable subjects for imitation. Satire and the epigram, for instance, were decidedly and, from the point of view of female authorship, inhospitably "masculine" in stance and attitude, as was the Ovidian elegy, with its frank eroticism and frequent celebration (or denigration) of the female body. Lady Bedford might be seen as an appropriate reader for Donne's satires, as Jonson points out in one epigram, but when he praises her in another poem for her "learned and manly soul," it is not because he thought she should put on the habit of the satirist. As Rosalind, playing the man and voicing the dominant view, says in *As You Like It*, "Woman's gentle brain / Could not drop forth such giant-rude invention" (IV, iii, 34–5).

At the same time, the kind of literary ambition revealed by a Drayton or a Jonson depended in large part on strategic and frequent ventures into the public arena of print. But for women, speaking through the medium of print was potentially a doubly fraught affair. Along with the usual class strictures operating in aristocratic circles, where the opportunities for literacy by women were greatest, went the accompanying perception that the public sphere was hardly the place for any woman to air her views. In her one act of publication, for instance, Mary Wroth found herself the target of a furious attack by Edward Denny, Baron of Waltham, for supposedly slandering him in the first part of her prose romance *Urania*, published in 1621; and Denny's method of attack, which Wroth turned against him, was to underscore her sexually "unnatural" appearance in print as "Hermaphrodite in show."[5] (Without admitting to his allegations, Wroth nonetheless stopped the sale of her book.) As the epigraph taken from King's poem again suggests, the perceived secondary status of women contributed to the wider cultural assumption that women exist as poets by permission, not by right ("wee scarce allow your Sex to prove / Writers"), and that the "self" King imagines being "planted" and multiplying ("peopled") does so within a restricted and private space ("this Little Book"), not as part of the public sphere. It is little wonder that scarcely a printed volume of poetry written by a woman appears in the earlier seventeenth century that does not find a way to apologize for its public appearance (and even, as happens with a Lanyer or Cavendish, to make that apology into the extended subject of the poetic occasion). Nor is it surprising that modern feminists frequently mark such published speech acts as "transgressive."

With access to the official educational institutions closed to them whatever their rank – women were not allowed to attend university, a point lamented by Martha Moulesworth – the domestic sphere of the home constituted the basic and in many instances the only classroom for women in this period. Given the literary prominence of a number of households in Tudor and Stuart England, this situation need hardly be construed as intellectually impoverishing. Writing in the middle of the Restoration, Bathsua Makin, one of the most learned women of the age and the former royal tutor of Elizabeth, daughter to Charles I, readily recited the names of women associated with some of the great households of the recent past as part of her argument that "Women have been good Poets": "the four Daughters of Sir *Anthony Cook*, also the Lady *Russel*, the Lady *Bacon*, the Lady *Killegrew* ... the beautiful and learned Lady *Mary*, Countess of *Pembrook*, the worthy Sister to that incomparable Person Sir *Philip Sidney* ... The Lady *Jane Grey*, and the Lady *Arabella* [Stuart]," as well as Queen Elizabeth and Lord Burleigh's "three Daughters."[6] Other names, too, a bit further down the social scale could be easily added: Elizabeth Cary, Viscountess Falkland and only child of a prosperous lawyer; Lady Anne Southwell, of a prominent family from Devon; or Lucy Hutchinson, the daughter of Sir Allen Apsley, Lieutenant of the Tower. But for a good many women drawn from the less educated classes, the domestic life – and its hardships – constituted the sole subject for verse: from the rhymed "sayings" of one Katherine Dowe, a dairy wife at Sibton Abbey, Suffolk,

> Arise earelie
> Serve God devoutly.
> Then to they [sic] work bustlie
> To thy meat joyfully
> To thy bed merilie
> And though thou fare poorely
> And thy lodging homelie
> Yet thank God highly,[7]

to the painful couplets by the twice married Lady Mary Carey as she prepares to bury yet another child,

> What birth is this; a poore despissed creature?
>   A little Embrio; voyd of life, and feature.[8]

To all but a select few women in the earlier seventeenth century, the notion of belonging to a "clan" or "tribe" other than one's immediate family would have seemed beyond the pale, and even in these instances the notion of "belonging" would have to be carefully qualified. Dryden's famous remark at the end of the century about Milton being Spenser's "poetical son" reminds us that the language of literary inheritance at this time is still the language of the dominant (male) culture.[9] As Bathsua Makin observes, examples of female poets could be traced as far back as Corinna of Thebes in the third century BC and Sappho in the sixth century BC (with a few references to Minerva thrown in for good measure), but the discontinuous nature of her comments makes another point as well. At this moment in history, there was no "tradition" of women's poetry that might parallel the version so comfortably enunciated by Dryden: no talk of female authors conversing with one another, no talk of one soul becoming "transfused" into the body of another.[10] In Makin's formulation, Bradstreet and Philips exist next to each other as contemporaries but not in "relation" to each other. Bradstreet comes first, with her own "Works" testifying independently to her qualities as a poet, then Philips. For Philips, however, "we need no other Encomium … than what Mr. *Cowley* gives"; her connection is not with Bradstreet but with the dominant tradition, although Makin also goes on to add in the manner of an afterthought, "besides, her Works in print speak for her."

Mary Wroth (1587?–1651?) and Aemilia Lanyer (1569–1645)

The problem of access to literary traditions and models was, of course, less severe for women with connections to literary families, and to some degree the difference between the two most interesting (and ambitious) female Jacobean poets – Mary Wroth and Aemilia Lanyer – can be accounted for in these terms: Wroth near the center, Lanyer on the periphery of elite society. Notwithstanding the spectacular collapse of her personal fortunes after the death of her husband, Sir Robert Wroth, in 1614 and a personal life that soon exceeded the conventional in the two illegitimate children she bore her rakish cousin William Herbert, the third Earl of Pembroke, Mary Wroth seems always to have written as a Sidney. She found thoroughly congenial the courtly, amatory genres favored by her famous uncle (and in slighter fashion by her father, Sir Robert Sidney), and as a woman, she exhibited the determination to write as shown earlier by her celebrated aunt and namesake, Mary Sidney, the Countess of Pembroke.[11] To be a Sidney in Jacobean England was already to belong to a literary tradition, as Jonson so clearly understood in writing "To Penshurst." Penshurst Place was also the home of Mary Sidney before she became Mary Wroth.

More specifically, being a Sidney meant writing sonnets and pastoral lyrics, a play for a private audience – in this case the Neoplatonic *Love's Victory* – and many, many pages of prose, interspersed with lyrics in imitation of *The Countess of Pembroke's Arcadia*. *The Countess of Montgomery's Urania*, published in a first installment in 1621 of some 350,000 words (a second installment of another 240,000 words is still in manuscript), is the *work* of a Jacobean (female) Sidney, buoyed up by an allegiance to both aunt and uncle. It is a beautiful folio volume, replete with a handsome title page spelling out the author's distinguished family connections, and it concludes with a separately paginated sonnet sequence, *Pamphilia to Amphilanthus*, Wroth's best known group of poems that also survives in a slightly longer and different arrangement in another manuscript.

If being a Sidney shaped Mary Wroth's poetic identity, and if, in turn, being seen by her contemporaries as one "in whom her *Uncle's* noble Veine renewes" – to borrow Joshua Sylvester's phrase – helped to enhance her place at James's court and to sustain her in her later exile from it, her verse has notable attributes of its own. Her sonnets are more inward and reflective than her uncle's, less given to dramatic and rhetorical playfulness, less consciously inventive with respect to other sonneteers, more autumnal or nocturnal in mood. (The last mentioned quality has received special emphasis in feminist readings of her poetry.)[12] Wroth is an exacting prosodist, but rarely do the stress patterns underscore the kind of extravagant emotionality so often encountered in Sidney. Nor does she seek to overwhelm by acts of technical virtuosity that, at one level, are meant to work their charms on the desired subject of address.

What has especially attracted readers of late, rather, is the recognition that the sonnets give expression to the woman's part in the Petrarchan scheme of wooing; sometimes they are even credited with no less an accomplishment than the invention of a female subjectivity.[13] Although Wroth's contemporaries seemed not to have been struck by this particular feature of her verse, *Pamphilia to Amphilanthus* has the distinction of being the first sonnet sequence in English to give voice to a woman's predicament in what had been until then a male literary domain:

> Am I thus conquer'd? have I lost the powers
>   That to withstand, which joy's to ruin mee?
>   Must I bee still while itt my strength devowres
>   And captive leads mee prisoner, bound, unfree?[14]

The familiar Petrarchan quandary of feeling helpless in love reverberates, in this instance, with an additional note of vexation and frustration, of the speaker's feeling doubly bound by Cupid and by convention:

> Love first shall leave mens phant'sies to them free,
>   Desire shall quench loves flames, spring hate sweet showres,
>   Love shall loose all his darts, have sight, and see
> His shame, and wishings hinder happy howres.

And doubly annoyed, as woman and lover, over her servility:

> Why should wee nott loves purblind charmes resist?
>   Must wee bee servile, doing what hee list?
>   Noe, seeke some hoste to harbour thee: I fly

> Thy babish trickes, and freedome doe profess;
>> Butt O my hurt, makes my lost hart confess
>> I love, and must: So farwell liberty.

But she is also unable to imagine for very long, or very emphatically, another alternative to her circumstances. Her flight is a brief and airy trespass, her return a muted and dutiful concession. In her desire to seek out some other "hoste," we are reminded of Herbert in "The Collar," but without the anger and snap.

"Predicament," in fact, seems to be the right word to describe the kind of emotional and circumstantial complexity revealed in a sonnet like this, one that perhaps helps to explain why a contemporary like Jonson might proclaim Wroth's artistry rather than her originality. As a number of modern readers have suggested, the sonnets do not assert a strongly eroticized female point of view to match or to rival the kind of rhetorical flourishings exhibited by male wooers.[15] There are no blazons, no attempts at seductive persuasion, no groveling at the feet of the beloved in *Pamphilia to Amphilanthus*. As her sonnet beginning "Like to the Indians, scorched with the Sun" suggests, Wroth's speaker bears "the marke of Cupids might" – the stigmata of eros – inwardly, "in hart as they in skin" bear the mark of Phoebus's light. And as these sonnets further illustrate, Wroth's poems frequently reaffirm the value of constancy: from a pledge of ceaseless "offrings to love while I Live," to the plain-speaking resolve of "I love, and must."

Indeed, more often than not we are struck by the frequent removal, not the reversal, of the usually explicit gender markings in this genre, as Wroth makes Pamphilia's own subjectivity, not Amphilanthus, the object of her focus, her pursuit. Pamphilia can flee – into the self (how is my situation comparable to that of a dark-skinned Indian whose part I once played in Jonson's 1606 *Masque of Blackness?*); or into darkness, in the poem beginning:

> Truly poore Night thou wellcome art to mee
>> I love thee better in this sad attire
>> Then that which raiseth some mens phant'sies higher
>> Like painted outsid[e]s which foule inward bee.

She regards herself not as a galley charged with forgetfulness but as

>> a ship, on Goodwines cast by wind,
> The more she strives, more deepe in sand is prest
> Till she bee lost; so am I, in this kind
> Sunk, and devour'd, and swallow'd by unrest.

But what she never does is pursue Amphilanthus: the Duchess of Malfi she is not. One might say, as Jonson implies, that courtly decorum, especially of a high

Sidneyan order, does not permit Wroth to be the aggressor, a Daphne chasing Apollo; that image might too readily become material for male erotic fantasy, as happens near the end of Carew's "A Rapture." Nor does Wroth regard her circumstances in any sustained sense as typically or representatively female. In her frequently anthologized sonnet, "When every one to pleasing pastime hies," it is the aristocratic activity at a country estate, not her sex, that provides the standards for establishing an even more aristocratic conception of the "self," as the first quatrain makes clear:

> When every one to pleasing pastime hies
>> Some hunt, some hauke, some play, while some delight
> In sweet discourse, and musique showes joys might
>> Yet I my thoughts doe farr above thes prise.

Wroth's is, in short, an art of the finely "spun" sentiment – to borrow a reso-nantly gendered image for writing verse from *Urania*[16] – that often comes trailing clouds of Sidneyan glory:

> You blessed starrs which doe heavns glory show,
>> And att your brightnes makes our eyes admire
>> Yett envy nott though I on earth beelow
>> Injoy a sight which moves in mee more fire;
>
> I doe confess such beauty breeds desire,
>> You shine, and cleerest light on us beestow,
>> Yett doth a sight on earth more warmth inspire
>> Into my loving soule, his grace to knowe;
>
> Cleere, bright, and shining as you are, is this
>> Light of my joye, fixt stedfast nor will move
>> His light from mee, nor I chang from his love,
> But still increase as th'eith [the height] of all my bliss.
>> His sight gives lyfe unto my love-rulde eyes
>> My love content because in his, love lies.

The difference between the first and second quatrains is one of degree not kind, a shift in emphasis that allows for both a greater clarification and an intensification of the effects of eros: "I doe confess such beauty breeds desire," says the star-gazing speaker, putting on her Astrophelian hat. And yet it is important to note that however warm the heart has become and whatever erotic intimations are ignited by her "confession," the emerging distinction between celestial beauty and earthly passion does not mean, for Wroth, that the body will become the book. In the concluding sestet, Wroth swerves away from this Donnean possibility in favor of defining a more delicate interweaving between the lovers that underscores a dynamic mutuality based on constancy.

As happens elsewhere in the sonnet sequence, the couplet unfolds a miniature labyrinth of love, one in which admitted subordination ("my love-rulde eye") still asks to be distinguished from a posture of abject dependency. The male lover who emerges in the latter portion of the poem is associated with sight, the (implied) female speaker with "life." He might give life to her love, but she gives "content," both peace *and* substance, to their love. As the sonnet subscribes to the conventions of male–female hierarchy in some ways – he is active, she is passive – so it also characteristically invites us to value an interiority, a content, associated with the speaker: to grant meaning and substance, in fact, to the "voice" doing the speaking in this particular sonnet and, by implication, in the sequence at large.

Wroth's many sonnets invite fine-tuned readings of this sort. The sensibility registered here is conscious of its "worth" – the pun was not lost on Wroth's contemporaries – and yet part of the appeal of the sonnets is their slightly less than "finished" feel: the greater latitude they allow for the process of exploring the inner life of passion, the quieter, though no less deeply felt, ebb and flow of emotions rather than the triumphant sounding of a monumental love:

> My hart is lost, what can I now expect,
>> An ev'ning faire; after a drowsie day?
>> (Alas) fond phant'sie this is nott the way
>> To cure a morning hart, or salve neglect.

Were Wroth writing verse today, one suspects she would be an aficionado of the half or slant rhyme, a practitioner of the art of imperfect closure that allows a little more breathing room from the heat of passion, a little more space for individual expression. Wroth's most memorable lines, in fact, are given to figuring the ebb and flow of eros in a context that also reminds us (as it perhaps reminded her contemporaries) of her Sidneyan high-mindedness as both poet and lover:

> In this strang labourinth how shall I turne?
>> Wayes are on all sid[e]s while the way I miss:
>> If to the right hand, ther, in love I burne;
>> Lett mee goe forward, therin danger is;

> If to the left, suspition hinders bliss,
>> Lett mee turne back, shame cries I ought returne
>> Nor fainte though crosses with my fortunes kiss;
>> Stand still is harder, although sure to mourne;

> Thus lett mee take the right, or left hand way;
>> Goe forward, or stand still, or back retire;
>> I must these doubts indure with out allay
>> Or help, but traveile find for my best hire;

Yet that which most my troubled sence doth move
Is to leave all, and take the thread of love.

Jonson very likely had in mind this and the following thirteen sonnets that form "A crowne of Sonetts dedicated to Love" when he invokes the image of a crown to begin his epigram "To Mary, Lady Wroth":

How well, fair crown of your fair sex, might he
    That but the twilight of your sprite did see,
And noted for what flesh such souls were framed,
    Know you to be a Sidney, though unnamed.

And just as likely, Jonson implies, the reader years hence will know her as a Sidney for her "crown" even if she herself remains unnamed. In the intricate weavings of the coronal form, we trace her lineage – her uncle included one example in *The Old Arcadia* – and perhaps her ambition to complete a sequence whose complicated artistry baffled her father. (Sir Robert Sidney managed to complete drafts of only four out of a probable thirteen poems.)[17] And in celebrating constancy as the highest rung in the Neoplatonic ladder of love, as happens most emphatically (and appropriately) in the crown of sonnets, Wroth locates herself squarely within a Sidneyan tradition of the idealizing court poet, whose skills are valued precisely because he (and now she) can feign notable images of virtue for others to emulate. As for the idea of the labyrinth of love quoted above, Wroth leaves her individual signature in the turns and counterturns of phrase and argument. Hesitant and yet resolute, she is more the Daedalian artist working out her amatory predicament than a female Theseus relying on her wits to escape love's clutches: a modest Britomart not too bold and yet, notwithstanding love's manifold trials, willing to embrace love's experience and "turn" it into verse.

Aemilia Lanyer, by contrast, is neither Daedalus nor Britomart. Until recently, in fact, what fame this daughter of a Venetian-born musician and his common-law wife possessed rested on A.L. Rowse's questionable nomination of her for the role of the "dark lady" in Shakespeare's sonnets. The evidence for the attribution is slim at best, but the association hints (darkly) at one of the major differences between Wroth and Lanyer. Although their paths must have crossed at court, the particular literary traditions and models open to Wroth were less accessible, although not quite closed, to Lanyer, who could claim only a marginal, not a lineal, connection to nobility. But claim it she did. *Salve Deus Rex Judaeorum* (1611), a slender quarto of 110 pages, is Lanyer's only publication and a chief source of the little we know about her, but it speaks volumes about Lanyer's desire to use poetry to create a place for herself and for women in the highly stratified, gender-conscious world of Jacobean society.

Here, for example, is the spacious opening stanza from the first of no less than ten dedicatory addresses (excluding her general preface "To the Vertuous

Reader"). All are directed to important women of the day, this one to Queen Anne:

> Renowned Empresse, and great Britaines Queene,
> Most gratious Mother of succeeding Kings;
> Vouchsafe to view that which is seldome seene,
> A Womans writing of divinest things:
> > Reade it faire Queene, though it defective be,
> > Your Excellence can grace both It and Mee.[18]

Compared to the shadowy, intricately wrought "rooms" of Mary Wroth's sonnets, Lanyer's verse seems emphatically available. The above stanza unfolds with the clean sweep of a bow, its announcement decorous but fully audible. What is announced, though, is not the presentation of a literary work alone or even an image of "A Womans writing of divinest things," but a view of what is "seldom seene": a not quite private showing of female authorship as a significant event in and of itself – not quite private because the woman writing to the queen here is also doing so in a style remarkable for its lucidity. We clearly observe a woman writing before the queen about becoming visible as a woman writer, or more precisely, about becoming visible because she is a woman writer. In 1611 – the year in which the King James Bible first appeared – this was a startling claim to make in public.

Much of our interest in *Salve Deus* is consequently of an historical or archeological nature. Who are the women addressed in the commendatory poems? What is Lanyer's relationship to them: the Lanyer identified on the 1611 title page as "Wife to Captaine *Alfonso Lanyer* Servant to the Kings Majestie," but also the Lanyer who once enjoyed "great pomp" as mistress to Henry Cary, Queen Elizabeth's Lord Chamberlain, and in a series of revealing conversations in 1597 with the astrologer Simon Forman, expressed anxiety over not having made a fortunate marriage.[19] And, of course, what did she hope to accomplish by dedicating poems to so many women: not just Queen Anne of Denmark and "great Britaines Queene," but, in the following order, Princess Elizabeth, the eldest daughter of the king and queen, "all vertuous Ladies in generall," James's first cousin, Lady Arabella Stuart, Ladie Susan Montgomery, Countess of Kent, Mary Sidney, Countess of Pembroke, Lucy, Countess of Bedford, Katherine (Howard), Countess of Suffolk, Anne (Clifford), Countess of Dorset, and finally and for good measure, the "vertuous reader" in general. When one adds to this list of commendatory poems the concluding "Description of Cooke-ham," Lanyer's personal recollection of her early days on the Clifford estate, we have a collection in which the framing material nearly equals in length the poem that is the occasion for the dedicatory addresses themselves: Lanyer's "complaint" on the Passion of Jesus that serves as the centerpiece and title for the volume, *Salve Deus Rex Judaeorum*.

As some of her modern readers have noted, Lanyer has taken more than a page out of the male practice of writing patronage verse as a way of climbing the social ladder at court, and there is an element of ludic ingenuity in making this material go as far as it can. But *Salve Deus* is not *A Tale of a Tub* or *Coriat's Crudities*. In keeping with the decorum of her main subject, Lanyer treats her commendatory material seriously, even reverently, inviting each of her potential patronesses to become a participant in a communal "feast" by sharing imaginatively in the Sacrifice, and insisting, all the while, on the special symmetry between the subject at the center – Jesus – and the female subjects on the margins, the women in the Bible and their latter-day reflections in Jacobean England. For however noble the latter are – and Lanyer thinks of her poetry as a "mirror" in which the inward, not the outward, beauty of each woman is on display – the women are also revealed as sharing a common bond not just in Jesus but also in Eve: the gender-specific sign of their subordinate place in the patriarchal world of Jacobean society.

Along with praise, in short, goes complaint – with a capital C (as in Daniel's *Complaint of Rosamond*). These two sides of an already antiquated "mirror" tradition were more associated, appropriately, with poetry written under the female Elizabeth (whose passing is nostalgically recalled at the outset of the Passion sequence) than with verse written under James. And if one side allows a class-conscious Lanyer to magnify her individual subjects in a way that respects social and class difference, that respects rank, in other words, as a valued category within English society, the other encourages a gender-conscious Lanyer to shrink the space that separates her from her patroness by emphasizing the common ground between them. Whatever their social and economic differences, they are fellow laborers in an essentially male vineyard. As Lanyer's remarks to Queene Anne suggest in a stanza that also alludes to "Faire *Eves* Apologie," these potentially conflicting demands can produce a text as complicated as Wroth's but for different reasons:

> Behold, great Queene, Faire *Eves* Apologie,
> Which I have writ in honour of your sexe,
> And do referre unto your Majestie,
> To judge if it agree not with the Text:
> And if it doe, why are poore Women blam'd,
> Or by more faultie Men so much defam'd?

A respect for rank and propriety requires that Lanyer observe an (unnatural) distinction in the pronouns in the second line. To have said "our sexe" rather than "your sexe," in the context of honoring the queen, would have seemed too familiar; it would have risked undermining the very structure supporting the queen's authority upon which Lanyer depends for her own authority. And yet, as Lanyer goes on to suggest, if in exercising her Minerva-like role as judge, the queen agrees with Lanyer's interpretation of "the Text," she would then validate not just the truth of the author's "complaint" but the unspoken

221

reality of this "other" bond between them: that of a reciprocated female loyalty.

Lanyer's verse might best be regarded then as giving voice to this "other" bond in a context that openly recognizes, and at times laments, the significant disparity in rank that divides the author from her potential patronesses. In this sense, Lanyer is both the creator of an imagined "female community" – to adopt momentarily Barbara Lewalski's phrasing – and the odd person out. She is the only one without any claim to title except as a woman "writing of divinest things"; but it is a title that has value in Jacobean England only as the value of woman is consciously amplified. We hear, therefore, of not one but many women, about their accomplishments in the past and present in many different capacities: ruler, nurturer, mother, moral guide, poet, visionary, with specific names attached to each. And we hear from many women within the poem lamenting the death of Jesus. We find, too, at the center of *Salve Deus* a Jesus with barely a drop of patriarchal blood in his body. As Lanyer reminds "The Vertuous Reader" of the Preface in a remark that illuminates the structure of her own account of the Passion narrative itself, the Son of God was "begotten of a woman, borne of a woman, nourished of a woman, obedient to a woman; and that he healed woman, pardoned women, comforted women: yea, even when he was in his greatest agonie and bloodie sweat, going to be crucified, and also in the last houre of his death, tooke care to dispose of a woman; after his resurrection, appeared first to a woman, sent to declare his most glorious resurrection to the rest of his Disciples" (pp. 49–50).

And we hear from one female witness in particular not mentioned in the above catalog. The most original and now most often anthologized portion of *Salve Deus* occurs when another "wife" is asked to speak. The woman known in the Passion story only as Pilate's wife is mentioned only in Matthew, and then only in a single sentence as follows: when Pilate "was set down on the judgment seat, his wife sent unto him, saying, Have thou nothing to do with that just man: for I have suffered many things this day in a dream because of him" (Matthew 27: 19). Compared to the more familiar activities of the Hebraic heroines or the New Testament women mentioned by Lanyer in "To the Vertuous Reader," the part played by Pilate's wife in the Bible is small indeed and is generally treated so by Scriptural commentators. The Geneva Bible does not even bother to gloss the incident, even though Calvin in his *Commentary on the Harmony of the Evangelists* called her dream an example of the "extraordinary inspiration of God" and defended her against "the commonly supposed [view] that the devil stirred up this woman in order to retard the redemption of mankind."[20]

Lanyer was probably drawn to "this woman," however, not because of Calvin's defense but for the same reason that her contemporary Lady Anne Southwell was: Pilate's wife was regarded as a domestic paragon, an example of the good wife offering counsel to her wayward husband.[21] She was obviously a figure who would be viewed sympathetically by Lanyer's immediate audience.

But if Lanyer was counting on this association, she also wished to amplify domestic counsel into cultural critique, as the voice of Pilate's wife becomes indistinguishable from Eve's, which blends with that of another female speaker, the "author" as identified on the title page where it can be seen as inseparable from the Jacobean patriarchy: "Mistris *Aemilia Lanyer*, Wife to Captaine *Alfonso Lanyer* Servant to the Kings Majestie." Hers is, as it were, the unauthorized version of the Fall, the Crucifixion, and the present historical moment. Generically, it is the complaint of female complaints. In what can only be described as a deeply subversive twist of the usual typological connections made between the Fall in the Garden and the Crucifixion in Golgotha, Lanyer sees in the crime that Pilate is about to commit an argument for redeeming women from their subservient place in the hierarchy. In Lanyer's new typology, Pilate's greater criminality "proves" Eve's greater innocence. His is crime done out of pure malice (and pusillanimity, as it turns outs; Pilate is seen to behave like a weak courtier); Eve's is done out of ignorance. His is committed in spite of a wife's admonition, hers without benefit of a husband's warning. If, moreover, with Calvin, Lanyer thinks of Pilate's wife as propelling, not retarding, the redemption (and therefore not acting as an agent of the devil), the redemption Lanyer imagines is more political than eschatological. It is in the here and now, not at some indefinite point in the future, and it centers specifically on women, not on mankind generally. The remarkable conclusion to this section is as follows:

> Then let us have our Libertie againe,
> And challendge to your selves no Sov'raigntie;
> You came not in the world without our paine,
> Make that a barre against your crueltie;
> Your fault beeing greater, why should you disdaine
> Our beeing your equals, free from tyranny?
>> If one weake woman simply did offend,
>> This sinne of yours, hath no excuse, nor end.

From the point of view of Biblical hermeneutics, some of Lanyer's arguments are stronger than others. Her defense that Eve sinned out of ignorance skips lightly over the fact that Eve also knowingly violated God's command (Genesis 3: 1); so, too, her claim that Eve's was the lesser crime because she was the weaker of the two risks making Eve seem only a reflex of Adam. But if Lanyer's entrance into the field of Biblical hermeneutics creates space for further responses, her attempts to use Eve's "Apologie" to redress the balance of power between the sexes is also more than another bid for patronage. The odd squaring, at the center of *Salve Deus*, of Pilate's cruelty to Jesus and the suffering of women at the hands of men that began with the Fall, takes Lanyer to the outer edges of traditional Biblical criticism and invites a view of gender equality that, in Jacobean England, is positively utopian. As Janel Mueller has argued, the feminist politics of *Salve Deus* are without immediate antecedents in the vernacular literature in England, although Lanyer's combative "defense" looks forward to the local *querelle des femmes* that was soon to erupt in the pamphlet literature by the likes of Joseph Swetnam and Rachel Speght and anticipates further down the line the radical egalitarianism of Mary Astell.[22]

As this stanza intimates, Lanyer is frequently on the verge of breaking boundaries, historical and rhetorical, which is one way to describe the present appeal of *Salve Deus*. And yet, as outward and forward-looking as Lanyer can sound, she is still very much bound up in the hierarchical culture she wishes, in some respects, to alter. Her "Description of Cooke-ham," appended to *Salve Deus* (but in some ways an easier introduction to her work), highlights the discrepancy between her visionary politics and the social realities of Jacobean culture. Sometimes regarded as another "first" for Lanyer, this time in the genre of the "country house poem," the 210-line "Cooke-ham" returns the reader to the private estate of the Countess of Cumberland, mother to the (now) better known Anne Clifford, with Lanyer using the occasion to trace out her own tenuous affiliations with this noble family. Like all of Lanyer's poetry, it has a distinctly sympathetic female slant, one made more poignant, even sentimental in places, by the note of exile sounded at the outset:

> Farewell (sweet *Cooke-ham*) where I first obtained
> Grace from that Grace where perfit Grace remain'd;
> And where the Muses gave their full consent,
> I should have powre the virtuous to content:
> Where princely Palace will'd me to indite,
> The sacred Storie of the Soules delight.
> Farewell (sweet Place) where Virtue then did rest,
> And all delights did harbour in her breast:
> Never shall my sad eies againe behold
> Those pleasures which my thoughts did then unfold.

As a memorial to an idyllic time in the recent past spent on the country estate, "Cooke-ham" redirects the explicitly religious concerns of *Salve Deus* toward a personal celebration of the landscape, now made special, if not sacred, by the hallowing presence of the mistress. In doing so, Lanyer anticipates a number of themes and attitudes soon to become central to the tradition of the "country-house" poem – the estate represented as a place that combines aesthetics and power fit for royalty:

> All interlac'd with brookes and christall springs,
> A Prospect fit to please the eyes of Kings:
> And thirteene shires appear'd all in your sight,
> Europe could not affoard much more delight;

(ll. 71–4)

but also, as develops later in the century, a place for private devotional meditation:

> What was there then but gave you all content,
> While you the time in meditation spent,
> Of their Creators powre, which there you saw,
> In all his Creatures held a perfit Law.

(ll. 75–8)

Given its assumed date of composition, sometime around 1609–10,[23] "Cooke-ham's" originary relationship to poems in the "estate" or "country house" tradition is also a matter of critical interest. But if there is a strong probability that Lanyer's poem predates Jonson's "To Penshurst" by a few years, it is equally the case that these two poems diverge significantly on crucial issues; for Jonson's describes his arrival on the scene, Lanyer's her departure from it. "To Penshurst," moreover, collapses the distinction between private and public spheres when the king is represented as coming on the scene, while "Cookeham" reinforces the distinction between the two: the "prospect" is fit to please a king's eye but is not itself visited by royalty. And most important, Lanyer does not – cannot? – represent herself as a poet seated at the table of the great, as Jonson so emphatically does. Whatever class differences there were between a Jonson and a Sidney, these could be temporarily surmounted in "To Penshurst" because Jacobean culture, thanks in part to Sidney, approved a vision of the classicized male poet with a recognized pedigree of his own. There was, however, no similar cultural niche for Lanyer in 1611. "A Womans writing of divinest things" is a title of distinction conferred only in retrospect by later cultures seeking to discover their own gendered, literary origins.[24] It did not provide entry into the great houses of the day – in this case the building is not even glimpsed by Lanyer – let alone a seat within at the table. In a very precise sense, Lanyer's poem is a farewell to a place to which she never belonged: "So great a difference is there in degree" (l. 106). As "The Description of Cookeham" makes clear, imagining a female community is not the same as being an inhabitant of that community. (The problem of social communion with the great is perhaps most evident in the strange tree-kissing episode recounted near the end of the poem.) In short, if we follow out a recent provocative suggestion that future criticism of "To Penshurst" needs to account for Jonson's act of locating his poem in "a field already occupied by a voice that speaks as a woman,"[25] then we also need to acknowledge the possibility that what Jonson saw was a house still waiting to be visited by a poet.

Anne Bradstreet (1612–72) and Martha Moulsworth (1577–16??)

While Wroth and Lanyer were spending their latter days pursuing activities other than writing verse, two women in the 1630s were finding further uses for poetry. Neither knew the other, nor did either show any familiarity with the poetry of Wroth or Lanyer. Indeed, in 1630, one was an eighteen-year old on her way from a Lincolnshire estate to New England; the other was approaching fifty-five, probably never having set foot outside of England. The contrasts need not stop with age and geography, since one went on to become a foundational poet for another nation and the other has only recently come to light, on the strength of a single poem. And yet for all their differences, they give two of the sharpest portraits of what might be loosely regarded as "matriarchal" poetry in the seventeenth century: poetry reflective of the concerns and interests of an educated woman writing within a traditional family structure as daughter, wife, mother, and even widow. For both Anne Bradstreet and Martha Moulsworth, it is not the court or the patronage system that motivates their poetry, that shapes their choice of genre and theme; nor is it their desire to identify themselves with an elite family, whether as a Sidney or a Clifford. Rather, it is the circumstantial nature of their relationship with other members of their family that lies at the core of their poetry.

For the Puritan Bradstreet, the fullest reckoning of that domestic and personal "vision" occurred gradually, only after she spent considerable energy wrestling with the Renaissance, to adopt Ivy Schweitzer's appropriately combative image of the Anne Bradstreet represented in *The Tenth Muse Lately Sprung Up In America* (1650).[26] This is the industrious but still dutiful daughter of Thomas Dudley and author of those seemingly endless "Quaternions" remembered by Milton's nephew Edward Phillips in his 1675 *Theatrum Poetarum* on themes derived largely from Raleigh and Du Bartas: "The Four Elements," "Of the Four Humours," "Of the Four Ages," "The Four Seasons," and, most ambitious of all, "The Four Monarchies." It is also the patriotic and "heroic" Bradstreet who writes belated elegies to Sidney, Du Bartas, and Queen Elizabeth, and the pious Bradstreet, reader and translator of Scripture as it bears on present political circumstances in England ("David's Lamentation for Saul and Jonathan") and, more generally, on the state of the world's good ("The Vanity of all Worldly Things," the title of the last poem in the 1650 volume that occupies the place of the traditional envoy).

It is not, however, the Bradstreet most often remembered today. The "worldly Puritan" who writes vigorously and movingly about the people closest to her, the more intimate Bradstreet who, in the New England wilderness, relinquishes her attachment to the English Renaissance in favor of writing about her immediate experiences as wife, mother, grandmother, and spiritual pilgrim: this Bradstreet comes fully into view only with the posthumously published second edition of her *Poems* (1678) in celebrated lyrics like "To My Dear and Loving Husband":

If ever two were one, then surely we.
If ever man were loved by wife, then thee;
If ever wife was happy in a man,
Compare with me, ye women, if you can.
I prize thy love more than whole mines of gold
Or all the riches that the East doth hold.
My love is such that rivers cannot quench,
Nor ought but love from thee, give recompense.
Thy love is such I can no way repay,
The heavens reward thee manifold, I pray.
Then while we live, in love let's so persevere
That when we live no more, we may live ever.

To some degree, Bradstreet's career rehearses in miniature the stylistic shift from Elizabethan "copia" to Jacobean concentration. When she left England in 1630, much of what was "new" about the seventeenth century had not yet appeared in print. But the shift to a more concentrated utterance in the poem to her husband is also inseparable in Bradstreet from a shift from public to private address. In the arena of domestic love, Bradstreet writes with Donnean assurance, predicating an eternity of love on a passionate commitment in the present. The control displayed in this poem develops unequivocally from the opening line; and if sincerity of expression replaces witty conceit as the means of making two into one, Bradstreet's is an eros that still presses outward, measuring itself against the competition ("Compare with me, ye women, if you can") across space and time and collapsing barriers along the way that tradition-ally denied women the role of the amatory aggressor. The special emphasis Puritans placed on the sacrament of marriage – Milton's "Hail, Wedded love" – gave Bradstreet access to a language of erotic courtship not available to women in the courtly tradition:

But when thou northward to me shalt return,
I wish my Sun may never set, but burn
Within the Cancer of my glowing breast,
The welcome house of him my dearest guest.
Where ever, ever stay, and go not thence,
Till nature's sad decree shall call thee hence:
Flesh of thy flesh, bone of thy bone,
I here, thou there, yet both but one.
("A Letter to Her Husband, Absent Upon Public Employment")

The passage is notable for illustrating how fully Bradstreet accepts the tradi-tional role of the loving spouse – and also the ease with which she enters into Adam's language in Genesis and claims it as hers, or rather, as theirs. She plays Eve speaking to her silent Adam, rehearsing the lines that bind them and which receive renewed point in the final answering rhyme: "I here, thou there, yet both but one."

Daughter, spouse, and mother, the domestic Bradstreet monitors the household, awaits arrivals, marks the many exits, registers the bittersweet passing of generations:

> I had eight birds hatched in one nest,
> Four cocks there were, and hens the rest.
> I nursed them up with pain and care,
> Nor cost, nor labour did I spare,
> Till at the last they felt their wing,
> Mounted the trees, and learned to sing.
> ("In Reference to her Children, 23 June, 1659")

And as a grandmother grieving the early deaths of her grandchildren, she is sufficiently seasoned in the ways of Calvinism to resist the emotional logic of her own utterance, but only just barely:

> No sooner came, but gone, and fall'n asleep,
> Acquaintance short, yet parting caused us weep;
> Three flowers, two scarcely blown, the last i' th' bud,
> Cropt by th' Almighty's hand; yet is He good.
> With dreadful awe before Him let's be mute,
> Such was His will, but why, let's not dispute.
> ("On My Dear Grandchild Simon Bradstreet")

So fully has Bradstreet internalized her maternal role that her concept of authorship as represented in the much anthologized "The Author to her Book" is inseparable from notions of childbearing and child rearing:

> Thou ill-formed offspring of my feeble brain,
> Who after birth didst by my side remain,
> Till snatched from thence by friends, less wise than true,
> Who thee abroad, exposed to public view,
> Made thee in rags, halting to th'press to trudge,
> Where errors were not lessened (all may judge).

We might think of this poem in a familiar genre – both Jonson and Herrick wrote epigrams to their books – as an example of the modesty topos with teeth. The circumstances referred to in the opening lines involve the surreptitious printing of *The Tenth Muse* by in-laws and friends, all male, who used the occasion to commend "Anne Bradstreet" to Old England from America, and like the lyric to her husband, but in a still plainer register, Bradstreet's poem is one to set the record straight and in more ways than one. We learn not simply how these poems came into print but whose poems they really are; and the claim of authorship is a matter of both nature and nurture – a mother's right to speak with blunt humor to and about her offspring, how she raised them and how she sent them out the door, with unsentimental apologies. Hers is a distinctly "different" send-off from what we find in either Jonson or Herrick, right down to the paternal disavowal at the end:

> At thy return my blushing was not small,
> My rambling brat (in print) should mother call,
> I cast thee by as one unfit for light,
> Thy visage was so irksome in my sight;
> Yet being mine own, at length affection would
> Thy blemishes amend, if so I could:
> I washed thy face, but more defects I saw,
> And rubbing off a spot still made a flaw.
> I stretched thy joints to make thee even feet,
> Yet still thou run'st more hobbling than is meet;
> In better dress to trim thee was my mind,
> But nought save homespun cloth i' th'house I find.
> In this array 'mongst vulgars may'st thou roam.
> In critic's hands beware thou dost not come,
> And take thy way where yet thou art not known;
> If for thy father asked, say thou hadst none;
> And for thy mother, she alas is poor,
> Which caused her thus to send thee out of door.

In this highly artful self-portrait of the author as mother, Bradstreet, the single parent, claims little for her poems except that they are indubitably and undeniably hers – warts, or rather joints, and all.

The idea of the Puritan female saint in the New World was clearly a motivating one for Bradstreet. We can only speculate as to why, at age 55, Martha Moulsworth decided to write her unusual "Memorandum," a 110-line poem in mostly pentameter couplets that survives in a single manuscript in a commonplace book in the Beinecke Library at Yale University. Moulsworth clearly did not think of herself as an "author" in Bradstreet's sense, although in "The Memorandum" she registers a sense of her early affinity with the muses; and while her modern editors note that "memorandum," from the Latin, means "[it is] to be remembered," it is not clear by whom or for what purpose.[27] By her own admission, those who meant most to her are no longer alive: "roote, & ffruite is dead, wch makes me sad," she ruefully notes at one point (l. 72). Nor do her observations amount to religious self-scrutiny. Although piety and numbers are important to Moulsworth, as we shall see, "The Memorandum" is not written in the spirit of someone preparing a final account.

Nonetheless, she does set down for the record the major events of her life to date – perhaps as a birthday present to herself. (At the outset, she tells us that she has begun her poem on her 55th birthday.) Names, dates, personal musings, marginal comments, Biblical allusions, proverbial sayings: all these notations help to make "Martha Moulsworth, Widow" into one of the most graphically present women of the period, a kind of Bess of Hardwick in verse.

> Thrice this Right hand did holly wedlocke plight
> And thrice this Left with pledged ringe was dight
> three husbands me, & I have them enjoyde
> Nor I by them, nor they by me annoyde
> all lovely, lovinge all, some more, some lesse
> though gonn their love, & memorie I blesse.

(ll. 43–8)

This is equanimity that comes with age: generous, accepting, socially aware, tonally nuanced. She is definitely a Martha, not a Mary, hospitable, almost to a fault:

> our Saviour christ her guesse [sic] to entertayne
> God gyve me grace my Inward house to dight
> that he wth me may supp, & stay all night.

(ll. 18–20)

A few lines later, after lamenting the exclusion of women from the universities – "Two Universities we have of men / o thatt we had but one of women then" (ll. 33–4) – and then speaking further of her related decline as a Latinist, she writes in the margin: "Lattin is not the most marketable mariadge mettall," and then goes on to add in verse:

> Had I no other portion to my dowre
> I might have stood a virgin to this houre
> Butt though the virgin Muses I love well
> I have longe since Bid virgin life ffarewell.

(ll. 39–42)

Moulsworth would surely know her way around an Austen novel – perhaps even around a Congreve comedy. Wry, pious, and witty, she enjoys wordplay, and with her third husband, her favorite, she enjoys the ways of the world:

> Was never man so Buxome to his wife
> Wth him I led an easie darlings life.
> I had my will in house, in purse in Store
> What would a women old or yong have more?

(ll. 65–8)

230

Only our sense of how we think "women" should sound in "autobiography" limits the interpretive latitude we might give to this passage, especially to the third line, for instance. Is "Martha Moulsworth" speaking like one of Shakespeare's women of the world here?

Charitable as she is, she also makes good on an earlier promise to use this occasion to bless the memory of each husband, which she does not simply by recalling their names and her associations with each, but by drawing attention to a coincidence that, in a sense, blesses them collectively: "My husbands all on holly dayes did die / Such day, such waie, they to the Sts [saints] did hye" (ll. 73–4). She then gives each his separate due in a way that happily illustrates her own wit: "The ffirst, the ffirst of Martirs did befall / St. Stevens ffeast to him was ffunerall (ll. 77–8) … the second on a double sainted day / To Jude, & Symon tooke his happy way" (ll. 81–2).

> The Last on St. Mathias day did wend
> unto his home, & pilgrimages ende
> this feast comes in that season wch doth bringe
> uppon dead Winters cold, a lyvelie Springe
>
> His Bodie winteringe in the lodge of death
> Shall ffeele A springe, wth budd of life, & Breath.
>
> (ll. 89–94)

One can easily understand why the hospitable widow Moulsworth might have been in demand as a wife. "All lovely, lovinge all, some more, some lesse," she reminds us that in heaven there are to be no favorites, citing in the margin as her authority Matthew 22: 18 (containing Jesus's repudiation of the hairsplitting inquiries into the logic of the Resurrection by the Sadducees):

> In vayne itt were, prophane itt were ffor me
> Wth Sadnes to aske wch of theis three
> I shall call husband in the Resurrection
> ffor then shall all in glorious perfection
> Like to th'immortall heavenlie Angells live
> Who wedlocks bonds doe neither take nor give.
>
> (ll. 97–102)

And just possibly the marital latitude in heaven is to be extended a little further on earth. The final eight lines, with their clever use of proverbs, describe a woman who well understands her value in silver:

> But in the Meane tyme this must be my care
> of knittinge here a fourth knott to beware
> A threefold cord though hardlie yett is broken

Another Auncient storie doth betoken
thatt seldome comes A Better; whie should I
Then putt my Widowehood in jeopardy?
The Virgins life is gold, as Clarks us tell
The Widowes silvar, I love silvar well.

(ll. 103–10)

Yes, a fourth knot, another husband, could spell trouble. According to the proverb in Ecclesiastes 4: 12 noted in the margin, "a threefold cord is not quickly broken," a saying that is further reinforced and yet also not perfectly clinched by another proverb: that "seldom comes the better." Seldom is not quite never. If this were Donne writing, we would be quick to honor the slight equivocation here and the force of the subsequent question, and perhaps, too, the repetition of "silvar" in the final line as a sign that she is hardly to be had for the asking, which does not quite mean that she would refuse all offers.

An Collins's *Divine Songs and Meditacions* (1653) and Anna Trapnel's *The Cry of a Stone* (1654)

Motherhood, widowhood, marriage: these "worldly" matters all but disappear or are radically refigured in the poetry of the reclusive An Collins and the Fifth Monarchist Anna Trapnel, two of the many women energized at mid-century by England's great political and religious upheavals, viewed from afar by Bradstreet and perhaps not at all by Moulsworth.[28] Collins's *Divine Songs and Meditacions* (1653) has the distinction of being the only collection of devotional poetry published by a woman in the early seventeenth century after the manner of Herbert. Trapnel, by contrast, is barely a poet at all in the usual sense. Her verses are of one kind, spiritual songs or hymns sung in emphatically simple ballad stanzas:

Oh he has said that he will reign,
Therefore Rulers shall flye,
Oh he hath said that he'l cast out
The fourth great Monarchy.

Oh he will shew unto the pure,
And such that are upright,
To manifest to these proud Walls,
That now to you are in sight.

O therefore Clergy, and you State,
Nothing at all you shall,
When that the Lord Christ he doth speak,
You utterly shall fall.

The worldly Bradstreet never got beyond the Fourth Monarchy.

But there is also little that is usual about this self-described female prophet, who begins *The Cry of a Stone* (1654), the work from which these verses are quoted, as follows:

> I am *Anna Trapnel*, the daughter of *William Trapnel*, Shipwright, who lived in *Poplar*, in *Stepney* Parish; my father and mother living and dying in the profession of the Lord Jesus; my mother died nine years ago, the last words she uttered upon her death-bed, were these to the Lord for her daughter. Lord! Double thy spirit upon my child; These words she uttered with much eagerness three times, and spoke no more.
>
> (p. 3)

Not three-times married but three-times called, Trapnel places herself within a strong matrilinear tradition. She acknowledges receiving a mother's blessing as Elisha received his from Elijah in 2 Kings 9: "I pray thee, let a double portion of thy spirit be upon me." And the blessing she receives points to the manifestly oral nature of her own performance: indeed, to her own prophetic authority. Trapnel is not a women writing of divinest things, seeking, as Lanyer did, to insert a feminist defense of Eve into the received tradition of the Fall. She is a woman in whom Scripture speaks, "a voyce within a voyce," as she remarks at one point in *The Cry of a Stone* (p. 42), and the object of her prophetic utterances is more sweepingly apocalyptic. Whether in prose or verse, she urges England's total spiritual renovation, which Fifth Monarchists believed was to conclude with the Second Coming of Jesus and the Rule of the Saints.

To a modern reader, of course, indeed to any one who did not witness the original twelve days during which an undernourished Trapnel uttered prayers and songs outside of Whitehall, "speaking every day, sometimes two, three, four and five hours together," as reported by "the Relator," the printed page is bound to seem a poor substitute for the actual performance. This is especially true with the verse, which is meant to be heard, not read, where its winnowing themes might get replicated in the rushing sounds of speech – the prophetic winds, as it were of God,

That shall enter in,
Into their Pallaces great,
A blustring Wind from the great God,
A whirlwind that's compleat.

That will tear them up by the roots,
And cast them on the ground,
Where they no greeness shall have here,
No sap shall be there found.

In the transcribed text, what does capture our attention, however, is not so much the surviving verse (powerful though it is in short blasts, it becomes quickly repetitious) as the image of the speaker "related" to us – of the trance-like Trapnel, especially as she shifts registers:

> besides her own word, the effects of a spirit caught up in the Visions of God, did abundantly appear in the fixedness, and immoveableness of her speech in prayer, but more especially in her songs: notwithstanding the distractions among the people occasioned by rude spirits, that unawares crept in, which was observed by many who heard her, who seemed to us to be as one whose ears and eyes were locked up, that all was to her as a perfect silence.
>
> (p. 14)

In the transition into print, singing is what gets lost; but the notion of speech escalating into song still plays a crucial (and disturbing)[29] role in authorizing Trapnel's own wide-angled visionary critiques of Cromwellian England. For in song the voice is at its most sharply pitched and prophetic: at its most "enlarged," to use the verb form of a word ("enlargement") repeated by the "relator," a word that, in religious parlance, had recently acquired the meaning of liberty as an "absence of constraint." (According to the *OED*, the first such usage occurs in 1648.)

For her repeated acts of prophesying, Trapnel was branded a slut, a Ranter, and a vagabond – all charges she denied. On a journey to Cornwall, she also found herself in trouble with the authorities, and her subsequent arrest, trial, and imprisonment in Bridewell form the subject of her *Report and Plea* (1654), a narrative told with a novelist's attention to the quotidian and a martyr's eye toward sufferings. Nothing so dramatic or high-pitched can be found in An Collins, whose constrained lyricism is a far cry from Trapnel's verse in almost every respect: conscientiously formal, doctrinally informed, indebted for inspiration more to the psalter than to the Book of Revelation. As she lets on in her prefatory address "To the Reader," she discovered her voice not through anything so emphatically charged as receiving a mother's dying blessing. She found it through the practice of writing poetry:

> I inform you that by divine Providence, I have been restrained from bodily employments, suting with my disposicion, which enforced me to a retired Course of life; Wherin it pleased God to give me such inlargednesse of mind, and activity of spirit, so that this seeming desolate condicion, proved to me most delightfull: To be breif, I became affected to Poetry, insomuch that I proceeded to practice the same; and though the helps I had therein were small, yet the thing it self appeared unto me so amiable, as that it enflamed my faculties, to put forth themselvs, in a practise so pleasing.[30]

As her prefatory remarks intimate, Collins composes verse in the manner of someone coming to terms with her craft and finding pleasure in the act of accomplishment. Her favorite stanzaic form, in fact, was rhyme royal, perhaps because of its associations through King James with devotional poetry. But Collins seems drawn to it also for the complicated structural and rhetorical challenges it posed: the alternating then interlaced patterns of rhyme brought to a conclusion, if not quite a close, with a final couplet, as in the following example, chosen almost at random from among the 102 stanzas of rhyme royal that make up the first two poems:

> Now touching that I hasten to expresse
> Concerning these, the ofspring of my mind,
> Who though they here appeare in homly dresse
> And as they are my works, I do not find
> But ranked with others, they may go behind,
> Yet for theyr matter, I suppose they bee
> Not worthlesse quite, whilst they with Truth agree.
>
> (ll. 78–84)

In part because Collins uses rhyme royal in two poems bearing titles more typical of those found in prose – "The Preface" (not to be confused with her prefatory address) and "The Discourse" – one senses here and elsewhere an "essay" being turned or massaged into verse. We are also reminded, in her apology for the appearance of her "ofspring" in "homly dress," of Bradstreet and of the comparable place the domestic holds in their conception of poetry. But the differences are equally illuminating. Collins is everywhere more tentative about her craft ("Now touching that," "I do not find," "I suppose they bee") and dependent upon an abstract notion of Truth as justification for deeming her work "not worthlesse quite." In this regard, although her verse (like this stanza) is frequently autobiographical in orientation, her poetry is rarely personal in Bradstreet's sense. It is "the ofspring of my mind," as she notes, not the "ill-formed offspring of my feeble brain," let alone the object of direct address (as in "Thou ill-formed offspring of my feeble brain"). As the distinction between "mind" and "brain" suggests (the one drawn from Neoplatonic lore, the other from physical science), Collins's poetry shows little of Bradstreet's interest in the graphic or the dramatic as responses to reality filtered through a strongly gendered lens, one as aware of the body as the soul.

Collins's ideal audience, rather, is one already conversant with the comforting truths of Christianity:

> You that indeared are to pietie
> And of a gracious disposicion are,
> Delighting greatly in sinceritie
> As your respects to godly ones declare;

For whose society you only care:
Dain to survay her works that worthlesse seem,
To such as honnest meanings dis-esteem.

(ll. 1–7)

This stanza appears at the beginning of "The Discourse," a seven-hundred line poem that outlines, in latitudinarian fashion, the principal experiences and truths of Protestant theology: the personal need for saving grace, the primary place of Scripture in the life of the Godly, a belief in the Trinity as well as the Decalogue, and so forth. Collins's most recent editor does suggest that these widely held "truths" also do not preclude the possibility of a more individualistic strain of worship since the value she places on the "rectified" mind illuminated by grace can seem, at times, barely distinguishable from the "inner light" of Quakerism.[31]

Still, in Collins the observing of a particular brand of Christianity is also less important than possessing a "gracious disposition ... delighting greatly in sincerity." These are, for her, the defining features of the Godly, and the defining characteristics of her ideal reader: someone who prizes the attempt more than the result, the message more than the medium. As Helen Wilcox has remarked, Collins is precisely the kind of poet implicitly encouraged by Herbert in "A true Hymne" when he speaks of God as supplying the "want" if the verse be "somewhat scant."[32] The "want" is never in doubt. Collins writes with undiluted respect for her subject, at times (to shift metaphors) simply restitching lines from Scripture to make a new quilt of verse. This is one way to describe the "homly" poetics involved in creating a stanza of rhyme royal for each of the ten commandments in "The Discourse" (ll. 407–77); or the decision to conclude the whole volume by weaving anew a verse paraphrase from that most familiar of Biblical texts, "the twelvth Chapter of Ecclesiastes," with its almond trees, silver cords, and golden bowl; or the desire to introduce into a subtitle the notion of "interlacing cordiall Comforts with fatherly Chastisments" in "A Song shewing the Mercies of God."

In an important sense with Collins, there is nothing new under the sun, except the opportunity to make new patterns out of familiar truths for an audience that, she believes, seeks comfort rather than surprise. Hence, the proliferation of stanzaic experiments that make her look but rarely sound like either Herbert or Vaughan (at least for more than a phrase or two). The interlacing of cordial comforts into a song showing the mercies of God, for instance, begins in the following manner:

As in the time of Winter
The Earth doth fruitlesse and barren lie,
Till the Sun his course doth run
Through Aries, Taurus, Gemini;
Then he repayres what Cold did decay,

Drawing superfluous moistures away,
And by his luster, together with showers,
The Earth becoms fruitful & plesant with flowers
That what in winter seemed dead
There by the Sun is life discovered.
      ("A Song shewing the Mercies of God to his people")

Herbert, too, begins a poem with an unrhymed first line ("Joseph's Coat"), and Collins's experimentation with line length and rhyme – internal rhyme is almost signatorial with her – shows sophistication beyond what one meets in the popular Sternhold and Hopkins translation of the Psalter. And thematically, the subject of natural and spiritual regeneration lies at, or near, the center of Vaughan's poetry. But to note these similarities is also to notice how quickly she veers away from either Vaughan's radical sublimity or what Helen Vendler calls Herbert's "named emotionalities":[33] grief, love, joy, and so on. As the above stanza suggests, Collins is interested in presenting patterns of continuity, not in expressing "private ejaculations," to quote from the subtitle that appears on both men's volumes.

In making these observations, I am not suggesting that Collins be held to a standard of verse that only Herbert can achieve, but I am suggesting that she saw her poetry as purposefully decorative and general rather than original and personal in spirit. Most of her images, metaphors, and themes belong to the common stock-in-trade of religious discourse, and precisely because of their familiarity, they serve as signs of her sincerity, including even her sometimes awkward grappling with form. In a sense, the experiments, noticeable as they are, remain the generic products of a poet for whom there is no room for guile. With poems as simply titled and constructed as "Another Song exciting to spirituall Mirth," no one endeared to piety is in danger of being led astray:

The Winter being over
In order comes the Spring,
Which doth green Hearbs discover
And cause the Birds to sing;
The Night also expired,
Then comes the Morning bright,
Which is so much desired
By all that love the Light;
This may learn
Them that mourn
To put their Griefe to flight.
The Spring succeedeth Winter,
And Day must follow Night.

For Collins, apart from the spiritual disconsolation endured by those who have forgotten God's "gracious Promise" that *"He doth not leave nor forsake them"* (Heb. 13: 5), and for whose explicit benefit and comfort she offers her songs and meditations, the only real danger to be confronted comes from the ungodly. In "A Song composed in time of the Civill Warre, when the wicked did much insult over the godly" and in its sequel, "Another Song," the vocal distance between Trapnel and Collins shrinks considerably, as the latter trades in her "homely" muse for the more impassioned utterances of prophecy:

> Therefore who can, and will not speak
>   Betimes in Truths defence,
> Seeing her Foes their malice wreak,
>   And some with smooth pretence
>
> And colours which although they glose
>   Yet being not ingraind,
> In time they shall their luster lose
>   As cloth most foully staind.

(ll. 17–24)

In contrast to Trapnel, however, it is not easy to align Collins with a particular political party in these two most political of her poems. She can sound at times like a royalist sympathizing for those whose lands were sequestered, or at least like an anti-Parliamentarian critical of the Oath of Allegiance; but she also borrows freely from the apocalyptic language more readily associated with radical Protestantism.[34] I am not sure it is possible to pin her down exactly here, in part because we lack a precise date for these poems in a period when dates are extremely important, but mainly because speaking in defense of Truth takes her outside of discrete political categories into the more open arena of Biblical prophecy. Just as Collins never defines the Godly in terms other than those who are endeared to piety, so the "wicked" are known largely through their perverse behavior. What remains crucial in her work, as in Milton's, is that the elect are "most severely try'd," as she says at the end of "A Song composed in time of the Civill Warre," and, as she says in the sequel, that "from those storms hath God preserved / A people to record his praise" (ll. 57–8). On the basis of the information in these poems, we are free to think of these "Saints" as Puritans or Protestants or, simply, "the Godly elect": the "endeared" who endured.

Margaret Lucas Cavendish (1623–73) and Katherine Philips (1632–64)

As exceptional as Trapnel and Collins were in venturing into print, scholars are discovering that they represent only a small portion of the women who wrote devotional verse in the seventeenth century. There is little danger, however, of overlooking two of the more celebrated women of the era, whose activities in print were regarded by contemporaries as not merely unusual or exceptional but singular. I mean, of course, the woman who sometimes regally referred to herself as "Margaret the First," or, alternatively, was referred to by others as "Mad Madge" – Margaret Lucas Cavendish, the Duchess of Newcastle, whose behavior and dress shocked contemporaries of both sexes, and whose vast literary output Virginia Woolf once likened to "some giant cucumber [spreading] itself over all the roses and carnations in the garden,"[35] but which also has entitled her to an increasingly appreciated place in history "as the first Englishwoman to write a substantial body of literature intentionally for publication."[36] And I mean, too, Cavendish's infinitely more respectable contemporary, "The Matchless Orinda," Katherine Philips, England's first publicly celebrated female poet. With each we leave behind the Biblically-based utterances of mid-century and enter the world of Restoration verse and visibility.

Their routes to "fame" – a favorite word of Cavendish's – could hardly be less alike, yet their separate pathways are deeply familiar ones in the seventeenth century. Philips, on the one hand, claimed the social and artistic privileges that traditionally belonged to an elite manuscript culture. Only after a "pirated" edition of her *Poems* was published in 1664 did the "Incomparable / Mrs. K.P." emerge into full view in a "corrected" version of 1667, and then only in the company of commendatory poems written by six different hands and prefaced by a posthumous epistle supplied by the modest Philips herself denying that her verse had ever been intended for an audience beyond a private few. With her sudden early death from smallpox in 1664, what was once "incomparable" had become "matchless." These double adjectives now decorated the title page of the folio editions of her *Poems* in 1667, 1669, and 1678, where, in addition to the new verse translations Philips had made of Corneille's *Pompey* and *Horace*, each of these handsome editions also included a carefully wrought engraved frontispiece of a bust of "Orinda" in a niche done by William Faithorne, the Elder, England's great engraver (Fig. 3).[37] As Edward Phillips said of Katherine Philips in his *Theatrum Poetarum*, hedging his bets only slightly, she was "the most applauded, at this time, Poetess of our Nation, either of the present or former Ages."[38]

Cavendish, on the other hand, plunged into the world of print with Wither-like gusto. Beginning with *Poems and Fancies*, her one book solely devoted to verse and published in 1653, and continuing for more than a decade, she wrote in a medley of genres: drama, philosophical prose, prose romance, biography, autobiography, science fiction, and the familiar letter (or *Sociable Letters*, as she called them); and on many topics, but especially those related to the New Sciences: matter, motion, atomism. She also struck a number of radically different poses for the Antwerp artist, Abraham van Diepenbeke, which were used, and sometimes reused, as frontispieces for individual works. The "Thrice Noble, Illustrious, and Excellent Princesse," as she came to be known after the Restoration, appears as imperious virago in *The World's Olio* (1655), *The Blazing World* (1668), and the *Plays* (1668); as modest domestic partner in a circle of storytellers for *Nature's Pictures drawn by Fancies Pencil* (1656); and as solitary

Figure 3 Poems by the most deservedly admired Mrs. Katherine Philips, the Matchless Orinda,
1667. Frontispiece engraving by William Faithorne, the Elder.
(Reproduced by permission of the William Andrews Clark Memorial Library.)

sage in *Philosophical and physical Opinions* (1655). In these much varied guises, moreover, Cavendish also wrote less as the passionate spouse of Sir William Cavendish, who was thirty years her senior when they married in 1645, and more as the Marchioness or Duchess of Newcastle, his companionate author and coequal in society. (Having had much of his property confiscated while living in exile overseas, Sir William was made Duke in 1665.) In the complicated world of sexual and party politics in mid-century, the "Matchless Orinda" might project a "royalist" identity for herself in her poetry while married to the Parliamentarian Colonel, James Philips, thirty-eight years her senior; but Margaret Lucas's actual "match" to a member of the nobility gave her a social position – a platform, it is tempting to say – that allowed her to speak her "fancy," to cite a key word of hers that runs throughout her writing.

And speak she did, especially in the prefaces: on behalf of her sex, against her sex, in favor of their essential difference from men, conscious of their general inferiority as a class. As Catherine Gallagher has noted in an important article entitled "Embracing the Absolute: The Politics of the Female Subject in Seventeenth-Century England," "it is an odd but indisputable fact that the seventeenth-century women whom we think of as the forerunners and founders of feminism were, almost without exception, Tories."[39] And the indisputably oddest example of this sympathetic alliance between monarchical allegiance and proto-feminist impulse is Margaret Cavendish. In Charles Lamb's formulation, Cavendish regarded herself as a female "sui generis," someone not to be bound, as Cavendish herself said of fancy, by "Rule and Method"; and to the extent that she felt free of the obligations and constraints of polite society, she further extended into the marketplace the sense of aristocratic privilege of predecessors like Mary Wroth. As an aristocrat, Cavendish both absorbed and participated in the radical social upheavals of the Civil War, although not its radical politics.[40]

Singular, absolutist, extravagant in almost every sense of a word being given new meaning at this particular juncture in history,[41] Cavendish does offer a flip side to her desire to be "empress of the world," to borrow her own fanciful self-characterization from *The Blazing World*. She imagines in verse (again I am following Gallagher) every world being a world of its own, every element as having its own organizing structure, each mind its peculiar similes, each gender its particular discursive realm. "*Poetry*, which is built upon *Fancy*, women may claim as a worke belonging most properly to themselves." This separatist credo, both self-empowering and self-diminishing, appears in the preface from *Poems and Fancies* addressed "To all Noble, and Worthy Ladies." And Cavendish's poetry, without doubt, is built on fancy: on the idea of having an opinion on almost any topic. "Of Vapour," "Of Dewes, and Mists from the Earth," "The Attraction of the Poles, and of Frost," "Quenching out of Fire," and, again, "Quenching, and Smothering out of Heat, and Light, doth not change the Property, nor Shape of Sharpe Atomes": I am quoting titles from poems on a single facing page (pp. 24–5). Indeed, the titles are themselves often works of manifest ingenuity: "It is hard to believe, that there are other Worlds in this

World," is followed by "Of many Worlds in this World," and then, for good measure, "A World in an Eare-Ring" and "Severall Worlds in Severall Circles." And so the poems often challenge the normal order of things:

> Who knowes, but *Fishes* which swim in the *Sea*,
> Can give a Reason, why so *Salt* it be?
> And how it *Ebbs* and *Flowes*, perchance they can
> Give *Reasons*, for which never yet could *Man*.
>
> ("Of Fishes")

Whether comparing the head to a barrel of wine or "similizing" fancy itself to a gnat (and thereby in manner outdoing Donne's flea), Cavendish doesn't flinch from treating most any subject in couplets: Lapland witches, dialogues between birds, the brain, the agile movement of water, a landscape, melancholy. In some regards the less consequential the topic the better, for what is weighty might only shackle Cavendish's "fancy," might rob it of its eagle-like power, its quest for an untrammeled purity:

> But at all other things let *Fancy* flye,
> And, like a *Towring Eagle*, mount the Skie.
> Or like the *Sun* swiftly the *World* to round,
> Or like pure *Gold*, which in the *Earth* is found.
> But if a drossie *wit*, let't buried be,
> Under the *Ruines* of all *Memory*.

Hers is rhyme with a sweep here, the conjunctions releasing or returning image upon image in the interest of developing crucial oppositions: a "drossie *wit*" lies with memory and ruin – subjects we might associate with history and elegy – while the "*Fancy*" flies high, untouched, uncontaminated by the contingent, the immediate, the actual. It is as if Descartes reappeared as a female poet and said: "Fancying therefore I am."

It is also only a small step in Cavendish from the gendered notion of fancy as female to an "aristocratic" view of poetry as an expression of nobility because it is easy and free:

> Give *mee* the *Free*, and *Noble Stile*,
> Which seems *uncurb'd*, though it be *wild*:
> Though *It* runs wild about, *It* care not where;
> It shews more *Courage*, then *It* doth of *Feare*,
> Give me a *Stile* that *Nature* frames, not *Art*:
> For *Art* doth seem to take the *Pedants* part.
> And that seems *Noble*, which is *Easie*, *Free*,
> Not to be bound with ore-nice *Pedantry*.
>
> ("The Claspe")

So much for the value of "sweet neglect" as articulated by Jonson in "Still to be neat" and further refined by Herrick in "Delight in Disorder." The spouse of one of England's most celebrated horsemen has decisively abandoned the court for the country, the "sweet" for the "complete" neglect of art, the "loosely flowing" for the "uncurb'd" and the "wild": what she calls the pedantic in favor of the courageous. One need only turn the page, moreover, to discover examples of the link between female fancy and noble country courage. Cavendish offers two poems on that most aristocratic of male topics, the hunt, but written from a perspective that also undoes the hunt as a celebrated masculine ritual.

"The Hunting of the Hare" may well be Cavendish's most interesting poem. It is certainly one of her most vigorously written, with the sympathy between the poet and "Poor Wat" reminding us that the Duchess of Newcastle was in the vanguard of those in the seventeenth century challenging an older anthropocentric view of nature.[42] ("The Hunting of the Stag" seems more formulaic and, after Denham's "Coopers Hill," predictably allegorical.) Right from the beginning in "The Hunting of the Hare," Cavendish succeeds at making us see the world from Wat's perspective:

Betwixt two *Ridges* of *Plowd-land*, lay *Wat*,
Pressing *his* Body *close to* earth *lay squat.*
His *Nose* upon his two *Fore-feet* close lies,
Glaring obliquely with his *great gray Eyes.*
His *Head* he alwaies sets against the *Wind*;
If turne his *Taile* his *Haires* blow up behind:
Which *he* too cold will grow, but he is wise,
And keepes his *Coat* still downe, so warm he lies.

The portrait is quickly drawn, the bold sketching more important than the fine detail; but a picture quickly emerges of Wat as more than a wood-cut for an Aesopian fable ("so warm he lies"), and we begin to see the hunt from the eyes of the hunted and our identification as part of a larger dramatic strategy to expose the ritual of the event for what to Cavendish it is: sensational, cruel, barbaric. After being chased for some sixty lines, Wat is caught:

For why, the *Dogs* so neere his *Heeles* did get,
That they their sharp *Teeth* in his *Breech* did set.
Then tumbling downe, did fall with *weeping Eyes*,
Gives up his *Ghost*, and thus poore *Wat* he dies.
Men hooping loud, such *Acclamations* make,
As if the *Devill* they did *Prisoner* take.
When they do but a *shiftlesse creature* kill;
To hunt, there needs no *Valiant Souldiers* skill.
But *Man* doth think that *Exercise*, and *Toile*,
To keep their *Health*, is best, which makes most spoile.

> Thinking that *Food*, and *Nourishment* so good,
> And *Appetite*, that feeds on *Flesh*, and *Blood*.

And so the poem continues, coursing its way through the "sport" of hunting. Cavendish's are obviously not the finely wrought perceptions (and ironies) of Marvell's "The Nymph complaining for the death of her Faun." The perspective here is not psychological and allegorical but moral, uncomplicated in the extreme, but in its expressed outrage also illustrating why Woolf might have found "the passion of poetry" beating in Cavendish's breast.

Still, fancy is a paradoxical figure for inspiration, as Cavendish no doubt understood. In what could almost serve as a gloss on her verse, Cavendish's contemporary and acquaintance, Thomas Hobbes, remarked to Davenant that although fancy "seemeth to fly from one Indies to the other, and from heaven to earth, and to penetrate into the hardest matter and obscurest places, into the future and into herself, and all this in a point of time; the voyage is not very great, herself being all she seeks." Almost everything but the Indies seems to find its way into the pages of *Poems and Fancies*. Indeed, the 210 or so pages make the book substantially longer than any earlier volume of poetry published by a woman, and the cook's tour through the natural world shows Cavendish entering into a domain as masculine as the hunt. In this, fancy is a great enabler of expression. The constant attention to "similizing" becomes a way for Cavendish to find her own angle into a traditionally male subject, as Bronwen Price has explained.[43] And it also fuels the light, playful, rustic entertainment within that most traditional of English subjects, fairy folklore associated with the countryside. In "The *Pastime* of the *Queen* of Fairies, when *she comes upon the* Earth *out of the* Center," Cavendish, in fact, can sound like Jonson or Herrick, to say nothing about Shakespeare and Milton; but her lyrical pursuit of the fanciful also reflects an independent, feminized, aristocratic sensibility, as the opening lines suggest:

> This lovely sweet, and beauteous *Fairy* Queen,
> Begins to rise, when *Vespers Star* is seen.
> For she is *kin* unto the *god* of Night,
> So to *Diana*, and the stars so bright.
> And so to all the rest in some degrees,
> Yet not so neer relation as to these.
> As for *Apollo*, she disclaims him quite,
> And swears she nere will come within his light.

But the mind that ventures in many directions, touching on many topics, refusing to be pedantic, also risks making fanciful thought its solitary subject, whether by actively pursuing the chimeras of fairy lore or by quietly glossing over the knotty character of personal or literary history. Books, people, events – things that might roughen the verse, making it more a part of lived experience, barely figure into Cavendish's verse. Even the elegies appearing in "A Register of Mournfull Verses" have an aura of unreality about them. We know too, for example, that she read Donne because she quotes a line of his in "Of Light, and Sight," but the allusion is conspicuous for its rarity; and while readers have long felt a link with Milton's *Poems*, at least with "L'Allegro" and "Il Penseroso" (no doubt because of their fanciful projections of mental states), these connections do not so much deepen as disappear upon close inspection. In the company of her other half, Cavendish belongs to a literary circle of two, or perhaps one, as the poem written by her husband for the engraved frontispiece to her *Philosophical and Physical Opinions* (1655) suggests.

The frontispiece portrait shows Margaret Cavendish in a private drawing room, at a table with a pen for writing and a servant's bell to ring, and facing outwards, being crowned by putti carrying laurels, but also separated from the viewer because of a sturdy railing interposed between her and us (Fig. 4). In the manner of describing an enigma, the poem reads:

> Studious She is all Alone
> Most visitants, when She has none,
> Her Library on which She looks
> It is her Head, her Thoughts her Books.
> Scorninge dead Ashes without fire
> For her owne Flames doe her Inspire.

As Gallagher has remarked, the utter solitude is strikingly – and I would add teasingly – different from traditional ways of representing female privacy and subjectivity (p. 30); for if the poem initially presents her looking outward on to a library which occupies the place of the viewer, the poem also quickly dissolves this connection – this "voyage" into the world, as Hobbes might say – by turning the library into her head, books into her thoughts. In this illusory exchange, Cavendish is suddenly represented not as the product of her reading in the manner, say, of Anne Clifford in the Clifford "Great Picture." She simply sits, hand not touching pen, staring outward, "herself being all she seeks."

Whereas the sometimes cross-dressing Cavendish is self-consciously inimitable (and for that reason exerted little influence on later authors), Katherine Philips is everywhere more user-friendly and influential, replete with her own "school" of followers, as Marilyn Williamson has noted.[44] Philips writes comfortably within already well-established categories of seventeenth-century verse. The familiar verse epistle is her favorite form, although she also practiced other lyrical modes in favor around mid-century – songs, dialogues, and epitaphs, for instance – and wrote on the high-minded subjects long considered appropriate to poetry: love, honor, loyalty, friendship, and so forth. Almost every one of her 130 or so poems comes bearing the tell-tale preposition "to" or "on" (or "upon") in the title. In pointed contrast to Cavendish, poetry that was not about an event or addressed to someone was almost unthinkable to Philips;

Studious She is and all Alone
Most visitants, when She has gone,
Her Library on which She looks
It is her Head her Thoughts her Books.
Scorninge dead Askes without fire
For her owne Flames doe her Inspire.

Figure 4 Margaret Cavendish, Duchess of Newcastle. Frontispiece portrait from *Philosophical and Physical Opinions* (1655) by Abraham van Diepenbeke, engraved by Peter van Schuppen.
(Reproduced by permission of the Huntington Library, San Marino, California.)

and one of the consequences of her gender-inclusive social vision is her acceptability by both male and female readers. In a sense, she is "incomparable"
precisely because she is comparable to what had been and was being written in
the dominant tradition. She can sound like the Donne of (among other poems)
"A Valediction, Forbidding Mourning":

> And as when one foot does stand fast,
> And t'other circles seeks to cast,
> The steddy part does regulate
> And make the wanderer's motion streight:
>
> So friends are onely Two in this,
> T' reclaime each other when they misse:
> For whose're will grossely fall,
> Can never be a friend at all.
> ("Friendship in Emblem, or the Seale, to my dearest Lucasia")[45]

She mastered the Jonsonian couplet, both tetrameter,

> Here what remaines of him does ly,
> Who was the world's epitomy,
>   ("Engraved on Mr. John Collyer's Tomb stone at Beddington")

and pentameter:

> Though you (Great Sir) be Heaven's immediate Care,
> Who shew'd your Danger, and then broke the Snare;
> And our first Gratitude to that be due,
> Yet there is much that must be pay'd to you.
>   ("To my Lord Duke of Ormond, Lord Lieutenant of Ireland")

She had songs set by Henry Lawes ("Friendship's Mysterys" among others) and
complimented the composer in turn ("To the truly noble Mr. Henry Lawes").
She was one of fifty-four (and the only woman) to have a commendatory poem
included in the 1651 edition of Cartwright's *Plays and Poems*. She praised
Vaughan on his poems, and received two back in turn, including an elegy. She
could strike a chivalric pose, like Lovelace, in "To My Lady Elizabeth Boyle,
Singing":

> Your voice, which can in moving strains
>   Teach beauty to the blind,
> Confines me yet in Stronger chains,
>   By being soft and kind.

(ll. 13–16)

247

She owned a copy of Suckling's *Fragmenta Aurea*, quoted Herrick in passing,[46] and even attempted one of the earliest imitations of a Cowley "Pindaric" in "An ode upon retirement, made upon occasion of Mr. Cowley's on that subject."

To describe Philips, even briefly, in light of her imitative versatility is to notice that she is singularly adroit among seventeenth-century female poets in assimilating – and centering herself within – those genres most prized by the dispersed court culture of the middle years of the seventeenth century; and in choosing to translate Corneille's *Pompey* at the beginning of the Restoration, she showed herself equally in step with the turn toward Neoclassicism under Charles II. It is also to note, moreover, that while Philips's emergence in print was ultimately framed and to a great degree controlled by men (like that of most women poets of this period), her ability to interpolate into her verse the conventional forms of male utterance helped to assure her a degree of acceptability within the dominant culture that no other female poet had yet experienced. Writing to people of both sexes, she spoke, as it were, "their" language: the established "poetic" language of the day.

But with a twist, as recent criticism has increasingly sought to underscore. Whether Philips should be regarded as the author of "'closet' lesbian verse" or as a pre-eminent example in the seventeenth century of a female poet dilating on the traditional subject of "romantic friendship,"[47] she is a liminal figure in the history of same-sex love and stands alone among poets in this chapter in directing much amatory verse to specific female friends. Perhaps more than any other poetry of the period, Philips's reminds us that amatory and amicable are cognates, the meaning of one experience crossing over and illuminating the other, as in the following opening lines from "*On* Rosania's *Apostacy, and* Lucasia's *Friendship*":

> Great Soul of Friendship, whither art thou fled?
> Where dost thou now chuse to repose thy head?

Is this friend to friend or lover to lover? Or take one of her most frequently anthologized lyrics, the precisely dated "To My excellent Lucasia, on our friendship. 17th. July 1651," which is short enough to quote in full. The initial choice of "live" for "love" in the first line keeps the mode of address decorous without altogether eliminating a sense of passion between friends:

> I did not live untill this time
>   Crown'd my felicity,
> When I could say without a crime,
>   I am not Thine, but Thee.
>
> This Carkasse breath'd, and walk'd, and slept,
>   So that the world believ'd
> There was a soule the motions kept;
>   But they were all deceiv'd.

For as a watch by art is wound
    To motion, such was mine:
But never had Orinda found
    A Soule till she found thine;

Which now inspires, cures and supply's,
    And guides my darken'd brest:
For thou art all that I can prize,
    My Joy, my Life, my rest.

Nor Bridegroomes nor crown'd conqu'rour's mirth
    To mine compar'd can be:
They have but pieces of this Earth,
    I've all the world in thee.

Then let our flame still light and shine,
    (And no bold feare controule)
As inocent as our design,
    Immortall as our Soule.

As Elaine Hobby has remarked, "the general terms of the poem are conventional,"[48] except perhaps for the boast differentiating the speaker's mirth from that of the conquering bridegroom, the pleasures of personal intimacy over the usual language of heterosexual conquest. The difference is one that frequently animates Philips's verse at its most original. Donne's hyperbolic (and now famous) claim in "The Sunne Rising" that "She is all States, and all Princes, I, / Nothing else is" reappears, for instance, in "Friendship's Mysterys, to my dearest Lucasia" as

We are our selves but by rebound
    And all our titles shuffled so,
    Both Princes, and both subjects too.

In finding a room of her own within the Donnean discourse of male heterosexual love, Philips has shuffled more than titles. She has turned the amatory occasion – disassembled its oracular components, as we might say today[49] – into an exploration of mutuality, extinguishing in the process the vertiginous Donnean rhetoric of "I," "thou," and "nothing" into a single, rebounding "we," with neither person possessing power over the other. Alongside "The Extasie" and its "dialogue of one" lies, as it were, another language in Philips, a dialogue between equals:

And thus we can no absence know,
    Nor shall we be confin'd;
Our active soules will dayly go
    To learne each other's mind.

Nay, should we never meet to sence,
Our soules would hold intelligence.
("To Mrs. Mary Awbrey at parting")

Philips was clearly not viewed by her established male contemporaries as unusual in voicing her affections for other women, as varied as these expressions were. (Along with celebrating the mutual pleasures of friendship, Philips also defended her female friends from slander, mourned their passing, commemorated the occasion of their marriages with marked ambivalence, and expressed injury when she felt slighted.) Her royalist friend, Sir Charles Cotteral, for instance, speaks only with praise when, in the preface to the authorized version of her *Poems* (1667), he remarks that "we might well have call'd her the English *Sappho*, she of all the female Poets of former Ages, being for her Verses and her Vertues both, the most highly to be valued" (p. 23). The language of Neoplatonic love is discreet by its nature: the pseudonyms, the assumed names of Orinda's principal female friends, Rosania (for Mary Aubrey) and Lucasia (for Anne Owens), allow a space for eros to be lightly encoded and explored and yet also erased. Think how different the poem "To my excellent Lucasia" quoted above would sound had Philips not written the final quatrain of the poem, with its deliberate Neoplatonizing. To conclude with "I've all the world in thee" would unequivocally write the language of same-sex passion on to the female body. But, culturally speaking, this version was not permissible in the narrow social sense, as Fadiman suggests, and perhaps, in a broader way, was not yet even thinkable.[50] "Orinda" remains "Orinda" and not Sappho.

A full exploration of Philips's writings helps to illuminate the dynamics of female friendship amid the intricately constructed world of royalist politics, especially as the Restoration evolved.[51] All early editions, for instance, begin with the contentious poem "Upon the double murther of K. Charles, in answer to a libellous rime made by V.P.," and then proceed with another ten poems expressing her unswerving loyalism to the crown, the most engaged being "On the 3d September 1651," which addresses the royalist defeat at Worcester and, for readers of Milton at least, draws the startling parallel between the fortunes of the king and those of Samson. But to look deep into the Restoration is also to begin to beg the comparison of Philips with Aphra Behn, England's first professional female writer, and to go beyond the boundaries of what is possible in a single chapter. So with a glance backward to the epigraph to this chapter, I want to conclude this survey with a less well-known poem by a female poet whose surviving output is too small to accord her a place in most modern discussions of women's poetry; and yet, as with Moulsworth's, one wishes for more.

The poem, by the royalist Anne King, deserves attention precisely because it is characteristic of the kind of verse written by an educated woman in the early seventeenth century, in this case some time during the 1650s. Never intended for publication, it is a study in female modesty, and yet it also describes, in its sufficient command of couplets, a woman of active purpose, answering to the needs of her particular community through skills typically accorded her sex: writing and drawing (talents Dryden would praise to the rooftops in his 1685 Pindaric ode to Anne Killegrew, "Excellent in the Two Sister-arts of Poesy and Painting"). Here the community involved the sequestered circle associated with Bishop King and his family during the interregnum, one that included, for a time, John Hales, the learned churchman, diplomat, and scholar, whom Clarendon hauntingly called "the most separated from the worlde of any man then livinge."[52] As recounted by Walton, Hales was to have had his picture made but was forced to leave the exiled community before it happened, and he died shortly thereafter. Responding to this lack, Anne King produced a drawing, an excellent likeness according to Walton, which has not survived, and this verse apology:

> Though by a Sodaine and unfeard surprise,
> thou lately taken wast from thy friends eies:
> Even in that instant, when they had design'd
> to keipe thee, by thy picture still in minde:
> least thou like others lost in deths dark night
> shouldst stealing hence vanish quite out of sight;
> I did contend with greater zeale then Art,
> This shadow of my phancie to impart:
> which all shood pardon, when they understand
> the lines were figur'd by a womans hand,
> who had noe copy to be guided by
> but Hales imprinted on her memory.
>   Thus ill cut Brasses serve uppon a grave,
>   Which less resemblance of the persons have.[53]

As a political and cultural document, the poem records the story of Hales's sudden departure: what his disappearance meant to his immediate community, with their fear that, without his picture, he would join the nameless many and be altogether lost to "deths dark night." It also tells a counter-story of sorts, of the balancing act Anne King plays within her community, and within the poem. Her own emergence as speaking subject near the middle of the poem helps to redress the void left by Hales. "I did contend with greater zeale then Art, / This shadow of my phancie to impart." King is not a Herculean Milton seeking, like Jove's great son, to rescue the dead from the grave, but she is also not without a "zeale" of her own. And while the appearance of her contending self is quickly tempered by the reference to her woman's hand, it is no small thing (although not quite as huge a thing as it would be with Margaret Cavendish) that the picture is a work produced from memory. For if "a dim view of women's powers of memory" was often the message inculcated in the official instructional literature of the Renaissance[54], memory in this poem is a sign of "mind" – of remembering, caring, and creating – and, faulty though the final product might be, these lines figured by a woman's hand, like the others we have been reading, also figure their way both through and around the dominant tradition in the process. For modern readers and women poets especially, it is perhaps this stubbornly fanciful image as much as any single act of creation that is their chief legacy as well.[55]

9

ANDREW MARVELL

"Here at the Fountain's Sliding Foot"

Or to suspend my sliding Foot
On the Osiers undermined Root
Marvell, "Upon Appleton House"

Literary histories have last chapters; literary history does not. And so it is with this book, reflecting on Andrew Marvell, "here at the Fountain's Sliding Foot" ("The Garden") – Marvell, the creation of much that was best in seventeenth-century poetry. Like Vaughan, he wrote some of his most celebrated poems around mid-century; the famous "Horatian Ode upon Cromwel's Return from Ireland" comes immediately to mind. And he seems to have had an even briefer apprenticeship (if apprenticeship is indeed a useful word to describe a poet who was largely indifferent to the notion of a literary career) before producing work of astonishing skill, judgment, and variety. Only a handful of his poems can be dated with much certainty, but to know that the "Horatian Ode" and "Upon Appleton House, to my Lord Fairfax" were written by someone in his late twenties, or at most early thirties, is to recognize a poet limited (a questionable word again) only by his own lack of literary ambitions and his cool regard for the approval of either a wide contemporary readership or posterity itself. "Fit audience find though few" is a remark Marvell would not have been especially concerned to make.

Such modesty can be disarming, particularly for modern readers who wish to identify authorship with literary production rather than literary performance. Indeed, in a culture as radically divided over issues of publication as seventeenth-century England, we might even regard Marvell as an accident almost waiting to happen. Were it not for the improbable charade involving his housekeeper, Mary Palmer, who posed as his wife, Mary Marvell, in order to lay claim to a portion of her "late dear Husband'[s]" estate,[1] we would scarcely have reason to remember Marvell, the poet, as more than the author of a few deftly worked commendatory or occasional poems. For the proof offered by Mary Palmer of her supposed marital link to Marvell (who died in 1678 without ever having married) also contains most of the verse upon which his modern reputation as a poet rests: that is, the posthumously published *Miscellaneous Poems* of 1681.[2]

But if Marvell almost did not "happen" as a poet, it is entirely appropriate that he did so in a volume with "miscellaneous" in its title: appropriate because the phrase conjures up the older sense of "miscellany" as a literary category referring to different "kinds" of composition (rather than mere odds and ends – one thinks immediately of the difference with Herrick); and appropriate, too, because for Marvell modesty and "miscellany," in this more restrictive sense, were hardly incompatible ideas. A man "of very few words," as Aubrey described him, and "in his conversation very modest,"[3] Marvell was not likely to be any less selective, any less careful, when it came to writing, especially writing verse. As Wallace Stevens remarked, "it is not every day that the world arranges itself in a poem,"[4] and for Marvell, a member of Parliament from Hull for the last eighteen years of his life, there were many fewer days for poetry than there were for Stevens.

But he also made almost every one count. As some of his best readers have noted, by which I mean readers most at home with much of the seventeenth century, the *Miscellaneous Poems* somehow manages to include at least one example – often the quintessential example – from nearly each of the major literary "kinds" popular in the period: amatory verse reminiscent of both Donne and Jonson at their most distinctive ("A Definition of Love" and "To his Coy Mistress"); the longest "country house" poem yet written in English – too "elusive," writes Donald Hall when he was "young and lazy" because too long, but "now its length is a luxury";[5] a few epitaphs in Latin and English; several verse epistles, including individual poems to the most famous Cavalier of the period (Lovelace) as well as to its most notorious Puritan (Milton); pastoral verse, fewer in number but more various than those in *England's Helicon*; some songs, perhaps used in masques or for other social occasions; a gospel hymn sung by religious exiles that would have pleased Crashaw in its respect for artifice and Wither for its purity of song; a meditative devotional lyric ("The Coronet") that reflects an intricate understanding of the problem of praise as set forth in Herbert's "Jordan [II]" and "The Wreath"; some satires that nearly span the century in their use of models (from Donne to Cleveland to Dryden); a number of poems inspired by current interest in emblem literature and the visual arts ("On a Drop of Dew" and "The Gallery" are probably the most familiar examples of each); and, of course, the "Horatian Ode," Marvell's most celebrated reworking of a traditional subject in English and perhaps the greatest political poem written in the seventeenth century.

With a lesser poet, so much attention to generic variety might become merely a Cromwellian march through the available modes of the day. It can also place unusual demands on any literary history since a chapter on Marvell can easily become a recapitulation of the major modes and historical events of the time. But a few simple points about Marvell are worth bearing in mind at the outset. The first is that Marvell is probably the most resourceful practitioner of the tetrameter line in English. Nearly half of his poetry – twenty out of the forty-five poems generally attributed to him – are strictly in tetrameter verse, while another eight make considerable use of the line. Take away the octosyllabic line, and it is tempting to say of the canon what Marvell said of the nuns' priory in "Upon Appleton House" at the moment of its disappearance: "as when th'Inchantment ends / The Castle vanishes or rends" (ll. 269–70). The second point is that in spite of the many obstacles presented by the canon itself, Marvell's poetry speaks, however indirectly at times, to the conditions of England in the middle decades better than that of any contemporary poet, including Milton himself. In this century, Marvell, the poet, might have initially come into vogue because of Donne, but he has shown remarkable lasting power because of his uncanny reach into his culture, because of his ability to frame, as it were, many of the more pressing concerns of his day.

These two issues, the more strictly technical and the more broadly cultural, are not unrelated. Both speak to the opportunistic use Marvell made of poetry: in the one case capitalizing on a metrical line that had become an increasingly important resource for lyric poets of the early seventeenth century;[6] in the other seizing upon poetry more generally as a way to celebrate, eulogize, or criticize – sometimes in a single poem – a number of the more important people and occasions in the seventeenth century. In part because Marvell was so successful at cultivating an image of himself in his verse as modest and deferential, almost morbidly bashful at times (hiding, for instance, his fishing "utensils" as if they were something else when he spots the "young Maria" walking the grounds of Appleton House), it is still possible to forget that he served and wrote poems about two of the most influential men in English history in Thomas Fairfax, Commander-in-Chief of the Parliamentary Army during the Civil War, and Oliver Cromwell, made Lord Protector of England in 1653; that in one of the poems he drew a portrait of the memorable scene of Charles's execution unrivaled for its compassionate yet unclouded view of events; that he was on familiar terms with the most important poet of the era; and that his commendatory poem written for the second edition of *Paradise Lost* in 1674 stands alone in commemorating in its native language the epic that was soon to be regarded as the greatest long poem in English. Marvell had a keen eye for spotting not only birds in flight but epochal moments in the making and the people associated with them. Indeed, Jonson might have been envious of the opportunities afforded this poet, a point perhaps not entirely lost on Marvell, who, in "Tom May's Death," represents Jonson denouncing the royalist-turned-Parliamentarian May precisely because May has so magnificently failed to rise to the poetic challenge presented by the radical historical changes being wrought in England at mid-century.

But Marvell rose to these challenges in his own peculiar and baffling way. His easy assimilation of past and current literary examples, for instance, points not to his derivative status as a poet but to his independence, a feature that, in turn, has led some modern literary historians sometimes to characterize Marvell "as the greatest minor poet in the English language." The phrase belongs to Hugh Kenner, although the idea can be traced back to Eliot;[7] and while I think it is risky to consider Marvell in any way a minor poet, especially in a book that has already reserved that laurel for Herrick and at a moment in our own history when that claim is being turned into a self-evident virtue, I think conjoining "greatest" with "minor" is just the kind of oxymoron that Marvell would have appreciated. It points to a composite of interests, indeed, to a "perspective," that both partially aligns him with his Cavalier contemporaries and yet profoundly differentiates him as well.

In this context, Marvell might be said to have made a virtue out of necessity, made "his destiny his choice," in a way that would have been impossible for either a Drayton or Milton, to name two other "patriotic" poets. As a great lyricist, as perhaps the quintessence of what we mean by a lyricist of the Renaissance, whose graceful conclusion he is often thought to supply, Marvell is nearly unrivaled in the respect he shows for small objects that are the frequent subject of Caroline lyric poetry. This practice, this habit of seeing, carries over especially into his pastoral poetry, in which Marvell generally eschews the more prophetic strains of Spenserian pastoral, exploited by Drayton and Milton, in favor of emphasizing the special features of lyric, often at their most emotionally wrought and intellectually complicated: the long, psychologically riven, elegiac moment of the Nymph's complaining for the death of her faun (in the poem with that title), for instance, or the plangent reflections of "The Mower's Song," which begins,

> My Mind was once the true survey
> Of all these Medows fresh and gay;
> And in the greenness of the Grass
> Did see its Hopes as in a Glass:
> When *Juliana* came, and She
> What I do to the Grass, does to my Thoughts and Me.

But even at its most concentrated and isolated, lyric does not function in Marvell as a perfectly enclosed form. "The difference in scale between Marvell and, say Herrick – good as Herrick is – " writes Barbara Everett, "might be summarized as the greater *openness* of a Marvell lyric. It contains more of life; of the world; of its time."[8] The Nymph's complaint, as many have remarked, is initiated by "wanton troopers" who seem to have wandered into her intensely private pastoral domain from a nearby battle (the usage of "trooper" first became current in the early 1640s); and though no one has been able to produce a completely satisfying, extended allegorical reading of the poem, most readers register the belief that the lyric is also – whether through allusion or echo or a combination of the two – deeply interfused with history and politics.

The same may be said for the mower poems. The mowers themselves don't generally speak more than they mean and therefore "glance" at a larger political world. With the exception of the mower in "The Mower against Gardens," they are as forlorn as any broken-hearted shepherd out of Theocritus or Sidney: perhaps even more so because of Marvell's acute concentration on the mowers' psychological as well as emotional "condition," a practice made possible by shifting the intellectually taut and self-focused concerns of the lyric as developed by Donne and Herbert onto the naive pastoral speaker. But the poems speak more than they mean, or at least they suggest they do even when they sometimes protest to the contrary, as in the following stanza gleaned from "The Mower to the Glo-Worms":

> Ye Country Comets, that portend
> No War, nor Princes funeral,
> Shining unto no higher end
> Than to presage the Grasses fall.

We do not have to produce a specific historical referent for war, a prince's funeral, or the fall (of Troy? Caesar? Charles? mankind?), to understand that Marvellian pastoral invites us to see double, inside and outside, the small with the large; and partly because Marvell likes to draw boundaries in order to erase them, he teases us into thinking that his mowers might be said to possess a leveling mentality, imaged in the shape of the scythes they carry and heard in their repeated "sighs": the pun is Marvell's in "Damon the Mower." And while, in turn, these pastorals do not insist that in order to understand them we must forge a link between the disappointed hopes of these "scythe" bearers, who seem drawn to their own doom, and the Leveller party in England, Marvell himself hints at this possibility by making the equation more exact in "Upon Appleton House."

In a sense, Marvell the amphibian keeps having his lyric cake and eating it too, swallowing it – to shift metaphors yet again – into a maze of other cultural, social, and religious concerns. In sharp contrast to Herrick's verse, which Marvell's resembles in so many superficial ways, the minor never quite remains minor, the accidental incidental. The mower in "The Mower's Song" fantasizes a tomb for himself in the manner of an aspiring member of the gentry:

> And thus, ye Meadows, which have been
> Companions of my thoughts more green,
> Shall now the Heraldry become
> With which I shall adorn my Tomb;
> For *Juliana* comes, and She
> What I do to the Grass, does to my Thoughts and Me.

So, too, at the end of her complaint, the Nymph presents herself as not simply the most exquisite of mourners, reckoning in the faun's tears a comparison (no less) with those of "the brotherless Heliades": the three daughters of Helios who, after mourning the death of their brother Phaeton, were turned into amber-dropping trees. She also seeks, in the Niobe-like statue she imagines of herself "cut in marble," a scale of gendered significance in – and through – representation denied her in life:[9]

> First my unhappy Statue shall
> Be cut in Marble; and withal,
> Let it be weeping too: but there
> Th'Engraver sure his Art may spare,
> For I so truly thee bemoane,
> That I shall weep though I be Stone:
> Until my Tears, still dropping, wear
> My breast, themselves engraving there.
> There at my feet shalt thou be laid,
> Of purest Alabaster made:
>   For I would have thine Image be
>   White as I can, though not as Thee.

In the construction of these "minor monuments" – both those within the poem and the poems themselves – we witness in part the legacy of Theocritean and Virgilian pastoral operating in its most distilled form: the incidental not being divided from but incorporating the significant; matters of pastoral retreat appearing inseparable from acts of personal assertion.[10] The wit and pathos of "The Mower's Song" might be said to result in the uncanny linking of the mower's greatest moment of self-assertion, the moment when the "I" appears (in a Spenserian alexandrine, no less), with the moment of his self-cancellation. With the swing of a scythe, he simultaneously presents himself as a reflex of what Juliana does to him, or more accurately, does "to my thoughts and me," Marvell's closing words, repeated in the refrain at the end of each stanza, signifying the self-division that is the poem's subject.

But the legacy of this kind of paradox need not be restricted to conventional pastoral in Marvell, much as "pastoral" in Marvell is too inclusive a way of thinking to be limited to poems with nymphs, shepherds, and mowers.[11] The small is constantly impinging on the large in Marvell; epic is continually being folded into lyric in ways that both distinguish Marvell from his many courtly (mostly royalist) contemporaries and explain why the master of octosyllabics might eventually become the defender of *Paradise Lost*. "On a Drop of Dew," to take perhaps the most microscopic of Marvell's poems, differs from its Neoplatonic counterpart in Vaughan ("The Retreate"), for instance, not simply because of the greater reflexive intricacy of Marvell's poem, astonishing as that is.[12] What the soul yearns for in Marvell – indeed remembers, recollects, and expresses – is nothing less than an heroic version of itself, a "greater Heaven in an Heaven less":

So the Soul, that Drop, that Ray
Of the clear Fountain of Eternal Day,
Could it within the humane flow'r be seen,
    Remembring still its former height,
    Shuns the sweat leaves and blossoms green;
    And, recollecting its own Light,
Does, in its pure and circling thoughts, express
The greater Heaven in an Heaven less.

Whereas Vaughan writes as a disenchanted visionary of the episcopal church, hoping in the "weaker glories" of "some *gilded Cloud*, or *flowre*," to spy "Some shadows of eternity," Marvell invites a concentration on the tiny so intent that he takes us to the vanishing point of vision itself – "Could it within the humane flow'r be seen" – then carries us through to the other side, in which the small suddenly becomes tall, a circling thought an image of heaven itself, and then further outward, on our way toward imagining a heavenly return almost as hugely triumphant as Cromwell's in the "Horatian Ode." With an exit that is more like an exodus, as the allusion to the manna of Exodus 16: 21 happily indicates, Marvell concludes his musings with a note of eager spiritual militancy. And with it, all the pent-up, "congeal'd" energy of the poem is exquisitely released in the penultimate line through the strong enjambment on "run" that helps further animate the emphatic "glories" of the last line:

Such did the Manna's sacred Dew destil;
White, and intire, though congeal'd and chill.
Congeal'd on Earth: but does, dissolving, run
Into the Glories of th' Almighty Sun.

In "On a Drop of Dew," the little globe and the global, the precious and the penultimate are yoked together in a manner that is characteristic of Marvell at his most "conceited" or emblematic; and in a way that is further characteristic of his thinking, the terms in which these different scales are expressed here have a tendency to spiral outwards and beget others: the difference between stasis and mobility, for instance, or between retreat and involvement, between self-reflection and self-immolation, between courtly and Puritan. And these differences in turn, or rather Marvell's perspective on these differences, reappear sometimes in highly refracted form in poem after poem. As Richard Poirier has observed in another context, "a poem 'gives you somewhere to go from,' not something on which to repose."[13] If size is often a matter of perspective in Marvell, breadth is a feature of the rebound.

    The exit which is an exodus in "On a Drop of Dew," for instance, leads in many directions. On the farthest horizon, imaginatively and geographically, lies the beautiful gospel song of "Bermudas," which begins in telescopic fashion:

Where the remote *Bermudas* ride
In th' Oceans bosome unespy'd,
From a small Boat, that row'd along,
The listning Winds receiv'd this Song.

The poem then shifts to a close-up view in which we overhear many voices in
perfect unison:

What should we do but sing his Praise
That led us through the watry Maze,
Unto an Isle so long unknown,
And yet far kinder than our own?
Where he the huge Sea-Monsters wracks,
That lift the Deep upon their Backs,
He lands us on a grassy Stage;
Safe from the Storms, and Prelat's rage.

Although the lyric might well have been composed while Marvell was tutor
to Cromwell's ward, William Dutton, and residing in the home of John
Oxenbridge, a Puritan divine who had himself traveled twice to the Bermudas,
the first time in 1635 in order to escape ecclesiastic persecution under Laud, it is
typical of Marvell's allusive habits that the basis for imagining the historical
context comes from within the poem. Whoever these gospellers are – and
Marvell wants them to remain mysteriously "remote" – they are Puritan émigrés
who have fled religious persecution. Their hymn of praise is a hymn of deliverance woven unobtrusively out of the psalms and yet celebrating a God whose
sense of decorative purity is also undeniably poetic:[14]

He gave us this eternal Spring,
Which here enamells everything;
And sends the Fowl's to us in care,
On daily Visits through the Air.
He hangs in shade the Orange bright,
Like golden Lamps in a green Night.
And does in the Pomgranates close,
Jewels more rich than *Ormus* show's.

Nature in the New World is imagined in the Old in the manner of a mid-
century "cabinet of rarities."

But for all the attention given to purity in this most Ariel-like of utterances
– and Marvell has gone so far in the direction of the ethereal as to cast "the listning Winds" as the primary audience for the song – he also manages, in a
characteristic twist, to turn his lyric inside out, as it were, and to give his poem
at the end a dynastic or epic touch:

He cast (of which we rather boast)
The Gospels Pearl upon our Coast.
And in these Rocks for us did frame
A Temple, where to sound his Name.
Oh let our Voice his Praise exalt,
Till it arrive at Heavens Vault:
Which thence (perhaps) rebounding, may
Eccho beyond the *Mexique Bay.*

Marvell speaks of "the Empire of the Ear" in "Musicks Empire." Here in "Bermudas," he imagines in small an empire of sound: the voice of the Puritan elect hoping their hymn of salvation and praise (the poem we have been over-hearing) will spread throughout the New World. By encouraging us to view their song as an expression of their sense of election in this expanding context, Marvell also resituates the heroic internally – as Milton will later do – and perhaps, as Annabel Patterson has suggested, as part of an ideologically moti-vated "correction" of Edmund Waller's sybaritic, mock-heroic, royalist "Battle of the Summer Islands," published in 1645. A carefully modulated modesty (the later parenthetical "perhaps" answering to the earlier parenthetical "boast") and the elegant simplicity of Marvell's octosyllabics together fine-tune our sense of the overblown in Waller's mock-heroic poem. Marvell does so, too, while still maintaining, indeed subtly insisting on, the link between the "purity" of the lyric experience and the patriotic associations of the gospellers. In our final glimpse of them, what was earlier described as only "a small boat" is now "the *English* boat." We also now understand, in one of Marvell's richest reversals, that the purpose of their labor – their rowing – is not so much to move them with Draytonian gusto toward the New World as to "guide" them in their singing or rather their "Chime," to use Marvell's harmonically suggestive word. This faraway "ring" to the Puritan's song might even have pleased Herbert, who spoke of hearing "Church-bels beyond the starres" in "Prayer [I]."

In the ever-elastic physics of Marvell's universe, sounds rebound within poems, across poems. Closer to home – to Marvell's Hull, at least – lies "To his Coy Mistress," the chime of the closing "sun/run" rhyme echoing in reverse the "run/sun" rhyme at the end of "On a Drop of Dew." The difference is subtle, even precious, but the emphasis on mobility at the end of his great *"carpe diem"* poem suggests a wish on Marvell's part not simply to outrun the sun as a sign of physical desire but also to outrun his many courtly contemporaries in this literary venture: to query the meaning of "seize" in "seize the day" by readmit-ting into the genre some of the original sexual energy from Catullus that got lost in translation. Milton, too, will later "seize" upon "seize" to describe, from Eve's perspective, the original moment of wooing in *Paradise Lost* (4: 488–9), and, in doing so, plant a suggestion of sexual desire that will ripple throughout the poem.

In fact, "To his Coy Mistress" has been so often celebrated for its combination of smooth surface and logical rigor that it is easy to forget that it differs from its principal Catullan prototype in English, Jonson's "Song to Celia," primarily because of the grand scale on which wooing is imagined. Only a single additional syllable per line distinguishes Marvell's sinewy octosyllabics from Jonson's "beheaded" tetrameter, but space and time in "Coy Mistress" are matters of perspective, not meter, and, familiar as the beginning has become, Marvell's casual assimilation of epic into lyric remains little short of breathtaking:

> Had we but World enough, and Time,
> This coyness Lady were no crime.
> We would sit down, and think which way
> To walk, and pass our long Loves Day.
> Thou by the *Indian Ganges* side
> Should'st Rubies find: I by the Tide
> Of *Humber* would complain.

In Marvell's playful reverie, there is no need to worry, as there is in Jonson, about fooling a few household spies. Domesticity has little place in an argument that moves from India to England, from the antediluvian to the end of time; and whereas Cowley will employ the familiar arithmetic-of-love in order to indicate how long he can survive on a sigh or a look in "My Dyet,"

> On a *Sigh* of Pity I a year can live,
>   One *Tear* will keep me twenty at least,
>   Fifty a gentle *Look* will give;
> An Hundred years on one *kind word* I'll feast:
>   A thousand more will added be,
> If you an Inclination have for me;
> And all beyond is vast *Eternity*,

counting in "Coy Mistress," with its languid pauses and quantum surges, expresses a connoisseur's hunger. So close and yet so far, we might imagine Marvell saying of Cowley, as he works his way artfully across time's horizon and then down the lady's body:

>   I would
> Love you ten years before the Flood:
> And you should if you please refuse
> Till the Conversion of the *Jews*.
> My vegetable Love should grow
> Vaster then Empires, and more slow.
> An hundred years should go to praise
> Thine Eyes, and on thy Forehead Gaze.

Two hundred to adore each Breast:
But thirty thousand to the rest.
An Age at least to every part,
And the last Age should show your Heart.
For Lady you deserve this State;
Nor would I love at lower rate.

In a way that could never have happened in the Jacobean court, the urbane and the apocalyptic are now partners in rhyme.

Like Herrick, Marvell too will play with the occasional polysyllabic word, as in the unforgettable "vegetable Love" quoted above. The difference, though, is that Marvell's polysyllables are usually associated not with shimmering surfaces but images of impending vastness ("Annihilating all that's made / To a green Thought in a green Shade," for instance) that disrupt what he elsewhere describes as the chaste purity of the English language:[15] the spaciousness of "desarts of vast eternity," for instance, in the next paragraph, when internal rhyme seems to expand our sense of "eternity" itself; or the long preservation of innocence that is nonetheless doomed in the memorably macabre phrase, "then Worms shall try / That long preserv'd Virginity." To look ahead for a moment to the "Horatian Ode," the polysyllabic "climacteric" and "indefatigably" seem even more loaded and portentous, performing thematically as specific repositories of energy – verbal equivalents of the shocking image of the "bleeding head" that is seen to animate and justify the revolutionary powers.

A full response to "Coy Mistress" would have to go beyond measuring epic longing (and epic tropes like the familiar "Times winged Charriot" in the middle section) and the polyphonic reach of diction and address the "climactic" finale itself, the collapse into the present "now." Here the violence imagined does seem nearly to overwhelm the urbane speaking subject of the previous lines.[16] Jonson had remarked, somewhat casually, upon "proving," while we may, the "sport of love" in his "Song to Celia." In Marvell, proving assumes a level of urgency (now ... now ... now ...) that Jonson had identified in *Volpone* – the original setting of his song – with the ravenous appetites of the villains in that play, the expression of which barely falls short of rape itself. Marvell does not allow for such nice moral discriminations in his conclusion. Sexual violence of a heroic, apocalyptic kind is the way to a new order, even if Marvell leaves us guessing about the specific means:

Now therefore, while the youthful hew
Sits on thy skin like morning dew,
And while thy willing Soul transpires
At every pore with instant Fires,
Now let us sport us while we may;
And now, like am'rous birds of prey,
Rather at once our Time devour,

Than languish in his slow-chapt pow'r.
Let us roll all our Strength, and all
Our sweetness, up into one Ball:
And tear our Pleasures with rough strife,
Thorough the Iron gates of Life.
Thus, though we cannot make our Sun
Stand still, yet we will make him run.

As the allusion to the riddle of Samson in Judges 14: 14 indicates ("Out of the eater came forth meat, and out of the strong came forth sweetness"), Marvell has exchanged the courtly qualifications of "if you please" and "some, I think," along with the playful roll of the tongue in "Shoulds't Rubies find," for Hebrew heroics; and while specific referents for the "one Ball" and "the Iron gates [or grates] of Life" are likely to remain matters of scholarly debate,[17] there can be little doubt about the general tenor of Marvell's argument here, or about its oblique connections to other moments in his poetry in which the act of defloration seems to be part of a larger, often barely specified, response to historical change – in this case, one to be embraced triumphantly.

* * *

Sounds rebound. So does sense. Pre-eminently a lyricist, Marvell seems born to vex linear thinking. A poem like "To his Coy Mistress" manages, as his poems so often do, to look in not one but two directions, reminding us (once again) that the dialogue and the dialogical are where Marvell most often lives, moves, and has his being. The 1681 *Miscellaneous Poems*, we might recall, is introduced by "A Dialogue Between The Resolved Soul, and Created Pleasure," and while Donne could represent ecstasy in the poem of that title as "a dialogue of one," Marvell usually insists on differentiating, as precisely as art can do, the one perspective from the other: the "Resolved Soul," in this case, defending himself in tight-lipped, heroic "tetrameter" couplets (if there is such thing, it is realized in this poem), against that most courtly of tempters, "Created Pleasure," who speaks alluringly of the five senses in a far more relaxed trochaic meter, made even looser by the occasional use of alternating rhymes.

Differentiating and exploring, or better yet, differentiating and experiencing: so pointed and concentrated is Marvell's lyric imagination that it often gives the double sense of an idea being simultaneously entertained and yet taken to its farthest limits and thereby exhausted in the process. Never was "vegetable Love" given a greater hearing, for instance, than in that wonderful off-shoot from "To his Coy Mistress," "The Garden." Or is it the other way around, the erotic pleasures associated with plants in "The Garden" finally discovering a "straight" outlet in "To his Coy Mistress"? In any event, Marvell would be almost unthinkable without "The Garden" in the same way that he would appear a far more diminished poet without its mirror opposite, "An Horatian Ode upon Cromwel's Return from Ireland," as if the sought-after sweetness and strength in "To his Coy Mistress" were suddenly unrolled, with lyric pleasure all going in one direction and power all in the other.

In an important sense, the two poems, different as they are from each other and because of their differences, are central to any full understanding of Marvell, even if what they illuminate is Marvell's ability to imagine living in the seemingly divided and distinguished worlds of lyric and epic. The one poem is undatable in its composition and dedicated to describing the timeless pleasures found in the "green" world. The other is precisely datable in the historical event it purportedly celebrates: the return of Cromwell from Ireland, which happened in May 1650, just before he set out for Scotland in July of the same year; it is committed to understanding and evaluating the great changes suddenly brought about in England.

"The Garden" has been typically described as private, the ode as public, and from this set of oppositions many others are quickly generated: the difference between feminine playfulness and masculine doing, between a Neoplatonic celebration of the mind and a Machiavellian consent to power, between a protoromantic defense of poetry reminiscent of Sidney's, and an Horatian recognition that poetry should not surrender itself either to fancy or annihilation but scrupulously evaluate what's "there."[18] If – to reverse the order of the comparison – the ode is "grim, witty, exuberant, explosive, savage, elliptical, elegiac, apocalyptic but not balanced and transcendent," as David Norbrook suggests,[19] then "The Garden" is pliant and whimsical, happily slippery rather than savagely elliptical, its nine stanzas (each with eight lines of eight syllables each) beautifully proportioned to reflect nine ways of thinking about – reflecting upon – the pleasures of horticultural retreat.

So sharply differentiated are these two poems and the experiences they explore that a critical history of Marvell's reception (and perhaps that of seventeenth-century verse more generally) could almost be written from the point of view of which poem has been more in favor at any given moment. It would no doubt begin with the excision from the 1681 Miscellaneous Poems of the "Horatian Ode" and Marvell's other two Cromwell poems by a printer possibly intimidated by Tory reprisals; but in the same way that Marvell's Puritan and political sympathies cannot be neatly limited to these three Cromwell poems[20] – the prelate still rages in "Bermudas" – so the imaginative boundaries separating "The Garden" and the ode are occasionally and strategically blurred: the one poem including within its perspective a glancing reflection of the world it would seem otherwise to deny.

In this context, "The Garden," whimsical and worldly, ought to be read (lightly) against a contemporary celebration of retreat like Mildmay Fane's "To Retiredness" from Otia Sacra (1648). Marvell's ironies and eccentricities – the very mental habits Fane declines – expose through overstatement the underlying claim that pastoral is the expression of "a mind ambition-free," as the Earl of Westmoreland puts it. Perhaps because pastoral had become sentimentalized in the seventeenth century,[21] Marvell was especially attuned to the element of "bad faith" in this gesture. As the opening stanza suggests, in its entangling wit, a posture that claims a complete renunciation of power only deflects and re-creates the totalizing impulse in another form. The perfect "garland of repose" imagined by the speaker "crowns" and "upbraids" all efforts at civic accomplishment in the respective areas of war, statesmanship, and poetry:

> How vainly men themselves amaze
> To win the Palm, the Oke, or Bayes;
> And their uncessant Labours see
> Crown'd from some single Herb or Tree.
> Whose short and narrow verged Shade
> Does prudently their Toyles upbraid;
> While all Flow'rs and all Trees do close
> To weave the Garlands of repose.

Marvell, of course, is the maker, not the victim of the maze. By taking the idea of pastoral – "vegetable Love" – excessively straight, he ensures that we see its eccentricities:

> No white nor red was ever seen
> So am'rous as this lovely green.
> Fond Lovers, cruel as their Flame,
> Cut in these Trees their Mistress name.
> Little, Alas, they know, or heed,
> How far these Beauties Hers exceed!
> Fair Trees! wheres'e'er your barkes I wound,
> No Name shall but your own be found.

And he ensures that we understand, too, how eccentricities are perhaps not always quite innocent, as in the much disputed central stanza, although it is also extremely difficult to know precisely where to draw the line between excessive pleasures and "fallen" behavior:

> What wond'rous Life in this I lead!
> Ripe Apples drop about my head;
> The Luscious Clusters of the Vine
> Upon my Mouth do crush their Wine;
> The Nectaren, and curious Peach,
> Into my hands themselves do reach;
> Stumbling on Melons, as I pass,
> Insnar'd with Flow'rs, I fall on Grass.

And how the mind, imagining a totalizing pastoral, is not without fantasies of "annihilation":

> Mean while the Mind, from pleasure less,
> Withdraws into its happiness:
> The Mind, that Ocean where each kind
> Does streight its own resemblance find;
> Yet it creates, transcending these,
> Far other Worlds, and other Seas;
> Annihilating all that's made
> To a green Thought in a green Shade.

In "The Garden," Marvell might be said to have his lyric cake because he eats it. The fullest admission of pastoral coincides simultaneously with the moment of "annihilation" itself, that strange Cromwellian word (like "*Clymacterick*") that seems to lie at the end of the labyrinth like the minotaur ready to devour the poem's horticultural offerings in a single apocalyptic gulp. At the farthest reach of worldly ambition, Marvell seems to say, lie ambitions of another kind – the fantasy of bodily transcendence "here at the Fountains sliding foot," or a belief in the absolute self: "Such was that happy Garden-state, / While Man there walk'd without a Mate." The latter attitudes, especially, might be said to underlie the many expressions of pastoral retreat in the 1640s and 1650s. But it would be wrong to think of "The Garden" as simply a work of genteel demystification, as has been sometimes claimed. If Marvell invites us to see, from many angles, the fictitiousness of the pastoral, he also stresses in the final stanza that our pleasures are also dependent upon recognizing their limitations. Gardens, like poems, are beautiful places to go from:

> How well the skilful Gardner drew
> Of flow'rs and herbes this Dial new;
> Where from above the milder Sun
> Does through a fragrant Zodiack run;
> And, as it works, th'industrious Bee
> Computes its time as well as we.
> How could such sweet and wholsome Hours
> Be reckon'd but with herbs and flow'rs!

That sentiment, in conjunction with the final stanza, almost serves as the perfectly adequate bridge to its apparent opposite in the "Horatian Ode": more trustworthy, in some regards, than a speculative chronology that attempts to pinpoint the moment when Marvell, once and for all (at least until the Restoration), crossed over to the Parliamentary side; more trustworthy because more responsive to the kind of reflective doubling that goes on elsewhere in Marvell's poetry. In fact, Marvell's unusual designation of the Ode as specifically

"Horatian" would seem to signal at the outset a range of interpretive possibilities. Having originally sided with Brutus and Cassius against the triumvirate of Antony, Lepidus, and Octavius in the Roman civil wars, but then eventually finding preferment under Augustus, with the patronage of Maecenas, to whom he dedicated the first three books of Odes in 23 BC, Horace seems almost a ready-made multivalent political symbol in 1650.[22] He could be thought of as figuring either republican or monarchical sympathies or as embodying an example of individual change in the context of wider historical fortunes; and at one point or another, as criticism this century has ably demonstrated, Marvell's poem touches on all three of these possibilities. Although few critics today are likely to read the "Ode" as a crypto-royalist lament for Charles, it is equally the case that readers who fail to register the multivalent tenor of Marvell's argument – and so disruptive and subtle are the tonal shifts that responses can vary significantly not only between readers but between readings – will also risk turning the "Ode" into panegyric of the kind written either by Crashaw and Cowley in the 1630s in their several salutes to the returning king[23] or by Marvell himself several years later in "The First Anniversary *of the Government under O.C.*"

These poems are fully shaped by the public events they wish to commemorate. The "Ode," by contrast, is a signal instance, in Barbara Everett's apt phrase, of Marvell's "thinking aloud," or perhaps "rethinking aloud." In this context we should regard the ending of "The Garden" as forming only an imperfect bridge to the "Ode." Beautiful as they are to go from, gardens – and the poetry and perspectives they generate – also never quite get left behind in Marvell, even when the poet suggests the contrary as in the celebrated opening to the "Horatian Ode":

> The forward Youth that would appear
> Must now forsake his *Muses* dear,
>   Nor in the Shadows sing
>   His Numbers languishing.
> 'Tis time to leave the Books in dust,
> And oyl th'unused Armours rust:
>   Removing from the Wall
>   The Corslet of the Hall.

The "Ode" is a measure of Marvell's reflective capacity as a poet to gauge the tremendous forces at work in history by registering their effects on poetry. No other poet of the period, it bears mentioning, put the case for a historically determined generic shift so succinctly, just as, some months earlier in his poem to Lovelace, no one had defended poetry against the "barbed Censurers" so sharply:

> The Ayre's already tainted with the swarms
> Of Insects which against you rise in arms.

Word-peckers, Paper-rats, Book-scorpions,
Of wit corrupted, the unfashion'd Sons.

But for Marvell to say that he is rejecting pastoral in favor of the heroic is also not quite the same thing as either rejecting pastoral outright or folding it seamlessly into the heroic as Milton does in his sonnet to Cromwell written less than two years later. When the older poet concludes his celebration by exhorting Cromwell, now that Scotland has been conquered, to save "free conscience" from "hireling wolves" at home, the turn in the sestet is in a characteristically Miltonic and inward direction, but the heroic idiom in which the new challenge is cast doesn't skip a beat. England's chief spiritual advisor continues to advise Cromwell, "our chief of men."

In the "Horatian Ode," the heroic beat is powerfully registered, especially in the drumming tetrameter couplets, but it occasionally skips a note – this is one way to describe the frequently softening effect of trimeter in this poem – or takes a long pause in between. The most obvious suspension is the lengthy inset dedicated to Charles's execution near the center, the poem's "sovereign moment" as it is sometimes called when Cromwell disappears altogether from sight. The note of hesitation sounded at the outset of the "Ode" when Marvell speaks of how the forward youth "must now forsake his *Muses* dear" – think of the tonal difference if Marvell had simply used the offhand "forget" instead of the reluctant "forsake" – gets resounded and expanded upon in the central panel:

That thence the *Royal Actor* borne
The *Tragick Scaffold* might adorn:
   While round the armed Bands
   Did clap their bloody hands.
He nothing common did or mean
Upon that memorable Scene:
   But with his keener Eye
   The Axes edge did try:
Nor call'd the *Gods* with vulgar spight
To vindicate his helpless Right,
   But bow'd his comely Head,
   Down as upon a Bed.

In this highly cinematic scene, Marvell momentarily substitutes one version of heroic behavior for another: the dignified fall of a prince who plays his part to the end replaces the military prowess of the cunning warrior embodied in Cromwell. But Marvell does not insist on reconciling the two or subordinating one form of heroic behavior to the other. In a sense, he doesn't need to because history has already made that judgment, and whether as apology or explanation

– and Marvell makes it extremely difficult to know exactly where to draw the line here – the poet urges that at this particular moment,

> 'Tis Madness to resist or blame
> The force of angry Heavens flame.

The climactic fusion of providential history and personal ambition has somehow transmuted "th'industrious Bee" of pastoral into the prodigious figure of Cromwell who "Could by *industrious* Valour climbe / To ruine the great Work of Time" (my italics).

Still, resistance to an easy or complete assent is what this poem is largely about. Just as Cromwell is given a moment in his "private Gardens," much is still due to the king: much but not everything. The eye that measures Charles (or for that matter Cromwell) is as exacting as the royal eye that measures the axe's edge. But in seeing events sharply, it also sees further, as was the case in "On a Drop of Dew." The moment of greatest sentiment in the "Ode" is registered in the figure of the "comely Head" bowed down "as upon a Bed," and it is given a full pause, as if responding in a more disciplined and compassionate key to the noise of the soldiers' gruesome clapping; but then that moment is passed through or by, neither forsaken nor forgotten, but seen instead to assume a foundational place in England's new history in a characteristically Marvellian way: the large gesture somehow implicated in the small, the "comely" now with the bloody, Caroline lyric with Roman epic:

> This was that memorable Hour
> Which first assur'd the forced Pow'r.
> > So when they did design
> > The *Capitols* first Line,
> A bleeding Head where they begun,
> Did fright the Architects to run;
> > And yet in that the *State*
> > Foresaw it's happy Fate.

The poet of the "Horatian Ode" would not have been surprised by Walter Benjamin's oft-quoted, postmodernist epigram: "there is no document of civilization which is not at the same time a document of barbarism," in part because Benjamin's response squares so perfectly with a Renaissance truism quoted by Marvell's countryman and contemporary, Marchamont Nedham: "all governments have had their beginning and foundation upon force and violence."[24] But Marvell would have called the events documented in his poem something else: post-Caroline pastoral. At this percipient moment in the poem and in English history, a "bleeding head" can spell again, as it once did, the grandeur of Empire. Marvell alludes here to an anecdote found in Pliny among others that ascribes prophetic import to the discovery of a man's head at the foundations of the temple of Jupiter Capitolinus. The conceit of yoking together two hetero-doxical ideas (death and birth) and cultures (Rome and England) seems a natural, or rather unnatural, outgrowth of an early, equally metaphorical moment in the poem where Cromwell gives a meteor-like Caesarian birth to himself while on the way to blasting Charles's "head at last":

> And, like the three-fork'd Lightning, first
> Breaking the Clouds where it was nurst,
>   Did thorough his own Side
>   His fiery way divide.

But the "bleeding Head" – "bleeding" is Marvell's addition that pushes the image in a slightly fetal direction – born out of this climactic event also spells a new set of political obligations and contingencies. Power (and "sway," as it turns out) is not simply resituated in a new political system. It is made a more promi-nent and problematic feature of it, an embodiment of Cromwell himself:

> Nor yet grown stiffer with Command,
> But still in the *Republick's* hand:
>   How fit he is to sway
>   That can so well obey.
> He to the *Commons Feet* presents
> A *Kingdome*, for his first years rents:
>   And, what he may, forbears
>   His Fame to make it theirs:
> And has his Sword and Spoyls ungirt,
> To lay them at the *Publick's* skirt.
>   So when the Falcon high
>   Falls heavy from the Sky,
> She, having kill'd, no more does search,
> But on the next green Bow to pearch;
>   Where, when he first does lure,
>   The Falckner has her sure.
> What may not then our *Isle* presume
> While Victory his Crest does plume!

The equipoise here is remarkable even for Marvell. The concluding optative couplet, balancing "presume" against "plume," gestures toward a utopia that is nonetheless dependent on a whole series of conditions continuing into the future involving Cromwell's subservience to the new republic that now bears, almost as a logo, the image of the falconer holding the falcon "sure." But in its representation of deadly brute force falling "heavy from the Sky," the simile cuts in another direction as well. For all the deftly woven comparisons between the king and Cromwell, in the end it is one thing to have had Charles on the throne, his head surrounded by laurels, and another thing to have Cromwell perched on a green bough preparing himself not for "longer flight" by "Casting the Bodies Vest aside" ("The Garden") but for attack. Poems give you a place to go from:

> But thou the Wars and Fortunes Son
> March indefatigably on

but also, while going, something to think about:

> And for the last effect
> Still keep thy Sword erect:
> Besides the force it has to fright
> The Spirits of the shady Night,
> The same *Arts* that did *gain*
> A *Pow'r* must it *maintain*.

Whatever the exact relationship between "The Garden" and the "Ode," neither poem serves as a last word on what is for Marvell a remarkably continuous, open-ended debate centering on those mid-century imponderables involving the active and the contemplative life, ambition and retirement, the heroic and the lyric: alternative modes of imagining England that were also immediate realities for Marvell, who, in the early 1650s, was tutor to Maria Fairfax on her father's estate at Nun Appleton in Yorkshire and also seeking a place in the new government under Cromwell. The end of the "Ode," in fact, manages to glance, like so many of Marvell's poems, in both directions. In the militant image of the erect sword frightening the spirits of the shady night, we can glimpse a view of Marvell, the defender of Cromwell in "The First Anniversary," exploiting, with renewed vigor, the extended reach of the pentameter couplet into contemporary affairs of state. But in the compressed verse of the "Ode" and the distance Marvell "*maintains*" on his heroic subject, the poem also leaves room for a fuller exploration of post-Caroline pastoral in the ninety-seven stanzas of octosyllabic verse that make up "Upon Appleton House." "Marvell's most original and ambitious poem," it is the most interesting long poem written in the 1650s, as the amount of recent scholarship amply testifies.[25]

But the poem's ambition is understood and carefully qualified by subject matter and circumstance. "Upon Appleton House" is Marvell's pre-eminent effort at aristocratic entertainment, but one written also in the aftermath of Charles's execution and Fairfax's decision, upon point of conscience, not to lead English troops into Scotland. The Lord General's wife, Anne Vere Fairfax, had spoken out against the execution of the king in a scene much remarked on by contemporaries, while Fairfax himself had only demurred. But he stated his opposition to heading up the Scottish campaign with a meticulousness worthy of Marvell: "It is probable there will be war between us, but whether we should begin this war and be on the offensive part, or only stand upon our own defense is that which I scruple." The remark was made in Whitehall on June 24, 1650, with Cromwell present, and when pressed further about his involvement, Fairfax added (in a now more Miltonic register), "I am to answer only for my own conscience, and what that yields unto as just and lawful, I shall follow; and what seems to me or what I doubt to be otherwise I must not do."[26] Marvell tactfully recorded this sentiment in the center of his poem, with an equally tactful reminiscence from Milton's *Comus*:

> For he did, with his utmost Skill,
> *Ambition* weed, but *Conscience* till.
> *Conscience*, that Heaven-nursed Plant,
> Which most our Earthly Gardens want.
> A prickling leave it bears, and such
> As that which shrinks at ev'ry touch;
> But Flowrs eternal, and divine,
> That in the Crowns of Saints do shine.
>
> (stanza 45)

Milton had spoken of *Haemony* as "a small unsightly root / But of divine effect ... / The leafe was darkish, and had prickles on it, / But in another Country ... / Bore a bright golden flow'r."

The circulation of compliments here points, I believe, to the wider issue of how "Upon Appleton House" ought to be read. In recent years a good deal of critical energy has been spent recovering historical information and political attitudes that tend to lie just below the surface of the poem, information that, in turn, helps to fill in gaps in our understanding: the circumstances surrounding Fairfax's retirement, his connection with Winstanley and hostility toward the Levellers, the possibility in the 1650s that Fairfax might return to active military service. Michael Wilding has been especially helpful in this regard, but his frequently reiterated and accurate conclusion about Marvell, that the poet often invites general analogies but usually blocks specific decoding, also has the effect of returning us, although with renewed appreciation, to the surface and to a continuing truth about the poem: that "Upon Appleton House" is a virtuoso performance in the recently established tradition of the country house poem.[27] It is a lesson in delight and instruction by a tutor-poet whom, of all things, Milton, the author of *Comus*, was shortly to recommend for a position as his assistant in Cromwell's government.

By delight and instruction, I mean something more than what is usually expected in the seventeenth century: something more like delight in instruction, as happens rather deliriously near the end of the poem, for instance, when Marvell casts himself in the role of the *"easie Philosopher"*:

Out of these scatter'd *Sibyls* Leaves
Strange *Prophecies* my Phancy weaves:
And in one History consumes,
Like *Mexique Paintings*, all the *Plumes*.
What *Rome, Greece, Palestine*, ere said
I in this light *Mosaick* read.
Thrice happy he who, not mistook,
Hath read in *Natures mystick Book*.

(stanza 73)

A whimsical pastiche of prophetic exotica – a "light *Mosaick*," deliciously punning, hovering between Pentateuchal illumination and airy design; this stanza is a set-up to annoy serious scholars of a Marxist inclination.[28] It is not about knowledge won through laborious study, as even "Il Penseroso" manages to be. But criticism of this kind is also quick to forget that the subtitle of "Upon Appleton House" is "to my Lord Fairfax." Along with his own attempts at "light" scholarship, Fairfax had also recently been the dedicatee of a travel narrative written by the Protestant minister Thomas Gage, one that included, along with the usual anti-cloister satire – this time of gambling friars not lesbian nuns – detailed descriptions of Mexico.[29] John Wallace's remark that "one may suspect that [the poem] contains personal allusions only Lord Fairfax would have understood"[30] seems right on the money.

And by calling Marvell's poem a virtuoso "performance," I mean, in this honorific context, to point to something more than the calculated, open-ended ease with which the persona moves, like quicksilver, about the estate and through the landscape: sometimes speaking as a tour guide with an antiquarian's knowledge of the family's past, relating "The Progress of this Houses Fate" (l. 84); at other times marking his abrupt descent into the nearby fields – "And now to the Abbyss I pass / Of that unfathomable Grass" (ll. 368–9); and at still other moments marking the spectacular effects of young Maria on nature in a stanza that begs to be quoted in full:

Maria such, and so doth hush
The *World*, and through the *Ev'ning* rush.
No new-born *Comet* such a Train
Draws through the Skie, nor Star new-slain.
For streight those giddy Rockets fail,
Which from the putrid Earth exhale,
But by her *Flames*, in *Heaven* try'd,
Nature is wholly *vitrifi'd*.

(stanza 86)

I mean, too, the many ways in which Marvell leaves his own signature in the poem, especially in the compressed ease with which he handles many different literary genres: epigram, of course, but now with a thematic focus on "size" that connects poet and patron and speaks to Fairfax's architectural, moral, and political circumstances:

> Humility alone designs
> Those short but admirable Lines,
> By which, ungirt and unconstrain'd,
> Things greater are in less contain'd.

One meets as well epic-romance of a wry quixotic kind, now in the general service of the Protestant reformation (stanzas 12–35); a courtly masque (stanzas 66–8); panegryic (stanzas 83–91); Horatian retreat with a serio-comic religious note enabled in part by a familiarity with the Polish Jesuit Casimir Sarbiewski (stanzas 71–5); even perhaps a little touch of night music from Milton's "Il Penseroso" (stanzas 65–6): "The Nightingale does here make choice / To sing the Tryals of her Voice … But I have for my Musick found / A Sadder, yet more pleasing Sound."

Whatever their precise literary origins, moreover, these different forms are also seen as perfectly congruent with one another (making "a light Mosaick") and happily naturalized; as much an expression of a patriotic conscience as the fabric of the house itself as described in the poem's opening couplet: "Within this sober Frame expect / Work of no Forrain Architect." In another way, too, we might regard these literary topoi as grounded in English soil and a further compliment to Fairfax even if he has disappointed his country. Many of the key texts associated with these different genres were housed on the estate itself, in the library at Bolton Percy, or the parish church of Nun Appleton, as Hilton Kelliher has shown.[31] And, of course, near the exact center of the poem is the evocation of a poet patriotic to the core:

> Oh Thou, that dear and happy Isle
> The Garden of the World ere while,
> Thou Paradise of four Seas,
> Which Heaven planted us to please,
> But, to exclude the World, did guard
> With watry if not flaming Sword;
> What luckless Apple did we tast,
> To make us Mortal, and The[e] Wast.

> Unhappy! shall we never more
> That sweet Militia restore,
> When Gardens only had their Towrs,
> And all the Garrisons were Flowrs,
> When Roses only Arms might bear,
> And Men did rosie Garlands wear?

Tulips, in several Colours barr'd,
Were then the *Switzers* of our *Guard*.

The *Gardiner* had the *Souldiers* place,
And his more gentle Forts did trace.
The Nursery of all things green
Was then the only *Magazeen*.
The *Winter Quarters* were the Stoves,
Where he the tender Plants removes.
But War all this doth overgrow:
We ord'nance Plant and Powder sow.

And yet their walks one on the Sod
Who, had it pleased him and God,
Might once have made our Gardens spring
Fresh as his own and flourishing.
But he preferr'd to the *Cinque Ports*
These five imaginary Forts:
And, in those half-dry Trenches, spann'd
Pow'r which the Ocean might command.

(stanzas 41–4)

Criticism on this tonally complex section of the poem almost always concentrates on determining Marvell's response to Fairfax's retreat. Is Marvell paying Fairfax a left-handed compliment? Is Fairfax right to prefer his "five imaginary Forts" to the *Cinque Ports*? To the extent that scholars weigh the patronage system in their analysis, they differ in the latitude they allow Marvell to "advise" his patron; but the one thing which is not at issue here, and perhaps because it is not it rarely attracts extra attention from the reader, is the elegantly complicated but unalloyed nature of Marvell's attachment to England. At the center of this "country house" poem is a lament for "country" in the widest sense, with the echo from John of Gaunt's dying speech in *Richard II* serving to predate the sentiments here to a time before Jonson's classically hierarchical celebration of ideal English society in "To Penshurst." More inclusive in its reiterated use of "we," this section is also, in an important sense, less bound by the past. For if Marvell's "we" all shared in tasting the "luckless Apple" that did make "us Mortal, and The[e] Wast," the ensuing fall is not presented as being necessarily absolute. Fairfax might have preferred his "conscience" to his country at this juncture in English history, but since England's renovation is imagined as dependent upon a fruitful conjunction between the right individual and God – and has nothing to do with social politics of a Jonsonian sort – the possibility remains open in the future for someone else, but not Fairfax, to make "our Gardens spring."

The uncanny way in which Marvell forecloses one possibility only to open up another characterizes more generally the vision of "Upon Appleton House," as a number of critics have observed. But there is a politics in this kind of mobility as well, one especially suitable to the mobility of the political moment and very different, say, from the kind of robust but blunt patriotism of a Drayton. "Upon Appleton House" quietly dramatizes tactfulness of the most extraordinary kind in its praise of Fairfax, as if Marvell, like the modern poet he is often seen to resemble – Yeats – was drawn to his task by the fascination of what is difficult. Milton's celebration of the warrior Fairfax in *The Second Defense*, though sympathetic, seems almost crude by comparison. Nothing is said in "Upon Appleton House" of Fairfax's ill health as a justification for retreat, just as Marvell takes the popular image of Fairfax as the warrior hero and deflects it away from the center of the poem and on to Fairfax's ancestral past. Nothing is said about the great Parliamentary victory at Naseby led by Fairfax; nothing about Fairfax's response to the execution of Charles; nothing about his wife's problematic role in her husband's decision to retire. She is known in this poem simply – and beautifully – as "Starry Vere." With the exception of the Miltonic celebration of conscience, all the big issues that might appeal to contemporary curiosity are left out, thwarted. By the standards then and now, Marvell would make a poor journalist in this poem.

So discreet and diplomatic is the poet in handling the Fairfax "situation" that we might almost begin to suspect that Marvell's modesty is the true subject of the poem. "Humility alone designs / [These] short but admirable Lines." In one of the most intriguingly "allegorical" moments in the poem, in fact, Marvell invites us to share his surprise over the toppling of the "Tallest Oak" in the forest by a hewel, or woodpecker, as if we were witnessing pastoral function as partisan political criticism:

> The good he numbers up, and hacks;
> As if he mark'd them with the Ax.
> But where he, tinkling with his Beak,
> Does find the hollow Oak to speak,
> That for his building he designs,
> And through the tainted Side he mines.
> Who could have thought the *tallest Oak*
> Should fall by such a *feeble Strok'*!

> (stanza 69)

The scene is eerily reminiscent of the king's execution in "An Horatian Ode," as is often noted. The closing exclamation even encourages us to think in terms of political parallels; but Marvell invites this response only to explain away in the next stanza the temptation to allegorize by producing a kind of semiotic overload. With a quick glance back and four couplets forward, Marvell arrives at a no-fault solution to partisan readings:

> Nor would it, had the Tree not fed

A *Traitor-worm*, but within it bred.
(As first our *Flesh* corrupt within
Tempts impotent and bashful *Sin*.)

And yet that *Worm* triumphs not long,
But serves to feed the *Hewels young*.
While the Oake seems to fall content,
Viewing the Treason's Punishment.

(stanza 70)

A Fairfax who brooded over his failure to avert the execution might find comfort in these lines. And yet it is also the case that the easiness in Marvell's philosophy here doesn't prevent him from participating elsewhere in a "game" of Cromwellian iconoclasm, as the nunnery episode indicates, or, for that matter, in a game of Miltonic disenchantment, although played for smaller stakes: "The wasting Cloister with the rest / Was in one instant dispossest" (stanza 34).

"Things greater are in less contained." That sentiment might easily serve as a motto for this poem – indeed for Marvell's lyric vision more generally; for as private and idiosyncratic as are the individual perspectives in "Upon Appleton House," Marvell's practice of identifying the lesser world of the estate is accomplished only by his continually looking over the shoulder at the larger world beyond. "He call'd us *Israelites*" cries "bloody *Thestylis*" (stanza 51), one of the supposedly imaginary mowers in the poem, the "he" being, of all people, Marvell the poet. In this novel, theatricalized rupture of the fictional frame, we witness the aggressive habits of the levelling mowers as they react against the casually expressed typologizing authority of the poet, but the scene also draws our attention, once again, to the analogical habits of Marvell's mind that have been operating throughout the poem. In this regard, it is perhaps not unreasonable that critics have sometimes regarded the young, chaste Maria as a belated figure for Elizabeth. Nor is it altogether surprising that the poem, in its dynastic glances backward and private celebrations of Maria's magical innocence, seems also to herald the end of courtliness as a potent literary mode altogether. Saying much in little, the poem seems always on the verge of saying more.

*   *   *

But humility alone also hardly guaranteed a place for Marvell beyond the grounds of Appleton House; or if it helped at all, it helped him merely to exchange "one tutorship for another," Cromwell's ward for Fairfax's daughter, as John Wallace has ruefully noted.[32] In any event, after Appleton House, it is Cromwell and Milton, rather than Fairfax, who occupy the lion's share of Marvell's literary thinking.[33] The redetermination in emphasis is no doubt due to Marvell's own desire to win a post in the new government, a shift that has often been greeted with puzzlement and disappointment for either personal or literary reasons by readers who are generally more comfortable thinking of Marvell as the last great gasp of the English Renaissance rather than one of the first to anticipate – or participate in – the creation of a public verse shortly to be associated with Dryden. I do not think it is altogether surprising that Marvell himself should partake in this outward "turn," however epochal such a shift in the dominant modes of poetic address has come to seem in retrospect. If the conjunction of the heroic and the worldly helps to distinguish the courtly Marvell from his Cavalier contemporaries, it is only a small step – adding an extra foot, in fact – for Marvell to make the heroic or the mock-heroic into the poem's generating perspective.

It is also the case, too, that the turn outward in these poems has less to do with Marvell's response to an incipient rise of a new, dominant mode of poetry than with the desire simply to speak out on a number of different occasions and for different reasons. Although Marvell could certainly write heroic couplets with the pointed symmetries of later Neoclassicists – these features are especially apparent, for example, in the satiric descriptions of the monarchs and the encomia to Cromwell in "The First Anniversary" – he seems more preoccupied with defending a version of the heroic that he sees under threat at a particular moment in history than he does with defining enduring heroic traits in and of themselves. (The same motivation lies behind the commendatory poem to Lovelace.) In this context, it might be helpful to think of the poems as cultural "interventions" – as attempts to save something perceived in the poem as having potentially significant value to many, not just to a few. In Marvell's case, moreover, the impulse has less to do with enunciating a set of continuous political beliefs than with ensuring a future for both the specific artifact – whether the state or a poem – and the individual architect or poet. Pragmatic, yes; idealistic, yes, but with a concentrated emphasis on distinguishing freedom from tyranny, acts of public significance from attempts at private gain, within a generally Protestant view of history and England's place in that scheme.

To underscore the problem of the heroic in these later poems is not to deny the poetry the deeply circumstanced political resonances that recent scholarship has been so good at detecting. Nor is it to question their rhetorical sophistication. But it is to suggest that part of their political and rhetorical strategy is to resist the tyranny of the local in favor of a more cosmopolitan or global perspective on the subject. In the case of "The First Anniversary," for instance, sensitive though Marvell is to the issue of Cromwell's official status as England's Protector rather than England's King, he invites us to consider these issues in light of a larger, more basic question. What would England be like without Cromwell at all? To think of the poem with this question in mind is to see, at once, its affinities with other "anniversary" poems; Donne's come readily to mind as they perhaps did to Marvell since Donne's poetry went through three editions in the brief time from 1649–1654. But it is also to mark out salient differences between the two, the most obvious being that Donne's is a full-scale anatomy of the world in the wake of Elizabeth Drury's actual death, the anatomy revealing in as many gruesome and witty ways possible "all coherence gone," while Marvell's "Anniversary" is only a dress rehearsal for Cromwell's demise, though a highly revealing one.

Near the center of the poem, almost always the location for crucial moments in his verse, Marvell recounts Cromwell's coach accident in Hyde Park on 24 September 1654. The event was matter for individual poems by Denham and Wither. Marvell, on the other hand, "interweaves," as he says, "this one Sorrow ... among / The other Glories of our yearly Song," and, indeed, sees this act of sorrow as if it were occasioned by an actual death and to be mourned appropriately: "So with more Modesty we may be True / And speak of the Dead the Praises due." The solemnities, replete with pathetic fallacy and "loud shrieks," invite us to imagine the funeral scene for Cromwell, but it also serves the wider goal of the poem by staging Cromwell's Elijah-like apotheosis from the "low world." The allusion to Elijah is only one of several to Biblical heroes in the poem (Gideon and Noah being the other obvious ones); and in conjunction with the earlier extended comparison of Cromwell to Amphion in the remarkable section on the creation of the Commonwealth (ll. 49–98), it helps to establish Cromwell's heroic status. (The Commonwealth section also presents, unequivocally, Marvell's credentials as a keen observer of the political state, just as he had been a keen participant in the pleasures of Fairfax's garden estate.)

What secures this vision of a heroic Cromwell crucial to England's future, however, is not Cromwell's imaginary Biblical heritage but something more like the opinion of the international community. Cromwell may be a Noah figure who has planted "the Vine / of Liberty" – "sober Liberty," as Marvell is quick to qualify; but he is equally quick to insist that a "*Chammish* issue still does rage" in the land, and nowhere more so than in the derisive responses by sectarians occasioned by Cromwell's "fall." Indeed, heresy materializes at this moment in the poem, as it were, with the slip of Cromwell's "Foot." Fifth Monarchists, Quakers, Ranters, Feake and Simpson: the whole bunch emerges as if their multiplying presence signifies the true meaning of Cromwell's Fall (and England's along with it). Their appearance, in turn, invites some of Marvell's most explosive invective:

> Accursed Locusts, whom your King does spit
> Out of the Center of th'unbottom'd Pit;
> Wand'rers, Adult'rers, Lyers, *Munser's* rest,
> Sorcerers, Atheists, Jesuites, Possest;
> You who the Scriptures and the Laws deface
> With the same liberty as Points and Lace:
> Oh Race most hypocritically strict!
> Bent to reduce us to the ancient Pict;
> Well may you act the *Adam* and the *Eve*;
> Ay, and the Serpent too that did deceive.
>
> (II. 311–20)

On one level, Marvell's is a vision of "all coherence gone"; but on another, the incoherence is only seen to underscore further England's need for Cromwell: to encourage not just a sigh of relief in the reader that Cromwell's "fall" has not been fatal but a renewed commitment to England's destiny as a world power.

* * *

Marvell's last two poems – at least the two that can be confidently assigned to him – take us deep into Restoration England. "The Last Instructions to a Painter" (1667) and "On Mr. Milton's *Paradise Lost*" (1674) might profitably be read together. As generically different as they are, both are ambitious, complicated poems; both represent profoundly immediate responses to other poems and the political worlds they invoke and inhabit; both assess problematic versions of the heroic; and both come to radically different conclusions. In "The Last Instructions to a Painter," the heroic might be described as everything that was missing from England after the return of monarchy. Indeed, a reader coming to this poem right after "The First Anniversary" and forgetful of the intervening ten years (and Restoration censorship) might readily respond: "Cromwell thou shouldst be living at this hour." Little remains of England as imagined in the earlier poem: not the Commonwealth as a "listening structure" in all that phrase implies – a Parliament made sturdier by debate, a country made stronger by hearing the voice from abroad – nor a ruler unwavering in his Protestantism and capable of making England into a world power. All is tainted and painted.

Marvell's extended verse essay in this popular Restoration mode delivers a portrait of England overblown with corruption. "The Last Instructions" presents a reverse image, if you will, of the "ship of state" in "Bermudas": no longer an open boat, guided by a common spirit as reflected in the aerial lightness of song, it is secretive, unwieldy, militarily impotent. As Marvell notes near the end of the poem, the factions at court have striven "to Isle the *Monarch* from his *Isle*" (l. 968), and England has become vulnerable to invasion from either the Dutch or the French. The immediate historical occasion prompting the poem was "the unmitigated naval disaster of 10–12 June 1667, when … the Dutch sailed up both the Thames and Medway, and burned the English fleet at Chatham."[34] But as Steven Zwicker has remarked, "it is the low-mindedness of this poem that carries its most urgent arguments":[35] one argument being to deconstruct, in domino fashion, preceding attempts by Waller (in "Instructions to a Painter") and Dryden (in "Annus Mirabilis") to mythologize England's heroic exploits at sea.

Another is to make the visual into a site of excess. The exaggerated fleshy body is now seen, as it were, through the new technological advances provided by the microscope (l.16). Here is the salacious and Brobdingnagian Henry Jermyn, once "Master of the Horse to Henrietta Maria in 1639, and at her request created Earl of St. Albans in 1660":[36]

Paint then St. *Albans* full of soup and gold,
The New *Courts* pattern, Stallion of the old.
Him neither Wit nor Courage did exalt,
But Fortune chose him for her pleasure salt.
Paint him with *Drayman's* Shoulders, butchers *Mien*,
Member'd like Mules, with Elephantine chine.
Well he the Title of St. *Albans* bore,
For never *Bacon* study'd Nature more.

(ll. 29–37)

The profusion of topical jokes defines both the immediate appeal of this kind of writing and the difficulties it presents to later readers (a "Drayman" was someone who drew a cart – a dray – and therefore had large shoulders; Bacon, of course, had been Viscount of St. Albans); but one also sees in these relentless reductions the satirical Marvell whom Swift, with reference to *The Rehearsal Transprosed* (1672–3), will later commend as a "great Genius."[37] As for heroic representations, they are either of the Dutch whose bravery seems designed more to offset England's manifold weaknesses – its soft underbelly – than to celebrate Dutch accomplishment (ll. 523–50); or of "the valiant Scot," Archibald Douglas, whose homoerotic description and extravagant death seem performed almost for the benefit of upbraiding a watchful George Monck (ll. 649–90).

Of course Cromwell is not living at the present hour. Charles II sits on the throne, or rather, doesn't. Marvell's last portrait is of the king, and if one purpose of this sprawling poem is to bring pressure to bear on Clarendon's unscrupulous behavior in the naval debacle – the closing allusion to his "foaming tusk" (l. 941) grotesquely suggests rapacious ambition worthy of a Richard III – it does so as part of a larger warning for the king to clean up his act, even his bedroom act, as Zwicker has argued, and to hear the drums of France now within earshot. To provoke him in this direction, moreover, Marvell summons a bit of the king's family history. In a scene that smacks of Senecan violence of an Elizabethan order, Charles is visited in a dream by victims from both sides of his family, grandfather and father alike:

Shake then the room, and all his Curtains tear,
And with blue streaks infect the Taper clear:
While, the pale Ghosts, his Eye does fixt admire
Of Grandsire *Harry*, and of *Charles* his Sire.
Harry sits down, and in his open side
The grizly Wound reveals, of which he dy'd.

(ll. 915–20)

Then, with a flick of his painterly wrist, Marvell draws a "line" that stands out from all the others in its sharply etched, luminous coloration:

And ghastly *Charles*, turning his Collar low,
The purple thread about his Neck does show.

(ll. 921–2)

Cromwell is dead, but his mark in history lives on, more substantial and less fleeting, at the present moment, than the English navy itself.

*   *   *

It might be of little consequence that the word "majesty" is never used in "The Last Instructions"; Charles is referred to as monarch or king. But the appearance of this word, for perhaps the only time in Marvell's verse,[38] in a poem commending the magnum opus of England's most notorious anti-monarchist is a little surprising; and we might be permitted to regard this example of the Marvellian "rebound" in operation for possibly the last time as also more than a hint of Marvell's deepest loyalties in the Restoration. The phrase from "On Mr. Milton's *Paradise Lost*" reads: "That Majesty which through thy Work doth Reign / Draws the Devout, deterring the Profane." What adds to the line's peculiar resonance is the fact that Milton's majesty is seen as a feature of his work: that it is said to permeate "thy Work," an honorific connection that might seem to be merely conventional praise except for two reasons. At least since the publication of Donne's *Poems* in 1633, commendatory verse had been associated with party politics, especially royalist politics in the Civil War, as evidenced in the many partisan poems accompanying the separate publications of the works of both William Cartwright (1651) and Beaumont and Fletcher (1647). And in yoking together "Majesty" with "Work," Marvell is also uniting what in politics had belonged to divided planes of reality: the king associated with the former by virtue of inherited title or "ancient rights" (and visible at least as a metaphor for kingly behavior in the Horatian Ode), and "indefatigable," industrious Cromwell with the latter.

We can in part locate Marvell's admiration for Milton by simply observing the place of this phrase in his poetry and in the poetry of the seventeenth century more generally. But what makes the poem seem more than a trick of oppositional politics at this point has to do with something else. If "On Mr. Milton's *Paradise Lost*" represents the most sustained, intelligent reading in verse of a single literary work in the seventeenth century, it is so in part because it is the closest thing we have to a "liberal" or non-conformist response to a literary text in the period: what Catherine Belsey would describe as the emerging humanist subject present in the act of reading. If the poem is a product of a particular historical period when Marvell was defending the rights of the individual conscience against ecclesiastical authority in *The Rehearsal Transprosed*, it seems only "natural," too, that the poem came of age again in the era of New Criticism and that it continues to attract attention into the present. Everything – including politics – hinges on individual judgment and taste; on thinking and rethinking; on Marvell as a *tabula rasa* filling his mind with Milton and the matter of his great poem:

> When I beheld the Poet blind, yet bold,
> In slender Book his vast Design unfold,
> *Messiah* Crown'd, *Gods* Reconcil'd Decree,
> Rebelling *Angels*, the Forbidden Tree,
> Heav'n, Hell, Earth, Chaos, All; the Argument
> Held me a while misdoubting his Intent,
> That he would ruine (for I saw him strong)
> The sacred Truths to Fable and old Song,
> (So *Sampson* groap'd the Temples Posts in spight)
> The World o'rewhelming to revenge his Sight.

Marvell's authority to issue judgments and bestow praise, or rather, commendation on the poem, does not result from the poem's adherence to existing rules or previous examples. (In Dryden's prefatory letter affixed to "Annus Mirabilis," Marvell had a full instance of just this kind of appeal to authority.) Authority is grounded, instead, and paradoxically, on the speaker's capacity for reflection; indeed, for reflecting on the act of reflection and recognizing changing responses as part of the process of reading:

> Yet as I read, soon growing less severe,
> I lik'd his Project, the success did fear;
> Through that wide Field how he his way should find
> O're which lame Faith leads Understanding blind;
> Lest he perplext the things he would explain,
> And what was easie he should render vain.
> Or if a Work so infinite he spann'd,
> Jealous I was that some less skilful hand
> (Such as disquiet alwayes what is well,
> And by ill imitating would excell)
> Might hence presume the whole Creations day
> To change in Scenes, and show it in a Play.

To identify the turns and counterturns in Marvell's response is not to devalue the many instances of respectful emulation in this poem: the assumption on Marvell's part of "a formal Miltonic syntax," as Rosalie Colie has emphasized; the marked allusion to Samson; the acute redeployment of resonant Miltonic phrases or words (like "surmise" or "transported").[39] As Marvell wrote in a letter to Cromwell about his ward: "Emulation … is the spur to virtue," and "modesty … is the bridle to Vice."[40] Here lies Marvell's genteel disdain for those presumptuously seeking, as we might say today, to make a movie out of *Paradise Lost*, or more blasphemously, to "show it in a Play," Marvell's disdain now underlining Milton's longstanding iconophobic prejudices. But it is also to note, too, that identifying Milton with "Majesty" is a matter for a fifth, not a first, paragraph. It is not a claim automatically asserted at the outset, nor is it enunciated as part of a proclamation for all time, in the manner of Jonson's celebration of Shakespeare. It is, rather, a position arrived at through internal deliberation or dialogue. It is the logical outcome of thinking about Milton's inimitability, a point earned, in this respect, by both the poet of *Paradise Lost* and by the thinking, writing subject. Yet Marvell's emphasis on individual evaluation is finally not exclusively rationalistic in its criteria: Milton's "Majesty ... Draws the Devout, deterring the Profane."

In putting his signature, or more exactly, his initials at the bottom of his response to Milton's poem, Marvell allows his own readers a rare opportunity to consider the distance he has travelled as a reader since the time his first and only other signed commendatory poem appeared in print: "To his Noble Friend Mr. Richard Lovelace, upon his Poems." The difference between the two poems in the same genre is almost as conspicuous as the difference between the two poets commemorated. In the earlier poem, Lovelace is "read" not as one Cavalier might read another but as the author of *Areopagitica* might read Lovelace, or rather not so much read him (for not a single poem is mentioned, and not a single stylistic trait celebrated), as defend the right to read him in the current post-Civil War climate of renewed suspicion and censorship. Lovelace might even be seen to represent an interesting though challenging test case for an "Areopagitican" Marvell, since Lovelace's devotion to the royalist cause was indisputable. That challenge may help to explain the most curious moment in the poem – the sudden arrival at the end of a bevy of women, naturally Lovelace's most ardent supporters – who have "Sally'd" forth to question the sincerity of the commendatory poet's intentions.

> They all in mutiny though yet undrest
> Sally'd, and would in his defence contest.
> And one the loveliest that was yet e're seen,
> Thinking that I too of the rout had been,
> Mine eyes invaded with a female spight,
> (She knew what pain 'twould be to lose that sight.)

This fanciful event then allows Marvell the opportunity to state, unequivocally, not his party allegiance as the lines might first suggest, but the truth of Lovelace's "cause," the right of *Lucasta* to appear in print at all:

> O no, mistake not, I reply'd, for I
> In your defence, or in his cause would dy.
> But he secure of glory and of time
> Above their envy, or mine aid doth clime.
> Him, valianst men, and fairest Nymphs approve,

His Booke in them finds Judgement, with you Love.

The poem on *Paradise Lost*, by contrast, is written with a Cavalier's respect for form, as exemplified in the concluding, urbane apology for using rhyme:

Well mightst thou scorn thy Readers to allure
With tinkling Rhime, of thy own Sense secure;
While the *Town-Bays* writes all the while and spells,
And like a Pack-Horse tires without his Bells.
Their Fancies like our bushy Points appear,
The Poets tag them; we for fashion wear.
I too transported by the *Mode* offend,
And while I meant to *Praise* thee, must Commend.
Thy verse created like thy *Theme* sublime,
In Number, Weight, and Measure, needs not *Rhime*.

But Marvell's attention to form here only emphasizes the spuriousness of always assuming an easy identity between political beliefs and artistic expression. By the end of the poem, rhyme is about the only thing that separates Marvell from Milton, so thoroughly has Marvell become Milton's reader, even the kind of uncloistered, conscientious reader Milton had once imagined all England becoming in the early days of the Revolution in *Areopagitica*: judicious, independent, individual.[41]

So individual is Marvell in his judgment, in fact, that rhyme can have a marked place in his poem: as a means of honoring Milton, as a way of signaling difference, as a method of identifying a special bond. Praise is fine; it's what the Irish are made to say about Cromwell in the Horatian Ode. But to commend, from the Latin "commendare," is a different matter; at once more formal and more intimate, it means to entrust, to commit to someone's charge (*Oxford English Dictionary*, first usage). It was the kind of thing Marvell had done in asking Milton to recommend him for the post of Assistant Latin Secretary under Cromwell; the kind of thing required of Milton when Marvell intervened at the beginning of the Restoration and helped to save him from a possible hanging.[42] As Aubrey said of Marvell, "he would not play the goodfellow in any man's company in whose hands he would not trust his life."[43] Rhyme matters for Marvell, not for reasons of technical display – Herbert has him beaten hands down – but as a self-defining impulse: because he understood better than any poet in English that it was possible to be original on the rebound.

NOTES

FOREWORD

1 See, for instance, *The Penguin Book of Renaissance Verse, 1509–1659*, ed. David Norbrook and H. R. Woudhuysen, Harmondsworth: Penguin Books, 1993.
2 Vendler, *Soul Says: On Recent Poetry*, Cambridge, MA: Harvard University Press, 1995, p. 3. The other remarks by Vendler woven into the next paragraph are taken from her brief introduction.
3 Heaney, *The Redress of Poetry: Oxford Lectures*, London: Faber and Faber, 1995, p. 8.

1   IRREMEDIABLY DONNE

1 Quoted from R.C. Bald, *John Donne: A Life*, Oxford: Clarendon Press, 1970, p. 139. The attribution of the quotation is questionable but has recently been assigned to Donne by Ernest W. Sullivan, II, "Donne's Epithalamium for Anne" in *John Donne's "desire of more": The Subject of Anne More Donne in His Poetry*, ed. M. Thomas Hester, Newark, DE: University of Delaware Press, 1996, pp. 35–8.
2 Bald, p. 134; spelling largely modernized. See also Dennis Flynn, *John Donne and the Ancient Catholic Nobility*, Bloomington, IN: Indiana University Press, 1995, ch. 5.
3 *Ben Jonson*, ed. Ian Donaldson, New York: Oxford University Press, 1985, p. 597.
4 *John Donne: The Epithalamions, Anniversaries, and Epicedes*, ed. W. Milgate, Oxford: Clarendon Press, 1978, p. 81. "Prince of wits" comes from "In Memory of Doctor Donne," attributed to Richard Busby (p. 97).
5 North, from *A Forest of Varieties: or Rather a Wyldernesse Concerning Petty Poetry*, in *Literary Criticism of Seventeenth-Century England*, ed. Edward W. Taylor, New York: Alfred A. Knopf, 1967, pp. 159–60.
6 Carey, *John Donne: Life, Mind and Art*, London: Faber & Faber, 1981, pp. 121–2.
7 See North's remarks "Concerning Petty Poetry" in Taylor, *Literary Criticism of Seventeenth-Century England*, p. 162: "I may be crabbed and rugged, but will never affect to bee so, especially in verses, whose true nature and use is to worke a kind of a Charme upon the mind, even with slightnesse of matter, by the well wrought and exquisite harmony of their Cadence, and sound."
8 "Life of Cowley" in *Samuel Johnson: Selected Poetry and Prose*, ed. Frank Brady and W.K. Wimsatt, Berkeley, CA: University of California Press, 1977, pp. 347–8.
9 *The Poems of Thomas Carew*, ed. Rhodes Dunlap, Oxford: Clarendon Press, 1949, pp. 72–3.
10 Dennis Flynn, "Donne's First Portrait: Some Biographical Clues?" *Bulletin of Research in the Humanities* 82 (1979): 7–17. See also Flynn, *John Donne and the Ancient Catholic Nobility*, ch. 8.
11 *Walton's Lives*, ed. A.H. Bullen, London: George Bell & Sons, 1884, p. 54.

12 On the connection between writing and social advancement in Donne, see Carey, *John Donne: Life, Mind, and Art*, chaps. 3–4; and Arthur Marotti, *John Donne: Coterie Poet*, Madison, WI: University of Wisconsin Press, 1986, *passim*.

13 Quoted from *The Later Renaissance in England*, ed. Herschel Baker, Boston, MA: Houghton Mifflin, 1975, p. 676.

14 John Hollander, "Donne and the Limits of Lyric" in *Vision and Resonance: Two Senses of Poetic Form*, New York: Oxford University Press, 1975, p. 46.

15 *John Donne: The Satires, Epigrams and Verse Letters*, ed. W. Milgate, Oxford: Clarendon Press, 1967, p. 66 ("To Mr. S.B.").

16 *The Collected Poems of Joseph Hall*, ed. A. Davenport, Liverpool: University of Liverpool Press, 1949, p. 97.

17 Milton, *An Apology Against a Pamphlet* in *The Complete Prose Works of John Milton*, ed. Don M. Wolfe *et al.*, 8 vols, New Haven, CT: Yale University Press, 1953–; vol. I, 1953, pp. 915–16.

18 *John Donne: The Satires, Epigrams and Verse Letters*, p. xvii.

19 James S. Baumlin, "Generic Context of Elizabethan Satire: Rhetoric, Poetic Theory, and Imitation," in *Renaissance Genres: Essays on Theory, History, and Interpretation*, ed. Barbara Kiefer Lewalski, Cambridge, MA: Harvard University Press, 1986, pp. 444–67.

20 *Ben Jonson*, p. 596.

21 The strongest claim of late for a radical reading of Satire III belongs to Richard Strier, *Resistant Structures: Particularity, Radicalism, and Renaissance Texts*, Berkeley, CA: University of California Press, 1995, ch. 6: "Impossible Radicalism I: Donne and Freedom of Conscience." An earlier version appeared as "Radical Donne: Satire III," *ELH* 60 (1993): 283–322. For a different view see Thomas Hester, *Kinde Pitty and Brave Scorne: John Donne's Satyres*, Durham, NC: Duke University Press, 1982.

22 Patricia Parker, "Suspended Instruments: Lyric and Power in the Bower of Bliss," in *Cannibals, Witches, and Divorce: Estranging the Renaissance*, ed. Marjorie Garber, Baltimore, MD: Johns Hopkins University Press, 1987, pp. 28–30.

23 Current assumptions of Donne's authorship are briefly noted by Janel Mueller, "Troping Utopia: Donne's brief for lesbianism," in *Sexuality and Gender in Early Modern Europe*, ed. James Grantham Turner, Cambridge: Cambridge University Press, 1993, pp. 182–207, especially 183–4.

24 Puttenham, *The Arte of English Poesie*, Amsterdam: Theatrum Orbis Terrarum, 1971, p. 20.

25 Alan Armstrong, "The Apprenticeship of John Donne: Ovid and the *Elegies*," *ELH* 44 (1977): 419–42.

26 Carey, *John Donne: Life, Mind and Art*, p. 107.

27 *John Donne: The Elegies and The Songs and Sonnets*, ed. Helen Gardner, Oxford: Clarendon Press, 1965, p. 174.

28 *Ben Jonson*, p. 596.

29 Interpretations of Donne's poetry as misogynistic abound; Camille Wells Slights argues a sensitive middle position that also finds female empowerment in Donne in "A Pattern of Love: Representations of Anne Donne" in *John Donne's "desire of more,"* pp. 66–88.

30 For a full exploration of Donne's fear of annihilation, see Robert N. Watson, *The Rest is Silence: Death as Annihilation in the English Renaissance*, Berkeley, CA: University of California Press, 1994, ch. 5 ("Duelling Death in the Lyrics of Love").

31 *Walton's Lives*, p. 54.

32 *Walton's Lives*, p. 55. The account, however, may be apocryphal; see David Novarr, *The Disinterred Muse: Donne's Texts and Contexts*, Ithaca, NY: Cornell University Press, 1980, pp. 172–3.

33 See John Stachniewski, "John Donne: The Despair of the 'Holy Sonnets'," *ELH* 48 (1981): 677–705; and Richard Strier, "John Donne Awry and Squint: The 'Holy Sonnets,' 1608–1610," *Modern Philology* 86 (1989): 357–84. A counter-response is R.V. Young, "Donne's Holy Sonnets and the Theology of Grace," in *"Bright Shootes of Everlastingnesse": The Seventeenth-Century Religious Lyric*, ed. Claude J. Summers and Ted-Larry Pebworth, Columbia, MO: University of Missouri Press, 1987, pp. 20–39.

34 See *John Donne: The Divine Poems*, ed. Helen Gardner, Oxford: Clarendon Press, 1952, p. 99.

35 My understanding of this poem has been especially helped by Donald M. Friedman, "Memory and the Art of Salvation in Donne's Good Friday Poem," *English Literary Renaissance* 3 (1973): 418–42.

36 Novarr, *The Disinterred Muse*, p. 158. The remark belongs to Donne's contemporary, John Chamberlain.

37 *Index of English Literary Manuscripts*, compiled by Peter Beal, 5 vols, London: Mansell, 1980, vol. I, p. 245.

38 *The Poems of Thomas Carew*, p. 74 ("In answer of an Elegiacall Letter upon the death of the King of *Sweden* from *Aurelian Townsend*, inviting me to write on that subject").

39 These respective positions have been most fully delineated by Barbara K. Lewalski, *Protestant Poetics and the Seventeenth-Century Religious Lyric*, Princeton, NJ: Princeton University Press, 1979, ch. 8; Jonathan Goldberg, *James I and the Politics of Literature*, Baltimore, MD: Johns Hopkins University Press, 1983, especially pp. 65–6, 107–12; and Marotti, *John Donne: Coterie Poet, passim*.

2 BEN JONSON AND THE ART OF INCLUSION

1 *Ben Jonson*, ed. Ian Donaldson, New York: Oxford University Press, 1985, p. 600. All further references to Jonson's works are to this edition.

2 Carew, "An Elegie upon the death of the Deane of Pauls, Dr. John Donne," in *The Poems of Thomas Carew*, ed. Rhodes Dunlap, Oxford: Clarendon Press, 1949, p. 73.

3 Roman Jakobson and Morris Halle, *Fundamentals of Language*, The Hague: Mouton, 1971, pp. 90–6.

4 *Ben Jonson*, p. 455, l. 64.

5 ibid., p. 609.

6 Richard Helgerson's *Self-Crowned Laureates: Spenser, Jonson, Milton and the Literary System*, Berkeley, CA: University of California Press, 1983, provides a comprehensive analysis of this process.

7 Eliot, "Ben Jonson," in *Selected Essays*, New York: Harcourt, Brace & World, 1932, p. 128.

8 *Ben Jonson*, pp. 595, 598.

9 Mark Bland, "William Stansby and the Production of *The Workes of Beniamin Jonson*, 1615–16," *The Library*, 6th ser., 20 (1998): 1–33.

10 A fuller reading of the title page will be found in Margery Corbett and Ronald Lightbown, *The Comely Frontispiece: The Emblematic Title-page in England, 1550–1660*, London: Routledge & Kegan Paul, 1979, pp. 145–50.

11 Bland, "William Stansby and the Production of *The Workes of Beniamin Jonson*, 1615–16," p. 19.

12 Puttenham, *The Arte of English Poesie*, 1589; repr. Amsterdam: Theatrum Orbis Terrarum, 1971, I: XXVII.

13 Richard Dutton, *Ben Jonson: To The First Folio*, Cambridge: Cambridge University Press, 1983, p. 14.

14 See, respectively, "A Sessions of the Poets" in *The Works of Sir John Suckling: The Non-Dramatic Works*, ed. Thomas Clayton, Oxford: Clarendon Press, 1971, and

Wilson, *The Triple Thinkers: Ten Essays on Literature*, New York: Charles Scribner's Sons, 1938, pp. 71–6. For an extensive and subtle refutation of a number of recent accounts of Jonson as court sycophant or "representative voice" of Jacobean absolutism, see Martin Butler, "'Servant, but not Slave': Ben Jonson at the Jacobean Court," *Proceedings of the British Academy* 90 (1995): 65–93. My own chapter was completed before Butler's fine article appeared, although we are clearly both resisting, from different angles, the prevalent view of seeing Jonson as either entirely complicitous with, or always already constrained by, a pervasive system of court patronage.

15 James A. Riddell, "Cunning Pieces Wrought Perspective: Ben Jonson's Sonnets," *Journal of English and Germanic Philology* 87 (1988): 193–212.

16 John Hollander, "Ben Jonson and the Modality of Verse," in *Vision and Resonance: Two Senses of Poetic Form*, New York: Oxford University Press, 1975, p. 173.

17 *Ben Jonson*, p. 596.

18 ibid., p. 595.

19 ibid.

20 ibid., p. 222.

21 *The Poems of Sir John Davies*, ed. Robert Krueger, Oxford: Clarendon Press, 1975, p. 377.

22 Alastair Fowler, "The Silva Tradition in Jonson's *The Forrest*," in *Poetic Traditions of the English Renaissance*, ed. Maynard Mack and George deForest Lord, New Haven, CT: Yale University Press, 1982, pp. 163–80.

23 For a full discussion of Jonson's place in this history, see Wesley Trimpi, *Ben Jonson's Poems: A Study of the Plain Style*, Stanford, CA: Stanford University Press, 1962.

24 *Ben Jonson*, p. 228.

25 For acute discussions of the social strains operating in this poem, see Don E. Wayne, *Penshurst: The Semiotics of Place and the Poetics of History*, Madison, WI: University of Wisconsin Press, 1984, and Michael C. Schoenfeldt, "'The Mysteries of Manners, Armes and Arts': 'Inviting a Friend to Supper' and 'To Penshurst,'" in *"The Muses Common-Weale": Poetry and Politics in the Seventeenth Century*, ed. Claude J. Summers and Ted-Larry Pebworth, Columbia, MO: University of Missouri Press, 1988, pp. 69–79.

26 Aemilia Lanyer's "The Description of Cooke-ham," published as the concluding poem to *Salve Deus Rex Judaeorum*, 1611, is not strictly speaking a "country house" poem, but a lament or farewell to a place. Although Jonson's familiarity with Lanyer's poem is now sometimes taken for granted in critical discussions of the two poems, no one, to my knowledge, has established that Jonson knew Lanyer's poetry. The relationship between the two poems is discussed in more detail below in Chapter 8.

27 See Martin Butler, "'Servant, but not Slave'," p. 83.

28 Greene, *The Light in Troy: Imitation and Discovery in Renaissance Poetry*, New Haven, CT: Yale University Press, 1982, ch. 13.

29 *Ben Jonson*, pp. 598, 596.

30 See especially T.J.B. Spencer, "Ben Jonson on his beloved, The Author Mr. William Shakespeare," in *The Elizabethan Theatre*, IV, ed. G.R. Hibbard, Hamden, CT: Archon Books, 1974, pp. 22–40; Lawrence Lipking, *The Life of the Poet: Beginning and Ending Poetic Careers*, Chicago: University of Chicago Press, 1981, pp. 138–46; and Richard S. Peterson, *Imitation and Praise in the Poems of Ben Jonson*, New Haven, CT: Yale University Press, 1981, ch. 4.

31 *The Poetical Works of William Basse, 1602–1653*, ed. R. Warwick Bond, London: Ellis & Elvey, 1893, p. 115.

32 *Ben Jonson*, p. 569; *Seventeenth-Century Poetry: The Schools of Donne and Jonson*, ed. Hugh Kenner, New York: Holt, Rinehart & Winston, 1964, p. 69.

33 *Ben Jonson*, p. 569. The recent rediscovery of Jonson's copy of the 1617 Folio of Spenser's *Faerie Queen: The Shepheards Calendar; Together With the Other Works of England's Arch Poet* has helped to counter, and to complicate, the "legendary" differences between the two poets as largely reported by Drummond. See James A. Riddell and Stanley Stewart, *Jonson's Spenser: Evidence and Historical Criticism*, Pittsburgh, PA: Duquesne University Press, 1995.

34 *Ben Jonson*, p. 586.

35 Stella P. Revard, "Pindar and Jonson's Cary–Morison Ode," in *Classic and Cavalier: Essays on Jonson and the Sons of Ben*, ed. Claude J. Summers and Ted-Larry Pebworth, Pittsburgh, PA: University of Pittsburgh Press, 1982, p. 17.

36 Anne Barton, *Ben Jonson, Dramatist*, Cambridge: Cambridge University Press, 1984, chaps 12, 14; and Robert N. Watson, *Ben Jonson's Parodic Strategy: Literary Imperialism in the Comedies*, Cambridge, MA: Harvard University Press, 1987, ch. 8.

37 Quoted from Peterson, *Imitation and Praise in the Poems of Ben Jonson*, p. 215.

3 PATRIOTIC AND POPULAR POETS

1 T.S. Eliot, *Selected Essays*, New York: Harcourt, Brace & World, 1964, p. 247 ("The Metaphysical Poets").

2 A handsomely produced modern selection has been edited by William B. Hunter, *The English Spenserians: The Poetry of Giles Fletcher, George Wither, Michael Drayton, Phineas Fletcher, and Henry More*, Salt Lake City, UT: University of Utah Press, 1977. Further selections of all but Taylor's poetry can be found in *The Later Renaissance in England: Nondramatic Verse and Prose, 1600-1660*, ed. Herschel Baker, Boston, MA: Houghton Mifflin, 1973. Joan Grundy, *The Spenserian Poets: A Study in Elizabethan and Jacobean Poetry*, London: Edward Arnold, 1969, provides a valuable introduction to the subject. The most important revaluation of the Spenserians is the chapter in David Norbrook, *Poetry and Politics in the English Renaissance*, London: Routledge & Kegan Paul, 1984, entitled "The Spenserians and King James, 1603–16." By including patriotic with popular poets in this chapter, I am departing a bit from the more canonical line of Spenserian poets as represented by Hunter and Grundy.

3 *The Works of Michael Drayton*, ed. J. William Hebel, 5 vols, 1931–41; repr. Oxford: Basil Blackwell, 1961, vol. IV: vi, and vol. III: 206, respectively. Further references to Drayton's works will be to this edition.

4 Representative of these phases, in chronological order, are two earlier books, Bernard Newdigate's *Michael Drayton and His Circle*, 1941, repr. Oxford: Basil Blackwell, 1961, and Richard F. Hardin's *Michael Drayton and the Passing of Elizabethan England*, Lawrence, KS: University of Kansas Press, 1973; then David Norbrook, *Poetry and Politics in the English Renaissance*, ch. 8 ("The Spenserians and King James"), Richard Helgerson, "The Land Speaks: Cartography, Chorography, and Subversion in Renaissance England," *Representations* 16 (1986): 51–85, and Jean R. Brink, *Michael Drayton Revisited*, Boston, MA: G.K. Hall, 1990; and, most recently, Thomas Cogswell, "The Path to Elizium 'Lately Discovered': Drayton and the Early Stuart Court," *The Huntington Library Quarterly* 54 (1991): 207–33, and Claire McEachern, *The Poetics of English Nationhood, 1590–1612*, Cambridge: Cambridge University Press, 1996, ch. 4 ("Putting the 'poly' back into *Poly-Olbion*: British union and the border of the English nation").

5 The *OED* describes "chorography" as "a term, with its family of words, greatly in vogue" in the seventeenth century, and proceeds to define it as "the art or practice of describing, or of delineating on a map or chart, particular regions, or districts; as distinguished from geography, taken as dealing with the earth in general, and (less distinctly) from topography, which deals with particular places, as towns."

6 Quoted in Newdigate, *Michael Drayton and his Circle*, p. 218.

7 Newdigate, *Michael Drayton and His Circle*, p. 218.

8 Carol Maddison, *Apollo and the Nine: A History of the Ode*, London: Routledge & Kegan Paul, 1960, pp. 290–6. Paul Fry, *The Poet's Calling in the English Ode*, New Haven, CT: Yale University Press, 1980, begins his study with Jonson.

9 Sidney, *A Defence of Poetry*, ed. J.A. Van Dorsten, Oxford: Oxford University Press, 1966, p. 46. For Drayton's bardic interests, see also Geoffrey G. Hiller, "'Sacred Bards' and 'Wise Druides': Drayton and His Archetype of the Poet," *ELH* 51 (1984): 1–15.

10 This point is developed more fully by Marlin E. Blaine, "Drayton's Agincourt in 1606: History, Genre and National Consciousness" in *Renaissance Papers 1996*, ed. George Walton Williams and Philip Rollinson, Columbia, SC: Camden House, 1997, pp. 53–65.

11 Richard F. Hardin, *Michael Drayton and the Passing of Elizabethan England*, p. 160, n.1.

12 See McEachern, *The Poetics of English Nationhood, 1590-1612*, ch. 4.

13 *The Works of Sir Thomas Browne*, ed. G. Keynes, 4 vols, London: Faber & Faber, 1964, vol. IV, pp. 194–5.

14 Pat Rogers, "Drayton's Arden and Windsor-Forest," *Papers on Language and Literature* 17 (1981): 284–91.

15 McEachern, *The Poetics of English Nationhood, 1590-1612*, p. 170.

16 Newdigate, *Michael Drayton and His Circle*, ch. 12.

17 Lewis, *English Literature in the Sixteenth Century, Excluding Drama*, 1954, repr. London: Oxford University Press, 1973, p. 535. For a considered encounter with Lewis, see also William A. Oram, "The Muses Elizium: A Late Golden World," *Studies in Philology* 75 (1978): 10–31.

18 Cogswell, "The Path to Elizium 'Lately Discovered,'" pp. 226–9. See also Newdigate, *Michael Drayton and His Circle*, pp. 210–22.

19 *The Whole Works of William Browne*, ed. W. Carew Hazlitt, 1869, repr. New York: Johnson Reprint Corp., 1970, vol. II, p. 98. Further references to Browne's poetry are to this edition.

20 Fowler, "Genre and Tradition," in *The Cambridge Companion to English Poetry: Donne to Marvell*, ed. Thomas N. Corns, Cambridge: Cambridge University Press, 1993, p. 89. The example he provides is from the second song from Book II of *Britannia's Pastorals*. The final lines of the song, not quoted by Fowler, conclude on a characteristic note of expansion:

> Yet of faire *Albion* all the westerne Swaines
> Were long since up, attending on the Plaines
> When *Nereus* daughter with her mirthfull hoast
> Should summon them, on their declining coast.

21 Cedric C. Brown and Margherita Piva, "William Browne, Marino, France, and the Third Book of *Britannia's Pastorals*," *RES* 29 (1978): 385–404.

22 Allan Holaday, "William Browne's Epitaph on the Countess of Pembroke," *Philological Quarterly* 28 (1949): 495–7.

23 Aubrey, *"Brief Lives," Chiefly of his Contemporaries*, ed. Andrew Clark, 2 vols, Oxford: Clarendon Press, 1898, vol. II, p. 306.

24 J. Milton French, "George Wither in Prison," *PMLA* 45 (1930): 959–66.

25 *"Brief Lives," Chiefly of his Contemporaries*, I, 221. David Norbrook, "Levelling Poetry: George Wither and the English Revolution, 1642–1649," *English Literary Renaissance* 21 (1991): 217–18, has questioned the truth of this anecdote. In a similar possibly erroneous manner, the *Dictionary of National Biography* assumes Wither is the subject of the following lines from "The Second Part of Absalom and Achitophel": "But Fagotted his Notions as they fell, / And if they Rhim'd and

Rattl'd all was well." The current editors of Dryden identify Elkanah Settle (1648–1724) as the referent. See *The Works of John Dryden*, ed. H.T. Swedenberg, Jr., *et al.*, Berkeley, CA: University of California Press, 1972, vol. 2, pp. 332–3. As was true for Dryden of the *Essay of Dramatic Poetry* quoted below, Wither can easily become synonymous with all that high art is not.

26 Dryden, *The Works of John Dryden* 17 (1971): 12. Dryden is speaking only indirectly about Wither; his direct target is probably Robert Wild. I owe this point to Margery Kingsley.

27 "On the Poetical Works of George Wither," in Charles Lamb, *Poems, Plays and Miscellaneous Essays*, 2 vols, Boston, MA: C.C. Brainard, n.d., vol. II, p. 241.

28 Allan Pritchard, "Abuses Script and Whipt and Wither's Imprisonment," *RES* 14 (1963): 337–45.

29 *The Poetry of George Wither*, ed. Frank Sidgwick, 2 vols, London: A.H. Bullen, 1902, vol. I, p. 73. Unless otherwise indicated, all references to Wither's poetry will be to this edition.

30 Allan Pritchard, "George Wither's Quarrel with the Stationers: An Anonymous Reply to The Schollers Purgatory," *Studies in Bibliography* 16 (1963): 27–42; and Norman E. Carlson, "Wither and the Stationers," *Studies in Bibliography* 19 (1966): 210–15.

31 See also Thomas O. Calhoun, "George Wither: Origins and Consequences of a Loose Poetics," *Texas Studies in Literature and Language* 16 (1974): 266–79.

32 From *Time Vindicated* in *Ben Jonson*, ed. C.H. Herford, Percy Simpson and Evelyn Simpson, 11 vols, Oxford: Clarendon Press, 1925–52, vol. 7, p. 659.

33 Wither, *Hallelujah, or Britain's Second Remembrancer*, ed. Edward Farr, London: John Russell Smith, 1857, p. 108.

34 Wither, *Britain's Remembrancer, Containing a Narration of the Plague lately Past*, London, 1628, repr. *Publications of the Spenser Society* nos 28–9, Manchester: Charles Simms, 1880, pp. 232–3.

35 *Britain's Remembrancer*, p. 85.

36 ibid., pp. 235–6.

37 A partial attempt was made by Charles S. Hensley, *The Later Career of George Wither*, The Hague: Mouton & Co., 1969. David Norbrook has written two important essays on Wither's later writings: "Levelling Poetry: George Wither and the English Revolution, 1642–1649" (cited earlier), and "'Safest in Storms': George Wither in the 1650s" in *Heart of the Heartless World: Essays in Cultural Resistance*, ed. David Margolies and Maroula Joannou, London: Pluto Press, 1995. See also Allan Pritchard, "George Wither: The Poet as Prophet," *Studies in Philology* 59 (1962): 211–30.

38 Norbrook, "Levelling Poetry: George Wither and the English Revolution, 1642–1649," p. 220. The remarks that follow are based on points made by Norbrook in his two essays.

39 Michael McKeon, *The Origins of the Novel*, Baltimore, MD: Johns Hopkins University Press, 1987, chaps 1, 2.

40 *Westrow Revived*, repr. in *Publications of the Spenser Society* no. 16, Manchester: Charles Simms, 1874, p. 47.

41 ibid., p. 32.

42 ibid., pp. 16–17.

43 Wood, *Athenae Oxonienses*, ed. Philip Bliss, 4 vols, 1813–20, London: F.C. and J. Rivington, vol. III, p. 192. Quarles's association with Puritanism is rejected by Michael Bath, *Speaking Pictures: English Emblem Books and Renaissance Culture*, London: Longman, 1994, p. 200.

44 Newdigate, *Michael Drayton and His Circle*, p. 221.

45 John Horden, "Francis Quarles (1592–1644): A Bibliography of his Works to the Year 1800," *Oxford Bibliographical Society* n.s. 2 (1948): 2.

46 Quoted from the *DNB* entry for Quarles, 1909 edn, p. 539.

47 *The Complete Works in Prose and Verse of Francis Quarles*, ed. Alexander B. Grosart, 3 vols, 1880, repr. New York: AMS Press, 1967, vol. III, p. 240. Unless otherwise noted, all references to Quarles's poetry are to this edition. There is a recent, useful edition of *Argalus and Parthenia*, ed. David Freeman, London: Associated University Presses, 1986.

48 B.S. Field, Jr., "Sidney's Influence: The Evidence of the Publication of the History of *Argalus and Parthenia*," *English Language Notes* 17 (1979): 98–102.

49 Fuller, *The Worthies of England*, ed. John Freeman, London: George Allen & Unwin, 1952, p. 183. Valuable introductory remarks on Quarles and the emblem tradition will be found in Rosemary Freeman, *English Emblem Books*, London: Chatto & Windus, 1948, ch. 5, "Quarles and His Followers"; and in Bath, *Speaking Pictures*, ch. 8, "Divine Opticks: Francis Quarles."

50 Cedric C. Brown, *John Milton's Aristocratic Entertainments*, Cambridge: Cambridge University Press, 1985, p. 23.

51 Much of the general information in this paragraph is taken from Philipp P. Fehl, "Poetry and the Entry of the Fine Arts into England: *ut pictura poesis*," in *The Age of Milton: Backgrounds to Seventeenth-Century Literature*, ed. C.A. Patrides and Raymond B. Waddington, Manchester: Manchester University Press, 1980, pp. 273–306. See also David Howarth, *Lord Arundel and His Circle*, New Haven, CT: Yale University Press, 1985; and A.R. Braunmuller, "Robert Carr, Earl of Somerset, as Collector and Patron," in *The Mental World of the Jacobean Court*, ed. Linda Levy Peck, Cambridge: Cambridge University Press, 1991, pp. 230–50.

52 Harold Jenkins, *Edward Benlowes (1602–1676): Biography of a Minor Poet*, London: The Athlone Press, 1952, chaps 7, 20.

53 Laura Stevenson, *Praise and Paradox: Merchants and Craftsmen in Elizabethan Popular Literature*, Cambridge: Cambridge University Press, 1984, p. 66.

54 Estienne, *The Art of Making Devices*, trans. Thomas Blount, London, 1650, p. 6.

55 Gordon S. Haight, "The Sources of Quarles's Emblems," *The Library* 16 (1936): 188–209.

56 Pope, *The Dunciad*, ed. James Sutherland, 1943; revised 2nd edn, London: Methuen, 1953, vol. I, pp. 139–40 (B version).

57 Ernest B. Gilman, *Iconoclasm and Poetry in the English Reformation: Down Went Dagon*, Chicago: University of Chicago Press, 1986, ch. 4.

58 *Ben Jonson*, ed. Ian Donaldson, New York: Oxford University Press, 1985, p. 538.

59 Most of Taylor's writings were reprinted by the Spenser Society as *The Works of John Taylor, The Water Poet, Reprinted from the Folio Edition of 1630*, 3 vols, Manchester, 1868–69; and *The Works of John Taylor, The Water Poet Not Included in the Folio Volume*, 5 vols, Manchester, 1870–8. To minimize confusion, quotations from the Folio edition are to *FW* and from the later writings are to *W*, in each case followed by volume and page number, and included in the text.

60 Stevenson, *Praise and Paradox*, pp. 55–7.

61 *Ben Jonson*, p. 608.

62 Quoted from Paul Fussell, *Abroad: British Literary Traveling Between the Wars*, New York: Oxford University Press, 1980, p. 200. See also Warren W. Wooden, "The Peculiar Peregrinations of John Taylor the Water-Poet: A Study in Seventeenth-Century British Travel Literature," *Prose Studies* 6 (1983): 3–20.

63 Aubrey, *"Brief Lives," Chiefly of His Contemporaries*, vol. II, p. 253.

64 Fussell, *Abroad*, p. 208.

65 Robert Southey, *Attempts in Verse, by John Jones, an Old Servant: with some Account of the Writer, Written by Himself: And an Introductory Essay on the Lives and Works of our Uneducated Poets*, London: John Murray, 1831, p. 85. The Huntington Library copy is signed "W. Wordsworth Rydal Mount."

4 CAROLINE AMUSEMENTS

1 *The Complete Works of William Hazlitt*, ed. P.P. Howe, 21 vols, London: J.M. Dent, 1930, vol. 5, p. 82 (from "Lectures on the English Poets").

2 A thoughtful, though apparently unconscious, variation is Richard Helgerson's *Self-Crowned Laureates: Spenser, Jonson, Milton and the Literary System*, Berkeley, CA: University of California Press, 1983. See also William Kerrigan and Gordon Braden, *The Idea of the Renaissance*, Baltimore, MD: Johns Hopkins University Press, 1989, pp. 193–4. Seeking to correct Helgerson's account, Lawrence Venuti, *Our Halcyon Dayes: English Prerevolutionary Texts and Postmodern Culture*, Madison, WI: University of Wisconsin Press, 1989, ch. 5, emphasizes the subversive quality of Caroline verse but ultimately ends up limiting this claim to a ruling elite contained by the royal ideology (pp. 258–9). His is not simply the familiar dilemma of New Historicism; in Caroline poetry, pleasure is not easily reconciled to virtue, except in the fictional world of the masque.

3 *The Poems of John Cleveland*, ed. Brian Morris and Eleanor Withington, Oxford: Clarendon Press, 1967, p. 41.

4 See Patricia Fumerton, *Cultural Aesthetics: Renaissance Literature and the Practice of Social Ornament*, Chicago: University of Chicago Press, 1991, especially chaps 1 and 5; and Jeffrey Knapp, *An Empire Nowhere: England, America, and Literature from Utopia to the Tempest*, Berkeley, CA: University of California Press, 1992.

5 *The Poems of Henry King*, ed. Margaret Crum, Oxford: Clarendon Press, 1965, p. 76 ("Upon the Death of my ever Desired Freind Dr. Donne Deane of Paules"). For a modern variation on King's elegy, see Peter Porter's "An Exequy" in his *Collected Poems*, Oxford: Oxford University Press, 1983.

6 Quoted from *Ben Jonson and the Cavalier Poets*, ed. Hugh Maclean, New York: W.W. Norton, 1974, p. 196.

7 As evidence of manuscript activity in this period, see Peter Beal's interesting comments on the popularity of William Strode and his Song ("I saw fair Cloris walk alone") in the *Index of English Literary Manuscripts, Volume II, 1625–1700, Part 2*, London: Mansell, 1993, p. 352. Some eighty-eight manuscript copies of Strode's poem survive, even though little of his verse was published until the twentieth century.

8 *The Poems of Thomas Carew*, ed. Rhodes Dunlap, Oxford: Clarendon Press, 1949, p. xxxiii. References to Carew's poetry will be to this edition.

9 *Ben Jonson*, ed. Ian Donaldson, Oxford: Oxford University Press, 1985 pp. 584–6.

10 Quoted in Dunlap, *The Poems of Thomas Carew*, p. li. Although Carew is lumped with Pope's "mob," Pope was elsewhere more ambivalent about Carew's status.

11 For the last point especially, see John Kerrigan, "Thomas Carew," *Proceedings of the British Academy* 74 (1988): 311–50.

12 See Sidney Gottlieb, "'Elegies Upon the Author': Defining, Defending, Surviving Donne," *John Donne Journal* 2 (1983): 23–38.

13 *The Poems of Thomas Carew*, p. liv.

14 ibid., p. xlvi.

15 Louis L. Martz, *The Wit of Love: Donne, Carew, Crashaw and Marvell*, Notre Dame, IN: University of Notre Dame Press, 1969, p. 90.

16 *The Poems of Thomas Carew*, p. xxxv.

17 *The Poems of Thomas Carew*, p. xlviii.

18 Norman K. Farmer, Jr., *Poets and the Visual Arts in Renaissance England*, Austin, TX: University of Texas Press, 1984, pp. 30–8.

19 For the first point, see Michael P. Parker, "Carew's Politic Pastoral: Virgilian Pretexts in the 'Answer to Aurelian Townsend,'" *John Donne Journal* 1 (1982): 101–16. For

the second, see Kevin Sharpe, *Criticism and Compliment: The Politics of Literature in the England of Charles I*, Cambridge: Cambridge University Press, 1987, pp. 134–51.

20 See Derek Hirst, *Authority and Conflict, England, 1603–1658*, Cambridge, MA: Harvard University Press, 1986, pp. 15–18, and *Seventeenth-Century Economic Documents*, ed. Joan Thirsk and J.P. Cooper, Oxford: Clarendon Press, 1972, 1–29.

21 *The Poems of Thomas Carew*, pp. xli, xxxix, respectively.

22 Hollander, *Melodious Guile: Fictive Pattern in Poetic Language*, New Haven, CT: Yale University Press, 1988, pp. 59–63.

23 *The Poems of Thomas Carew*, p. 263.

24 *The Works of Sir John Suckling*, ed. Thomas Clayton, Oxford: Clarendon Press, 1971, pp. xxvii–xxviii. All further references to Suckling's non-dramatic works will be to this edition.

25 See Clayton, "'At Bottom a Criticism of Life': Suckling and the Poetry of Low Seriousness" in *Classic and Cavalier: Essays on Jonson and the Sons of Ben*, ed. Claude J. Summers and Ted-Larry Pebworth, Pittsburgh, PA: University of Pittsburgh Press, 1982, pp. 219–20.

26 *Aubrey's Brief Lives*, ed. Oliver Lawson Dick, 1949, repr. Ann Arbor, MI: University of Michigan Press, 1962, p. 287.

27 *The Works of Sir John Suckling*, pp. 3, 105 respectively.

28 For an anatomy of this term, with examples taken largely from this period, see Patricia Meyer Spacks, *Gossip*, Chicago: University of Chicago Press, 1985.

29 *The Works of John Dryden*, ed. H. T. Swedenberg, Jr., *et al.*, Berkeley, CA: University of California Press, 1956– , vol. 17, p. 14.

30 Leavis, "The Line of Wit," in *Revaluation: Tradition & Development in English Poetry*, London: Chatto & Windus, 1962, pp. 10–41.

31 Hazlitt's comments on Suckling's Ballad appear, respectively, in *Works* 6: 56 and 5: 83.

32 Gordon Braden, *The Classics and English Renaissance Poetry*, New Haven, CT: Yale University Press, 1978, pp. 255–8 (appendix). Braden's separate chapter on Herrick is also now the starting place for studying this familiar line of descent.

33 All further references to Herrick's poetry are to *The Poetical Works of Robert Herrick*, ed. L.C. Martin, Oxford: Clarendon Press, 1956.

34 *Robert Herrick: The Hesperides & Noble Numbers*, ed. Alfred Pollard, 2 vols, London: Lawrence & Bullen, 1891, vol. 1, p. xi.

35 Louise Schleiner, "Herrick's Songs and the Character of *Hesperides*," *ELR* 6 (1976): 77–91.

36 J. Max Patrick, "'Poetry perpetuates the Poet': Richard James and the Growth of Herrick's Reputation," in *"Trust to Good Verses": Herrick Tercentenary Essays*, ed. Roger B. Rollin and J. Max Patrick, Pittsburgh, PA: University of Pittsburgh Press, 1978, p. 232.

37 Eliot, "What is Minor Poetry," in *On Poetry and Poets*, New York: Farrar, Straus, and Cudahy, 1952, pp. 43–4.

38 See John L. Kimmey, "Order and Form in Herrick's *Hesperides*," *JEGP* 70 (1971): 255–68; Kimmey, "Robert Herrick's Persona," *SP* 67 (1970): 221–36; and Ann Baynes Coiro, *Robert Herrick's "Hesperides" and the Epigram Book Tradition*, Baltimore, MD: Johns Hopkins University Press, 1988.

39 Fowler, "Robert Herrick," *Proceedings of the British Academy* 66 (1980): 245.

40 *The Book of Common Prayer, 1559*, ed. John E. Booty, Charlottesville, VA: University Press of Virginia, 1976, p. 18 ("Of Ceremonies, Why Some be Abolished and Some Retained").

41 Eliot, "What is Minor Poetry," p. 43.

42 The most substantial reading of Herrick's title belongs to Coiro, *Robert Herrick's "Hesperides" and the Epigram Book Tradition*, ch.1; an earlier version of this chapter appeared in *ELH* 52 (1985): 311–36.

43 Castiglione, *The Book of the Courtier*, trans. Charles S. Singleton, New York: Doubleday, 1959, p. 66.

44 *Sir Thomas Browne: Religio Medici and Other Works*, ed. L.C. Martin, Oxford: Clarendon Press, 1964, p. 124.

45 Claude J. Summers, "Herrick's Political Counterplots," *Studies in English Literature* 25 (1985): 165–82.

46 The most thoughtful exposition of this view is Leah S. Marcus, *The Politics of Mirth: Jonson, Herrick, Milton, Marvell, and the Defense of Old Holiday Pastimes*, Chicago: University of Chicago Press, 1986, ch. v. See also Peter Stallybrass, "'Wee feaste in our Defense': Patrician Carnival in Early Modern England and Robert Herrick's *Hesperides*," *English Literary Renaissance* 16 (1986): 234–52.

47 *The Poetical Works of Robert Herrick*, p. xvi. See also Coiro, *Robert Herrick's "Hesperides" and the Epigram Book Tradition*, pp. 178–9, for further reasons for questioning the view of Herrick as a strict Laudian.

48 *The Poems of Richard Corbett*, ed. J.A.W. Bennett and H.R. Trevor-Roper, Oxford: Clarendon Press, 1955, p. 50.

49 I have made this point in greater detail in "Robert Herrick: A Minority Report," *The George Herbert Journal* 14 (1990): 16–18.

50 See Martin's extended note to ll. 57–70 in *The Poetical Works of Robert Herrick*, pp. 514–15.

51 Others would include his cousin Thomas Stanley (1625–78), John Hall (1627–57), and Charles Cotton (1630–87) – all better known in their day and ours as important translators rather than as original poets.

52 Further references to Lovelace's poems are to *The Poems of Richard Lovelace*, ed. C.H. Wilkinson, Oxford: Clarendon Press, 1930.

53 Quoted from *The Poems of Richard Lovelace*, p. lxiii.

54 *Richard Lovelace: Selected Poems*, ed. Gerald Hammond, Manchester: Carcanet Press, 1987, pp. 10–12.

55 See Annabel Patterson, "Fables of Power," in *Politics of Discourse: The Literature and History of Seventeenth-Century England*, ed. Kevin Sharpe and Steven N. Zwicker, Berkeley, CA: University of California Press, 1987, pp. 271–96.

56 Norman K. Farmer, *Poets and the Visual Arts in Renaissance England*, Austin, TX: University of Texas Press, 1984, p. 57.

57 Miner, *The Cavalier Mode from Jonson to Cotton*, Princeton, NJ: Princeton University Press, 1971, p. 291.

58 Noted in Allen, *Image and Meaning: Metaphoric Traditions in Renaissance Poetry*, 1960; revised edn, Baltimore, MD: Johns Hopkins University Press, 1968, p. 161, n. 27. Allen's early analysis has had considerable impact on later intepretations of the poem. His framing assumption, however, that "this poem was written and sent by Lovelace to his fellow poet and royalist, Charles Cotton, sometime after the collapse of the great cause and the execution of King Charles" (p. 152), is certainly open to question on bibliographical grounds. *Lucasta* was licensed on February 4, 1647/8; Charles was not executed until nearly a year later on January 30, 1648/9. Some three months after that, on May 14, 1649, *Lucasta* was entered with the Stationers' Registers (Wilkinson, p. lxxii).

59 Along with the studies of Lovelace cited above, see also Bruce King, "Green Ice and a Breast of Proof," *College English* 26 (1965): 511–15.

60 *The Poetical Works of Robert Herrick*, pp. 225, 333.

61 *The Poems of Richard Lovelace*, p. lii.

5 SUBSTANCE AND STYLE IN GEORGE HERBERT'S *THE TEMPLE*

1 All references to Herbert's writings are to *The Works of George Herbert*, ed. F.E. Hutchinson, Oxford: Clarendon Press, 1945. The quotation is from "The Pearle."

2 Quoted from *The Herbert Allusion Book: Allusions to George Herbert in the Seventeenth Century*, compiled and edited by Robert H. Ray in *Studies in Philology* 83 (1986): 131–2. (From Baxter's *Poetical Fragments*, 1681.)

3 See, respectively, Amy Charles, *A Life of George Herbert*, Ithaca, NY: Cornell University Press, 1977, and Diana Benet, "Herbert's Experience of Politics and Patronage in 1624," *George Herbert Journal* 10 (1986/7): 33–46; and also Joseph H. Summers, *George Herbert: His Religion and Art*, Cambridge, MA: Harvard University Press, 1954, ch. 2.

4 Keith Wrightson, *English Society, 1580–1680*, London: Hutchinson, 1982, ch. 7, especially pp. 209–12.

5 *Walton's Lives*, ed. A.H. Bullen, London: George Bell & Sons, 1884, p. 318. Ray, *The Herbert Allusion Book*, p. v, notes the surprising fact to modern readers that "The Church-porch" was Herbert's most popular poem in the seventeenth century.

6 *Coleridge on the Seventeenth Century*, ed. R.F. Brinkley, Durham, NC: Duke University Press, 1955.

7 For an illuminating account of the catholicity of Herbert's readership, see Joseph H. Summers, "George Herbert and Anglican Traditions," *George Herbert Journal* 16 (1992–3): 21–39.

8 Vendler, *The Poetry of George Herbert*, Cambridge, MA: Harvard University Press, 1975, p. 118.

9 ibid., p. 120.

10 Richard Strier, "'John Donne Awry and Squint': The 'Holy Sonnets,' 1608–1610," *Modern Philology* 86 (1989): 357–84.

11 Hooker, "A Learned Discourse of Justification," in *Of the Laws of Ecclesiastical Polity*, 2 vols, London: J.M. Dent & Sons, 1907, vol. I, p. 58.

12 Joseph H. Summers, "From 'Josephs coat' to 'A true Hymne,'" *The George Herbert Journal* 2 (1978): 11.

13 "The Parson Preaching" in *A Priest to the Temple, or, The Country Parson*, in *Works*, p. 233.

14 Recent work of interest that assesses from a variety of angles the circumstantial nature of Herbert's poetry includes Stanley Stewart, *George Herbert*, Boston, MA: G.K. Hall, 1986, especially ch. 3; Marion Singleton, *God's Courtier: Configuring a Different Grace in George Herbert's "Temple,"* Cambridge: Cambridge University Press, 1987; Sidney Gottlieb, "The Social and Political Backgrounds of George Herbert's Poetry" in *"The Muses Common-Weale": Poetry and Politics in the Seventeenth Century*, ed. Claude J. Summers and Ted-Larry Pebworth, Columbia, MO: University of Missouri Press, 1988, pp. 107–18; and, most thoroughly, Michael C. Schoenfeldt, *Prayer and Power: George Herbert and Renaissance Courtship*, Chicago: University of Chicago Press, 1991, especially p. 227 for remarks on "Love [III]" muffling disputes.

15 Stevens, *Opus Posthumous*, ed. Milton J. Bates, New York: Alfred A. Knopf, 1989, p. 184.

16 I owe this point and much of my sense of contrasting discourse in Herbert to Chana Bloch, *Spelling The Word: George Herbert and the Bible*, Berkeley, CA: University of California Press, 1985, especially pp. 12–45. (See p. 15 for her identification of the refrain with Psalm 38.)

17 Schoenfeldt, *Prayer and Power: George Herbert and Renaissance Courtship*, Chicago: University of Chicago Press, 1991, pp. 61–3, makes this argument with considerable subtlety. We do not differ at all about whether "Jordan [I]" should be read as "plain"

in meaning, which it is not, only about the purpose of difficulty in the poem, which he views more as an elaborate reflex to absolutist power than to issues of moral and artistic intentions. Where he emphasizes the inherent instability of "My God, my King," I would argue that Herbert is already there ahead of him with his stress on "plainly."

18 For my emphasis here and later on Herbert's different audiences, I am indebted to an early reading of this poem by Summers, *George Herbert: His Religion and Art*, p. 112.

19 In attributing the reference of the pronoun ("He") to God, I follow Summers, *George Herbert: His Religion and Art* and Richard Strier, *Love Known: Theology and Experience in George Herbert's Poetry*, Chicago: University of Chicago Press, 1983, p. 203.

20 Strier, *Love Known*, p. 208. In an essay to which I am more generally indebted, Robert Shaw's, "Farewells to Poetry," *Yale Review* 70 (1980): 187–205, discusses "The Forerunners" in the context of other "Farewell" poems by Herrick, Yeats, and Stevens. As will be clear to those familiar with his essay, I found his discussion of authorship in Herbert's poem especially suggestive.

21 Vendler, *The Poetry of George Herbert*, p. 267.

22 Fish, *Self-Consuming Artifacts: The Experience of Seventeenth-Century Literature*, Berkeley, CA: University of California Press, 1972, ch. 3 ("Letting Go: The Dialectic of the Self in Herbert's Poetry").

23 Michael J. Colacurcio, "'The Corn and the Wine': Emerson and the Example of Herbert," *Nineteenth-Century Literature* 42 (1987): 1–28.

24 *Works*, p. 233 ("The Parson preaching").

25 James Merrill, *Recitative: Prose by James Merrill*, ed. J.D. McClatchy, San Francisco: North Point Press, 1986, p. 33.

6 THE ONCE AND FUTURE POET

1 Thomas N. Corns, "Milton's Quest for Respectability," *MLR* 77 (1982): 769–79. See also Corns, *Uncloistered Virtue: English Political Literature, 1640–1660*, Oxford: Clarendon Press, 1992, ch. 3.

2 All references to Milton's work are to *John Milton: Complete Poems and Major Prose*, ed. Merritt Y. Hughes, Indianapolis, IN: The Odyssey Press, 1957. The quotation is from *The Reason of Church Government as Urged Against Prelaty*, p. 671. I have also consulted the Scolar Press Facsimile edition of Milton's *Poems 1645*.

3 Revard, *Milton and the Tangles of Neaera's Hair: The Making of the 1645 "Poems,"* Columbia, MO: University of Missouri Press, 1997.

4 Quoted in *John Milton: The Complete Poetry and Major Prose*, p. 1021.

5 *Selections from Ralph Waldo Emerson*, ed. Stephen E. Whicher, Boston, MA: Houghton Mifflin, 1957, p. 158 (from "Self-Reliance").

6 Martz, "The Rising Poet, 1645," in *The Lyric and Dramatic Milton*, ed. Joseph H. Summers, New York: Columbia University Press, 1965, pp. 3–33.

7 *Samuel Johnson: Selected Poetry and Prose*, ed. Frank Brady and W.K. Wimsatt, Berkeley, CA: University of California Press, 1977, p. 429.

8 Wilding, "John Milton: The Early Works," in *The Cambridge Companion to English Poetry: Donne to Marvell*, ed. Thomas Corns, Cambridge: Cambridge University Press, 1993, p. 221. See also David Loewenstein, "'Fair Offspring Nurs't in Princely Lore': On the Question of Milton's Early Radicalism," *Milton Studies* 28 (1992): 37–48. By contrast, Barbara K. Lewalski regards Milton as unquestioningly "radical" from his earliest years as a poet. See her "How Radical was the Young Milton?" in *Milton and Heresy*, ed. Stephen B. Dobranski and John P. Rumrich, Cambridge, Cambridge University Press, 1998, ch. 3.

9 Barker, "The Pattern of Milton's 'Nativity Ode,'" collected in *Milton: Modern Judgements*, ed. Alan Rudrum, London: Macmillan, 1969, p. 49.

10 Budick, *The Dividing Muse: Images of Sacred Disjunction in Milton's Poetry*, New Haven, CT: Yale University Press, 1985, ch. 2 ("Pattern of Division in the Nativity Ode," especially pp. 21–2.

11 See Revard, *Milton and the Tangles of Neaera's Hair*, pp. 79–83.

12 Peter Lake, "Anti-popery: The Structure of a Prejudice," in *Conflict in Early Stuart England: Studies in Religion and Politics 1603–1642*, ed. Richard Cust and Ann Hughes, London: Longman, 1989, pp. 72–3.

13 *Samuel Johnson: Selected Poetry and Prose*, p. 429.

14 Christopher, "Subject and Macrosubject in *L'Allegro* and *Il Penseroso*," *Milton Studies* 28 (1992): 27.

15 See Edward R. Weismiller, "Studies of Verse Form in the Minor English Poems," in *A Variorum Commentary on the Poems of John Milton*, ed. A.S.P. Woodhouse and Douglas Bush, New York: Columbia University Press, 1972, vol. II (part 3), pp. 1026–37.

16 Quoted from Christopher Grose, *Milton and the Sense of Tradition*, New Haven, CT: Yale University Press, 1988, p. 40.

17 Quoted from "The Redress of Poetry," in Seamus Heaney, *The Redress of Poetry: Oxford Lectures*, London: Faber and Faber, 1995, p. 1.

18 *Samuel Johnson: Selected Poetry and Prose*, p. 430.

19 *Poems upon Several Occasions, English, Italian, and Latin, with Translations*, by John Milton, London: James Dodsley, 1785, p. 338. For an extended inquiry into the effects of retitling Milton's sonnet "When I consider," see Dayton Haskin, *Milton's Burden of Interpretation*, Philadelphia, PA: University of Pennsylvania Press, 1994, pp. 90–117.

20 Prince, *The Italian Element in Milton's Verse*, Oxford: Clarendon Press, 1954, p. 96.

21 *The Complete Prose Works of John Milton*, ed. Don M. Wolfe *et. al.*, 8 vols, New Haven, CT: Yale University Press, 1953–82, vol. I , p. 319.

22 W.R. Parker, *Milton: A Biography*, 2 vols, Oxford: Clarendon Press, 1968, vol. I, ch. 5.

23 See Cedric C. Brown, *John Milton's Aristocratic Entertainments*, Cambridge: Cambridge University Press, 1985, ch. 1, for a careful account of the context.

24 See Barbara Breasted, "*Comus* and the Castlehaven Scandal," *Milton Studies* 3 (1971): 201–24, and the response by John Creaser, "Milton's *Comus*: The Irrelevance of the Castlehaven Scandal," *Notes and Queries* 31 (1984): 307–17. Brown, *John Milton's Aristocratic Entertainments*, pp. 175–8, is also skeptical about the extent to which Milton's masque is informed by the scandal.

25 *Samuel Johnson: Selected Poetry and Prose*, p. 429.

26 Fletcher, *The Transcendental Masque: An Essay on Milton's "Comus,"* Ithaca, NY: Cornell University Press, 1971, pp. 195–209.

27 Norbrook, "The Reformation of the Masque," in *The Court Masque*, ed. David Lindley, Manchester: Manchester University Press, 1984, pp. 94–110.

28 Maryann Cale McGuire, *Milton's Puritan Masque*, Athens, GA: University of Georgia Press, 1983, ch. 4 ("Merriment Well Managed: Chastity as a Rule of Life"), helpfully distinguishes Milton's version of chastity from that celebrated in court masques under Henrietta Maria.

29 *John Milton: The Complete Poetry and Major Prose*, p. 832.

30 On the complicated subject of Milton's revisions, see Brown, *John Milton's Aristocratic Entertainments*, ch. 6, and the appendix (pp. 171–8).

31 For a selection of representative modern responses, see the many essays collected in *Milton's "Lycidas": The Tradition and the Poem*, ed. C.A. Patrides (1961; revised edn., Columbia, MO: University of Missouri Press, 1983). For "Lycidas" as a poem of "crisis," see J. Martin Evans, *The Road from Horton: Looking Backwards in "Lycidas,"* University of Victoria: ELS Monograph Series No. 28, 1983; for "Lycidas" as a poem

of mourning, see Peter Sacks, *The English Elegy: Studies in the Genre from Spenser to Yeats*, Baltimore, MD: The Johns Hopkins University Press, 1985, pp. 90–117.

32 Brown, *Milton's Aristocratic Entertainments*, ch. 7 ("The Sense of Vocation in the 1630s"), and David Norbrook, *Poetry and Politics in the English Renaissance*, London: Routledge & Kegan Paul, 1984, ch. 10 ("The Politics of Milton's Early Poetry").

33 See Parker, *Milton: A Biography*, I: 155; and John Leonard, "'Trembling Ears': The Historical Moment of Lycidas," *JMRS* 21 (1991): 59–81.

34 Ransom, "A Poem Nearly Anonymous," in *Milton's "Lycidas"*, p. 75.

35 Quoted from the entry for "Monody" in the *Princeton Encyclopedia of Poetry and Poetics*, ed. Alex Preminger, 1965; enlarged edn, Princeton, NJ: Princeton University Press, 1974, p. 529.

36 Milton privileges poetry over logic and rhetoric as "being less subtle and fine but more simple, sensuous, and passionate" in *Of Education* (1644). See *The Complete Poetry and Major Prose*, p. 637.

37 Fish, "*Lycidas*: A Poem Finally Anonymous" in *Milton's "Lycidas": The Tradition and the Poem*, p. 335.

38 Sacks, *The English Elegy*, p. 114.

39 *John Milton: The Complete Poetry and Major Prose*, p. 637.

40 The exact meaning of "the Genius of the shore" and the next two lines has been much debated. Lawrence Lipking, "The Genius of the Shore: Lycidas, Adamastor, and the Poetics of Nationalism," *PMLA* 111 (1996): 205–21, argues for the nationalistic over the global or "sublunary" reach of Milton's sentiments here, and concludes, learnedly but rather fantastically in my view, that the poet, continuing King's "mission," seeks to "enlist fresh recruits" in order "to convert the Irish" (p. 212).

7 ARENAS OF RETREAT

1 Rich, *Blood, Bread, and Poetry: Selected Prose, 1979–1985*, New York: W.W. Norton, 1986, p. 170.

2 Quoted from "Regeneration," p. 397. Further quotations of Vaughan's writings are from *The Works of Henry Vaughan*, ed. L.C. Martin, 2nd edn, Oxford: Clarendon Press, 1957. Serious students of Vaughan will also want to consult the more recent, annotated editions by Alan Rudrum (Harmondsworth: Penguin, 1976) and Louis Martz (Oxford: Oxford University Press, 1986).

3 Although there is much criticism on the subject of retreat and retirement in the seventeenth century, my most immediate debt is to Lois Potter, *Secret Rites and Secret Writings: Royalist Literature, 1641–1660*, Cambridge: Cambridge University Press, 1989.

4 See James D. Simmonds, *Masques of God: Form and Theme in the Poetry of Henry Vaughan*, Pittsburgh, PA: University of Pittsburgh Press, 1972; and my *Henry Vaughan: The Unfolding Vision*, Princeton, NJ: Princeton University Press, 1982. For interesting treatments of *Thalia Rediviva*, focusing on "Daphnis: an Elegiac Eclogue," see Cedric C. Brown, "The Death of Righteous Men: Prophetic Gesture in Vaughan's 'Daphnis' and Milton's *Lycidas*," *The George Herbert Journal* 7 (1983–4): 1–25; and Graeme J. Watson, "Political Change and Continuity of Vision in Henry Vaughan's 'Daphnis. An Elegiac Eclogue,'" *Studies in Philology* 83 (1986): 158–81.

5 *The Works of Henry Vaughan*, p. 186.

6 ibid., p. 392.

7 ibid., p. 217 ("To the Reader" of *Flores Solitudinus*).

8 ibid., p. 391.

9 Seamus Heaney, *The Redress of Poetry: Oxford Lectures*, London: Faber & Faber, 1995, p. 9.

10 For a fuller exploration of Herbert's formalistic influence on Vaughan, see my *Henry Vaughan: The Unfolding Vision*, ch. 4.

11 Quoted from *Anthroposophia Theomagica* in *The Works of Thomas Vaughan*, ed. Alan Rudrum, Oxford: Clarendon Press, 1984, p. 52. Important discussions of Vaughan's hermeticism date from Elizabeth Holmes's *Henry Vaughan and the Hermetic Philosophy*, Oxford: Blackwell, 1932, and include several valuable articles by Alan Rudrum: "The Influence of Alchemy in the Poems of Henry Vaughan," *Philological Quarterly* 49 (1970): 469–80; and "An Aspect of Vaughan's Hermeticism: The Doctrine of Cosmic Sympathy," *Studies in English Literature* 14 (1974): 129–38. The best general discussion of Vaughan and the pastoral belongs to Georgia B. Christopher, "In Arcadia, Calvin ... A Study of Nature in Henry Vaughan," *Studies in Philology* 70 (1973): 408–26.

12 Harold Skulsky, "The Fellowship of the Mystery: Emergent and Exploratory Metaphor in Vaughan," *Studies in English Literature* 27 (1987): 89–107.

13 Davies, *Henry Vaughan*, Glamorgan: Poetry Wales Press, 1995, p. 112.

14 John N. Wall, *Transformations of the Word: Spenser, Herbert, Vaughan*, Athens, GA: University of Georgia Press, 1988, p. 301. The seminal article on the subject of searching in Vaughan is by Louis Martz, "Henry Vaughan: The Man Within," *PMLA* 78 (1963): 40–9.

15 Greenblatt, *Marvelous Possessions: The Wonder of the New World*, Chicago: University of Chicago Press, 1992, especially ch. 2.

16 See, for example, Joseph H. Summers, "Some Apocalyptic Strains in Marvell's Poetry," in *Tercentenary Essays in Honor of Andrew Marvell*, ed. Kenneth Friedenreich, Hamden, CT: Archon Books, 1977, 180–203.

17 For two recent studies comparing Vaughan's apocalyptic thinking with that of conservative and radical contemporaries, see, respectively, Claude J. Summers, "Herrick, Vaughan, and the Poetry of Anglican Survivalism" in *New Perspectives on the Seventeenth Century English Religious Lyric*, ed. John R. Roberts, Columbia, MO: University of Missouri Press, 1994, pp. 46–74, and Nigel Smith, *Literature and Revolution in England, 1640–1660*, New Haven, CT: Yale University Press, 1994, pp. 269–71. An exhaustive analysis of the subject appears in Philip West's 1998 Cambridge University dissertation, *Scripture Uses: Henry Vaughan's "Silex Scintillans" [1650, 1655] and its Contexts*, ch. 6 ("Perfection Postponed"). Some of my remarks are partially anticipated in *Henry Vaughan: The Unfolding Vision*, ch. 7.

18 *George Herbert and Henry Vaughan*, ed. Louis L. Martz, New York: Oxford University Press, 1986, p. 504.

19 John Cook, *King Charles his Case: Or an Appeal to all Rational Men, Concerning his Tryal at the High Court of Justice*, London, 1649, pp. 35–6. I owe this reference to Thad Bower.

20 *The Works of Henry Vaughan*, p. 346.

21 F.E. Hutchinson, *Henry Vaughan: A Life and Interpretation*, Oxford: Clarendon Press, 1947, pp. 124–5.

22 Peter Brown, *The Body and Society: Men, Women, and Secular Renunciation in Early Christianity*, New York: Columbia University Press, 1988, pp. 193–5.

23 Two recent articles, from very different angles, will give the reader a spectrum of interpretive possibilities elicited by this poem. See Graeme J. Watson, "The Temple in 'The Night': Henry Vaughan and the Collapse of the Established Church," *MP* 84 (1986): 144–61; and Geoffrey Hill, "A Pharisee to Pharisees: Reflections on Vaughan's 'The Night,'" *English* 38 (1989): 97–113.

24 Kermode, *The Uses of Error*, London: Collins, 1990, p. 431. See also his earlier influential essay, "The Private Imagery of Henry Vaughan," *Review of English Studies*, n.s. 1 (1950): 206–25.

25 See, for instance, Alan Rudrum, "Vaughan's 'The Night': Some Hermetic Notes," *Modern Language Review* 64 (1969): 14–15. In his 1976 Penguin edition of Vaughan's poetry, Rudrum attempts to fortify this position further (and in turn a Behmenist reading of "The Night") while nonetheless citing the *OED*'s authority to the contrary. His reasoning seems to be that since Vaughan often views creatures sympathetically, it is therefore "typical of Vaughan that he should refuse to adopt a convention of speech which would imply contempt of one of God's humbler creatures." But Vaughan could occasionally view the creatures contemptuously in order to indicate his criticisms of man (see "Idle Verse," for instance, or the "mole" in "The World"), and he seems to have done so on this occasion. It is perhaps indicative of the shaky argument that Rudrum introduces his gloss with a "perhaps." Pettet's remarks (also cited) would not seem to support this position either since Pettet, somewhat illogically, is speaking of a "worm" rather than of a "glowworm" in the gloss he produces from Psalm 22 ("But I am a worm, and no man.")

26 Potter, *Secret Rites and Secret Writing*. See also the particularly interesting essay by Janet E. Halley, "Versions of the Self and the Politics of Privacy in *Silex Scintillans*," *The George Herbert Journal* 7 (1983–4): 51–71.

27 Watson, "The Temple in 'The Night'," 154–5, takes up the issue of persecution in some detail. For Calvin's place in this debate, see Carlos M.N. Eire, *War Against the Idols: The Reformation of Worship from Erasmus to Calvin*, Cambridge: Cambridge University Press, 1986, ch. 7.

8 FROM WROTH TO PHILIPS

1 The most useful introduction to the subject remains *Kissing the Rod: An Anthology of Seventeenth-Century Women's Verse*, ed. Germaine Greer *et al.*, London: Virago Press, 1988. Helpful recent critical surveys include two complementary essays in *Women and Literature in Britain, 1500–1700*, ed. Helen Wilcox, Cambridge: Cambridge University Press, 1996: see ch. 8 by Helen Hackett, "Courtly Writing by Women," and ch. 9 by Elizabeth H. Hageman, "Women's Poetry in Early Modern Britain." For the most part, criticism of women's poetry has been conducted without making literary value judgments, but notions of a "canon" are beginning to emerge in works like *Major Women Writers of Seventeenth-Century England*, ed. James Fitzmaurice, Josephine A. Roberts, Carol L. Barash, Eugene R. Cunnar and Nancy A. Gutierrez, Ann Arbor, MI: University of Michigan Press, 1997. Although poetry is only one of the genres represented here, the anthology provides a useful critical and bibliographical assessment of the state of scholarship in the field as well as relevant bibliographies for each author.

2 Quoted from Margaret J.M. Ezell, "The Myth of Judith Shakespeare: Creating the Canon of Women's Literature," *New Literary History* 21 (1990): 583.

3 See Patricia Crawford, "Women's Published Writings 1600–1700," in *Women in English Society 1500–1800*, ed. Mary Prior, London: Methuen, 1985, p. 214.

4 *Ben Jonson*, ed. Ian Donaldson, Oxford: Oxford University Press, 1985, p. 599.

5 *The Poems of Lady Mary Wroth*, ed. Josephine A. Roberts, Baton Rouge, LA: Louisiana State University Press, 1983, p. 32. See also Wendy Wall, *The Imprint of Gender: Authorship and Publication in the English Renaissance*, Ithaca, NY: Cornell University Press, 1993, ch. 5.

6 Makin, *An Essay to Revive the Antient Education of Gentlewomen*, 1673; repr. Los Angeles: The Augustan Reprint Society, no. 202, William Andrews Clark Memorial Library (1980): 20. Makin's listings are not always easy to follow; Ladies Russell, Bacon and Killegrew are probably three of the five, not four, daughters of Sir Anthony Cooke and Anne Fitzwilliam Cooke. Along with the *DNB* entry for Cooke, see Frances Teague, *Bathsua Makin, Woman of Learning*, Lewisburg, PA:

Bucknell University Press, 1998, pp. 169, 173. The best-known of the daughters is Ann Bacon, second wife of Nicholas Bacon, mother of Francis, and English translator of Bishop John Jewel's *Apologia Ecclesiae Anglicanae*, 1562.

7 Quoted from Juliet Fleming's review of Lewalski's *Writing Women in Jacobean England*, *The Huntington Library Quarterly* 57 (1994): 203–4.

8 Quoted from *Kissing the Rod: An Anthology of Seventeenth-Century Women's Verse*, p. 158.

9 Dryden, "Preface to the Fables" [1700] in *Essays of John Dryden*, ed. W.P. Ker, 2 vols, Oxford: Clarendon Press, 1926, vol. 2, p. 247.

10 The idea of a conscious tradition of female poetry is a later historical development, although how much later is a matter for debate: see, for instance, Cheryl Walker, *The Nightingale's Burden: Women Poets and American Culture before 1900*, Bloomington, IN: Indiana University Press, 1982; Isobel Armstrong, *Victorian Poetry: Poetry, Poetics and Politics*, London: Routledge, 1993, ch. 12 ("'A Music of Thine Own': Women's Poetry – An Expressive Tradition?"); and, most relevant to the present inquiry, Carol Barash, *English Women's Poetry, 1649–1714: Politics, Community, and Linguistic Authority*, Oxford: Clarendon Press, 1996, introduction.

11 This point is developed by Margaret P. Hannay, "'Your vertuous and learned Aunt': The Countess of Pembroke as a Mentor to Mary Wroth" in *Reading Mary Wroth: Representing Alternatives in Early Modern England*, ed. Naomi J. Miller and Gary Waller, Knoxville, TN: University of Tennessee Press, 1991, pp. 15–34.

12 See Ann Rosalind Jones, *The Currency of Eros: Women's Love Lyric in Europe, 1540–1620*, Bloomington, IN: Indiana University Press, 1990, pp. 141–8, and Wall, *The Imprint of Gender: Authorship and Publication in the English Renaissance*, pp. 330–40.

13 See Nona Fienberg, "Mary Wroth and the Invention of Female Poetic Subjectivity," in *Reading Mary Wroth: Representing Alternatives in Early Modern England*, pp. 175–90.

14 Quotations from Wroth's poetry are taken from *The Poems of Lady Mary Wroth*, ed. Josephine A. Roberts, Baton Rouge, LA: Louisiana State University Press, 1983.

15 See, for instance, Barbara Kiefer Lewalski, *Writing Women in Jacobean England*, Cambridge, MA: Harvard University Press, 1993, p. 253, and Jeff Masten, "'Shall I turne blabb?': Circulation, Gender, and Subjectivity in Mary Wroth's Sonnets," in *Reading Mary Wroth: Representing Alternatives in Early Modern England*, pp. 67–87.

16 *The First Part of the Countess of Montgomery's Urania*, ed. Josephine A. Roberts, Binghamton, NY: Medieval and Renaissance Texts and Studies for the Renaissance English Text Society, 1995, p. 350.

17 *The Poems of Robert Sidney*, ed. P.J. Croft, Oxford: Clarendon Press, 1984, pp. 26–7, 174–81.

18 Quotations from Lanyer's poetry are from *The Poems of Aemilia Lanyer*, ed. Susanne Woods, New York: Oxford University Press, 1993; the passage from the commendatory poem to Queen Anne occurs on p. 3. For biographical information about Lanyer, see Woods's Introduction.

19 *The Poems of Aemilia Lanyer*, pp. xx–xxi.

20 *Commentary on the Harmony of the Evangelists, Matthew, Mark, and Luke*, trans. Rev. William Pringle, 3 vols, Edinburgh: Calvin Translation Society, 1846, vol. 3, p. 283. It should be noted that Calvin rejects this common view, as does Lanyer.

21 *The Southwell–Sibthorpe Commonplace Book*, ed. Jean Klene, C.S.C., Tempe, AZ: Medieval and Renaissance Texts and Studies, 1997, p. 81. In *Of the Nobilitie and Excellencie of Womankynde*, 1542, a text with important parallels to Lanyer's, Cornelius Agrippa noted the heroic labors of Pilate's wife. See Esther Gilman Richey, *The Politics of Revelation in the English Renaissance*, Columbia, MO: University of Missouri Press, 1998, p. 66.

22 See Mueller, "The Feminist Poetics of Aemilia Lanyer's 'Salve Deus Rex Judaeorum,'" in *Feminist Measures: Soundings in Poetry and Theory*, ed. Lynn Keller and Cristanne Miller, Ann Arbor, MI: University of Michigan Press, 1994, pp. 230–4.

23 *The Poems of Aemilia Lanyer*, p. xxv.

24 On this point in particular, see Judith Scherer Herz, "Aemilia Lanyer and the Pathos of Literary History," in *Representing Women in Renaissance England*, ed. Claude J. Summers and Ted-Larry Pebworth, Columbia, MO: University of Missouri Press, 1997, pp. 121–35.

25 Fleming, *The Huntington Library Quarterly*, p. 201.

26 Schweitzer, "Anne Bradstreet Wrestles with the Renaissance," *Early American Literature* 22 (1988): 291–312. Quotations from Bradstreet's poetry are from *The Works of Anne Bradstreet*, ed. Jeannine Hensley, Cambridge, MA: Harvard University Press, 1967. Readers interested in the exact contents of *The Tenth Muse* will want to consult the facsimile edition introduced by Josephine K. Piercy, Gainesville, FL: Scholars' Facsimiles & Reprintings, 1965.

27 *"My Name Was Martha": A Renaissance Woman's Autobiographical Poem*, ed. with commentary by Robert C. Evans and Barbara Wiedemann, West Cornwall, CT: Locust Hill Press, 1993, p. 9. All references to Moulsworth's poem are to this edition.

28 See Elaine Hobby, "'Discourse so Unsavoury': Women's Published Writings of the 1650s," in *Women, Writing, History, 1640–1740*, ed. Isobel Grundy and Susan Wiseman, Athens, GA: The University of Georgia Press, 1992, pp. 16–32.

29 Diane Purkiss, "Producing the Voice, Consuming the Body: Women Prophets of the Seventeenth Century" in *Women, Writing, History, 1640–1740*, p. 141.

30 *An Collins: Divine Songs and Meditacions*, ed. Sidney Gottlieb, Tempe, AZ: Medieval and Renaissance Texts and Studies for the Renaissance English Text Society, 1996, p. 1. Further references to Collins's poetry are to this edition.

31 *An Collins: Divine Songs and Meditacions*, pp. xvii–xviii.

32 Wilcox, "'You that Indeared are to Pietie': Herbert and Seventeenth-Century Women," in *George Herbert in the Nineties: Reflections and Reassessments*, ed. Jonathan F.S. Post and Sidney Gottlieb, Fairfield, CT: George Herbert Journal, Special Studies & Monographs, 1995, p. 209.

33 Vendler, "Herbert and Modern Poetry: A Response," in *George Herbert and the Nineties*, p. 85.

34 See Gottlieb's commentary, pp. 111–14.

35 Woolf, *A Room of One's Own*, New York: Harcourt, Brace & World, 1929, p. 65.

36 Marilyn L. Williamson, *Raising Their Voices: British Women Writers, 1650–1750*, Detroit, MI: Wayne State University Press, 1990, p. 37.

37 A student of William Peake, painter to Charles I, Faithorne produced engraved portraits of many famous people. Those from the middle to the late seventeenth century include Charles I, Henrietta Maria, Cromwell, Davenant, Cowley, Fairfax, and Milton. For a partial list of his work, see *A Catalogue of an Exhibition of Portraits Engraved by William Faithorne*, New York: Grolier Club, 1893; Philips is number 88. A more comprehensive, detailed list can be found in Louis Fagan, *A Descriptive Catalogue of the Engraved Works of William Faithorne*, London: Bernard Quaritch, 1888.

38 Quoted from *The Collected Works of Katherine Philips*, ed. Patrick Thomas, G. Greer, and R. Little, 3 vols, Brentford: Stump Cross Books, 1990–3, vol. I, p. 24. Further references to Philips's poetry are to this edition and volume.

39 Gallagher, "Embracing the Absolute: The Politics of the Female Subject in Seventeenth-Century England," *Genders* 1 (1988): 24–39. Quotations from Cavendish's *Poems and Fancies* are from the original 1653 edition.

40 For an excellent account of Cavendish's problematic place in the political and intellectual milieu of the mid-seventeenth century see John Rogers, *The Matter of Revolution: Science, Poetry, and Politics in the Age of Milton*, Ithaca, NY: Cornell

University Press, 1996, ch. 6. In justifying her own abrupt appearance in print, Cavendish also seems to have had access to the censorious manuscript exchange between Mary Wroth and Edward Denny because she aired part of it in the preface "To All Noble, and Worthy Ladies" in *Poems and Fancies*. Details of the exchange between Denny and Wroth can be found in *The Poems of Lady Mary Wroth*, pp. 31–5. Roberts cites Cavendish's *Sociable Letters*, 1664 as the source for this reference to Wroth. My attention was drawn to the earlier uses of the quotation by James Fitzmaurice, "Fancy and the Family: Self-characterizations of Margaret Cavendish," *HLQ* 53 (1990): 198–209.

41 The *OED* cites a number of uses of "extravagant" from the middle to the latter part of the seventeenth century having to do with going beyond normal limits. "Extravagant" was also a word apparently circling around Cavendish and *Poems and Fancies* from the outset, as is made clear by Dorothy Osborne in her letter to her future husband, William Temple: "Let mee aske you if you have seen a book of Poems newly come out, made by my Lady New Castle. For god sake if you meet with it send it mee[.] They say tis ten times more Extravagant then her dresse. Sure the poore woman is a little distracted[.] She could never been soe rediculous else as to venture at writeing book's and in verse too." See *Dorothy Osborne: Letters to Sir William Temple*, ed. Kenneth Parker, Harmondsworth: Penguin Books, 1987, p. 75, Letter 17. I have modernized the punctuation somewhat.

42 Keith Thomas, *Man and the Natural World: Changing Attitudes in England, 1500–1800*, Harmondsworth: Penguin, 1984, p. 170.

43 Price, "Feminine Modes of Knowing and Scientific Enquiry: Margaret Cavendish's Poetry as Case Study," in *Women and Literature in Britain, 1500–1700*, ed. Helen Wilcox, ch. 6.

44 See Williamson *Raising Their Voices: British Women Writers, 1650–1750*, ch. 2, "Orinda and Her Daughters."

45 Quotations from Philips's poetry are from *The Collected Works of Katherine Philips, The Matchless Orinda*, vol. I, ed. Patrick Thomas, Brentford: Stump Cross Books, 1990. Volumes II and III print her letters and translations, respectively. The latter are edited by G. Greer and R. Little.

46 *The Collected Works of Katherine Philips, The Poems*, p. 9. For the quotation from Herrick's "Gather Ye Rosebuds," see *The Letters*, p. 60.

47 See, respectively, Elaine Hobby, "Katherine Philips: Seventeenth-Century Lesbian Poet" in *What Lesbians Do in Books*, ed. Elaine Hobby and Chris White, London: The Women's Press, 1991, p. 201, and Lillian Faderman, *Surpassing the Love of Men: Romantic Friendship and Love Between Women from the Renaissance to the Present*, London: The Women's Press, 1985, p. 71; for a restatement of this position see Faderman, *Chloe Plus Olivia: An Anthology of Lesbian Literature from the Seventeenth Century to the Present*, New York: Viking Penguin, 1994, pp. 3–6, 17–19. Faderman's views with regard to Philips are further questioned by Emma Donoghue, *Passions Between Women: British Lesbian Culture, 1668–1801*, London: Scarlet Press, 1993, pp. 111–12.

48 Hobby, "Katherine Philips: Seventeenth-Century Lesbian Poet," p. 201.

49 Eavan Boland, *Object Lessons: The Life of the Woman and the Poet in our Time*, New York: W.W. Norton, 1995, p. 216.

50 See Donoghue, *Passion Between Women*, pp. 19–20, and the possibility that "lesbianism was unthinkable unless linked to other symptoms or concepts, such as Spain, Roman Catholicism or witchcraft." Marvell's seemingly sexually active cloister of nuns in "Upon Appleton House" helps to bolster this point. See also James Holstun, "'Will You Rent Our Ancient Love Asunder?': Lesbian Elegy in Donne, Marvell, and Milton," *ELH* 54 (1987): 835–67. Hobby, pp. 189–90, draws attention to Cowley's couplet in "On *Orinda's* Poems" as an instance of "significant contemporary anxiety" about equating Philips with Sappho: "They talk of Sappho,

but alass, the shame! / Ill manners soil the lustre of her Fame." But in the context of the admittedly obscure syntax of the stanza, the "ill manners" to which Cowley refers seem to apply to those who speak of Sappho, not to Sappho's behavior:

> They talk of Nine, I know not who,
> Female Chimera's that o'er Poets reign,
> I ne'r could find that fancy true,
> But have invok'd them oft I'm sure in vain:
> They talk of Sappho, but alass, the shame!
> Ill manners soil the lustre of her fame:
> Orinda's inward virtue is so bright,
> That like a Lanthorn's fair-inclosed Light,
> It through the paper shines where she does write.

Cowley's elegy "On the Death of Mrs. Katherine Philips" mentions Sappho but, again, without expressing anxiety over Sappho's sexual behavior. See *The Complete Works in Verse and Prose of Abraham Cowley*, 2 vols, ed. A.B. Grosart, New York: AMS Press, vol. I, pp. 154, 165.

51 For an extended discussion of these issues, see Barash, *English Women's Poetry, 1649–1714*, ch. 2.

52 Quoted from Douglas Bush, *English Literature in the Earlier Seventeenth Century, 1600–1660*, 2nd edn, Oxford: Clarendon Press, 1962, p. 341, n. 1. Walton's remarks about this incident can be found in *The Poems of Henry King*, ed. Margaret Crum, Oxford: Clarendon Press, 1965, p. 22.

53 Quoted from *Kissing the Rod*, p. 181.

54 Ferguson, "Renaissance Concepts of the 'Woman Writer,'" in *Women and Literature in Britain, 1500–1700*, p. 154.

55 See Alice Fulton, "Unordinary Passions: Margaret Cavendish, The Duchess of Newcastle," in *Feeling as a Foreign Language: The Good Strangeness of Poetry*, St. Paul, MN: Grey Wolf Press, 1999.

9 ANDREW MARVELL

1 This remark and subsequent quotations from Marvell's poetry are taken from *The Poems and Letters of Andrew Marvell*, ed. H.M. Margoliouth, 3rd edn, Oxford: Clarendon Press, 1971.

2 After three hundred years, the exact boundaries of the Marvell canon are still a bit up for grabs: but along with those works printed in the *Miscellaneous Poems*, including the three Cromwell poems suppressed from all but two of the extant 1681 copies, and those verses printed in his lifetime bearing his signature, the other poems that scholars generally accept as Marvell's are "The last Instructions to a Painter" and "The Loyall Scot."

3 Quoted from *Andrew Marvell*, ed. Frank Kermode and Keith Walker, Oxford: Oxford University Press, 1990, p. xiii.

4 Quoted from *Adagia* in *Opus Posthumous*, ed. Milton J. Bates, New York: Alfred A. Knopf, 1989, p. 191.

5 Hall, "The Manyness of Andrew Marvell," *Sewanee Review* 97 (1989): 431.

6 Although Marvell's skill with the tetrameter line is generally recognized, there is no detailed study of this feature of his verse, as there is for Milton. Helpful remarks appear in J.B. Leishman, *The Art of Marvell's Poetry*, 2nd edn, London: Hutchinson, 1968, pp. 10, 163–5, 209, 234, 246; and George Saintsbury, *A History of English Prosody*, London: Macmillan, 1923, vol. II, ch. 4. See also Elbert N.S. Thompson, "The Octosyllabic Couplet," *Philological Quarterly* 18 (1939): 257–68.

7 Kenner (ed.), *Seventeenth Century Poetry: The Schools of Donne and Jonson*, New York: Holt, Rinehart, & Winston, 1964, p. 444.

8 Everett, "The Shooting of the Bears: Poetry and Politics in Andrew Marvell," in *Andrew Marvell: Essays on the Tercentenary of his Death*, ed. R.L. Brett, Oxford: Oxford University Press, 1979, p. 69.

9 For a recent feminist reading of this poem, see Barbara L. Estrin, "The Nymph and the Revenge of Silence," in *On the Celebrated and Neglected Poems of Andrew Marvell*, ed. Claude J. Summers and Ted-Larry Pebworth, Columbia, MO: University of Missouri Press, 1992, pp. 101–20.

10 An excellent discussion of these features can be found in Judith Haber, *Pastoral and the Poetics of Self-Contradiction: Theocritus to Marvell*, Cambridge: Cambridge University Press, 1994, ch. 4.

11 This is the beginning premise of Donald M. Friedman's *Marvell's Pastoral Art*, Berkeley, CA: University of California Press, 1970, ch. 1.

12 On the issue of reflexiveness in this poem and in Marvell generally, see Christopher Ricks, "Its Own Resemblance," in *Approaches to Marvell: The York Tercentenary Lectures*, London: Routledge & Kegan Paul, 1978, pp. 108–35.

13 Poirier, "Pragmatism and the Sentence of Death," *Yale Review* 80 (1992): 94.

14 See Annabel Patterson, "'Bermudas' and 'The Coronet': Marvell's Protestant Poetics," *ELH* 44 (1977): 479–99.

15 See "To his worthy Friend Doctor Witty Upon his Translation of the Popular Errors."

16 For an account of this poem in a context of emerging liberal humanism, see Catherine Belsey, "Love and death in 'To his Coy Mistress,'" in *Post-Structuralist Readings of English Poetry*, ed. Richard Machin and Christopher Norris, Cambridge: Cambridge University Press, 1987, pp. 105–21.

17 Along with the commentary in Kermode and Walker on this passage, see also Dale B.J. Randall, "Once More to the G(r)ates: An Old Crux and a New Reading of 'To His Coy Mistress,'" in *On the Celebrated and Neglected Poems of Andrew Marvell*, ed. Claude J. Summers and Ted-Larry Pebworth, Columbia, MO: University of Missouri Press, 1992, pp. 47–69.

18 For the latter point, see especially Thomas M. Greene, "The Balance of Power in Marvell's 'Horatian Ode,'" *ELH* 60 (1993): 394–5.

19 Norbrook, "Marvell's 'Horatian Ode' and the Politics of Genre" in *Literature and the English Civil War*, ed. Thomas Healy and Jonathan Sawday, Cambridge: Cambridge University Press, 1990, p. 147.

20 See, for instance, Annabel Patterson, "Miscellaneous Marvell," in *The Political Identity of Andrew Marvell*, ed. Conal Condren and A.D. Cousins, Aldershot: Scolar Press, 1990, pp. 188–212.

21 Haber, *Pastoral and the Poetics of Self-Contradiction*, p. 98.

22 Although written slightly later, "The Life of Horace," in Alexander Brome's *The Poems of Horace Consisting of Odes, Satyres, and Epistles*, London, 1666, reflects the practice of reading Horace as a contemporary, in this case treating him as a lapsed royalist, as someone who had taken the wrong side, only to be pardoned by a munificent Augustus (A3–A4).

23 See, respectively, "Rex Redux," and "On his Majestie's Return out of Scotland."

24 Nedham, *The Case of the Commonwealth of England, Stated*, ed. Philip A. Knachel, Charlottesville, VA: University Press of Virginia, p. 32. Nedham is quoting from Jean Bodin's *Les Six Livres de la république*, I. 6. Benjamin's remark can be found in Stephen Greenblatt's *Marvelous Possessions: The Wonder of the New World*, Chicago: University of Chicago Press, 1991, p. 128.

25 The phrase belongs to John M. Wallace, *Destiny His Choice: The Loyalism of Andrew Marvell*, Cambridge: Cambridge University Press, 1968, p. 232.

26 *The Writings and Speeches of Oliver Cromwell*, ed. Wilbur Cortez Abbot, 4 vols, Cambridge, MA: Harvard University Press, 1937–47, vol. II, p. 270.

27 Michael Wilding, *Dragons Teeth: Literature in the English Revolution*, Oxford: Clarendon Press, 1987, p. 163.

28 James Turner, *The Politics of Landscape: Rural Scenery and Society in English Poetry 1630–1660*, Cambridge, MA: Harvard University Press, 1979, p. 76.

29 Gage, *The English-American Travail by Sea and Land: or, a New Survey of the West-India's*, London: 1648. Among other points made in "The Epistle Dedicatory," Gage strenuously urges Fairfax "to employ the Souldiery of this Kingdom upon such just and honourable designes in those parts of America" so that the New World will be liberated "From *Spanish* Yoke, and *Romes* Idolatry." (The last phrase is from Thomas Chaloner's prefatory poem.) Chapter XII is devoted to a description of "the famous City of Mexico." The anti-cloister satire occurs on pp. 26–7. Issues of patronage have been ignored by Fairfax's biographers, in marked contrast to the detailed treatment given to his many battles. One wonders whether "Bermudas" might not belong to Marvell's time at Appleton House.

30 Wallace, *Destiny His Choice: The Loyalism of Andrew Marvell*, p. 232.

31 Kelliher, *Andrew Marvell: Poet and Politician*, London: British Museum Publications Ltd, 1978, p. 48.

32 Wallace, *Destiny His Choice: The Loyalism of Andrew Marvell*, p. 107.

33 Criticism of Marvell and Cromwell abounds; the mutually – and undeniably – fruitful relationship between Milton and Marvell, however, remains one of the most elusive chapters in literary history. One almost always feels, while reading Marvell, in frequent touch with only the tip of a Miltonic iceberg. Christopher Hill provides a biographical overview in "Milton and Marvell" in *Approaches to Marvell: The York Tercentenary Lectures*, ed. C.A. Patrides, London: Routledge & Kegan Paul, 1978, ch. 1.

34 Annabel Patterson, *Marvell and the Civic Crown*, Princeton, NJ: Princeton University Press, 1978, p. 158.

35 Zwicker, "Virgins and Whores: The Politics of Sexual Misconduct in the 1660s," in *The Political Identity of Andrew Marvell*, p. 97.

36 *The Poems and Letters of Andrew Marvell*, p. 351.

37 *Andrew Marvell: The Critical Heritage*, ed. Elizabeth Story Donno, London: Routledge & Kegan Paul, 1978, p. 55.

38 The only other time that "majesty" appears as a noun is in "The Statue in Stocks-Market," whose inclusion in *The Poems and Letters of Andrew Marvell* is "in spite of the want of evidence" (p. 394). See *A Concordance to the English Poems of Andrew Marvell*, ed. George R. Guffey, Chapel Hill, NC: The University of North Carolina Press, 1974, p. 302.

39 In addition to Colie's brief remarks in *"My Ecchoing Song": Andrew Marvell's Poetry of Criticism*, Princeton, NJ: Princeton University Press, 1970, pp. 6–8, I have learned much from the more specialized studies of the poem by Joseph Anthony Wittreich, Jr., "Perplexing the Explanation: Marvell's 'On Mr. Milton's *Paradise Lost*'," in *Approaches to Marvell*, ch. 13, and Kenneth Gross, "'Pardon Me, Mighty Poet': Versions of the Bard in Marvell's 'On Mr. Milton's *Paradise Lost*'," *Milton Studies* 16 (1982): 77–96.

40 *The Poems and Letters of Andrew Marvell*, vol. II, p. 304.

41 My thinking on this issue has been sharpened by Sharon Achinstein, *Milton and the Revolutionary Reader*, Princeton, NJ: Princeton University Press, 1994, pp. 58–70.

42 Patterson, *Marvell and the Civic Crown*, p. 31.

43 Quoted in *Andrew Marvell*, ed. Kermode and Walker, pp. xiii–xiv.

INDEX

Abbot, Wilbur Cortez 308
Achinstein, Sharon 309
Aesop 126
Agrippa, Cornelius 304
Alcaeus 49
Alciati, Andrea 77, 88
Allen, Don Cameron 297
Anacreon 60, 127
Anne of Denmark, Queen 220, 221, 304
Apsley, Sir Allen 213
Archilochus 49
Ariosto 175
Armstrong, Alan 288
Armstrong, Isobel 304
Arundel, Earl of *see* Howard, Thomas
Astell, Mary 224
Aubrey, John x, 69, 76, 105, 156, 159,
    193, 254, 292, 294, 296
Aubrey, Mary 250
Augustus 268, 308
Austen, Jane 230

Bacon, Lady Ann 213, 303, 304
Bacon, Sir Francis 28
Bacon, Nathaniel 79
Bacon, Sir Nicholas 79, 304
Baker, Herschel 288, 291
Bald, R.C. 287
Barash, Carol 303, 304, 307
Barker, Arthur 164, 299
Barlow, Francis 80
Barnes, Barnabe 4; *Divine Centurie of
    Spirituall Sonnets, A* 17
Barth, Robert 112
Barton, Anne 291
Basse, William 43, 290
Bastwick, John 184

Bates, Milton J. 298, 307
Bath, Michael 293
Baumlin, James S. 288
Baxter, Richard 136, 137, 298
Bayly, Lewis: *Practice of Piety* 137
Beal, Peter 289, 295
Beaumont, Francis 42, 283
Beaumont, John 42
Bedford, Countess of (Lucy Harrington) 8,
    35, 36, 56, 212, 220
Behn, Aphra 250
Belsey, Catherine 283, 308
Benet, Diana 298
Benjamin, Walter 270, 308
Benlowes, Edward: *Theophila* 80
Bennett, Charles 81
Bennett, J.A.W. 297
Berkeley, George xii
Bess of Hardwick 230
Bible: Ecclesiastes 232; Exodus 259;
    Genesis 192, 227; Hebrews 204; John
    206; Joshua 202; Judges 264; 2 Kings
    233; Mark 304; Luke 304; Matthew
    113, 174, 187, 222, 231, 304;
    Revelation 166, 202, 203, 234; Song of
    Songs 206, 208
Bishop, Elizabeth ix
Blaine, Marlin E. 292
Bland, Mark 289
Bliss, Philip 293
Bloch, Chana 144, 298
Blount, Thomas 294
Boccaccio 175
Bodin, Jean 308
Boethius 200
Boland, Eavan 306
Bond, R. Warwick 290
Book of Common Prayer, The 296

Book of Sports, The 122
Booty, John E. 296
Borges, Jorge Luis xii
Bower, Thad 302
Braden, Gordon 295, 296
Bradstreet 210, 214, 226–9, 233, 235, 305;
    "Author to her Book, The" 149, 151,
    228; "Four Elements, The" 226; "Four
    Monarchies, The" 226; "Four Seasons,
    The" 226; "In Reference to her
    Children" 228; "Letter to Her
    Husband, Absent Upon Public
    Employment, A" 227; "Of the Four
    Ages" 226; "Of the Four Humours"
    226; "On My Dear Grandchild Simon
    Bradstreet" 228; Poems 226; Tenth Muse
    Lately Sprung Up In America, The 226,
    228; "To My Dear and Loving
    Husband" 226–7; "Vanity of all
    Worldly Things, The" 226
Brady, Frank 287, 299
Brathwait, Richard: Barnabees Journall 87
Braunmuller, A.R. 294
Breasted, Barbara 300
Breton, Nicholas 42, 67
Brink, Jean R. 291
Brinkley, R.F. 298
Brome, Alexander 308
Brome, Richard 42
Brooke, Christopher 22, 42, 68
Brown, Cedric 292, 294, 300, 301
Brown, Peter 302
Browne, Sir Thomas 64, 292, 297; Urn-
    Burial 118
Browne, William 42, 55, 56, 66–9, 70, 71;
    Britannia's Pastorals 66–7, 68, 70;
    Shepheard's Pipe, The 68; "Thirsis'
    Praise of His Mistress" 67; "Epitaph on
    Mary Sidney" 68–9
Browne, William 292
Brute 63, 66
Brutus 268
Brydges, William 77
Buckingham, Duke of (George Villiers)
    65, 79
Budick, Sanford 165–6, 300
Bullen, A.H. 287, 298
Bunyan, John 75
Burleigh, Lord 213
Burton, Henry 184
Burton, Robert 89; Anatomy of Melancholy
    167

Busby, Richard 287
Bush, Douglas 300, 307
Butler, Martin 290
Butler, Samuel: Hudibras 31

Calhoun, Thomas O. 293
Calvin, John ix, 302, 303, 304;
    Commentary on the Harmony of the
    Evangelists 222; Institutes of the Christian
    Religion 141, 173, 207
Camden, William 26, 33–4, 88; Britannia
    34, 63
Campion, Thomas 31
Caravaggio 79
Carew, Thomas 21, 24, 42, 46, 93, 94–105,
    107, 108, 109, 112, 123, 127, 192, 217,
    287, 289, 295, 296; "Aske me no more"
    104–5; "Caelia Singing" 99; Coelum
    Britannicum 95, 176; "Elegy upon the
    Death of Dr. Donne, Dean of Paul's" 3,
    21–2, 91, 95–7; "In Answer of an
    Elegiacal Letter, upon the Death of the
    King of Sweden, from Aurelian
    Townshend, Inviting Me to Write on
    that Subject" 100–1; "Mediocritie in
    love rejected" 98–9, 124; "Rapture,
    The" 11, 100, 101; "Spring, The" 99;
    "To Ben Jonson: Upon Occasion of His
    Ode of Defiance Annexed to His Play
    of The New Inn" 97–8; "To My Friend
    G.N., From Wrest" 101; "To my worthy
    friend Master Geo. Sands, on his
    translation of the Psalmes" 102–3; "To
    Saxham" 101–2; "Upon a Ribbon" 99
Carey, John 2, 11, 287, 288
Carey, Lady Mary 213
Carleton, Sir Dudley 94
Carlisle, Lucy Countess of 99, 107, 109
Carlson, Norman 293
Carr, Robert 70, 294
Cartwright, William 192, 283; Plays and
    Poems 247
Cary, Elizabeth, Viscountess Falkland 213
Cary, Henry 220
Cary, Lucius 48–53, 62, 134
Cassius 268
Castiglione 117, 297
Catullus 41, 261
Cavendish, Margaret Lucas 210, 212,
    238–45, 251, 305, 306, 307;
    "Attraction of the Poles, and of Frost,
    The" 241; Blazing World, The 239, 241;

"Claspe, The" 242; "Hunting of the Hare, The" 243–4; "It is hard to believe, that there are other Worlds in this World" 242; *Nature's Pictures drawn by Fancies Pencil* 239; "Of Dewes, and Mists from the Earth" 241; "Of Fishes" 242; "Of Light, and Sight" 245; "Of many Worlds in this World" 242; "Of Vapour" 241; "Pastime of the Queen of Fairies…" 244; *Philosophical and physical Opinions* 241, 245, 246; *Plays* 239; *Poems and Fancies* 239, 241, 244; "Quenching out of Fire" 241; "Quenching and Smothering out of Heat, and Light" 241; "Register of Mournfull Verses, A" 245; "Severall Worlds in Severall Circles" 242; "World in an Eare-Ring" 242; *World's Olio, The* 239

Cavendish, Sir William 241

Caxton, William 128

Cecil, Robert 39

Chaloner, Thomas 309

Chamberlain, John 289

Chapman, George 42

Charles I, King 26, 46, 49, 58, 65, 79, 91, 93, 94, 99, 119, 123, 126, 131, 181, 213, 250, 255, 268, 269, 271, 272, 277, 302, 305

Charles II, King 248, 282–3

Charles, Amy 298

Chaucer 58, 60, 68

Christopher, Georgia 170, 300, 302

Churchyard, Thomas: *Worthies of Wales, The* 63

Cicero 35

Clarendon, Earl of (Edward Hyde) 102, 251, 282

Clark, Andrew 292

Clayton, Thomas 289, 296

Cleveland, John 92, 93, 254, 295

Clifford, Anne, Countess of Dorset 220, 224, 245

Cogswell, Thomas 291, 292

Coiro, Ann Baynes 296

Colacurcio, Michael 299

Coleridge, Samuel Taylor 78, 81, 137, 138, 298

Colie, Rosalie 284, 309

Collins, An 210, 234–38, 305; "Another Song exciting to spirituall Mirth" 237, 238; "Discourse, The" 235–6; *Divine Poems and Meditacions* 232, 234; "Preface, The" 235; "Song composed in time of the Civill Warre, A" 238; "Song shewing the Mercies of God to his people, A" 236–7

Condren, Conal 308

Congreve, William 230; *Way of the World, The* 106

Cook, John 203, 302

Cooke, Anne Fitzwilliam 303

Cooke, Sir Anthony 213, 303

Cooper, J.P. 296

Copernicus 2

Corbett, Margery 289

Corbett, Richard 297; "The Faeries Farewell" 121; *Iter Boreale* 87

Corinna of Thebes 214

Corneille: *Horace* 239; *Pompey* 239, 248

Corns, Thomas 156, 292, 299

Coryat, Thomas: *Coryats Crudities* 85, 87, 221

Cotteral, Sir Charles 250

Cotton, Charles 127, 133, 297

Courthope, William 100

Cousins, A.D. 308

Cowley, Abraham 93, 106, 127, 214, 248, 268, 287, 305, 306, 307; *Davideis* x; "My Dyet" 262

Cranach, Lucas 79

Crashaw, Richard x, 156, 163, 207, 254, 268, 295; *Delights of the Muses* 157; *Steps to the Temple* 157

Crawford, Patricia 303

Creaser, John 300

Croft, P.J. 304

Cromwell, Oliver 55, 74, 259, 260, 265, 269–72, 273, 278–84, 286, 305, 307, 308, 309

Crum, Margaret 295, 307

Cumberland, Countess of 224

Cunnar, Eugene 303

Cust, Richard 300

Cyprian, St. 205–6

Daniel, Samuel 21, 26–27, 31; *The Civile Warres betweene the two houses of Lancaster and York* 27, 56; *Cleopatra* 27; *Complaint of Rosamond, The* 27, 56, 221; *Ideas Mirrour* 56; *Sonnets to Delia* 4, 27, 56; *Letter from Octavia, A* 27; *Musophilus* 27; *Workes* 27

Dante 175

Davenant, William 244, 305; *Gondibert* x
Davenport, A. 288
Davies, John 5, 8, 31–2, 290
Davies, Stevie 198, 302
Defoe, Daniel 75
Dell, William 121
Deloney, Thomas: *Jack of Newbury* 85
Denham 69, 74, 106, 280; *Coopers Hill* 62, 243
Denny, Edward, Baron of Waltham 212, 305, 306
Dent, Arthur: *Plain Man's Pathway to Heaven* 137
Derby, Countess of 77, 175
Descartes 242
Desmond, Earl of 48
Dick, Oliver Lawson 296
Dickinson, Emily 137
Diepenbeke, Abraham van 239, 246
Digby, Sir John 105
Digby, Sir Kenelm 105
Digby, Venetia 46
Diodati, Charles 163
Dionysius the Areopagite 206–7
Dobranski, Stephen 299
Donaldson, Ian 287, 289, 294, 295, 303
Donne, John ix, x, xi, 1–22, 25, 41, 42, 55, 56, 57, 58, 71, 81, 94, 95, 96, 97, 98, 99, 100, 102, 106, 107, 124, 125, 127, 136, 137, 139, 153, 162, 172, 175, 192, 207, 210, 211, 212, 232, 242, 254, 255, 257, 279, 287–9, 292, 295, 299, 306, 307; "Aire and Angels" 12; "Anagram, The" 10; "Anatomy of the World, The" 54; "Anniversarie, The" 14; "Breake of Day" 12; "Canonization, The" 5, 8; "Confined Love" 12; "Dampe, The" 12; "Divine Meditation 5" 17; "Divine Meditation 11" 17; "Divine Meditation 13" 17; "Divine Meditation 14" 17, 18; "Divine Meditation 17" 18; "Divine Meditation 19" 17; "Elegy 7" 10; "Elegy 19" 10–11; "Extasie, The" 249; *First and Second Anniversaries* 5, 8, 13, 16–17, 54, 86; "Flea, The" 5, 12–13, 93; "Good-morrow, The" 5, 13–14, 24; "Goodfriday, 1613: Riding Westward" 16, 18–19; "Hymne to Christ, at the Authors last going into Germany, A" 20, 149–50; "Hymne to God my God, in my sicknesse, A" 20–1, 149; "Hymne to God, the Father, A" 17, 77–8; "Indifferent, The" 8; "La Corona" 17–18; "Lecture upon the Shadow, A" 5; "Legacie, The" 12; "Litanie, A" 18; "Love's Growth" 8; "Loves Alchemie" 13; "Nocturnall upon S. Lucies Day, A" 14, 15–16, 17; "On his Mistris" 10; *Poems* 283; "Relique, The" 12; "Sapho to Philaenis" 9; "Satire I" 6–7; "Satire II" 5; "Satire III" 6; "Satire IV" 8; "Sunne Rising, The" 12, 13, 92, 249; "Sweetest love, I do not goe" 14; "Triple Foole, The" 12, 98; "To his Mistris Going to Bed" ("Elegy 19") 10–11; "Valediction: forbidding Mourning, A" 15, 247; "Valediction: Of my Name in the Window, A" 1; "Valediction: of Weeping, A" 15;
Donoghue, Emma 306
Dorset, Earl of 65
Dorset, Countess of (Mary Sackville) 65
Douglas, Archibald 282
Dowe, Katherine 213
Drake, Sir Francis 66
Drayton, Michael 41, 42, 43, 49, 55, 56–65, 66, 70, 71, 73, 76, 87, 94, 101, 107, 111, 120, 184, 212, 256, 291, 292; "Ballad of Agincourt, The" 60, 61–2; *Battle of Agincourt, The* 64, 65; *Heroical Epistles* 57; *Idea* 59; *Ideas Mirrour* 4, 59; *Matilda* 56; *Moon-Calfe, The* 59; *Muses Elizium, The* 58, 65; "Nearer to the Silver Trent" 58; *Nymphidia, the Court of Fayrie* 58, 65; "Ode Written in the Peake, An" 61, 62–3, 114; *Owle, The* 57; *Piers Gaveston* 56; *Poems Lyrick and Pastorall* 57, 60; *Poly-Olbion* 54, 56, 62, 63, 64, 65, 66, 86, 88; "Since there's no help, come let us kiss and part" 59; "Skeltoniad, A" 60; "Song XXVI" 64–5; "To Himselfe, and the Harpe" 60; "To Master George Sandys, Treasurer for the English Colony in Virginia" 56; "To the Virginian Voyage" 61
Drummond, William 23, 26, 31, 41, 52, 211, 291
Drury, Elizabeth 279
Dryden, John x, 43, 46, 131, 213, 214, 254, 278, 293, 296, 304; "Annus Mirabilis" 281, 284; *Essay of Dramatic Poesy* 69, 106; "To the Pious Memory

of the Accomplished Young Lady Mrs.
    Anne Killigrew" 251
Du Bartas, Guillaume 86, 226
Dudley, Thomas 226
Dunlap, Rhodes 287, 289, 295
Dürer, Albrecht 79
Dutton, Richard 289
Dutton, William 260

Ecclesiasticus 52
Edward VI, King 37
Egerton family 176, 182
Egerton, John 175
Egerton, Thomas 1
Eire, Carlos M.N. 303
Eliot, T.S. 12, 22, 26, 54, 93, 115, 256,
    289, 291, 296
Elizabeth, daughter of King Charles I 213
Elizabeth, Princess 68, 70, 76
Elizabeth, Queen xi, 26, 48, 56, 57, 58, 60,
    63, 65, 66, 211, 213, 221, 226, 278
Emerson, Ralph Waldo 153, 299
Englands Helicon 67, 254
Erasmus 303
Essex, Robert Devereux (son) 76
Essex, Earl of (Robert Devereux) 3, 57, 70,
    126
Esther 76
Estienne, Henri 81, 111, 294
Estrin, Barbara 308
Evans, J. Martin 300
Evans, Robert C. 305
Everett, Barbara 256, 268, 308
Ezell, Margaret J.M. 303

Faderman, Lillian 306
Fagan, Louis 305
Fairfax, Anne Vere 272, 277
Fairfax, Maria 255, 272, 274, 278
Fairfax, Thomas, Lord General 255,
    272–8, 305, 309
Faithorne, William, the Elder 239, 240,
    305
Fane, Mildmay, Earl of Westmoreland:
    Otia Sacra 118; "To Retiredness" 265
Farmer, Norman K. 295, 297
Farr, Edward 293
Fehl, Philipp 294
Felltham, Owen Resolves 201
Fennor, William 85
Ferguson, Margaret 307
Ferrar, Nicholas 70, 135, 137

Ferrar, William 70
Field, B.S. 294
Fienberg, Nona 304
Fish, Stanley 151, 187, 299
Fitzmaurice, James 303, 306
Fleming, Juliet 304, 305
Fletcher, Angus 179, 300
Fletcher, Giles 291
Fletcher, John 192, 283
Fletcher, Phineas 291
Flynn, Dennis 287
Forman, Simon 220
Fowler, Alastair 67, 113, 290, 292, 296
Foxe, John: Book of Martyrs The 84, 205
Frederick, Elector Palatine 68, 70, 76
Freeman, David 294
Freeman, John 294
Freeman, Rosemary 294
French, J. Milton 292
Friedenreich, Kenneth 302
Friedman, Donald 289, 308
Fry, Paul 292
Fuller, Thomas 43, 59, 294; Worthies of
    England 77
Fulton, Alice 307
Fumerton, Patricia 295
Fussell, Paul 294

Gage, Thomas 274, 309
Gallagher, Catherine 241, 245, 305
Gamage, Barbara 40
Garber, Marjorie 288
Gardner, Helen 288, 289
Gasford, Laird of 88
Geneva Bible 167, 187, 193, 222
George, St. 200
Gilman, Ernest B. 294
Giorgione 126
Godolphin, Sidney 98
Goldberg, Jonathan 289
Gorbuduc 65
Gottlieb, Sidney 295, 298, 305
Greek Anthology, The 30
Greenblatt, Stephen 200, 302, 308
Greene, Thomas 41, 290, 308
Greer, Germaine 303, 305, 306
Grenville, Sir Richard 66
Grey, Lady Jane 211, 213
Griffin, Bartholomew: Fidessa 4
Grosart, Alexander 81, 294
Grose, Christopher 300
Gross, Kenneth 309

Grundy, Joan 291, 305
Guevara, Antonio de: *Praise and Happinesse of the Countrie-Life, The* 200
Guffey, George R. 309
Guilpen, Everard 22, 31–2
Gustavus Adolphus, King 101
Gutierrez, Nancy 303
Guy of Warwick 89

Haber, Judith 308
Habington, William 192
Hackett, Helen 303
Hageman, Elizabeth H. 303
Haight, Gordon 294
Hakluyt, Richard 61; *Principall Navigations* 87
Hales, John 251
Hall, Donald 254, 307
Hall, John 297
Hall, Joseph 5, 7, 22, 207, 288; *Virgidemiarum* 5–6
Hallam, Henry 63
Halle, Morris 289
Halley, Janet E. 303
Hals, Franz 130
Hammond, Gerald 297
Hannay, Margaret 304
Hannibal 50
Hardin, Richard 291, 292
Harvey, Christopher: *The Synagogue: Or, The Shadow of the Temple* 157
Haskin, Dayton 300
Haydocke, Richard 79
Hazlitt, W. Carew 292
Hazlitt, William 91, 295, 296
Healy, Thomas 308
Heaney, Seamus 171, 194, 287, 300, 301; "Redress of Poetry" xii
Hebel, J. William 291
Helgerson, Richard 289, 291, 295
Henrietta Maria, Queen 58, 79, 91, 99, 281, 300, 305
Henry V, King 61–2
Henry VIII, King 121
Henry, Prince 62, 66, 67, 68, 70
Hensley, Jeannine 305
Hensley, Charles S. 293
Herbert, George ix, x, xi, 8, 30, 72, 95, 135–55, 157, 173, 192, 193, 206, 207, 232, 257, 286, 297, 298–9, 301, 302, 305; "Aaron" 138–40; "Affliction" xii, 152; "Altar, The" 140; "Bitter-sweet" 136; "British Church, The" 208; "Charms and knots" 140; "Church Militant, The" 142; "Church Porch, The" 137; "Church, The" 137, 154; "Church-floor, The" 147; "Collar, The" 138, 152, 216; "Death" 154; "Dedication, The" 151; "Deniall" 147; "Dialogue, A" 154; "Doomsday" 154; "Easter-wings" 140; "Elixir, The" 140, 152; "Flower, The" 152, 153; "Forerunners, The" 103–4, 136, 142, 148–51; "H. Scriptures, The" 196; "Heaven" 154; "Jesu" 153; "Jordan I" 142, 144–5, 146; "Jordan II" 142, 144, 145, 146, 154, 254; "Joseph's Coat" 237; "Judgment" 154; "Love III" 138, 142, 154–5; "Love Unknown" 153, 155; "Odour, The" 153; "Peace" 197; "Pearle, The" 135; "Prayer I" 140, 209; "Pulley, The" 140; "Quidditie, The" 142, 143; "Quip, The" 142, 143–4, 148, 150; "Redemption" 153–4; "Sacrifice, The" 140, 152, 155; *Temple, The* 21, 46, 55, 91, 135–55, 157; "Time" 140; "To All Angels and Saints" 140; "True Hymn, A" 142, 145–7, 236; "Vertue" xi, 148; "Windows, The" 142; "Wreath, The" 254
Herbert, Edward, Lord of Cherbury 22, 94
Herbert, Magdalen 137
Herbert, William, Third Earl of Pembroke 38, 214
Herford, C.H. 293
Herrick, Robert ix, 30, 55, 65, 90, 101, 111–23, 124, 127, 129, 130, 134, 136, 151, 191, 192, 228, 244, 248, 254, 256, 257, 263, 296, 297, 299, 302, 306; "Amber Bead, The" 116–17; "Ode for him [Ben Jonson], An" 113; "Argument of his Book, The" 114; "Corinna's going a maying" 122–3; "Delight in Disorder" 117, 243; "Discontents in Devon" 114, 115; *Hesperides* 93, 111–13, 116, 117, 118, 119, 120, 140, 192; "His Grange" 116; "His Poetrie his Pillar" 119; "His Prayer to Ben Johnson" 121–2; "His returne to London" 120; "His Wish to privacie" 112; "Hock-cart, The" 120; *Noble Numbers* 112, 123; "Rest Refreshes" 115; "To Daffadills" 115; "To his Tomb-

maker" 118; "To his Verses" 149; "To Prince Charles upon his coming to Exeter" 119; "To The King, Upon his coming with his Army into the West" 119; "Upon Julia's Clothes" 117–18; "Upon the losse of his Mistresses" 119; "Vine, The" 117; "Welcome to Sack, The" 119–20

Herz, Judith Scherer 305
Hester M. Thomas 287, 288
Heywood, Elizabeth 3
Heywood, John 3
Hibbard, G.R. 290
Hill, Christopher 309
Hill, Geoffrey 302
Hiller, Geoffrey 292
Hirst, Derek 296
Hobbes, Thomas 244, 245
Hobby, Elaine 249, 305, 306
Hoccleve, Thomas 68
Holaday, Allan 292
Holbein, Hans 79
Holinshed, Raphael 88
Holland Philemon 66
Holland, Abraham 66
Hollander, John 104–5, 288, 290, 296
Hollar, Wenceslaus 79
Holmes, Elizabeth 302
Holstun, James 306
Homer 49, 87
Hooker, Richard 139, 140, 298
Hope, A.D.: "The Elegy, Variations on a Theme of the Seventeenth Century" 12
Horace 6, 28, 30, 33, 41, 49, 60, 111, 127, 308; *Ars Poetica* 9, 25, 43; "Epode 2" 46; "Satire I.4" 43; "Satire I.9" 7; "Satire I.10" 43;
Horden, John 293
Hoskins, John: *Directions for Speech and Style* 4
Howard, Frances 70
Howard, Henry, Earl of Northampton 69, 70
Howard, Katherine, Countess of Suffolk 220
Howard, Thomas, Earl of Arundel 79, 88
Howarth, David 294
Howe, P.P 295
Hughes, Ann 300
Hughes, Merritt 184, 299
Hugo, Hermann: *Pia Desideria* 80

Hunter, William 291
Hutchinson, F.E. 298, 302
Hutchinson, Isabella 133
Hutchinson, Lucy 213
Hyne, Thomas: *Life and Death of Dr. Martin Luther, The* 76

Jakobson, Roman 24, 289
James I, King 22, 26, 27, 30, 34, 45–6, 57, 58, 59, 63, 64, 70, 102, 126, 215, 220, 221, 235, 291; *Workes of King James, The* 27
James, Richard 296
Jenkins, Harold 294
Jeremiah 121
Jermyn, Henry, Earl of St. Albans 99, 281–2
Jewel, John 304
Joannou, Maroula 293
Job 76, 81
Johnson, Samuel 3, 89, 160, 170, 171, 176, 189, 287, 299, 300; "Life of Milton" 156
Jonah 76
Jones, Ann Rosalind 304
Jones, Inigo 26
Jones, John 294
Jonson, Ben: x, xi, xii, xvi, 2, 3, 5, 7, 8, 12, 13, 21, 22, 23–53, 55, 56, 57, 58, 60, 62, 64, 66, 69, 71, 76, 84, 87, 95, 96, 97, 98, 99, 102, 111, 115, 117, 121, 123, 124, 134, 144, 151, 176, 192, 210, 211, 212, 219, 228, 244, 247, 254, 255, 287, 288, 289–91, 292, 293, 294, 295, 297, 303, 307. Poems: "Celebration of Charis, Her Triumph, A" 31, 46–7, 92; "Come My Celia" 32, 41; "Crowne of Sonnets dedicated to Love, A" 219; "Epistle to Master John Selden, An" 23; "Execration, Upon Vulcan, An" 46; "Fit of Rhyme against Rhyme, A" 31, 46; "Fragment of Petronius Arbiter, A" 46; *Heroologia* 31; "Hour-Glass, The" 31; "Inviting a Friend to Supper" 25, 38, 86; "My Picture Left in Scotland" 31; "Ode to James, Earl of Desmond. Writ in Queen Elizabeth's Time, Since Lost, and Recovered" 48; "On his Son" 149; "On Lucy, Countess of Bedford" 36; "On My First Daughter" 37; "On Something that Walks Somewhere" 35; "On *The New Inn*. Ode. To Himself"

49–50; "On the Famous Voyage"; "Praises of a Country Life, The" (Horace, "Epode 2") 46; "Sir William Burlase, The Painter to the Poet" 31; "Song: To Celia" 32, 262, 263; "Sonnet to the Noble Lady, the Lady Mary Worth [Wroth], A" 31; "Speech according to Horace, A" 46; "To Brain-Hardy" 33; "To Heaven" 32; "To John Donne (Epigram 96)" 54; "To King James" 33–34; "To Mary, Lady Wroth" 219; "To My Mere English Censurer" 36; "To My Muse" 35; "To Penshurst" xii–xiii, 32, 37, 38–40, 101, 155, 214, 225, 276; "To Sir Annual Tilter" 33; "To Sir Thomas Roe" 36; "To the Immortal Memory and Friendship of That Noble Pair, Sir Lucius Cary and Sir H. Morison" 32, 47, 48, 49–53, 94, 127; "To the Memory of My Beloved, The Author, Mr. William Shakespeare: And What He Hath Left Us" 42–5, 188–9, 284; "To the Reader" 32, 42; "To the Same" 41; "To William Camden" 33–4. Plays and Masques: *Alchemist, The* 38, 46; *Bartholomew Fair* 25, 46; *Catiline* 38; *Cynthia's Revels* 24; *The Devil is an Ass* 47; *Every Man in his Humour* 25, 28; *Golden Age Restored, The* 30; *Masque of Blackness, The* 25, 216; *New Inn, The* 46, 48–50, 95; *Poetaster* 25; *Time Vindicated* 69, 72; *Volpone* 26, 41. Collections: *Conversations with Drummond* 41; *Discoveries* 47, 49, 84; *Epigrams, The* 28, 31, 35, 37, 38, 42; *Forest, The* 28, 32, 37, 41; *Underwood, The* 32, 46, 47; *Workes* 26–30, 42, 43, 109
Junius, Franciscus: *De pictura veterum* 79
Juvenal 6, 200

Keats, John: "Ode to Psyche" 165
Keller, Lynn 304
Kelliher, Hilton 275, 309
Kenner, Hugh 46, 256, 290, 307
Ker, W.P. 304
Kermode, Frank 302, 307, 308, 309
Kerrigan, William 295
Keynes, G. 292
Killigrew, Lady 303
Killigrew, Thomas 99, 213
Kimmey, John L. 296

King, Anne 250–2
King, Bruce 297
King, Edward 161, 174, 182–3
King, Henry 2, 211, 212, 251, 295; "Exequy, The" 93, 188; "Upon a Table-book presented to a Lady" 210
Kingsley, Margery 293
Klene, Jean 304
Knachel, Philip 308
Knapp, Jeffrey 295
Krueger, Robert 290

Lake, Peter 300
Lamb, Charles 69, 72, 241, 293
Langland, William: *Piers Plowman* 6
Lanyer, Aemilia 210, 211, 212, 214, 219–25, 226, 233, 290, 304, 305; *Salve Deus Rex Judaeorum* 57, 219–24; "To Cooke-ham" 220, 224–5
Lanyer, Alfonso 220, 223
Laud, Archbishop 91, 120–2, 157, 260
Lawes, Henry 160, 175, 176, 179, 184, 247
Lear, Edward 88
Leavis, F.R. 107, 296
Leicester, Earl of (Robert Dudley) 1
Leishman, J.B. 307
Lely, Peter 126–7, 134
Leonard, John 301
Leonardo 79
Lepidus 268
Lewalski, Barbara 222, 288, 289, 299, 304
Lewis, C.S. 65, 292
Lightbown, Ronald 289
Lilburne, John 74
Lipking, Lawrence 290, 301
Little, R. 305, 306
Lodge, Thomas 5; *Phillis: Honoured with Pastorell Sonnets, Elegies, and amorous delights* 9
Loewenstein, David 299
Lok, Henry: *Sundry Christian Passions Contained in Two Hundred Sonnets* 17
Lomazzo, Gian Paolo: *Trattato dell' arte de la pittura* 79
Lord, George deForest 290
Lovelace, Richard 48, 94, 123–34, 147, 191, 192, 247, 254, 279, 285, 297; "A la Bourbon" 124; "Amnytor's Grove" 127; "Ant, The" 132–3; "Calling Lucasta from her Retirement" 125; "Falcon, The" 132; "Grasshopper Ode: To my Noble Friend, Mr. Charles

Cotton, The" xiii, 127–31, 133, 157; "Gratiana dauncing and singing" 125; "Her Reserved looks" 131; "La Bella Bona Roba" 124–5; "Loose Sarabande, A" 132; "Love made in the first Age: To Chloris" 132; *Lucasta* 124, 127; "Lucasta laughing" 131; *Lucasta: Posthume Poems* 126, 131; "On Sanazar's being honoured with six hundred Duckets by the Clarissimi of Venice" 132; "To Althea, from Prison" 125; "To Lucasta, Going to the Warres" 125; "To my Worthy Friend Mr. Peter Lilly" 126–7; "To Peter Lely [poem #2]" 133–4; "Triumphs of Philamore and Amoret, The" 133

Lucan 22

Luther 139

Machin, Richard 308

Mack, Maynard 290

Maclean, Hugh 295

Maddison, Carol 292

Maecenas 268

Makin, Bathsua 213, 214, 303

Marcus, Leah 122, 297

Margolies, David 293

Margoliouth, H.M. 307

Mark Antony 268

Marlowe, Christopher 8, 11; *Hero and Leander* 55, 78; "Passionate Shepherd to His Shepherdess, The" 55, 169

Marotti, Arthur 288, 289

Marshall, William 3, 82, 105, 160

Marston, John 5, 8, 70

Martial 30, 36, 37, 38, 41, 46, 111, 116

Martin, L.C. 296, 297, 301

Martz, Louis 160, 203, 295, 299, 301, 302

Marvell, Andrew ix, xi, 42, 65, 91, 126, 191, 202, 253–86, 292, 295, 297, 299, 302, 306, 307–9; "Bermudas" 67, 259–61, 265, 281; "Coronet, The" 254; "Damon the Mower" 257; "Definition of Love, The" 254; "Dialogue Between the Resolved Soul, and Created Pleasure" 264; "First Anniversary of the Government under O.C., The" 268, 279–80, 281; "Gallery, The" 254; "Garden, The" 253, 264, 265–7, 268, 272; "Horatian Ode upon Cromwell's Return from Ireland, An" xii-xiii, 79, 129, 253, 254, 259, 263, 265, 267–72,

277, 283; "Last Instructions to a Painter, The" 281–2, 283; *Miscellaneous Poems* 254, 264, 265; "Mower against Gardens, The" 257; "Mower to the Glow-Worms" 257; "Mower's Song, The" 256, 257, 258; "Musicks Empire" 261; "Nymph Complaining for the Death of her Fawn, The" 125, 244, 256, 258; "On a Drop of Dew" 125, 254, 258–9, 261, 270; "On Mr. Milton's *Paradise Lost*" 281, 283–6; "Picture of Little T.C. in a Prospect of Flowers, The" 125; *Rehearsal Transprosed, The* 282, 283; "To His Coy Mistress" 11–12, 254, 261–4, 265; "To His noble Friend Mr. Richard Lovelace upon his Poems" 124, 285; "To his worthy Friend Doctor Witty" 308; "Tom May's Death" 255; "Upon Appleton House" 39, 132, 253, 255, 257, 272–8

Marvell, Mary *see* Palmer, Mary

Marx, Karl ix

Mary, Queen of Scots 57

Masten, Jeff 304

May, Tom 255

McClatchy, J.D. 299

McEachern, Claire 292

McGuire, Maryann Cale 300

McKeon, Michael 293

Merrill, James 155, 299

Middleton, Thomas 76

Milgate, W. 287, 288

Millay, Edna St. Vincent 13

Miller, Cristanne 305

Miller, Naomi J. 304

Milton, John: x, xi, xvi, 6, 7, 26, 30, 35, 55, 57, 77, 81, 90, 91, 95, 99, 112, 124, 133, 142, 156–89, 203, 205, 207, 214, 227, 238, 244, 250, 251, 254, 256, 278, 283–6, 288, 295, 297, 299–303, 301, 305, 306, 309; *Arcades* 77, 175; *Areopagitica* 130, 156, 191, 285, 286; "At a Solemn Music" 158–9; "Avenge O Lord" 171; *Comus see Mask Presented at Ludlow Castle*; *Divorce Tracts* 156; "Donna Leggiadra" 162; *Eikon Basilike* 161, 209; "Epitaph on the Marchionessof Winchester, An" 162; "How soon hath time" 171–4; "Il Penseroso" 162–3, 167–71, 174, 245, 275; "L'Allegro" 63, 162–3, 167–71, 174, 245; "Lycidas" 52, 95, 156, 160,

164, 174, 175, 182–9; *Mask Presented at Ludlow Castle, A* 160, 161, 174, 174–82, 183, 184, 197, 273; "Methought I Saw" 171; *Of Education* 189; "On Shakespeare" 162; "On the Morning of Christ's Nativity" 68, 130, 157, 163–7, 172, 176, 178; "On the University Carrier" 163; "On Time" 163; *Paradise Lost* x, 158, 159, 160, 164, 169, 173, 179, 180, 187, 255, 258, 261; *Paradise Regained* 158, 160; "Passion, The" 161; *Poems* 93, 156, 157, 160, 163, 171, 174, 245; "Psalm 114 (trans.)" 175; *Reason of Church Government, The* 157, 161, 171, 190; *Samson Agonistes* 158, 160; *Second Defense of the English People, The* 181; "Upon the Circumcision" 163; "When I Consider" 171

Miner, Earl 127, 297

Moliére 110

Montgomery, Ladie Susan, Countess of Kent 220

More, Anne 1, 15, 287, 288

More, George 1

More, Henry 291

More, Sir Thomas 3

Morison, Sir Henry 48–53, 62

Morris, Brian 295

Moseley, Humphrey 156, 157, 158, 192

Moulsworth, Martha x, 213, 229–32, 250, 305; "Memorandum, The" 229–32

Mount, W. Wordsworth Rydal 294

Mueller, Janel 223–4, 288, 304

Nashe, Thomas: *Piers Penniless* 86

Nedham, Marchamont 270, 308

Newdigate, Bernard 291, 292, 293

Nicodemus 206–9

Nieremberg, Juan Eusebius 193

Norbrook, David 74, 180, 265, 287, 291, 292, 293, 300, 301, 308

Norris, Christopher 308

North, Dudley 2–3, 287

Northumberland, Earl of 1

Novarr, David 288, 298

Ogilby, John 126

Oram, William 292

Osborne, Dorothy 306

Ovid 8, 9, 10, 87, 288; *Elegies* 11; *Heroides* 57

Owens, Anne 250

Oxenbridge, John 260

Palmer, Mary 253

Parker, Kenneth 306

Parker, Michael P. 295

Parker, Patricia 288

Parker, W.R. 300, 301

Parr, Thomas 84

Pater, Erra *Prognostycacion for Ever, A* 78

Patrick, J. Max 296

Patrides, C.A. 294, 300, 309

Patterson, Annabel 261, 297, 308, 309

Paul, St. 81, 115

Paulinus, St. 193, 209

Peacham, Henry 77, 79

Peake, William 305

Pebworth, Ted-Larry 290, 296, 298, 305, 308

Peck, Linda Levy 294

Pembroke, Earl of 70

Persius 6

Peterson, Richard 290, 291

Petrarch 31, 98

Petronius 46

Pettet, E.C. 303

Philips, James 241

Philips, Katherine 192, 210, 214, 245–50, 305, 306; "Engraved on Mr. John Collyer's Tomb stone at Beddinton" 247; "Friendship in Emblem, or the Seale, to my dearest Lucasia" 247; "Friendship's Mysterys" 247; "Ode upon retirement, made upon Occasion of Mr. Cowley's on that subject, An" 248; "On Rosania's Apostacy, and Lucasia's Friendship" 248; *Poems* 239; *Pompey*(trans.) 248; "To Mrs. Mary Awbrey at parting" 249–50; "To My excellent Lucasia, on our friendship" 248–9; "To My Lady Elizabeth Boyle, Singing" 247; "To my Lord Duke of Ormond, Lord Lieutenant of Ireland" 247; "To the truly noble Mr. Henry Lawes" 247

Phillips, Edward 124, 127, 134, 226; *Theatrum Poetarum* x, 239

Philostratus 32

Piddack, John 88

Piercy, Josephine K. 305

Pilate's wife 222–3

Pindar 48–50, 60, 127, 291

Piva, Margherita 292
Pliny 270
Poirier Richard 259, 308
Pope, Alexander 8, 43, 131, 294, 295;
    Dunciad, The 69, 81; "Windsor Forest"
    64
Porter, Peter 295
Post, Jonathan F.S. 301, 302, 305
Potter, Lois 301, 303
Preminger, Alex 301
Price, Bronwen 244, 306
Prince, F.T.: *Italian Element in Milton's*
    Verse, The 173, 300
Pringle, William 304
Prior, Mary 303
Pritchard, Allan 293
Propertius 9, 10
Prynne, William 184
Purkiss, Diane 305
Puttenham, George 288, 289: *Arte of*
    English Poesie 9, 28

Quarles, Francis 55, 56, 72, 76–84, 99,
    293, 294; *Argalus and Parthenia* 77–9;
    Divine Fancies 77; *Emblems* 77, 79–84;
    Feast for Wormes, A 76; *Shepheardes*
    Oracle, The 77; *Sions Elegies* 76; *Sions*
    Sonets 76; *Solomon's Recantation* 76
Quarles, Ursula 76

Raleigh, Sir Walter 11, 42, 226; *History of*
    the World 27
Randall, Dale B.J. 308
Randolph, Thomas 93, 172
Ransom, John Crowe 184, 301
Raphael 79, 126
Ray, Robert 298
Revard, Stella 158, 291, 299, 300
Reynolds, John 57, 58
Rich, Adrienne 190, 191, 301
Richard III, King 282
Richey, Esther Gilman 304
Ricks, Christopher 308
Riddell, James A. 290, 291
Rivington, J. 293
Roberts, John R. 302
Roberts, Josephine A. 303, 304, 306
Roe, Sir John 35, 36
Roe, Sir Thomas 36
Rogers, John 305
Rogers, Pat 292
Rogers, W. Harry 81

Rollin, Roger B. 296
Rollinson, Philip 292
Rowse, A.L. 219
Rubens, Peter Paul 79
Rudrum, Alan 299, 301, 302–3
Rumrich, John 299
Russell, Lady 213, 303
Rutland, Countess of 211

Sacks, Peter 188, 301
Sackville family 65
Said, Edward 190
Saintsbury, George: *Minor Caroline Poets*
    93, 193, 307
Samson 76, 250, 264, 284
Sanazarro 134
Sanderson, Sir William: *Graphice, or The*
    Use of the Pen and Pensil 79
Sandys, George 56, 58, 72, 102–3, 104,
    134; *Relation of a Journey begun in 1610*
    containing a description of the Turkish
    Empire etc. 87
Sappho 87, 214, 306
Sarbiewski, Casimir 275
Sawday, Jonathan 308
Saxton, Christopher 64
Schleiner, Louise 296
Schoenfeldt, Michael C. 290, 298
Schuppen, Peter Van 246
Schweitzer, Ivy 226, 305
Sejanus 30
Selden, John 63, 65
Seneca 35, 44, 52
Settle, Elkanah 293
Shakespeare, William xi, 21, 25, 26, 42,
    43, 45, 56, 65, 96, 172, 188, 189, 219,
    244, 284, 290; *As You Like It* 212;
    Midsummer Night's Dream, A 85, 176;
    Richard II 276; *Tempest, The* 45, 176
Sharpe, Kevin 296, 297
Shirley, James 93
Sidgwick, Frank 293
Sidney family 37–9, 62, 144
Sidney, Lady Dorothy 161
Sidney, Mary Countess of Pembroke 68–9,
    136, 211, 213, 214, 220
Sidney, Sir Philip x, 2, 4, 8, 9, 25, 26, 53,
    55, 57, 61, 78, 106, 136, 211, 213, 225,
    257, 265, 292; *Arcadia* 68, 77, 214;
    Astrophil and Stella 4, 37, 56, 75, 140,
    145, 217; *Defense of Poesy* 60;

Sidney, Sir Robert 37, 38, 39, 214, 219, 304
Sidney, Sir William 37
Simmonds, James 301
Simonides 80
Simpson, Evelyn 293
Singleton 298
Skelton, John 68
Skulsky, Harold 302
Slights, Camille Wells 288
Smith, Nigel 302
Smith, William: *Chloris* 4
Southey, Robert 90, 294
Southwell, Lady Anne 213, 222
Southwell, Robert: *St. Peter's Complaint* 136
Spacks, Patricia Meyer 296
Speed, John 88
Speght, Rachel 224
Spencer family 26
Spencer, T.J.B. 290
Spenser, Edmund x, 4, 9, 21, 25, 26, 47, 53, 55, 63, 65, 66, 86, 100, 158, 162, 172, 176, 179, 188, 214, 256, 291, 295, 301, 302; *Amoretti* 4; *Astrophel* 188; *Colin Clouts Come Home Again* 56; *Faerie Queene, The* 4, 6, 57, 67, 180, 200; *Mother Hubbard's Tale* 57; *Prothalamion* 88, 185; *Shepheardes Calendar, The* 63
Stachniewski, John 289
Stallybrass, Peter 297
Stanley, Thomas 93, 112, 127, 297
Stansby, William 27, 289
Statius 49
Steen, Jan 122
Sternhold and Hopkins Psalter 71, 72, 237
Stevens, Wallace 135, 142, 254, 298, 299, 307
Stevenson, Laura 294
Stewart, Stanley 291, 298
Strier, Richard 288, 289, 298, 299
Strode, William 295
Stuart, Lady Arabella 213, 220
Suckling, Sir John 30, 47, 94, 105–11, 112, 123, 124, 127, 144, 145, 289, 296; *Account of Religion by Reason* 106; "Against Fruition" 105, 109; "Ballad upon a Wedding" 110; *Fragmenta Aurea* 105, 106, 248; *Last Remaines, The* 105; "Sessions of the Poets, A" 107, 109–10; "Sonnet I" 108; "Sonnet II" 107–8;

"Upon My Lady Carliles Walking in Hampton Gardens" 107, 109; "Upon St. Thomas his unbeliefe" 106; "Why so pale and wan fond Lover?" 108
Sullivan, Ernest, Jr. 287
Summers, Claude J. 120, 189, 290, 296, 297, 298, 302, 305, 308
Summers, Joseph 298, 299, 302
Sutherland, James 294
Swedenberg, H.T., Jr. 293, 296
Swetnam, Joseph 224
Swift, Jonathan 89, 282; *Tale of a Tub, A* 221
Swinburne, Algernon Charles 112
Sylvester, Joshua 215

Tasso, Torquato 22
Taylor, Edward 287
Taylor, John ix, 55, 56, 84–90, 92, 94, 294; *Dogge of Warre, A* 87; *The Fearul Summer, or London's Calamitie* 86; *Laugh and be Fat* 86; *Mad Verse, Sad Verse, Glad Verse, and Bad Verse* 85; *Motto* 87; *Part of This Summers Travel* 88; *Pennilesse Pilgrimage* 86, 88; *Sir Gregory Nonsense, His Newes from No Place* 87; *Taylor on Thames Isis* 88–90; *Taylor's Travels to Prague in Bohemia* 88; *The description of naturall English Poetry* 86; *Very Merrie Wherrie-Fery Voyage, or Yorke for my Money, A* 88; *Voyage in a Paper-boat from London to Quinborough, A* 88
Teague, Frances 303
Temple, William 306
Tennyson, Alfred 81; "The Princess" 104
Theocritus 257
Thirsk, Joan 296
Thomas, Dylan: "Fern Hill" xi
Thomas, Keith 306
Thomas, Patrick 305, 306
Thompson, Elbert 307
Tibullus 9, 111
Titian 79, 126, 134
Touchet, Mervyn, Lord Audley 175
Townsend, Aurelian 100, 105, 295
Traherne, Thomas x
Trapnel, Anna 210, 232, 233–4, 238; *Cry of a Stone, The* 233–4; *Report and Plea* 234
Trevor-Roper, H.R. 297
Trimpi, Wesley 290

Turner, James Grantham 288, 309
Typus Mundi 80

Unfortunate Lovers (anonymous) 77
Ussher, Archbishop 76

Van Dorsten, J.A. 292
Van Dyck, Anthony 79, 99, 126
Van Pass, Crispin 82
Vaughan, Henry 68, 95, 133, 190–209,
    236, 237, 247, 253, 259, 301–3; "Abels
    blood" 203–5, 208; "Ad Posteros" 203;
    "Ass, The" 205; "Cock-crowing" 196;
    "Constellation, The" 202;
    "Corruption" 202–3; "Daughter of
    Herodias" 194; "Dawning, The" 202;
    Flores Solitudinis 191; *Hermetical Physick*
    191; "I Walked the Other Day (To
    Spend My Hour)" 197–9; *Life of
    Paulinus* (trans.) 205, 207; "Love, and
    Discipline" 207; "Men of War, The"
    205; "Morning-watch, The" 196;
    Mount of Olives, The 191, 193; "Night,
    The" 191, 206–9; *Olor Iscanus* 191,
    192, 203; "Palm-tree, The" 205;
    "Peace" 202; *Poems* 192; "Proffer, The"
    205–6; "Regeneration" 194–6;
    "Religion" 199, 201, 202; "Retreate,
    The" 195, 200–2, 258; "Righteousness"
    205; "Rules and Lessons" 196; "Search,
    The" 202; "Seed growing secretly, The"
    207; *Silex Scintillans* 136, 192–205; *Silex
    Scintillans, Part II* 191, 205–9; "St.
    Mary Magdalene" 194; "Stone, The"
    202; *Thalia Rediviva* 193; *The Praise and
    Happinesse of the Countrie-Life* (trans.)
    200; "They are all gone into the world
    of light" 191; "Timber, The" 194; "To
    the River Isca" 193, 195; "Upon a
    Cloke lent him by Mr. J. Ridsley" 193;
    "Water-fall, The" 195–6; "White
    Sunday" 190; "World, The" 191, 202
Vaughan, Thomas 196
Vaughan, William 191
Vendler, Helen xi-xii, 139, 149, 237, 287,
    298, 299
Venuti, Lawrence 295
Virgil 22, 49, 87, 188; *Georgics* 67
Vitruvius: *Elements of Architecture, The* 79

Waddington, Raymond 294

Walker, Cheryl 304
Walker, Keith 307, 308, 309
Wall, John N. 302
Wall, Wendy 303, 304
Wallace, John 278, 308, 309
Waller, Edmund 74, 106, 160, 161, 261;
    "Instructions to a Painter" 281
Waller, Gary 304
Walpole, Horace 77
Walton, Izaak 4, 22, 251, 288, 298, 307;
    Compleat Angler, The 55
Warner, William: *Albions England* 63
Warton, Thomas 172
Watson, Graeme J. 301, 302, 303
Watson, Robert N. 288, 291
Wayne, Don E. 290
Webster, John: *Duchess of Malfi* 70, 216
Weever, John 35
Weismiller, Edward 300
Westminster Assembly 193
Whicher, Stephen E. 299
White, Chris 306
Whitney, Geoffrey 77
Wiedemann, Barbara 305
Wilcox, Helen 236, 303, 305, 306
Wild, Robert 293
Wilde, Oscar 105
Wilding, Michael 273, 299, 309
Wilkinson, C.H. 131, 297
Williams, George Walton 292
Williamson, Marilyn 245, 305
Wilson, Edmund 30, 290
Wimsatt, W.K. 287, 299
Winstanley, Gerrard 273
Wiseman, Susan 305
Wither, George 55, 68, 69–76, 81, 82, 84,
    92, 100, 142, 146, 162; *Abuses Stript
    and Whipt* 69, 70, 72, 86, 280, 291, 292,
    293; *Britain's Remembrancer* 73–4;
    Campo-Musae 74, 76; *A Collection of
    Emblemes, Ancient and Moderne* 72;
    Epithalamion 70; *Fair Virtue, The
    Mistresse of Phil'arete* 70, 71–2;
    *Hallelujah, or Britain's Second
    Remembrancer* 72–3; *Hymns and Songs
    of the Church, The* 71, 72; *Juvenilia* 72;
    Motto 69, 70, 72, 86; *Prince Henries
    Obsequies* 70; *Psalms of David, The* 72;
    "Shall I, wasting in despair" 71;
    Shepherd's Hunting, The 69, 70; *Vox
    Pacifica* 74; *Westrow Revived, a Funeral
    Poem Without Fiction* 75

Withington, Eleanor 295
Wittreich, Joseph Anthony, Jr. 309
Wolfe, Don M. 288, 300
Wood, Anthony à 76, 131, 293
Wooden, Warren W. 294
Woodhouse, A.S.P. 300
Woods, Susanne 304
Woolf, Virginia 211, 244, 305
Wordsworth, William 81, 200
Wotton, Sir Henry 22, 79, 175, 180
Woudhuysen, H.R. 287
Wrightson, Keith 298
Wroth, Mary 2, 31, 38, 210, 212, 214–19, 226, 241, 303, 304, 305, 306; "In this strang labourinth how shall I turne?"
218; "Like to the Indians, scorched with the Sun" 216; *Pamphilia to Amphilanthus* 215–17; *Urania* 214, 217–19; "When every one to pleasing pastime hies" 217
Wroth, Sir Robert 214
Wyatt, Sir Thomas 5

Yeats, W.B. 22, 277, 299, 301; "The Circus Animal's Desertion" 148
Young, R.V. 289
Young, Thomas 173

Zwicker, Steven 281, 282, 297, 309